INSTITUTE FOR INTEGRATED
ENERGY SYSTEMS (IESVic)
University of Victoria
P.O. Box 3055
Victoria, B.C. V8W 3P6 Canada

D1617338

NATURAL VENTILATION IN BUILDINGS

NATURAL VENTILATION IN BUILDINGS

A DESIGN HANDBOOK

EDITOR
FRANCIS ALLARD

PROJECT COORDINATOR
MAT SANTAMOURIS

CONTRIBUTORS
**SERVANDO ALVAREZ • ELENA DASCALAKI • GERARD GUARRACINO
EDUARDO MALDONADO • SALVATORE SCIUTO • LUK VANDAELE**

European Commission
Directorate General for Energy
Altener Program

Published by James & James (Science Publishers) Ltd,
35-37 William Road, London NW1 3ER, UK

First published in 1998
Reprinted 2002

A catalogue record for this book is available from the British Library

ISBN 1 873936 72 9

Printed in the UK by The Cromwell Press

Contents

Preface

This book is the result of a cooperative action carried out within the framework of the ALTENER Programme of the European Commission, Directorate General XVII, for Energy.

The ALTENER Programme concerns the promotion of renewable energy sources in the Community. The actions that are promoted in the framework of this programme are:

- studies and technical evaluations for defining technical standards or specifications;
- measures to support the Member States' initiatives for extending or creating infrastructures concerned with renewable energy sources;
- measures to foster the creation of an information network for better coordination between national, Community and international activities;
- studies, evaluations and appropriate measures aimed at assessing the technical feasibility and the advantages for the economy and the environments of the industrial exploitation of biomass for energy purposes.

The general goal of the present AIOLOS project was to create a specific educational material on the efficient use of passive ventilation for buildings that can be transferred to all education activities and can be used by all the professionals involved in the field of buildings. The present book aims to provide building professionals with all necessary knowledge, tools and information on the efficient use of natural ventilation in buildings in order to decrease the energy consumption for cooling purposes, increase the indoor thermal comfort levels and improve indoor air quality.

This book has three main objectives:

- To report and provide basic scientific knowledge to date on natural ventilation process as well as the existing methods and tools developed in research programmes during the last years.
- To show realistic examples of applications carried out and evaluated in various European countries, and to define technical barriers and limits of application of the technique.
- To provide designers with both easy-to-handle guidelines, necessary in the first steps of design, and software able to evaluate their project and to provide quantitative analysis of their solutions.

The overall task has been carried out by a group of Educational and Scientific Institutions involved in various European research projects in the field of rational use of energy in buildings and the improvement of passive solutions for cooling. This group has been coordinated by the Central Institution for Energy Efficiency Educational team of University of Athens represented by M. Santamouris and E. Dascalaki.

The following teams and institutions have to be acknowledged for their valuable contributions:

- M. Grosso of the Polytechnico di Torino and S. Sciuto and C. Priolo of Conphoebus, Italy;
- G. Guarracino, M. Bruant and V. Richalet of Lash/ENTPE, Lyons, France;
- E. Maldonado and J.L. Alexandre of the University of Porto, Portugal;
- S. Alvarez of the University of Seville, Spain;
- P. Wouters, L. Vandaele and D. Ducarme at BBRI, Belgium;
- K. Limam and M. Abadie of the University of La Rochelle, France, who contributed more specifically to the final edition.

We also would like to acknowledge the help of F. Haghigat of Concordia University, who provided the first comments and suggestions for this book.

Any comments with regard to the contents and structure of this book are welcome.

F. ALLARD, Editor

1

Introduction

1.1   WHY NATURAL VENTILATION?

Proper design of energy-conscious buildings requires a balance between two things:

- the thermal performance of the building envelope and the appropriate selection of techniques for heating, cooling and daylighting;
- an acceptable quality of the indoor climate in terms of thermal comfort, ventilation effectiveness or indoor air quality.

In general, these criteria are the basis of guidelines of good practice or standards which demonstrate the evolution of social and technical trends.

Looking back at the past 25 years, we notice a strong evolution of these requirements. In all western countries and more specifically in Europe, until 1973, there was no real policy for the rational use of energy in building design. Energy was cheap and available and building thermal performance and quality were mainly the result of good practice.

After the oil crisis of 1973, we can observe the enhancement of energy policies in all western countries as they became conscious of the limit of energy availability. The main result of this crisis in term of building activity was therefore to reduce significantly global energy consumption, mainly used for heating and air conditioning, while neglecting its impact on the comfort and health of building occupants. The main concepts of the new national regulations, developed in parallel by various countries at this period, were focused on a strong reduction of the energy needs for building heating and air conditioning, and the solution proposed was to increase significantly the envelope insulation level and to reduce air infiltration by sealing the building envelope in order to reduce the building energy losses. This period also saw the real development of building research in western countries. The main consequence of the new regulations was a significant reduction of energy consumption in the building sector. However, this was accompanied by an increasing number of disorders, mainly due to humidity condensation and the growth of mould, which affected the health of the occupants, to overheating in summer or in intermediate seasons, which affected the thermal comfort of the occupants, and finally poor indoor air quality due to low air-change rates, which impacted the productivity and performance of the occupants of buildings.

The 1980s started with preoccupations about the consequences of the first regulations on energy conservation, which emphasized only the reduction of energy consumption. The results were the emergence of the sick building syndrome and building-related sickness among building occupants. This reminded researchers, policymakers and designers that the first function of a building is to protect the occupants against harsh outdoor climate and to provide a comfortable and healthy environment for these occupants and only then to conserve energy. This was the start of the new era, called 'energy efficiency' in a global context.

This evolution began in the 1990s and it is now clear that energy conservation cannot be dissociated from the quality of the indoor and outdoor environment. Therefore, the concept of global design of the building is emerging with all environmental aspects taken into account, not only from the performance point of view but also on the basis of many other quality criteria. These environmental criteria have even led to major modifications in manufacturing and technology, such as the abandonment of CFCs (chlorofluorocarbons) in HVAC (heating, ventilating and air-conditioning) systems, and in state policies requiring designers to justify the use of active air conditioning. These criteria also highlight the necessity of full integration of the building site characteristics and potential in the design and this leads naturally to a focus on more integration of passive concepts of heating, cooling or, more generally, indoor climate conditioning [1].

With these various aspects taken into account, natural ventilation appears to be a very attractive solution to ensure both good indoor quality and acceptable comfort conditions in many regions. During the ZEPHYR architectural competition [2] held by the European Community in 1994, it was very clear that most of the projects used natural ventilation as the basic technique for passive cooling and for providing an acceptable indoor environment.

Furthermore, natural ventilation seems to provide an answer to many complaints from users concerning mechanical ventilation, which appears to be noisy, to create health problems (sick building syndrome is usually associated with mechanical HVAC systems), to require routine maintenance and to consume energy. In contrast, natural ventilation is preferred by the occupants, since it is energy efficient (no need of a mechanical system), it can be easily integrated into buildings and it provides a healthier and more comfortable environment if integrated correctly [3].

1.2   NATURAL VENTILATION FOR INDOOR AIR QUALITY AND TEMPERATURE CONTROL

Ventilation plays an important role in providing good indoor air quality and thermal comfort of the occupants.

1.2.1   Natural ventilation for indoor air quality control

Natural ventilation as a strategy for achieving acceptable indoor air quality is essentially based on the supply of fresh air to a space and the dilution of the indoor pollution concentration [4]. Optimum indoor air quality may be defined as air which is free of pollutants that cause irritation, discomfort or ill health in the occupants. A poor environment can manifest itself as a sick building, in which occupants may experience mild illness symptoms during the period of occupation. Health-related air quality standards are typically based on risk assessment and are either specified in terms of maximum permitted concentration or a maximum permitted dose. Higher concentrations are usually permitted for short-term exposure than are permitted for long-term exposure.

The quantity of ventilation needed to ensure an acceptable indoor air quality depends on the amount and the nature of the dominant pollutant source in a space. If the emission characteristics are known, it is possible to calculate the ventilation rate necessary to prevent the pollutant concentration from exceeding a pre-defined threshold concentration. Figure 1.1 gives a sketch of such a strategy [5]. The pollution level decreases exponentially with the airflow rate. If we know the recommended pollution level, we can easily define the recommended airflow rate.

In practice, it is important to identify the dominant pollutant source. This is the pollutant that requires the highest ventilation rate to control it. Thus, if

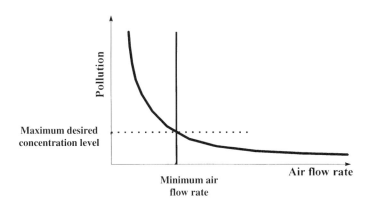

Figure 1.1. Natural ventilation for indoor air quality

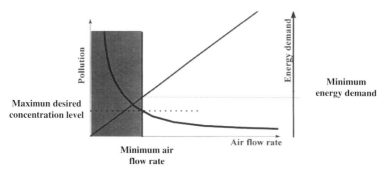

Figure 1.2. Combined evolution of pollution level and energy demand

a sufficient ventilation level is achieved to control the dominant pollutant, it will be sufficient to maintain the remaining pollutants below their respective threshold concentrations.

In naturally ventilated buildings, no energy is needed for moving the air; the only energy required is that necessary to warm up the air during the heating season. In this configuration, the energy demand will increase directly with the ventilation rate, which, in a natural ventilation configuration, varies as a function of time and depends on the wind characteristics and the thermal state of the building. At the same time, occupant behaviour, such as opening or closing windows and doors, has a substantial impact on the total energy consumption of a building. Figure 1.2 shows the effect of the airflow rate on both pollution level and energy demand.

Just as it is essential to ensure an acceptable indoor air quality by having a sufficient air supply, it is also mandatory to avoid airflow rates that are too high. Therefore, optimization is essential in order that a combined low energy demand and an acceptable indoor quality can be achieved while keeping ventilation rates within a certain range.

1.2.2   Natural ventilation and thermal comfort in summertime

Thermal sensation plays a key role in the perception of comfort and, as with any comfort parameters, is highly subjective. A comprehensive review of thermal comfort can be found in Chapter 8 of *ASHRAE Fundamentals* [6]. Human thermal comfort is defined as the conditions in which a person would prefer neither warmer or cooler surroundings. It is a rather complex concept, since it depends on various parameters that collectively define comfort conditions.

The parameters that influence the overall comfort can be grouped into three categories:

- physical parameters, which include the air temperature and the thermal conditions of the environment (mean radiant temperature or surface temperatures), the relative humidity of the air, the local air

velocity (mean and turbulent), the odours, the colours of the surroundings, the light intensity and the noise level;
- physiological parameters, which include age, sex and specific characteristics of the occupants;
- external parameters, which include human activity, clothing and social
conditions.

Among these, the local environment, represented by the dry-bulb temperature, humidity and air velocity, plays a leading role in thermal comfort. It can be assessed in terms of many combinations of these physical parameters, together with the clothing level and the activity of the subject [6].

Occupants' thermal comfort cannot be represented only by the simple heat balance of the human body; many psychological processes also have to be taken into account. However, the positive or negative influence of each parameter on the body's thermal equilibrium makes it possible to define various strategies in order to achieve acceptable thermal comfort conditions. Clothing is, of course, one of the easiest parameters that an individual can adjust to achieve the required level of comfort.

Modifying the air movement around the human body can also help to control the thermal comfort level. Air movements determine the convective heat and mass exchange of the human body with the surrounding air. In summer, higher air velocities will increase the evaporation rate at the skin surface and consequently enhance the cooling sensation. Although natural ventilation can shift the thermal comfort zone to regions of higher air temperatures, the recommended upper limit of indoor air movement is usually 0.8 m s^{-1}. Above this value, loose paper may be disturbed. Such air speeds permit one to maintain a space about 2°C warmer, at for example 60% relative humidity, and still maintain optimum comfort. This means that occupants can be in good thermal comfort conditions at higher air temperatures.

The second and direct effect of natural ventilation on comfort conditions is to eliminate or reduce internal gains and to limit the way in which the air temperature increases inside a building. This is the traditional cooling strategy in moderate or southern climates, where buildings have large openings to the outside. In this kind of configuration, the air-change rates become very high and the indoor air temperature tends to become equal to that outdoors. This situation usually applies to light building structures and, to be efficient, this strategy has to be coupled with good solar shading in order to limit the wall surface radiation within the building.

This technique is very efficient when the outdoor temperatures are in the range of a comfort zone. However, this strategy cannot work in buildings which need a higher control of indoor air velocities during the occupancy period. Then, another technique is to cool down the structure of the building when the building is not occupied. This technique is known as night-time ventilation. The building structure is cooled down during the night, providing a heat sink that is available during the occupancy period. This sink absorbs the

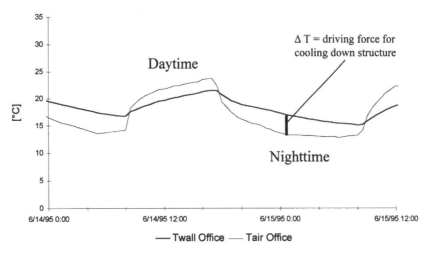

Figure 1.3. Cooling potential due to nighttime ventilation

heat gains due to occupancy or equipment and maintains an acceptable indoor condition. Figure 1.3 shows an example of this cooling potential [5].

1.3   EASY-TO-USE NATURAL VENTILATION?

Natural ventilation is very attractive for designers or architects because it offers robust solutions capable of providing an acceptable indoor air quality and meeting comfort needs throughout the full range of climate conditions. In most cases, the minimum ventilation rates needed for indoor air quality are easily reached and the maximum ventilation rates needed for summer thermal control of the building are well identified.

Natural ventilation appears as a logical and suitable strategy for many types of buildings, such as low-rise dwellings, schools, small or medium-sized offices, recreation buildings and public buildings in moderate or mild climates. The open-window environment associated with natural ventilation is often popular and offers a wide range of creative design to architects, especially in pleasant environments. Natural ventilation also appears very cost-effective compared with the capital, maintenance and operational costs of mechanical systems and it does not need any plant room space. In such an environment, any short periods of summer discomfort will be easily tolerated by the user of the building.

However, 'natural' also means that behaviour will be random and efficient control of the building will be difficult. The physical phenomena to take into account usually correspond to simple concepts like thermal mass, but they are not easy to handle because of the many uncertainties, for instance the randomness of indoor airflow patterns and the difficulty of determining the surface heat transfer between the air and the walls.

Furthermore, in many urban environments, outdoor air conditions and acoustics may not be acceptable because of air pollution and noise [7]. In these conditions, natural ventilation can be unsuitable or will need a special design in order to avoid a direct link between indoor and outdoor environments. When a special design using ducts is necessary, the duct dimensions are much bigger than those of mechanical systems. In order to be effective, natural ventilation also needs a high degree of permeability within the building. For certain buildings this can cause security risks and conflicts with fire or safety regulations. In the case of deep-plan or multiroomed buildings, fresh air delivery or good mixing may not be possible without some special design considerations.

These few examples show clearly that, while natural ventilation is very attractive, good design of naturally ventilated buildings needs to take into account many phenomena and criteria that are not necessarily easy to handle.

This book is largely aimed at the designers, architects, policy-makers and engineers who need to acquire a broad background knowledge about natural ventilation. Each chapter presents specific aspects of the problem and can be easily understood without particular reference to adjacent chapters.

Following the present Introduction, the contents of the book are:

Chapter 2, which provides the fundamentals and necessary information for understanding the effect of wind on a building and an introduction to the thermal behaviour of buildings.

Chapter 3, which focuses on the modelling of natural ventilation, from simple rules of thumb to computational fluid dynamics (CFD), and introduces intermediate models, which are the basis of the design tools provided within the book.

Chapter 4, which presents various diagnostic techniques and their use for natural ventilation studies.

Chapter 5, which gives the limit of natural ventilation and identifies critical barriers.

Chapter 6, which describes design guidelines and technical techniques for the implementation of natural ventilation.

Chapter 7, which presents some examples of naturally ventilated buildings studied during the European ALTENER/AIOLOS project.

Chapter 8, which introduces the AIOLOS software.

REFERENCES

1. Santamouris, M. and D. Asimakopoulos (1996). *Passive Cooling of Buildings*, James & James (Science Publishers), London.
2. ZEPHYR European Architectural Ideas Competition (1994). Energy Research Group, School of Architecture, University College Dublin.

3. Liddament, M. (1996). *A Guide to Energy Efficient Ventilation*. Air Infiltration and Ventilation Centre, Coventry, UK.
4. Liddament, M. (1990). 'Ventilation and building sickness – a brief review', *Air Infiltration Review*, Vol. 11, No. 3, *pp. 4–6.*
5. Wouters, P., L. Vandaele and D. Ducarme (1996). 'What do we mean with natural ventilation?', AIOLOS Workshop, Lyons, November 1996.
6. *ASHRAE Fundamentals* (1993). American Society of Heating, Refrigeration and Air Conditioning, Atlanta.
7. Maldonado, E. (1996). 'Syntheses of barrier and challenges: Why natural ventilation?', AIOLOS Workshop, Lyons, November 1996.

2

Fundamentals of natural ventilation

Edited by F. Allard and S. Alvarez

**2.1   WIND CHARACTERISTICS AND THE EFFECT OF WIND
ON BUILDINGS**

2.1.1   Climate and microclimate: the different climatic scales

The World Meteorological Organization [1] defines climate as a 'totality of meteorological elements that, in their usual succession and at a given period, characterise the state of the atmosphere'. Different scales of climate should then be distinguished.

2.1.1.1   The global scale
With a range of thousands of kilometres, this scale is related to the general astronomical characteristics of the earth (the spherical form of the planet, the inclination of the axis of rotation relative to the ecliptic plane, the rotation around the sun) that induce variations in the main climatic characteristics of the planet according to the latitude and the season. At the same time climate is subject to local variations due to the balance in the distribution of sea and land on the planet.

The radiative balance of the ground and the presence of an important source of humidity determine the hygrothermal characteristics of the air above the ground. If these conditions are stable for rather a long period and over a sufficiently important surface, a homogeneous mass of air will be generated and transported by the general air circulation.

According to Peguy [2], there are eight types of air mass over the total surface of the globe: arctic air; continental (dry) or maritime (humid) polar air, warming or not; continental (dry) or maritime (humid) tropical air; and equatorial air. Beyond the limits of the regions where these air masses are formed, the climate is influenced by the more or less rapid passages of the air

---

Main contributors: F. Allard, K. Limam, M. Abadie and S. Alvarez

masses through each region. This occurs particularly in temperate regions, such as western Europe, where there is a conflict between various air masses.

The main characteristics of a climate are the air temperature, the wind and the precipitations. As reported in Queney [3], the maximum temperature levels occur during summer in continents at subtropical latitudes (in July 30°C in Mexico, 35°C in South West Asia and the Sahara; in January 30°C in Australia, South West Africa and Paraguay) and the minimum temperatures occur during winter in continents at high latitudes (in January –40°C in Siberia and Greenland; in July –40°C in the Antarctic). The annual thermal amplitude reaches more than 40°C at the centre of the continents in the northern hemisphere, while it is less than 5°C in the maritime regions located between the two tropics.

2.1.1.2   The regional scale
This scale stretches over some hundreds of kilometres. Regional climatic features are influenced by the landscape layout, i.e. the spacing of and distance from mountains, the proximity of an oceanic zone and the location of the region with respect to the operating centres of the general air circulation.

2.1.1.3   The local scale
The local scale, also called the topoclimatic scale, stretches over approximately ten kilometres. The regional climate is modulated following the morphology of the landscape, i.e. the presence of a valley or a group of hills or the vicinity of the sea. Thus, the general wind regime is modified. This is the scale of thermal breezes, pluviometric ridges and diurnal thermal effects.

These local climates occur as a result of the balance between the climatic conditions on the regional scale and the modifications induced by, for example, urban areas, the proximity of the sea or of a great lake and the landscape (valley, hill, etc.).

The sea has a higher thermal inertia than the land. This is due to the higher heat capacity of the water, so that the seasonal temperature variation of the water layer is about 8°C; a diurnal variation of 1–2°C should be added to the seasonal one. Heat is therefore stored in the oceanic water during the summer and released to the air during the winter. When a moderate wind blows from the sea, the coastal strip of land is warmed.

Furthermore, as the diurnal inland variation of the radiative balance is much greater, especially under clear-sky conditions, the amplitude of the thermal diurnal variation at about 10 to 20 km from the shore is reduced by the maritime air that blows toward the shore. Temperature differences of about 3°C in 10 km may be observed close to the shore such that:

- during winter, the diurnal thermal amplitude increases owing to the minimum temperature increase;
- during summer, the diurnal thermal amplitude decreases owing to higher minimum temperatures and lower maximum temperatures;
- in the presence of a strong wind and an overcast sky, the temperature differences are smaller.

When the airflow reaches a shore, it is slowed down by the roughness of the ground, which causes rising air movements. As the maritime air has a high concentration of condensation nuclei (salt), precipitations are more abundant in the land close to the coast; this is called the 'ridge phenomenon'.

A stretch of water may also induce an increase in the partial vapour pressure, especially if the evaporation and transpiration of the surrounding vegetable shelter is weaker than the direct evaporation of the stretch of water.

As it crosses the sea–earth discontinuity, the airflow is slowed down by the roughness of the ground. At the same time, the flow deviates to its left in the northern hemisphere.

2.1.1.4 The microclimatic scale

This scale is only few hundred metres wide. It is the only scale where man can modify the climate in a lasting manner by using artificial systems, such as windbreak hedges and protection slopes, or by adapting town planning to the dominant winds, the sunshine, the presence of water, etc.

Moreover, horizontal pressure gradients that correspond to the horizontal temperature differences created by the effects of these microclimates induce specific air movements.

2.1.2   Wind structure near the ground

2.1.2.1 The atmospheric boundary layer

Recordings of the time variation of the wind velocity (Figure 2.1) show that the wind is a highly variable and irregular physical phenomenon. Such random behaviour is designated by the term *turbulence*. In the low atmospheric layers, turbulence is generated by any ground obstacle as well as by thermal airflow instabilities. Turbulence decreases with increasing height.

The instantaneous wind velocity should therefore be calculated using a statistical approach. This means:

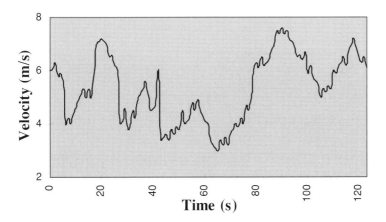

Figure 2.1. Typical record of the wind velocity near the ground

- The wind velocity can be written as the sum of an average and a fluctuating term. For the longitudinal component $u(t)$ we obtain:

$$u(t) = \overline{u} + u'(t) \tag{2.1}$$

where: $u(t)$ is the instantaneous term, $\overline{u}$ is the average term and $u'(t)$ is the fluctuating part.

- The average wind velocity is given by:

$$\overline{u} = \frac{1}{T} \int_{t_0}^{t_0+T} u(t)\, \mathrm{d}t \tag{2.2}$$

- The average process is assumed to be independent of time and the period T is such that the average operator should converge in a quadratic mean; in the lower part of the atmosphere, the experimental value of T ranges typically between 10 minutes and one hour.
- The vertical and lateral mean velocity components of an homogeneous flow over a flat surface are zero owing to adherence and non-permeability conditions. The instantaneous velocity vector $V(t)$ components are:

$$\overline{u} + u'(t), \quad \overline{v} + v'(t), \quad \overline{w} + w'(t)$$

where $u'(t)$ is the longitudinal fluctuation, $v'(t)$ is the lateral fluctuation, and $w'(t)$ the vertical fluctuation.

- If the effects of thermal stratification on the wind velocity can be neglected (general case for building applications), then, to a first approximation, the flow direction is assumed to be constant in the immediate vicinity of the ground (in a layer 100 m deep). By orienting the x axis according to the mean flow direction, the mean velocity will depend only on the height z above the ground.

For a horizontal homogeneous steady flow, and with the molecular viscosity term neglected, the Navier–Stokes equations lead to:

$$u\frac{\partial u}{\partial x} + v\frac{\partial v}{\partial y} + w\frac{\partial w}{\partial z} = 0 \tag{2.3}$$

The continuity equation for an incompressible flow gives:

$$\frac{\partial u}{\partial x} + \frac{\partial v}{\partial y} + \frac{\partial w}{\partial z} = 0 \tag{2.4}$$

Introducing the Reynolds decomposition of the velocity vector (equation 2.1) into the Navier–Stokes equations yields:

$$\frac{\partial (u'w')}{\partial z} = 0 \tag{2.5}$$

From this equation it can be seen that the turbulent momentum flux is constant with height. Integrating equation (2.5) between the ground ($z = 0$) and height z yields:

$$-u'w' = \frac{\tau_0}{\rho} \tag{2.6}$$

where τ_0 is the friction stress at the ground. τ_0 is usually equal to Δu^{*2}, u^* being a velocity scale called the *friction velocity*. Reynolds decomposition enables us to introduce turbulence effects into the mean airflow equations. Reynolds stresses should nevertheless be expressed in terms of mean velocity in order to keep the system of equations closed.

The first-order closure is based on the analogy between turbulent and molecular motions. Locally, the fluctuating velocity u' varies linearly with the distance of displacement l while w' is of the same order of magnitude as u'. This is Prandtl mixing length theory, expressed by equation (2.7):

$$u' \cong -\frac{\overline{\partial u}}{\partial z} l \text{ and } w' = -cu' \tag{2.7}$$

where:

$$cl^2 \left(\frac{\overline{\partial u}}{\partial z} \right)^2 = u^{*2} \tag{2.8}$$

and $\sqrt{c}l = kz$ where $k = 0.4$ (von Karman constant).

The mean velocity can therefore be calculated from:

$$\frac{\overline{\partial u}}{\partial z} = \frac{u^*}{kz} \tag{2.9}$$

The mean velocity equals zero ($\bar{u} = 0$) at the reference height $z = z_0$ where z_0 is the roughness length (a characteristic of the ground surface).

The mean wind velocity is thus a logarithmic function of the height above the ground:

$$\bar{u}(z) = \frac{u^*}{k} \ln \left(\frac{z}{z_0} \right); \tag{2.10}$$

u^* and z_0 are obtained experimentally. The velocity profile in semi-logarithmic coordinates is a straight line of slope k/u^* and y component at origin $\ln z_0$.

The roughness height is an aerodynamic characteristic of the ground surface. For an identical geostrophic velocity and an identical height above the ground, the average velocity will decrease for an increasing roughness of the ground. The roughness height is thus a function of the nature of the ground and the geometry of existing obstacles.

Table 2.1. Roughness height and class [4]

Type of surface	Roughness height	Roughness class
Sea, snow, sand	0.0005	I
Sea with very strong wind	0.005	II
Short grass	0.01	III
Cultivated open fields	0.05	IV
High plants, open country	0.10	V
Countryside and spread habitat	0.25	VI
Peripheral urban zone	0.50	VII
Mean city centre, forest	1.00	VIII
Metropolitan centre, tropical forest	4.00	IX

Table 2.1 presents a range of experimental values obtained on homogeneous sites of large horizontal extension [4].

A logarithmic variation law relating the wind speed to height is obviously applicable only above a height z^* where the flow can 'see' irregularities of the ground; z^* corresponds to the effective thickness of the turbulent substratum and is usually equal to $1.5h_0$ where h_0 is the average obstacle height [5].

Furthermore, when the density of obstacles is high, i.e. they occupy more than 25% of the total ground area, the apparent level of the ground alongside the flow is raised. This problem is solved by introducing the concept of displacement height in the formulation of the vertical velocity profile:

$$\overline{u}(z) = \frac{u^*}{k} \ln\left(\frac{z - d_0}{z_0}\right) \tag{2.11}$$

To a first approximation $d_0 = (0.7)h_0$.

2.1.2.2 Data transfer at a homogeneous site

In practice, available data on wind characteristics come from standard meteorological measurements that are taken at stations near airports. In an airport environment the roughness class is IV. A reference velocity, u_{ref}, is defined as the mean velocity measured at a height of 10 m at a site having a homogeneous roughness, z_{0ref}, equal to 0.05 m:

$$\overline{u}_{ref} = \frac{u_{ref}^*}{k} \ln\left(\frac{10}{z_{0ref}}\right) \tag{2.12}$$

The main difficulty is to express the speed of the wind at the studied site in terms of what is measured at the meteorological station ($\overline{u}_{ref}$). To a first approximation, the velocity of the geostrophic wind can be assumed to be identical above the two sites.

This relationship between the two speeds can then be written:

$$\bar{u}(z) = \lambda(z_0)\bar{u}_{\text{ref}} \ln\left(\frac{z}{z_0}\right) \tag{2.13}$$

with: $\lambda(z_0) = \dfrac{u^*}{u_{\text{ref}}^*} \dfrac{1}{\ln\left(\dfrac{10}{z_{0\text{ref}}}\right)}$ (2.14)

where u^*/u^*_{ref} remains to be determined. Similarity considerations on the scale of the atmospheric boundary layer make it possible to express the geostrophic wind velocity as:

$$u_g = \sqrt{u_{g_x}^2 + u_{g_y}^2} \tag{2.15}$$

which takes into account characteristic parameters of the boundary layer (the roughness length z_0, the Coriolis parameter f, and the friction velocity u^*). Simiu [6] proposed the following formula for the geostrophic wind velocity:

$$u_g^2 = \frac{u^{*2}}{k}\left(\left(\ln\left(\frac{u^*}{fz_0}\right) - B\right)^2 + A^2\right) \tag{2.16}$$

This relationship results from a balance between the force of the geostrophic pressure gradient and the friction force on the surface of the ground. A and B are estimated experimentally: $A = 4.5$ and $B = 1.7$. This expression gives a rough estimate of the atmospheric boundary layer height ($\delta = 0.3u^*/f$) and of the angular deviation between the geostrophic flow and the flow at ground level:

$$\sin \alpha = -\frac{Au^*}{ku_g} \tag{2.17}$$

Setting the geostrophic velocity corresponding to the studied site equal to the one at the meteorological station, one deduces the following (non-linear) relationship between the corresponding friction velocities:

$$\frac{u^*}{u_{\text{ref}}^*} = \frac{\sqrt{\left(\ln\left(\dfrac{u^*_{\text{ref}}}{fz_{0\text{ref}}}\right) - B\right)^2 + A^2}}{\sqrt{\left(\ln\left(\dfrac{u^*}{fz_0}\right) - B\right)^2 + A^2}} \tag{2.18}$$

Table 2.2 gives the values of the coefficient $\lambda(z_0)$ for the different types of terrain roughness (Table 2.1). λ is the reference roughness $z_{0\text{ref}} = 0.05$ calculated using the approximate formula proposed by ESDU 82026 [7]:

Table 2.2. $\lambda(z_0)$ values [7]

Type of surface	Coefficient	Roughness class
Sea, snow, sand	0.14	I
Sea with very strong wind	0.15	II
Short grass	0.17	III
Cultivated open fields	0.19	IV
High plants, open country	0.20	V
Countryside and spread habitat	0.21	VI
Peripheral urban zone	0.22	VII
Mean city centre, forest	0.24	VIII
Metropolitan centre, tropical forest	0.25	IX

$$\frac{u^*}{u^*_{ref}} = \frac{\ln\left(\dfrac{10^5}{z_{0ref}}\right)}{\ln\left(\dfrac{10^5}{z_0}\right)} \tag{2.19}$$

2.1.2.3 Local velocity modifications

The site environment is rarely homogeneous; each site is thus characterized over a range of a few kilometres by its position in the relief (hill, valley, etc.), the nature of the terrain (geographical distribution of urban zones, the close-cropped countryside, extended areas of water, etc.) and over a range of a few hundred metres by the presence of nearby obstacles (hedges, trees, houses, etc.).

To take these particular site characteristics into consideration, three specific coefficients are usually introduced for the definition of the average local wind velocity as a function of the reference mean velocity. These coefficients take into account a local change of roughness, a local modification of the relief and the presence of a singular obstacle:

$$\bar{u}(x,z) = u_{ref}\, C_R(x, z, z_0) C_T(x, z) C_S(x, z) \tag{2.20}$$

where $C_R(x, z, z_0)$ is the roughness coefficient, $C_T(x, z)$ is the topography coefficient and $C_S(x, z)$ is the wake coefficient.

CHANGES OF ROUGHNESS

Let us consider the atmospheric boundary layer above a flat surface where the terrain presents a discontinuity of roughness at $x = 0$ (Figure 2.2).

In Figure 2.2 $\bar{u}_1(z)$ is the equilibrium undisturbed velocity over ground with homogeneous roughness z_{01}. Downstream of the discontinuity where the roughness changes to z_{02}, the wind velocity $\bar{u}_2(x, z)$ is disturbed at a height $\delta(x)$, called the thickness of the internal boundary layer, which is a function of the distance x (the fetch). The modification of the structure of the flow is due to the modification of the level of production of turbulent energy by friction along

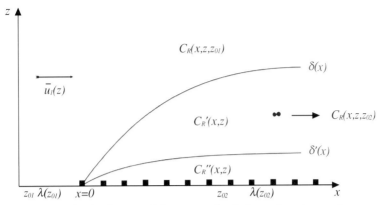

Figure 2.2. Evolution of the atmospheric boundary layer after a change of roughness

the ground according to the rate of dissipation of this turbulent energy in the air. When the fetch becomes very important (at around 10 km), the flow stabilizes at a new equilibrium state corresponding to a homogeneous roughness surface, z_0. For this surface of homogeneous roughness z_0, the roughness coefficient is given by:

$$C_R(x, z, z_0) = \lambda(z_0) \ln\left(\frac{z}{z_0}\right) \qquad (2.21)$$

This expression is applied before the discontinuity ($x < 0$, with $z_0 = z_{01}$), above the internal boundary layer ($x > 0$ and $z \geq \delta(x)$), with $z_0 = z_{01}$) and after the discontinuity ($x > 10^4$ m, with $z_0 = z_{02}$). Inside the internal boundary layer, the vertical profile of the wind velocity can be approximated by a three-layer model (Figure 2.3).

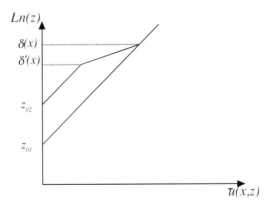

Figure 2.3. Vertical velocity profile in the internal boundary layer after a change of roughness

The internal boundary layer thickness develops according to:

$$\frac{\delta(x)}{z_{0max}} = 0.38\left(\frac{x}{z_{0max}}\right)^{0.83}$$

(2.22)

where $z_{0max} = \max(z_{01}, z_{02})$.

For the internal substratum of thickness $\delta'(x) = c'\delta(x)$, i.e. for $z < \delta'(x)$, the roughness coefficient is given by:

$$C_R''(x, z) = \lambda(z_{01})\ln\left(\frac{z}{z_0}\right)\frac{\ln\left(\frac{c\delta(x)}{z_{01}}\right)}{\ln\left(\frac{c\delta(x)}{z_{02}}\right)}$$

(2.23)

For the intermediate layer $(\delta'(x) \le z \le \delta(x))$, a log–linear interpolation of the velocity between the superior layer and the internal substratum makes it possible to obtain an expression for the roughness coefficient:

$$C_R'(x, z) = C_R''(x, \delta'(x)) + (C_R(x, \delta(x)) - C_R''(x, \delta'(x)))\frac{\ln(z/\delta'(x))}{\ln(1/c')}$$

(2.24)

Constants c and c' have been adjusted from experimental results: $c = 10$ and $c' = 0.2$.

This model may be applied to various changes of roughness.

EFFECTS OF THE LOCAL RELIEF
When a mass of air approaches a hill with a moderate magnitude, an important part of the flow is deviated upwards along the upwind slope and flows downwards along the downwind slope, while the complementary part of the flow passes the obstacle around the sides. This particular flow pattern creates a zone of high pressure near the ground and in the vicinity of the summit, and a low-pressure zone at the foot of the slopes. This pressure variation corresponds to an inverse variation of kinetic energy of the fluid, creating a region of higher velocity at the proximity of the summit and a low-speed region and strong turbulence at the foot of the hill.

Figure 2.4 shows an air velocity u_0 approaching a hill. H_a and H_s represent the upwind and downwind heights, while L_a and L_s give the projections of the hill's upwind and downwind slopes. In the following discussion, the origin of the x axis is placed at the top of the hill. The height of the obstacle above the ground is denoted z and the roughness of the ground z_0.

If $\bar{u}_0(\Delta z)$ is the horizontal average incident velocity and $\Delta\bar{u}(x, \Delta z)$ its perturbation, the fractional rate of higher velocity is defined by:

$$\Delta S(x, \Delta z) = \frac{\Delta\bar{u}(x, \Delta z)}{\bar{u}_0(\Delta z)}$$

(2.25)

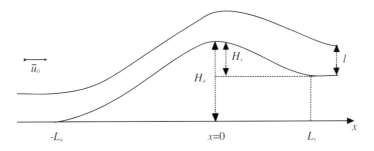

Figure 2.4. Wind structure over an isolated hill

and the topography coefficient by: $C_T(x, \Delta z) = 1 + \Delta S(x, \Delta z)$

For hills with slopes of small inclination ($H/L \ll 1$), the flow can be separated into two layers, internal and external. In the external layer, with a characteristic scale L, the perturbation of the flow is irrotational and non-viscous, while in the internal layer of thickness l, the perturbation of the flow is created by the pressure field of the external layer and determined essentially by turbulent transfers. Both experimental work and theory show that:

$$\frac{l}{z_0} = 0.3 \left(\frac{L}{z_0} \right)^{0.67}$$

(2.26)

where $L = \frac{1}{2} \min(L_a, L_s)$ and $L/z_0 \geq 10^3$.

The topography coefficient indicates that the effect of increased velocity in the vicinity of the summit is proportional to the upwind and downwind slopes of the hill up to a limit of $H_{a,s}/L_{a,s} \leq 0.3$:

$$C_T(x, \Delta z) = 1 + \gamma \left(\frac{H_a}{L_a} + \frac{H_s}{L_s} \right) \left(\frac{\ln\left(\frac{L}{z_0}\right)}{\ln\left(\frac{l}{z_0}\right)} \right)^2 f(x) g(x, \Delta z)$$

(2.27)

If the slope of one of the sides is greater, a detachment of the flow occurs, which significantly modifies its structure. In this case: $H_{a,s}/L_{a,s} = 0.3$; when the hill is a plateau possessing only an upwind slope, one considers $L_s \to \infty$ and $H_s = 0$. The function $g(x, \Delta z)$ describes the damping effect of the altitude on the perturbation of the flow:

$$g(x, \Delta z) = \left(\frac{1}{1 + a(x)\dfrac{\Delta z}{L}} \right)^2$$

(2.28)

Table 2.3. α(x) as a function of the relief shape

$\alpha(x)$	Upwind zone ($x \leq 0$)	Downwind zone ($x \geq 0$)
Hill	$2\left(1-\dfrac{x}{L_a}\right)^2$	$2\left(1-\dfrac{x}{L_s}\right)^2$
Valley	$\dfrac{8}{\left(1-\dfrac{x}{L_a}\right)^2}$	$\dfrac{8}{\left(1+\dfrac{x}{L_s}\right)^2}$
Plateau	$2\left(1-\dfrac{x}{L_a}\right)^2$	$\dfrac{4}{1+\left(\dfrac{x}{L_s}\right)^2}$

Table 2.3 gives the coefficient $\alpha(x)$, for different types of topography.

Function $f(x)$ represents the variation of the velocity perturbation along the axis of the flow direction. Table 2.4 gives the value of $f(x)$ for a hill with two sides and different forms of the relief.

Table 2.4. The expression for f(x) according to the form of the relief

Position x	Plateau with $H_a = 0$	Plateau with $H_s = 0$	Hill
$-1.5L_a \leq x \leq -L_a$	–	$f(x) = -0.4x/L_a - 0.6$	$f(x) = -0.6 - 0.4x/L_a$
$-L_a \leq x \leq 0$	–	$f(x) = 1.2x/L_a + 1$	$f(x) = 1 + 1.2x/L_a$
$0 \leq x \leq 3L_a$	–	$f(x) = -0.3x/L_a + 1$	–
$0 \leq x \leq L_s$	$f(x) = x/L_s$	–	$f(x) = 1 - 1.4x/L_s$
$L_s \leq x \leq 1.5L_s$	$f(x) = -2x/L_s + 3$	–	$f(x) = -0.6 + 0.2x/L_s$

Coefficient γ takes the three-dimensional character of the flow into account ($\gamma = 0.6$), while, for the case of a valley with $x = 0$ at the bottom of the valley, $\gamma = -0.4$. In all other cases, $\gamma = 1$.

Like the average flow of the air, the turbulent part of the flow is also affected by its passage over a hill. In the internal layer ($z/l \leq 1$) the dissipation of turbulent energy is important and thus the turbulence depends on the local balance between the production and the dissipation. In the external layer ($z/l \geq 1$) eddies are just deformed by the average flow and are weakly dependent on local conditions.

THE EFFECT OF A SINGLE OBSTACLE

The presence of an obstacle such as a hedge, a wall or a house, mainly disturbs the flow of air downwind by creating a wake characterized by a decrease of the average velocity and an increase of turbulence. If it is assumed that the wind is flowing along the *x* axis, whose origin is placed at the level of the downwind

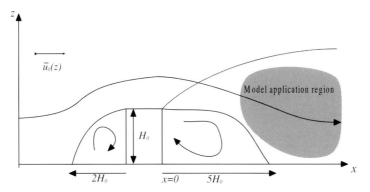

Figure 2.5. Structure of the flow around an isolated obstacle

side of the obstacle, and if the height above the ground is denoted z and the roughness of the ground z_0 (Figure 2.5), the wake coefficient is then defined by:

$$C_s(x, z) = 1 - \frac{\Delta\bar{u}(x, z)}{\bar{u}_0(z)} \qquad (2.29)$$

where $\bar{u}_0(z)$ is the horizontal average incident velocity and $\Delta\bar{u}(x, z)$ the velocity perturbation.

Let H_0 be the height of the obstacle, L_0 its lateral extension, and P_0 the porosity of the obstacle. Then $\Delta\bar{u}(x, z)/\bar{u}_0(z)$ is obtained experimentally for a single two-dimensional obstacle as a function of the roughness $(H_0/z_0 \geq 50)$:

$$\frac{\Delta\bar{u}(x, z)}{\bar{u}_0(z)} = 9.8\left(\frac{\xi}{H_0}\right)^{-1}\left(\frac{z}{H_0}\right)^{-0.14}(1-P_0)\eta\exp(-0.67\eta^{1.5}) \qquad (2.30)$$

where $\eta = \left(\frac{z}{H_0}\right)\left(K\frac{\xi}{H_0}\right)^{-0.47}$ and $K = \dfrac{0.32}{\ln\left(\dfrac{H_0}{z_0}\right)}$ $\qquad (2.31)$

The three-dimensional character of the flow is then introduced with the help of an additional variable ξ. A larger obstacle with $H_0 \leq L_0$ will induce a less extended wake.

If the flow incidence above the obstacle (θ) is not normal, then:

$$\xi = 0.83\frac{x}{\cos\theta} \quad \text{if } L_0/H_0 \geq 10 \qquad (2.32)$$

$$\xi = 7.14\frac{x}{\cos\theta}\left(\frac{L_0}{H_0}\right)^{-0.85} \quad \text{if } L_0/H_0 \leq 10 \qquad (2.33)$$

For the two-dimensional case, L_0 is infinite and $\theta = 0$.

2.1.3   Wind in an urban environment

2.1.3.1 General aspects

In an urban environment, the presence of numerous obstacles significantly increases the roughness of the ground as compared to a rural environment and thus increases the effect of friction on the airflow. The concept of vertical variation of wind velocity as a function of the nature of the terrain, presented in section 2.1.1, also applies to the city from a height approximately equal to twice that of the average roof level.

For moderate to strong winds, and for a height of 20 m above the ground a reduction of 20% to 30% in the average wind speed is observed when moving from the countryside into an urban environment. Conversely, the turbulence intensity increases by 50% to 100%. With strong winds, the friction due to the city also creates a cyclonic rotation of the flow (up to 10°).

Another effect of the urban boundary layer, in the case of moderate winds, is to provoke an upward movement of the air. This vertical velocity can reach 1 m s^{-1}.

Weak winds are 5% to 20% more frequent in a city than in the countryside. However, for wind velocities less than a threshold of 4 m s^{-1}, the wind velocity is higher in the centre than in the periphery of the city. This can be attributed to turbulence generated by the numerous obstacles and to the relatively unstable state that characterizes the urban boundary layer as compared to that in a rural atmosphere.

Furthermore, as the temperature increases when moving from the country-side into the city centre, the air converges at the centre of the city under the effect of the pressure gradient induced by the horizontal temperature difference. Thus, the continuity of the flow creates an upward movement of air, which stops at a given height. The countryside breeze, which mainly blows in the late evening and the early morning, can reach 2 to 3 m s^{-1}.

2.1.3.2 The heat-island concept

The urban heat-island effect is related to summer temperatures in urban areas being higher than in rural surroundings. Factors influencing the heat-island effect include climate, topography, physical layout and short-term weather conditions.

The heat-island effect can be partly explained by the relative scales of the different terms of the energy balance at a given place:

$$R_N = Q_C + Q_E + Q_S \tag{2.34}$$

where R_N is the net radiative balance at the ground, Q_S the sensible heat, Q_E the latent heat and Q_C the heat transferred to the ground by conduction.

Atmospheric pollution is the main cause of solar radiation differences observed between rural and urban environments. Pollution, characterized by an increase in the concentration of aerosols and nuclei of condensation, also increases cloud generation.

In the presence of clouds, the net atmospheric radiation at ground level increases, because clouds are a powerful source of thermal radiation and create a greenhouse effect. The effect of aerosols, though much weaker, is similar to that of clouds.

The thermal radiation emitted by the ground is associated with its surface temperature as well as with the emissivity of soil. Nevertheless, the ground surface temperature is usually higher in a city centre than in the countryside, which corresponds to the higher level of long-wavelength radiation in an urban zone. Measurements carried out in the USA indicate that the radiative flux measured at noon in a city centre is 20% higher than that recorded in the countryside; during the night, the difference is about 10%.

Absorbed solar energy is stored in building structures and, owing to the high thermal inertia of these structures, it is gradually restored to the atmosphere. Furthermore, cities benefit from the contribution of the anthropogenic energy, which can be higher than the solar contribution in winter, but does not exceed 15% of the total energy balance, R_N, in summer. Finally, the sewage system prevents the water from evaporating and at city level reduces the latent heat losses by evaporation.

We usually assume the following typical percentages for the various terms of the energy balance:

$$\text{countryside:} \qquad \frac{Q_C}{R_N} \cong 0.15 \qquad\qquad \frac{Q_E}{R_N} \cong 0.57 \qquad (2.35)$$

$$\text{urban zone:} \qquad \frac{Q_C}{R_N} \cong 0.27 \qquad\qquad \frac{Q_E}{R_N} \cong 0.29 \qquad (2.36)$$

Increasing urbanization and industrialization have therefore exacerbated the heat-island effect. Deficiencies in development control have important consequences, as the increasing number of buildings have crowded out vegetation and trees. For example, as Athens has grown, open spaces have been reduced to 2.7 m^2 per capita, while the corresponding numbers for Paris, Rome, and London are 8.4, 9.9 and 15 respectively, [8]. Also, New York city has lost 175,000 trees, or 20% of its urban forest, in the ten last years [9].

Population is also a parameter influencing heat-island intensity. Urban population has risen from 600 million in 1900 to 2 billion in 1986 [9]. If the same trend continues, it is expected that more than 50% of the world population will live in cities by the end of the century, whereas 100 years ago only 14% lived in cities. In the USA, it is estimated that more than 90% of the population will live in or around urban areas by the end of this century [9]. In Greece, the urban population has increased from about 3 million in 1951 to 5 million in 1981 [10]. Urbanization problems of developing countries have become dramatic. Already, 21 of the 34 cities with more than 5 million inhabitants are in developing countries [9]. Estimates show that 11 of those cities will have populations of between 20 and 30 million by the end of the century [9].

Studies correlating urban population and maximum difference in urban and rural temperatures for 11 European and 18 North American cities have shown that there is a very strong correlation between the city size and the heat-island intensity [11]:

$$\Delta\theta \cong \frac{\phi^{1/4}}{\bar{u}_r^{1/2}} \qquad (2.37)$$

where u_r is the regional speed of the wind, ϕ is the population of the city and $\Delta\theta = T_U - T_C$.

It is necessary to note the importance of the size of the city (represented by ϕ in the above formula) and the wind as a determining factor in the formation of the heat island; over a given threshold, the effect of the heat island disappears: the limits of wind velocity that allow the development of a heat island are strongly related to the size of the city:

$$u_{\text{lim}} = 3.4 \log \phi - 11.6 \, (\text{m s}^{-1}) \qquad (2.38)$$

For a city of 100,000 inhabitants, $\Delta\theta_{\text{max}} = 6°C$ and $u_{\text{lim}} = 5$ m s^{-1}.

Increasing urban temperatures have a direct effect on energy consumption and outdoor air quality. In fact, it has been found that higher urban temperatures increase electricity demand and the production of carbon dioxide and other pollutants.

The heat-island effect in warm and hot climates exacerbates cooling energy use in summer. It has been reported [9] that for US cities with populations larger than 100,000 the peak electricity load increases 1.5% to 2% for every 1°F increase in temperature. Estimates show that for Los Angeles almost 300 MW are additionally needed for a 1°F increase of the temperature [9]. If it is taken into account that urban temperatures during summer afternoons in the USA have increased by 2 to 4°F during the last 40 years, it can be assumed that 3% to 8% of the current urban electricity demand is used to compensate for the heat-island effect alone. Unfortunately, similar data are not available for European cities.

In order to evaluate the heat-island and other urban effects, experiments have been carried out in Montreal [12] and more recently in Athens. A series of 20 temperature and humidity stations has been installed in the extended Athens area. The grid of stations covers the very-high-density central urban area, the lower-density residential areas and the suburban surroundings of Athens.

Hourly temperatures and humidities are measured using tiny electronic sensors. The experiment started in June 1996 and is being carried out in the framework of the POLIS research programme of the Directorate General XII of the European Commission.

All the sensors have been calibrated against an absolute temperature scale. They have also been calibrated against one another on a relative scale in order to identify any possible differences, and readings from the sensors are adjusted in terms of the results of this calibration. All data have been documented and computer files have been created.

In the following, some of the results obtained from the very first analysis of the data obtained are given and discussed.

The main results are :

- Very high temperature differences have been found between the suburban and urban stations during the daytime and especially on hot days. These differences are between 5 and 17°C. Figure 2.6 shows the plots of the recorded temperature differences between the temperatures at the Kifisia suburban station and those at 12 urban stations as a function of the temperature of the corresponding urban station. As can be seen, the trend is always that the temperature difference increases as the temperature of the urban station increases.
- Temperatures recorded in the station at the National Garden, a completely green but urban environment, are much lower during the daytime than the corresponding temperatures of some nearby stations. In some cases the difference is close to 10°. However, this trend is not valid for some other nearby urban stations, such as the Ermou station (a pedestrian street) or the Solonos station. This still remains to be investigated.
- During the night-time, the temperature difference between urban and suburban stations is important. For some stations, the difference can be as much as 4°.
- An important difference is found at night between the National Garden station and the surrounding urban stations. This difference can be as much as 5°.

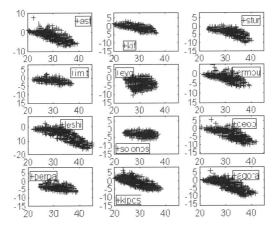

Figure 2.6. Temperature difference for August between a suburban (Kifisia) and 12 urban stations, plotted against the temperature of the corresponding urban station

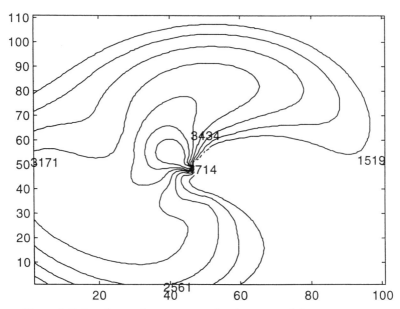

*Figure 2.7. Iso-degree-hours curves for August and for a temperature
base of 26°C*

Based on the measured data, monthly degree hours (d.h.) have been calculated
for each station and for various temperature bases. The 'iso-degree hours'
curves for August for the temperature base of 26°C are given in Figure 2.7. As
shown, the number of degree hours during August and for the temperature
base of 26°C varies between 1327 and 4714. The lowest value is observed in
a suburban station located at about 15 km north-east of Athens. The highest
values are observed in the very central area of Athens and particularly at a
station characterized by major traffic congestion.

For September, and for the same temperature base, the number of degree
hours varies between 86 and 1949. The highest value is from the same urban
station, while the minimum value is observed at a suburban station located
about 10 km south of Athens.

The cumulative frequency distribution of the measured temperatures has
also been calculated. It is found that for August, the frequency of the time with
a temperature higher than 26°C varies between 0.962 and 0.566. The
highest value is observed at an urban station located in one of the main
central streets of Athens, while the minimum is from an urban station
located inside the central park of Athens. For September, the corresponding
values are 0.572 and 0.096 and are from a very central and a suburban station
respectively.

The above numbers are indicative and demonstrate just some elements of the
complete thermal situation in a big urban area during the summer. More
advanced climatological analysis is actually being carried out, to provide
further analysis of the obtained results.

2.1.4   The effect of wind on buildings

Airflow around buildings affects worker safety, process and building equipment operation, weather and pollution protection at inlets, and the ability to control the environmental factors related to temperature, humidity, air motion and contaminants. As seen above for an isolated obstacle, wind causes surface pressures that vary around buildings, changing intake and exhaust system flow rates, natural ventilation, infiltration and exfiltration, and interior pressure. The mean flow patterns and wind turbulence passing over a building can even cause a recirculation of exhaust gases to air intakes.

The flow in the internal viscous boundary layer is dominated by the effect of viscosity. Depending upon the Reynolds number, the flow in this region is either laminar or turbulent. When a turbulent flow hits a sharp edge, such as a corner of a rectangular building, layer separation occurs immediately. Nevertheless, the effect of the Reynolds number is extremely small for rectangular buildings, because it is no longer the dominating factor in controlling the separation and wake width [13].

2.1.4.1 *Wind pressure distribution on buildings*

The relationship, for free stream flow, between velocity and related pressure at different locations of the flow field is obtained from Bernoulli's equation.

If constant density along a streamline at a given height is assumed, Bernoulli's equation can be simplified to:

$$P_{stat} + 0.5\rho v^2 = \text{Constant} \tag{2.39}$$

The pressure coefficient Cp at point $M(x, y, z)$ with the reference dynamic pressure P_{dyn} corresponding to height z_{ref}, for a given wind direction θ can be described by:

$$Cp_s(z_{ref}, \theta) = [P - P_0(z)].[P_{dyn}(z_{ref})]^{-1} \tag{2.40}$$

$$P_{dyn}(z_{ref}) = 0.5\rho_{out}v^2(z_{ref}) \tag{2.41}$$

where
$\quad P$ = the measured pressure

$\quad P_0$ = reference atmospheric pressure

Figure 2.8 shows the distribution of Cp on a building. Numerous articles on wind pressure distribution as input data for infiltration models have been published [14], but only a few deal with wind pressure distribution modelling as a method of calculating Cp. Allen [15] described a calculation method showing how the variation of pressure coefficients with wind angle can be represented by a Fourier series. Results are shown only for wall average Cp values, except for a location at relative building height of 0.85 m where the

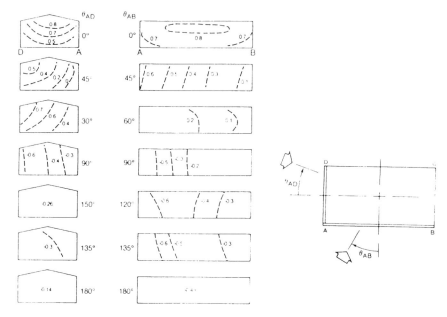

Figure 2.8. Example of the distribution of Cp on a building

horizontal distribution is plotted for a specific environmental situation. In addition, the dependence of the Fourier series on side ratio and wind shelter is demonstrated. A general remark is given about the need for further investigation, mainly concerning the fluctuating pressures arising from turbulence, different building shapes and the sheltering effect of neighbouring buildings.

Bala'zs [16] developed a software package called CPBANK containing a set of Cp data files for different predefined building geometries and exposures. A program handles a search of Cp values for a selected set of wind directions for any building similar to the CPBANK types. These data are taken from a series of measurement carried out in the wind tunnel laboratory of the Hungarian Institute of Building Science (ETI).

Swami and Chandra [17] developed two algorithms, one for low-rise buildings and another for high-rise buildings. For low-rise buildings, data from eight different investigators were analysed and surface average pressure coefficients were found by non-linear regression on a function of wind incidence angle and the side ratio (correlation coefficients: 0.8). For high-rise buildings, local pressure coefficients were used by fitting more than 5000 data points. The regression is represented by only one equation with location coordinates of a surface element as variables. Swami and Chandra's algorithm is therefore useful for surface average pressure coefficients on low-rise buildings or for Cp along the vertical centreline on a facade of an isolated high-rise building in the case of normally approaching wind and suburban terrain roughness. It is not useful for the wider needs of multizone airflow model applications.

Modelling wind pressure distribution according to a parametric approach means finding an algorithm calculating the variation of Cp over the building envelope surfaces as wind direction and architectural and environmental conditions are varied. As a result of the stochastic behaviour of the distribution of pressure coefficients around a building, such an algorithm should be based on empirical correlations of time-averaged Cp values from wind-tunnel tests chosen as reference data sets.

Wall-averaged Cp values are given only for wide intervals of wind angle [18, 19]. A parametric wind-pressure distribution model can yield Cp values at any point on the surface for any specific wind angle if there is sufficient data. Three types of parameters are suggested, as shown in Table 2.6.

Table 2.6. Parameters affecting the distribution of Cp

Wind	Environment	Building geometry
Wind velocity profile exponent ($\forall$)	Plan area density (PAD)	Frontal aspect ratio (FAR)
Wind incident angle (2)	Relative building height (RbH)	Side aspect ratio (SAR) Element positioning coordinates Roof slope tilt angle(N)

2.1.4.2 Regression analysis of the distribution of Cp

Within the framework of the European PASCOOL/Joule Project, a regression analysis of the Cp coefficient was carried out and a program called CPCALC+ has been implemented [20].

The Cp data sets were selected from a literature review and from specific experiments which were carried out within the frame of this project [21]. These data sets were analysed on the basis of the following features:

- number of parameters considered;
- range of values for each parameter;
- similarity of parameter values between different tests;
- lack of experimental data for specific parameters.

The regression analysis was carried out both for real Cp values, in order to define reference Cp profiles, and for normalized Cp values, with the reference values set equal to 1.

The relevant fitting equations were used to calculate Cp correction coefficients, which are the basis of the algorithm included in the model.

The Cp distribution over the building envelope and the Cp variation range with respect to the reference values were analysed by fitting the normalized Cp values in relation to each parameter. If $i_1, i_2, \ldots, i_n$ are parameters considered as independent variables, and C_1, C_2, . . ., C_n are parameters considered as constants, the dependent variable, i.e. the normalized Cp, is:

$$\text{Cp}_{\text{norm}}(i_1, i_2, \ldots, i_n) = \text{Cp}_{C_1, C_2, \ldots, C_m}(i_1, i_2, \ldots, i_n) / \text{Cp}_{C_1, C_2, \ldots, C_m}(i_{1\text{ref}}, i_{2\text{ref}}, \ldots, i_{n\text{ref}})$$

$$(2.42)$$

where $m = 1$ or 2, $n = 1$ in the one-dimensional regression (walls and roof) and $n = 2$ in the two-dimensional regression (roof).

The parameters were sorted according to their interrelations within the reference data sets (Table 2.7). As a correlation factor for the curve fitting, 0.95 was the minimum value when a one-directional regression was used, while 0.70 was the minimum value when two-directional regression was used (only for roofs).

Table 2.7. Parameter grouping in the regression analysis

Factor influencing the distribution of Cp	Independent variables		Constants (C)*
	Type	Reference value	
Terrain roughness	∀	0.22 (walls), 0.20 (roofs)	zh (walls), y (roof)
Density of surrounding buildings	PAD	0.0	zh(walls), y (roof)
Height relative to the surrounding buildings	RbH	1.0	zh(walls),y (roof), PAD
Building geometry: walls	FAR	1.0	zh, PAD
	SAR	1.0	zh, PAD
Building geometry: flat roof	FAR, PAD		y
	SAR, PAD		y
Wind direction: walls	xl	0.5	zh, 2
Wind direction: flat roof	2	0°	y
Lateral distribution		0.5	y, 2
Roof tilt and wind direction	N	0°	y
Roof tilt and lateral distribution	N		y, 2

* Parameters with varying fixed value; for each regression, every other parameter has the reference value.

By using this strategy, the various contributions of the terrain roughness, plan area density, relative building height, aspect ratio, wind direction and slope angle of the roofs were studied and modelled, as well as integrated into a user friendly program CPCALC+.

2.2   INDOOR CLIMATE

From a thermodynamic point of view, a building can be considered as a set of various systems coupled together. These systems may be rooms, walls, equipment, etc. Thus, the thermodynamic equilibrium of each system can be defined for a set of state variables, namely the pressure, the temperature, the mass or the various species concentrations.

In this section, we will focus on the equilibrium of a zone of one building. We define a zone as a geometric entity limited by an envelope, which might be a room or a combination of rooms with identical thermal behaviour. First, we will describe the main physical phenomena that define the behaviour of this zone. Second, we will translate these phenomena with the help of comprehensive equations. Then, we will describe the physical phenomena influencing the air transport in a building and finally we will introduce the concept of thermal inertia.

2.2.1   Thermal balance of a room

2.2.1.1   *Short description of the main phenomena and couplings in a zone*

As depicted in Figure 2.9, the final equilibrium of a zone (the definition of its state variables) depends on the interaction of climatic conditions and internal data relative to the use or the occupation of the zone. In this figure, the links between external or internal data with the state variables defining the thermodynamic equilibrium of the zone represent transfer phenomena. Thus, to solve the complete problem, we must solve two different kinds of physical equations:

- transfer equations that define, from a knowledge of the state variables, the various flows (heat, mass, chemical species, etc.);
- balance equations that define the state, namely pressure, temperature or various chemical species concentration, from the quantification of the various flows acting on a zone.

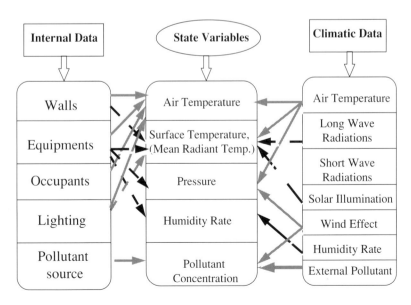

Figure 2.9. Physical phenomena and couplings in a room

In this application, we usually deal with three balance equations:

- energy
- mass, and
- pressure

and we study four different transfer phenomena:

- thermal diffusion (or conduction)
- convection (or advection)
- radiation (electromagnetic transfer), and
- mass.

In order to simplify this approach, let first us consider the thermal equilibrium of a single room.

2.2.1.2 Energy balance equation

Figure 2.10 shows a sketch of the thermal equilibrium of a room. In this sketch,

E_s represents short-wavelength radiation;
Φ_{cv} is the convective flux exchanged between the internal surfaces and the air;
Φ_{pc} is the total convective internal gains (occupants + equipment);
Φ_{ci} is the total conductive flux through the walls;
Q_m is the total mass flow rate of air at temperature T_e;
V is the volume of the room;
T_a is the air temperature;
T_{s_i} is the interior surface temperature.

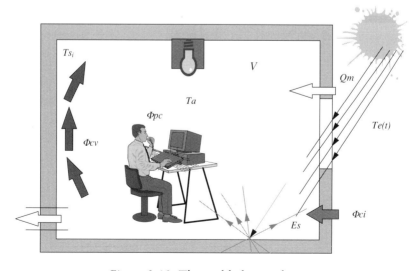

Figure 2.10. Thermal balance of a room

Then the global enthalpy balance of the room leads to:

$$VCp\frac{dT_a}{dt} = \Phi_{pc} + \sum_{i=1}^{nS} hc_i S_i \left(T_{s_i} - T_a\right) + Q_m Cp(T_e - T_a) \qquad (2.43)$$

where Q_m represents the total air mass flow rate coming from outside. In the general case, this flow rate comes from outdoors and also from connecting rooms at different temperatures and pressures.

The convective flux exchanged between the room air and each surface of the internal envelope of the room depends on the surface temperature of each internal surface. This temperature, T_{s_i}, is also defined by the thermal balance of each surface:

$$-\lambda \mathbf{n}.\mathrm{grad}\,T\big|_s = hc_i\left(T_{s_i} - T_a\right) - \alpha_i E_i + \Phi_{net_i} \qquad (2.44)$$

where:

λ is the thermal conductivity of the surface material;
$\mathbf{n}$ is the external normal of surface S_i;
hc_i is the convective exchange coefficient at surface S_i;
α_i is the thermal absorptivity of surface S_i for short-wave radiation;
E_i is the short-wavelength radiative flux density incident on surface S_i, (mainly solar and lighting);
Φ_{net_i} is the net long-wave radiation exchange between surface S_i and other surfaces.

Figure 2.11 shows a sketch of this balance.

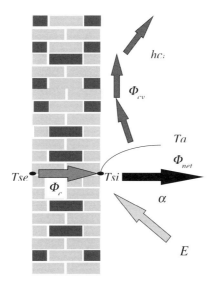

Figure 2.11. Thermal balance of a room surface

2.2.2   Mass transfer prediction

In the thermal balance of a room (equation 2.43) Q_m is the mass airflow rate coming from outside. In a general case, there are two main contributions of mass flow rates to the enthalpy balance of a room: the airflows coming from outdoors (infiltration or fresh air ventilation), and the interzonal airflow rates due to the air mass transfer between the various zones of a building.

In order to describe these mass transfers between zones of a building or between the indoor spaces and outdoors, a state variable, the pressure P and the transfer equation between two zones or from outside should be defined for each zone.

2.2.2.1   The driving forces

For steady, incompressible and non-viscous flow, the Navier–Stokes equations are integrated and reduced to a simpler expression combining the transport effect upon a field of density of the velocity of the flow, the pressure gradient effect and the gravity effect:

$$\tfrac{1}{2}\rho V^2 + P + \rho gz = \text{Constant} \tag{2.45}$$

This equation, combining the local values of pressure, velocity and density fields, is known as Bernoulli's equation. It is the fundamental equation necessary to understand and predict the behaviour of airflows in a building in terms of its natural environment. The next step is to define precisely the effects of these internal and external climatic parameters on the mass transfers.

THE EFFECT OF THE WIND

As discussed in the preceding section, wind creates a pressure distribution around a building with respect to the atmospheric pressure. This pressure is calculated by correcting the average dynamic pressure of the wind by a pressure coefficient Cp depending mainly on the building shape, the wind direction and the influence of nearby buildings and the natural environment [22]:

$$P_s = \text{Cp}P_v \tag{2.46}$$

where:

$P_v = \tfrac{1}{2}\rho V_H^2$; V_H is the mean wind velocity at upwind building height and ρ the outdoor air density as a function of atmospheric pressure, temperature and humidity.

THE STACK EFFECT

Another physical phenomenon that influences the infiltration and/or the ventilation rates of buildings is the buoyancy or stack effect. This phenomenon

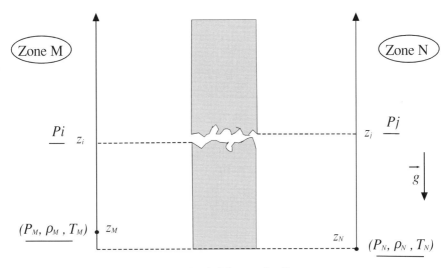

Figure 2.12. The stack effect

is due to density differences between inside and outside a building or between zones. In this application, the air density is mainly a function of temperature and moisture content of the air [23]. Figure 2.12 depicts leakage between two zones M and N.

The reference heights are respectively z_M and z_N. The reference pressure, temperature and humidity are respectively P_M, T_M and H_M, and P_N, T_N and H_N. The relative heights of the leakage in each zone are respectively z_i and z_j.

The local pressure difference between the two sides of the opening is $P_i - P_j$ with respect to the reference pressure of each zone:

$$P_i - P_j = P_M - P_N + P_{st} \qquad (2.47)$$

where P_{st} is the pressure difference created by the stack effect:

$$P_{st} = \rho_M g (z_M - z_i) - \rho_N g (z_N - z_j) \qquad (2.48)$$

In this equation, ρ_M and ρ_N are the air densities in zones M and N respectively.

2.2.2.2 Flow equations
ONE-WAY FLOW THROUGH A SIMPLE CRACK OR OPENING

Using Bernoulli's equation, one can directly obtain a theoretical expression for the velocity of a flow due to a pressure difference. The theoretical mass flow rate induced by this pressure difference is :

$$m'_t = \rho A \sqrt{\frac{2\Delta P}{\rho}} \qquad (2.49)$$

where A is the area of the cross section of the flow tube. In fact the flow is obviously affected by the geometrical characteristics of the opening. For a simple geometrical configuration, it is possible to introduce a discharge coefficient C_d relating the real mass flow rate, m', to the theoretical one. Thus,

$$m' = C_d \rho A \sqrt{\frac{2\Delta P}{\rho}} \qquad (2.50)$$

Furthermore, it appears that for leakages or openings of complex geometry, the dependency of the pressure difference is even more complicated. Therefore, an empirical power law function is usually considered.

$$m' = K\Delta P^n \qquad (2.51)$$

The flow exponent n ranges between 0.5 (fully developed turbulent flow) and 1 (laminar flow). The flow coefficient K includes in its definition the geometrical characteristics of the leakage and the discharge effect and can be interpreted physically as the flow rate induced by a unitary pressure difference. It is usually determined by measurement.

2.2.2.3 *Mass conservation equation*
Under assumed steady-state conditions, the conservation of mass inside each zone must be ensured by considering all elementary flows passing through the various leaks.

$$m'_{\text{vent}} + \sum_{k=1}^{N_k} m'_k = 0 \qquad (2.52)$$

where N_k is the total number of distinct leakage openings in the zone m'_{vent} is the extracted or supply mass flow rate due to a mechanical system and m'_k is the individual mass flow rate through leakage opening k.

2.2.2.4 *Large openings*
We call a large opening an internal or external opening that can be characterized by a two-way flow. To represent the behaviour of a large opening, we can use the concept that we have already used for a one flow opening, an explicit definition of the flow by a Bernoulli flow regime assumption, or any other correlation of natural or mixed convection corresponding to the studied configuration [24]. In order to integrate the behaviour of such an opening, the easiest way, however, is to represent its behaviour by non-linear flow equations based on the evaluation of the pressure fields on the two sides of the opening. Thus, the first possibility is then to describe the large opening as a series of parallel small one-way flow openings and to use the preceding method for each opening. This method has been used by Walton [25] and Roldan [26].

Another approach is to interpret directly the whole behaviour of this large opening in terms of a set of non-linear equations describing this typical scheme.

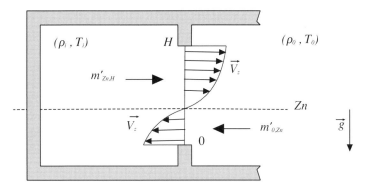

Figure 2.13. The basic problem of gravitational flow through a vertical opening

Since the pioneer work of Brown and Solvason, many authors have dealt with this solution. Figure 2.13 describes the basic problem.

For an incompressible, inviscid and steady flow, from Bernoulli's equation, the horizontal velocity V_z along a streamline is given by:

$$V_z = \left[2 \left(\frac{\rho_0 - \rho_i}{\rho_0} \right) \right]^{0.5} \tag{2.53}$$

If Z_N is the height of the neutral plane, the mass flow rate below this neutral plane is given directly by integrating the velocity profile between the origin and Z_N:

$$m'_{0,Z_N} = C_d \int_0^{Z_N} \rho_0 V_z W \, dz \tag{2.54}$$

where C_d, the discharge coefficient, takes into account the local contraction of the flow through the opening and the friction effects along its solid limits. The position of the neutral plane is then given by writing the mass conservation equation through this opening, which leads to:

$$\frac{Z_N}{H - Z_N} = \left(\frac{\rho_i}{\rho_0} \right)^{1/3} \tag{2.55}$$

Finally, a direct integration delivers the value of the outgoing airflow:

$$m'_{0,Z_N} = C_d \frac{W}{3} \left(8gH^3 \rho'_i \Delta\rho \right)^{0.5} \tag{2.56}$$

where:

$$\rho'_i = \frac{\rho_i}{\left[1 + \left(\dfrac{\rho_i}{\rho_0} \right)^{1/3} \right]^3} \tag{2.57}$$

In this model, the air densities are mainly functions of the air temperature and humidity. This basic model has been used by numerous authors and it can be coupled with an air supply on one side of the opening or with a thermal gradient on both sides of the opening [24]. More recently, it has been improved by adding a new correction factor to take into account the direct effect of wind on this opening. This correction factor deduced from the experimental work carried out during the PASCOOL project by Santamouris [27] is used instead of the discharge coefficient C_d and this new formulation leads to identical equations.

2.2.3   Basic elements of heat transfer through a wall

2.2.3.1 *Basic phenomena: the Fourier law and the heat conduction equation*

This phenomenological hypothesis can be presented easily by saying that there exists a linear relation between the heat flux density vector φ and the temperature gradient at any location of a solid. Furthermore, the heat is conducted from hot regions to cold regions, thus:

$$\varphi = -\lambda \operatorname{grad} T \tag{2.58}$$

where λ is the thermal conductivity of the material.

If we consider an elementary volume dV without internal heat source, taking into account all the heat fluxes transferred through its own surface, we can build a balance equation of its enthalpy, defining its equilibrium. This balance equation is usually used in its differential form, called the heat conduction equation:

$$\operatorname{div}(\lambda \operatorname{grad} T) = \rho \mathrm{Cp} \frac{\partial T}{\partial t} \tag{2.59}$$

If the thermal conductivity λ can be assumed as constant (the usual case in building physics), then equation (2.59) takes a simpler form:

$$\lambda \Delta T = \rho \mathrm{Cp} \frac{\partial T}{\partial t} \tag{2.60}$$

or

$$a \Delta T = \frac{\partial T}{\partial t} \tag{2.61}$$

where a is the thermal diffusivity of the material.

2.2.3.2 *Thermal behaviour of a wall subject to periodic boundary conditions: the thermal inertia concept*

Naturally ventilated buildings are subject to indoor periodic conditions with a more or less steady outdoor environment. In order to analyse the thermal

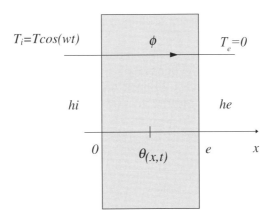

*Figure 2.14. A single wall subject to a periodic
air temperature variation*

behaviour of the building walls in such a configuration, let us consider a single wall of homogeneous and isotropic material subject on its internal surface to a sinusoidal air temperature variation $T_i = T \cos \phi t$ and on its external surface to a steady temperature T_e. Figure 2.14 shows this configuration.

The general solution of this problem can be found in any textbook [28]:

$$\theta(x, t) = T(t)(A \exp(\alpha x) + B \exp(-\alpha x)) \tag{2.62}$$

with $\alpha^2 = i\omega/a$ and $T(t) = T \exp i\omega t$.

Boundary conditions are on the internal surface:

$$\varphi(0, t) = -h_i \left[\theta(0, t) - T_i \right] \tag{2.63}$$

and on the external surface:

$$\varphi(e, t) = \left(h_e \left[\theta(e, t) - T_e \right] \right) \tag{2.64}$$

If $T_i = T \cos \omega t$ and $T_e = 0$, $\theta(x, t)$, this gives:

$$\theta(x, t) = T_i(t) \frac{\cosh \alpha(e - x) + \dfrac{h_e}{\lambda \alpha} \sinh \alpha(e - x)}{\left(1 + \dfrac{h_e}{h_i} \right) \cosh \alpha e + \left(\dfrac{he}{\lambda \alpha} + \dfrac{\lambda \alpha}{h_i} \right) \sinh \alpha e} \tag{2.65}$$

where e is the wall thickness, α is the thermal diffusivity and $\lambda \alpha / h$ is the Biot number.

At this stage we can introduce the effective thickness, $\delta = \sqrt{2a/\omega}$. This thickness corresponds to an amplitude of the temperature variation equal to the internal amplitude divided by 2.72. This term will be discussed in the next section.

If the thickness of the wall, e, is much higher than δ (which is usually the case in buildings), we can consider the behaviour of this layer as an isolated form. Then we can ignore the relative influence of outdoor conditions and heat transfer at the indoor surface, and the general expression becomes:

$$\theta(x, t) = T \exp\left[-\frac{x}{\delta}\right] \cos\left(\omega t - \frac{x}{\delta}\right) \tag{2.66}$$

or:

$$\theta(x, t) = T \exp\left[-\frac{x}{\delta}\right] \cos\omega\left(t - \frac{x}{\omega\delta}\right) \tag{2.67}$$

This expression indicates that the thermal behaviour of the wall is characterized by an exponential decrease of the amplitude of the indoor temperature variation. The new amplitude at a location x will be $T(x) = T \exp[-x/\delta]$ with a linear time delay $\tau = x/\omega\delta$. These two phenomena are characteristics of the so-called thermal inertia of the wall.

Then the amplitude correction factor is:

$$\text{Ac} = \exp-x\sqrt{\frac{\pi}{aP}} \quad \text{or} \quad \text{Ac} = \exp-\frac{x}{\lambda}\sqrt{\frac{\pi}{P}}\,b \tag{2.68}$$

where P is the period of the indoor temperature variation and b is the effusivity of the wall, $b = \sqrt{\lambda\rho C}$. The time delay, τ, becomes

$$\tau = \frac{x}{2}\sqrt{\frac{P}{a\pi}} \quad \text{or} \quad \tau = \frac{x}{2\lambda}\sqrt{\frac{P}{\pi}}\,b \tag{2.69}$$

To evaluate the heat flux density at any point in the wall, we will use the Fourier assumption directly and calculate the derivative of the temperature field at this point. A similar expression for the heat flux density can be obtained:

$$\varphi(x, t) = T\frac{\lambda\sqrt{2}}{\delta}\exp\left(-\frac{x}{\delta}\right)\cos\omega\left[t - \left(\frac{x}{\delta\omega} + \frac{\pi}{4\omega}\right)\right] \tag{2.70}$$

We can see from these equations that, while, in the steady state condition, knowledge of the thermal conductivity is sufficient to characterize the thermal behaviour of an homogeneous wall, in a periodic regime knowledge of the thermal effusivity b is needed.

For construction materials, this effusivity b ranges between 1 and 15, and it is very important to distinguish clearly this quantity from thermal insulation. For a constant insulation level (e/λ = constant) the thermal effusivity which characterizes the damping of the amplitude and the time delay will increase with the density and the specific heat capacity of the material.

For example, if only the insulation property is considered, a concrete wall of 40 cm thick is equivalent to a particle wood wall of 3.7 cm. However, if the thermal inertia is also considered, for the concrete wall the amplitude correction factor for a diurnal temperature variation will be 0.07 and the phase delay around 10 hours, while for the wood structure the amplitude correction factor for a diurnal temperature variation will be 0.59 and the phase delay about 2.23 hours. These numbers show clearly how important the thermal inertia phenomenon is in regulating the indoor conditions of a room.

2.3   COOLING POTENTIAL OF NATURAL VENTILATION

2.3.1   Introduction

In addition to providing good indoor air quality, ventilation plays a major role in maintaining acceptable thermal comfort and improving energy performance. The thermal behaviour of a building is strongly coupled to ventilation and air infiltration. At the same time, airflow depends on the different thermal levels of the building zones. In the absence of wind, these differences are the only driving forces for ventilation.

Use of natural ventilation during the **daytime** has three objectives:

- cooling of the indoor air as long as outdoor temperatures are lower than the indoor temperatures;
- cooling of the structure of the building;
- a direct cooling effect over the human body (through convection and evaporation).

If the natural ventilation takes place during the **night-time**, the objective is to use the thermal mass of the building as an intermediate storage medium, which enables us to use during the day the coolness stored during the previous night. (This is only applicable to office buildings where the building is not occupied during the night.)

2.3.2   Natural ventilation and comfort

2.3.2.1   *Review of the heat transfer processes over the human body*

Figure 2.15 shows the major heat flows over the human body, where: H_D is the direct, H_d is the diffuse and H_R is the reflected solar radiation absorbed by the subject; ΔR_S and ΔR_C represent the long-wave radiation exchange with surrounding surfaces; C_V is the air convection and E represents evaporation.

The thermal balance of a human body results in:

$$E_{sw} = M(1-\eta) + (\Delta R + C_V) - C_{res} - E_{res} - E_{dif} \qquad (2.71)$$

where $M(1-\eta)$ is the net metabolic heat production, C_{res} and E_{res} are respectively the sensible heat and the latent heat due to respiration. E_{dif} is the skin diffusion heat. The sweating regulation term, E_{sw}, closes the thermal

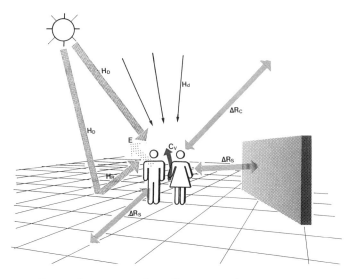

Figure 2.15. Major heat flows over the human body

balance and gives a measure of the adaptive effect of the organism and, in consequence, of the level of comfort.

The terms on the right-hand side of equation (2.71) can be calculated using different assumptions and correlations. Next, a brief overview of all the expressions used is included (all the energy values are expressed in W m^{-2}) [29]:

- radiation + convection:

$$(R+C) = \tau_{cl}\alpha_{sk}\left(F_D H_D + F_d H_d + F_r H_r\right) + h f_{cl} F_{cl}\left(T_o - T_{sk}\right) \qquad (2.72)$$

- respiration:

latent: $E_{res} = 0.0173M\left(5.87 - HR_a P_v\left(T_a\right)\right)$ $\qquad (2.73)$

sensible: $C_{res} = 0.014M\left(34 - T_a\right)$ $\qquad (2.74)$

- skin diffusion:

$$E_{dif} = 0.41\left(P_v\left(T_{sk}\right) - HR_a P_v\left(T_a\right)\right) \qquad (2.75)$$

where:

τ_{cl} is the clothing short-wave transmissivity (~0.11);
α_{sk} is the skin short-wave absorptivity (~0.7);
F_D is the body fraction seen from the sun (~0.5);
F_d is the view factor between person and sky;

F_r is the view factor between person and surroundings;

H_D, H_d, H_r are the direct, diffuse and reflected solar radiation (W m^{-2})

f_{cl} is the clothing area factor $(f_{cl} = 1 + 0.30I_{cle})$;

F_{cl} is the clothing intrinsic thermal efficiency $(F_{cl} = 1/0.155hf_{cl}I_{cle})$;

I_{cle} is the clothing effective insulation $(I_{cle} = 0.524\sum I'_{cl} + 0.056)$ (clo);

h is the convective-radiative transfer coefficient $(h = h_c + h_r)$ (W m^{-2} K^{-1});

h_c is the convective transfer coefficient (W m^{-2} K^{-1});

h_r is the radiative transfer coefficient (W m^{-2} K^{-1});

T_{sk} is the skin average temperature (°C);

T_o is the operative temperature $(T_o = (h_r T_r + h_c T_a)(h_r + h_c))$ (°C);

T_a is the ambient air temperature (°C);

T_r is the equivalent average radiant temperature (°C);

HR_a is the relative humidity of the ambient air (%);

$P_v(T)$ is the water vapour pressure of the air at a temperature T (kPa).

Figure 2.16 is a scheme showing the effect of the environmental variables on thermal comfort. A given comfort level can be achieved using multiple combinations of these variables.

2.3.2.2   The impact of the air velocity and the wall surface temperatures on the occupant's thermal comfort

The air velocity around the human body and the surface temperatures of the walls modify respectively the convective and the long-wave radiative terms of the balance equation.

The modification of the convective term is due to the increase of the convection heat transfer coefficient. Figure 2.17 Shows h_c as function of the room air velocity assuming $h_c = 2.7 + 8.7v^{0.67}$ [30].

To evaluate the combined effect of the air velocity and the wall surface temperatures, let us assume a standard indoor comfort situation characterized by an indoor air temperature of 25°C, 50% relative humidity, surface temperature of the walls of 25°C and no air velocity around the occupants. The same result for the energy balance over the human body (that is, the same comfort conditions) can be obtained by different combinations of the variables below.

For instance, Figures 2.18 and 2.19 show isocomfort graphs with some of the possible combinations obtained with a ventilation strategy (all the points pertaining to the isocomfort surface have the same comfort conditions).

Inspection of the figures reveals that, for instance, we obtain the same conditions as in the standard situation with:

- an indoor temperature of 28°C if the air velocity is 0.4 m s^{-1};
- an indoor temperature of 30°C if the wall surface temperatures are 23°C and the air velocity is 0.4 m s^{-1}.

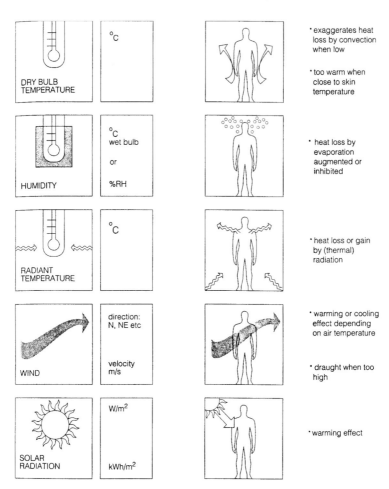

Figure 2.16. Environmental variables and their effect on thermal comfort (adapted from Yanna [36])

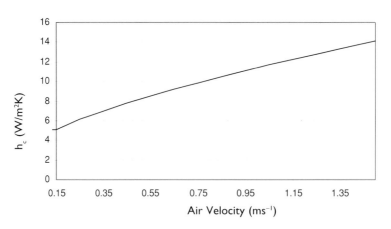

Figure 2.17. Convection heat transfer coefficient

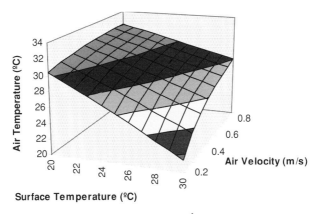

Figure 2.18. Isocomfort curve

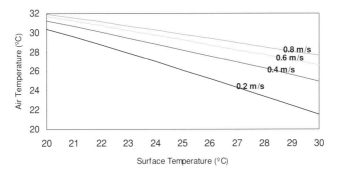

*Figure 2.19. Isocomfort curve parametrized as a function
of the air velocity*

2.3.3 Natural ventilation and building performance

2.3.3.1 Coupling heat transfer and airflow processes in buildings

PHENOMENA AND COUPLING

In general terms, the simulation of thermal and fluid mechanical behaviour of buildings calls for the definition of the transient behaviour of the building components under the impact of exterior and interior conditions.

The impact of the exterior environment is related to:

- solar radiation;
- outdoor air temperature;
- other external temperatures of sky, ground and surrounding surfaces;
- wind conditions;
- outdoor air humidity;
- outdoor concentration of pollutants.

The impact of the interior environment is related to:

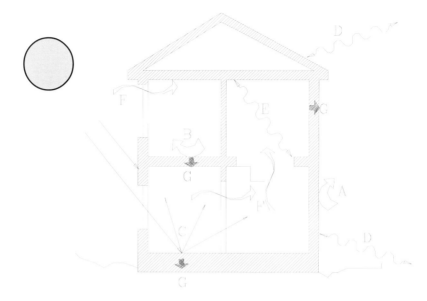

Figure 2.20. Scheme showing all the mechanisms involved in thermal building behaviour

- heat gains derived from lighting, occupants and equipment;
- sources of humidity and pollutants;
- sensible and latent effects of existing conditioning equipment.

A building can be described as a complex system made up of different solid elements forming an enclosed space. In this system we can identify a set of heat and mass transfer mechanisms, as follows (Figure 2.20):

A   external convection (usually forced) between the external surfaces and the outdoor air;

B   internal convection (usually natural or mixed) between the internal surfaces of the envelope components, the occupants, the lighting fixtures, etc. and the indoor air;

C   short-wave radiation coming from the sun and, in some cases, from internal heat sources;

D   external long-wave radiation between the envelope surfaces and the sky, surrounding buildings and the ground;

E   internal long-wave radiation between internal surfaces;

F   airflow through cracks and large openings between different enclosures of the building and between these and outdoors;

G   conduction through the building elements (internal and external).

The problem of simulating a building is very complex because of the combined effect of heat and mass transfer mechanisms. This coupling is handled on the three following levels:

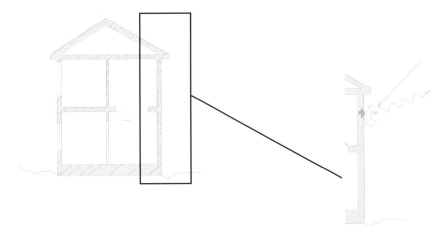

Figure 2.21. Scheme showing all the mechanisms involved in the behaviour of an exterior surface

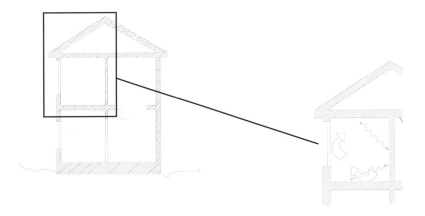

Figure 2.22. Scheme showing all the mechanisms involved in the interior zones

- Heat is transferred through the building shell by the combined effect of conduction, convection and radiation on the external elements (Figure 2.21).
- All the internal surfaces of an enclosure are coupled directly through the radiation mechanism and indirectly through the convection mechanism to the indoor air (Figure 2.22).
- Interzonal coupling is attributed to conduction (through walls separating two rooms), radiation (through semi-transparent media between two spaces) and/or airflow between enclosures (Figure 2.23).

In the following sections the combined effect of the above mechanisms will be described in a general way, considering all the variables involved, as well as the mathematical representation of their interrelation.

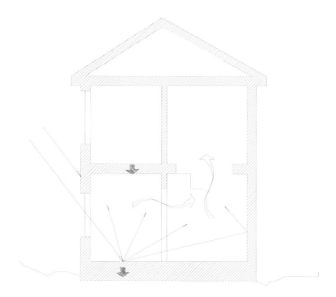

Figure 2.23. Scheme showing all the physical mechanisms involved in interzone coupling

SURFACE THERMAL BALANCES

Each internal or external isothermal surface temperature is defined by satisfying the thermodynamic equilibrium for the surface submitted to conduction, convection and radiation heat transfer (long- and short-wave radiation).

conduction   =   convection + short-wave radiation +
                 long-wave radiation

Replacing the net flux Φ_{neti} by its expression in equation (2.44):

$$-\lambda_i \left.\frac{\partial T_{\text{air}}}{\partial x}\right|_i = h_{Ci}(T_i - T_{\text{air}}) - \alpha_i E_i + \sum_{j=1}^{N_i} C_{i,j}^{R}(T_i^4 - T_j^4) \qquad (2.76)$$

where:

   $C_{i,j}^{R}$ is the long-wave radiant exchange term between the surface i and
        the surface j;
   N_i is the number of surfaces in the enclosure of the element i.

CONDUCTION: Modelling of conduction heat transfer in buildings is based on splitting the boundary of a building element into a finite number of layers N, having uniform temperature and uniform heat flow.

   This approach gives results that are closer to reality when increased discretization of the boundary is used. However, on most occasions, it implies a large number of simplifications in the modelling, while preserving total rigour (for instance one-dimensional conduction through walls).

The temperatures of the N layers are identified as the coupling variables.

The surface conduction heat fluxes at the boundary and the corresponding surface temperatures are related by the following formula:

$$\mathbf{q}(t) = \left[A(t)\right]\mathbf{T}_S + \mathbf{P}(t) \tag{2.77}$$

where the matrix $[A(t)]$ and the vector $\mathbf{P}(t)$ are calculated at each simulation step (for constant material properties, $[A(t)]$ is constant). This formula represents all the modelling techniques found in the literature.

CONVECTION: The convective heat transfer (q_{cv}) is expressed as a function of the temperature difference between the surface (T_s) and the air near the surface (T_{air}):

$$q_{cv} = h_{cv}(T_s - T_{air})$$

The proportionality constant h_{cv} is the convective heat transfer coefficient or film coefficient. This well known formulation is used by the majority of the modellers.

The main problems that modellers find in this transfer mechanism is not the formulation itself but the precise knowledge of convective heat transfer coefficients in each situation.

RADIATION: After linearization of the long-wave radiative exchanges, the heat flow by radiation (q) at the interior surfaces of an enclosure with opaque, semi-transparent or completely transparent elements can be formulated as:

$$\mathbf{q}_{rad} = [K]\mathbf{T} + [C_1]\mathbf{E}_{ext} + [C_2]\phi \tag{2.78}$$

where:

> $\mathbf{q}_{rad}$ is the vector of the radiant heat flow;
> $\mathbf{T}$ is the vector of the surface temperatures in the enclosure;
> $\mathbf{E}_{ext}$ is the vector of the exterior irradiation for every surface of the enclosure (only for (semi-) transparent elements);
> ϕ is the vector with irradiation (solar radiation, internal gains, etc.) for every surface of the enclosure, and
> $[K]$, $[C_1]$ and $[C_2]$ are matrices for the radiant redistribution calculated according to the method used.

The above equation is applied (with different matrices) for both long-wave and short-wave radiation.

ROOM MASS BALANCES

These are the enthalpy balances in each enclosure or zone. The enthalpy balance of each zone imposes the time variation of the zone enthalpy, so that it is equal to the total net heat entering the zone either by surface convection (coming from the internal gains or from the interior surfaces of the enclosure) or by air convection (air movements from/to outdoors or from/to other zones):

Time variation infiltration (of) enthalpy	=	Internal gains convection	+	Interior surface convection	+	Convected ventilation enthalpy $z = 1, \ldots, \text{NZ}$

$$V^z C_p \frac{\mathrm{d}\left(\rho^z T_a^z\right)}{\mathrm{d}t} = Q_{ig}^z + \sum_{k=1}^{NS_z} h_{cvk} S_k \left(T_{sk} - T_a^z\right) + \sum_{j=0}^{NZ} \dot{m}_{jz} C_p T_a^j - \sum_{j=0}^{NZ} \dot{m}_{zj} C_p T_a^z \quad (2.79)$$

where the superscript z denotes the zone index, NZ is the total number of zones of the building, and NS_z is the number of surfaces convecting to zone z and:

V is the volume of the zone;
C_p is the specific heat of the air;
ρ is the density of the air;
T_a is the temperature of the air;
T_{sk} is the temperature of the surface k in the zone;
Q_{ig} is the convective energy from the internal gains;
h_{cvk} is the film coefficient for the surface k in the zone;
m_{jz} is the mass flow from the zone j toward the zone z (0 is the outdoor environment).

MATRIX FORMULATION OF THE THERMAL PROCESSES
The mathematical interpretation of the thermal processes in buildings leads to a system of two different equations expressing:

- surface heat balance at every isothermal internal surface;
- heat balances of the air of each zone (fully mixed).

The unknowns in this system of equations are, obviously, the internal surface temperatures and the zone air temperature.

As an example, let us consider a two-zone building (see Figure 2.24) with eight internal surfaces in zone 1, where temperatures are included in the vector

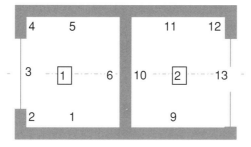

Figure 2.24. Cross section of the example building showing the numbering of surfaces

$\{T_1\}$, seven internal surfaces in zone 2 where temperatures are included in the vector $\{T_2\}$, and the two air temperatures of the zones included in the vector $\{T_{zone}\}$.

Let all the temperatures be included in a single vector $\{T\}$ that will contain first $\{T_1\}$, next $\{T_2\}$ and in the two final positions $\{T_{zone}\}$. The heat balance equations can be rewritten together in a matrix system as $[A]\,\{T\} = \{B\}$, where is a matrix containing the coefficients of all the system equations, $\{T\}$ is a vector containing the temperatures as described previously and $\{B\}$ is a vector containing all independent terms.

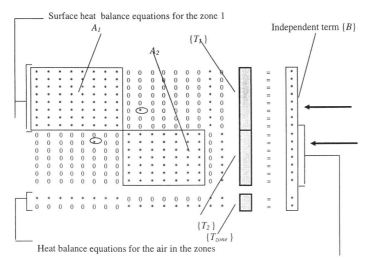

Figure 2.25. Structure of the final equations

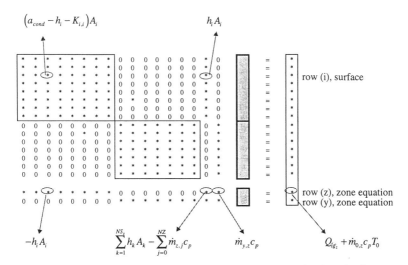

Figure 2.26. Structure of the final equations showing the detail of some of the non-zero terms

Figure 2.25 shows the whole final matrix for a two-zone building with an opaque element between zones. In this scheme, the asterisks represent non-zero terms. Figure 2.26 shows the detail of some of the non-zero terms.

The two indicated with an arrow are the two surface balances of an interior wall having one side in each zone. For a building with an internal opening, the surface balance equations will have more non-zero terms. Haghighat and Chandrashekar [32] developed a procedure for automatic formulation of these matrices.

2.3.3.2   Influence of the airflow on the thermal performance

SURFACE BALANCE EQUATIONS

At the level of the *surface balance equations*, the direct effect of the airflow rate appears in the film coefficients. The value of the film coefficients depends on the air velocity near the walls. Figure 2.27 compares the film coefficients [31] at interior walls under forced convection for different air velocities with those corresponding to still air. As can be seen, the film coefficients increase significantly with the air velocities. This fact improves to a great extent the structural cooling promoted by night ventilation strategies, as we will see later.

ROOM AIR BALANCE EQUATIONS: DAYTIME VENTILATION

At the level of the air balance equations, the major effect of the airflow rate appears in the convected enthalpy of the inlet outdoor air.

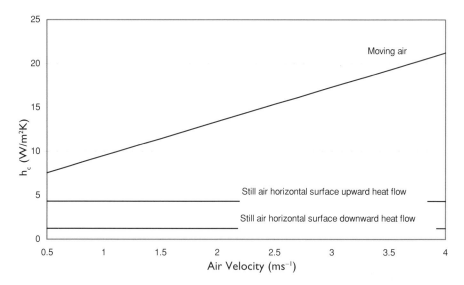

Figure 2.27. Variation of the film coefficients with the air velocity for internal walls [31]

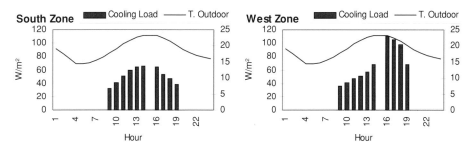

Figure 2.28. Load profiles for different zones of an office building

For example, we will examine the potential effect of this term on a hypothetical office building in Porto, Portugal, for which an indoor set-point temperature of 25°C has been prescribed. Figure 2.28 shows the cooling load profiles of two different zones of such building for a typical cooling day. Figure 2.29 shows the cooling power that could be provided for different combinations of the ventilation air and the indoor/outdoor temperature difference.

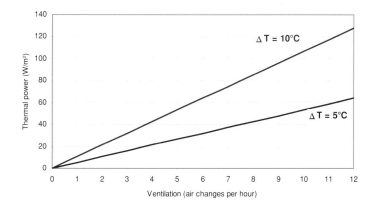

Figure 2.29. The cooling power of ventilation

As can be seen, the order of magnitude of the cooling requirements is comparable to that of the cooling energy that could be provided by ventilation so that it is certain that a ventilation strategy would cover a significant fraction of the cooling requirements at a seasonal level. The extent of this fraction is very dependent on the climate and on the balance-point temperature of the building being analysed.

For the same building, Figure 2.30 shows, for the Iberian peninsula, the regional variation of the fraction of the cooling requirements covered by daytime ventilation, assuming an average ventilation rate of 9 ach (air changes per hour).

For a given climate, the basic problem is to determine whether natural ventilation during the daytime is a suitable option for a building in which the balance-point temperature [33] is considerably lower than the indoor set-point

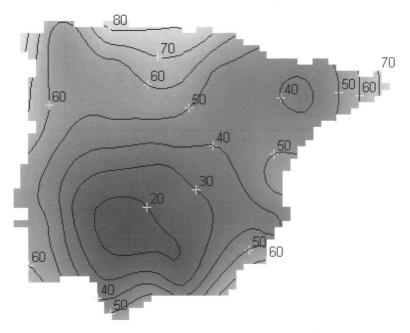

*Figure 2.30. Energy savings percentage (%) due to a daytime
ventilation strategy (9 ach)*

temperature. This rarely happens in residential buildings (except if the design
of the envelope and the orientation of the building are very unfavourable for
the cooling season), but is very common in commercial and institutional
buildings. The shaded areas of Figure 2.31 show the periods in which daytime
ventilation is potentially applicable.

NIGHT VENTILATION

Night ventilation strategies imply the existence of intermediate storage which
makes it possible to use during the day the coolness produced during the
previous night.

The thermal levels involved are three: the outdoor air temperature ($T_{outdoor}$), the
storage medium temperature ($T_{storage}$) and the building indoor temperature (T_{indoor}).

Although the estimation of the night ventilation potential requires the
simultaneous calculation of both surface and air temperatures, we will next
develop a simplified evaluation procedure based on the concept of *Storage
Efficiency* (SE). This concept can be used as a crude design tool to compare the
performance of alternative designs and to assess the effect of varying key
parameters. The coolness which is stored for use to offset heat loads is
proportional to the storage capacity of the building fabric times, SE.

At a certain moment during the night-time, assuming no internal loads, the
amount of energy absorbed by the fabric is given by:

$$Q(t) = YA(T_{storage} - T_{indoor}) = \dot{m}c_p(T_{indoor} - T_{outdoor}) \qquad (2.80)$$

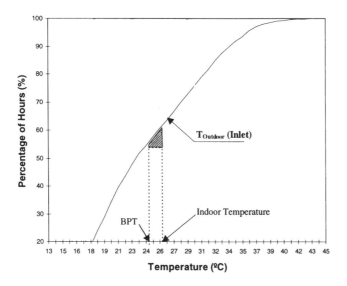

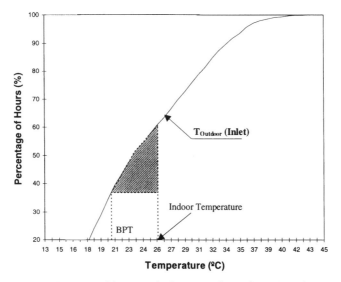

Figure 2.31. Usable periods for a residential (top) and an office building (bottom) for a daytime natural ventilation application

where YA is an average product of the admittance [34] of the walls multiplied by its effective area. The indoor air temperature is a representative average value that in any case will be higher than the outdoor air temperature.

The energy transferred can be written as:

$$Q(t) = \dot{m}c_p(T_{\text{storage}} - T_{\text{outdoor}})\,\text{NTU}/(\text{NTU}+1) \qquad (2.81)$$

where $NTU = YA / \dot{m}c_p$ from equation (2.80) is a dimensionless number commonly used in the analysis of heat exchangers and is termed 'number of thermal units'.

An accurate calculation of Y would be complex, and the worth of such calculation would be questionable due to the uncertainty of the convective heat transfer coefficients. However, an approximate value can be obtained by making the following assumptions:

- All the surfaces of the space are at the same temperature (i.e. radiant heat transfer is very much less than the convective heat transfer);
- Resistance of heat flow between the air and surfaces is very much greater than the resistance to heat flow within the fabric.

On the basis of these assumptions Y can be approximated by the convective heat transfer within the space.

An estimate of the storage temperature can be made for a typical night-time period of the location and we will assume that the building requirements are high enough for the storage temperature at the end of the previous daytime period (when the building required cooling) to be equal to the indoor set-point temperature.

The corresponding differential equation would be:

$$-(Mc_p)_f \frac{dT_{storage}(t)}{dt} = \dot{m}c_p(T_{storage}(t) - T_{outdoor}(t))\,NTU/(NTU+1) \quad (2.82)$$

where $(Mc_p)_f$ is the thermal capacity of the fabric involved.

If a constant outdoor temperature during a night-time cooling period of t hours is assumed, the solution of the differential equation is:

$$T_{storage}(t) = T_{storage}(0)\exp(-\frac{NTU}{NTU+1}.CR) \quad (2.83)$$

where $CR = \dot{m}c_p t / (Mc_p)_f$ is a capacity ratio.

The storage efficiency SE can be now defined as the actual amount of energy absorbed by the fabric divided by the maximum amount of energy potentially absorbed. In numerical terms:

$$SE = \frac{T_{storage}(0) - T_{storage}(t)}{T_{storage}(0) - T_{outdoor}} = 1 - \exp(-\frac{NTU}{NTU+1}.CR) \quad (2.84)$$

Figure 2.32 shows the storage efficiency as a function of NTU and CR.

EXAMPLE. Coming back to the hypothetical building office building in Porto, we can get for the typical cooling day:

> Daily cooling requirements: 500 W h^{-1} m^{-2} (south zone); −600 W h^{-1} m^{-2} (west zone).

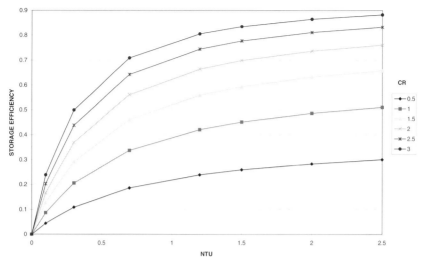

Figure 2.32. Dependence of the storage efficiency on NTU and CR

Outdoor temperature during night-time: ~15°C from 4 a.m. to 9 a.m. (five hours).

As the indoor set-point temperature is 25°C, and if the building has a medium weight construction [31] with approximately 340 kg m⁻² of floor area, the maximum amount of energy stored will be:

340 kg m^{-2} × 980 Jkg^{-1}°C^{-1} × (25–15) × 1 h/3600 s = 925 kWh m^{-2}

If we want, for instance, to evaluate the percentage of the cooling requirements covered with a ventilation rate of, say, 20 ach , we have:

$$\dot{m}c_p = 20 \times 3\,\text{m}^3\,\text{m}^{-2} \times 1000\,\text{J kg}^{-1}°\text{C}^{-1} \times 1\,\text{h}/3600\,\text{s} = 16.6$$

$$(Mc_p)_f = 340\,\text{kg m}^{-2} \times 980\,\text{J kg}^{-1}°\text{C}^{-1} \times 1\,\text{h}/3600\,\text{s} = 92.5$$

$$CR = 16.6 \times 5/92.5 = 0.89$$

For an NTU = 1, the SEF, from Figure 2.32, would be of about **0.36** which means:

$$925 \times 0.36/500 = 0.666$$

$$925 \times 0.36/600 = 0.555$$

say, 66.6% of the cooling requirements for the southern zone and 55.5% for western one.

As one example, let us suppose that we double the storage capacity of the building, all other factors being kept the same. In that case we have a new CR equal to 0.445 and a new SE of **0.21**.

The contribution to the cooling requirements would be:

$$1850 \times 0.21 / 500 = 0.777$$

$$1850 \times 0.21 / 600 = 0.647$$

Obviously, analogous sensitivity analysis can be performed with the other design variables, such as ventilation rate, effective area of the fabric, film coefficients, length of the ventilation period, or with any combination of these.

2.3.3.3 Influence of the thermal performance on the airflow

In the fluid-mechanical network models, the dynamic state of each zone is represented by a reference pressure. The flow equations define the different links existing in the pressure network that defines the building behaviour. The air mass balance in each zone then constitutes a non-linear system of equations combining these pressures:

$$F_j^F = \left(P^1, \ldots, P^J, \ldots, P^{NZ} \right) = 0 \tag{2.85}$$

To be rigorous, this equation must include the air density of each node. These densities are mainly functions of both absolute pressures and temperatures through the state equation of the air.

As an example, Figure 2.33 shows the effect of the temperatures on the airflow for a common opening [35].

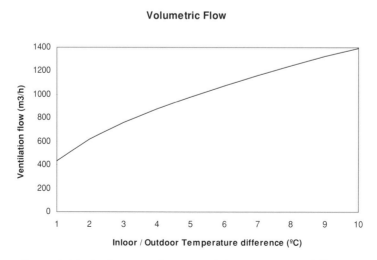

Figure 2.33. Airflow as a function of the temperature difference

2.3.3.4 *Solution strategies*

Despite the importance of airflow, thermal models have tended to adopt a very simplistic approach to the incorporation of ventilation and air infiltration. This can result in questionable predictions. At the most basic level, air change is incorporated as an assumed fixed value or an assumed, time-varying 'duty cycle'. In cases when air change is completely dominated by the installed ventilation system, such an approach can be acceptable. Conversely, if the building is naturally ventilated, such an approach is completely inadequate.

Techniques for including airflow algorithms into thermal calculation models are summarized in Figure 2.34. These methods include:

- **Sequential coupling.** This is the most straightforward of methods and involves separately running a network and thermal transport calculation model (Figure 2.34(a)). The network model is run first, using assumed values (e.g. design values) of room air temperature. The resultant air change rate or airflow characteristics are then incorporated into the

(a) Sequential

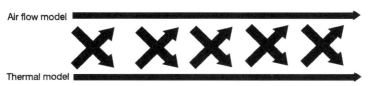

(b) Ping pong'

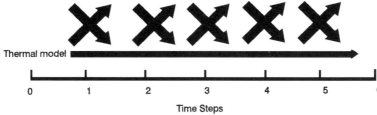

(c) Integrated

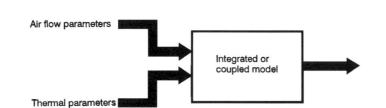

Figure 2.34. Combined air change and thermal calculation techniques [37]

thermal simulation model. It is necessary to ensure that air temperatures predicted by the thermal model are consistent with those used in the network model. This exercise should be repeated for a representative range of weather conditions so that the thermal transfer profile can be established for a complete design period (e.g. heating and/or cooling season).

- **Inter-model 'iteration' or 'ping-pong'.** This approach involves concurrently running a network (or computational fluid dynamics – CFD – model) and a thermal model. The simulation is run over a series of time steps. At each step, the thermal model is used to calculate air temperatures, which are transferred to the next time step of the network airflow model, while the network model is used to evaluate airflow rates for incorporation into the next step of the thermal model (Figure 32(b)). The advantage of this method is that two independent models can be used, yet a measure of coupling is provided. Results can be time-step dependent, especially if large openings are involved. Solutions should therefore be obtained for two or more step sizes (gradually reducing step size) until convergence is confirmed.
- **Direct coupling – full integration.** This involves solving the flow and thermal transport equations simultaneously in a directly coupled energy-balance model (Figure 2.32(c)). Such approaches are still under development. The nearest methods involve computational fluid-dynamic strategies in which energy 'flow' equations representing conduction, convection and radiant transfer are incorporated as part of the total flow network.

The limitations of these approaches are:

- Thermal calculation models are extremely complex and very dependent on the quality and interpretation of input data.
- The addition of an airflow model adds considerably to the overall level of complexity and risk of error.
- Much more development work is needed, particularly in providing guidance on data and the use of data, before combined models can be applied to routine applications.

REFERENCES

1. *Traité de Physique du Bâtiment* (1995). Centre Scientifique et Technique due Bâtiment, Tome I, p. 657. Louis Jean, Gap.
2. Peguy, Ch.P. (1970). *Précis de Climatologie*. Masson & Cie, Paris.
3. Queney, P. (1974). *Eléments de Météorologie*. Coll. Ecole Nationale Supérieure de Techniques Avancées. Masson & Cie, Paris.
4. Wieringa, J. (1991). 'Updating the Davenport Roughness Classification', 8th International Conference on Wind Engineering, London, Ontario, Canada, *Journal of Wind Engineering and Industrial Aerodynamics*, Vol. 4, pp. 357–368.

5. Sacré, C. (1988). Ecoulements de l'Air au-dessus d'un Site Complexe, 1ère partie: Etat des Connaissances Actuelles. Rapport CSTB EN-CLI 88. 12L, CSTB, Nantes.
6. Simiu, E. (1973). 'Logarithmic Profiles and Design Wind Speeds', *Journal of the Engineering Mechanics Division*, pp. 1073–1083.
7. ESDU 82026 (1982). 'Strong Winds in the Atmospheric Boundary Layer – Part 1: Mean Hourly Wind Speeds'. Engineering Sciences Data.
8. Papayannis, T. (1981). *Greece, Urban Growth in the 80's*. KEPE Editions, Ippokratous Str., Athens.
9. United States Environmental Protection Agency (1992). *Cooling our Communities. A Guidebook on Tree Planting and Light Coloured Surfacing*. United States Environmental Protection Agency, Washington, DC.
10. OCDE (1983), *Environmental Policies in Greece*. OCDE, Paris.
11. Oke, T.R. (1987). 'City Size and Urban Heat Island. Perspectives on Wilderness: Testing the Theory of Restorative Environments'. *Proceedings of the Fourth World Wilderness Congress*, vol. 7, pp. 767–779.
12. Oke, T.R. (1978). *Boundary Layer Climates*, 2nd edn. Methuen, New York.
13. Aynsley, R.M., W. Melbourne and B.J. Vickery. (1977). *Wind Tunnel Testing Techniques, Architectural Aerodynamics*, pp. 163. Applied Science Publishers, London.
14. Kula, H.G and H.E. Feustel. (1988). 'Review of Wind Pressure Distribution as Input Data for Infiltration Models', Lawrence Berkeley Laboratory Report LBL-23886, Berkeley, USA.
15. Allen, C. (1984).'Wind Pressure Data Requirements for Air Infiltration Calculations', Technical Note AIVC 13, Air Infiltrations and Ventilation Centre, Bracknell, UK.
16. Bala'zs, K. (1987). 'Effect of Some Architectural and Environmental Factors on Air Filtration of Multistorey Building', *3rd ICBEM Proceedings*, Vol. III, pp. 21–28. Presses Polytechniques Romandes, Lausanne, Switzerland.
17. Swami, M.V. (1987).'Procedures for Calculating Natural Ventilation Airflow Rates in Buildings', ASHRAE Research Project 448-RP, Final Report FSEC-CR-163-86, Florida Solar Energy Centre, Cape Canaveral, USA.
18. Wiren, B.G. (1985). 'Effects of Surrounding Building on Wind Pressure Distributions and Ventilation Losses for Single-Family Houses', *Bulletin* M85 (December), p. 19, National Swedish Institute for Building Research, Gavle, Sweden.
19. Liddament, M.W. (1986). *Air Infiltration Calculation Techniques – An Application Guide*. Air Infiltration and Ventilation Centre, Bracknell, UK.
20. Grosso M. (1994). Draft final report on CPCALC, PASCOOL European Project.
21. Saraiva, J.G. and F. Marques da Silva (1993–94). 'Determination of Pressure Coefficients over Simple Shaped Building Models under Different Boundary Layers', Minutes of the PASCOOL – CLI Meetings, Florence, May 1993, Segovia, November 1993; in *Wind Tunnel Reports*, Lisbon, January, March 1994.
22. Allard, F. and M. Herrlin. (1989). 'Wind Induced Ventilation', *ASHRAE Transactions*, Vol. 95, pp. 722–728.
23. Feustel, H. *et al.* (1990). COMIS (Conjunction of Multizone Infiltration Specialists) fundamentals, AIVC Technical Note 29, 115pp.
24. Allard, F. and Y. Utsumi. (1992). 'Airflow through Large Openings', *Energy and Buildings*, Vol. 18, pp. 113–145.
25. Walton, G.N. (1982). 'A computer Algorithm for Estimating Infiltration and Inter-Room Airflows', US Department of Commerce, National Bureau of Standards.
26. Roldan, A. (1985). 'Etude Thermique et Aéraulique des Enveloppes de Bâtiments'. Thèse de Doctorat, INSA de Lyon.

27. Santamouris, M and A. Argiriou (1996). PASCOOL Project Final report, EC DGXII, Ventilation and Thermal Mass Subtask Final Report, F. Allard and K. Limam eds.
28. Sacadura, J.F. (1993). 'Initiation aux Transferts Thermiques', 4th edn. Technique et Documentation Edit, Paris.
29. McIntyre, D.A. (1980). *Indoor Climate*. Applied Science Publishers, London.
30. Colin, J. and Y. Houdas (1967). 'Experimental Determination of Coefficient of Heat Exchange by Convection of the Human Body', *Journal of Applied Physiology*, Vol. 22, p. 31.
31. *ASHRAE Fundamentals* (1993). Chapters 3 and 22. ASHRAE, Atlanta, GA.
32. Haghighat, F. and M. Chandrashekar. (1987).'A System Theoretical Model for Building Thermal Analysis', *ASME Journal of Solar Energy Engineering*, Vol. 109, No. 2, pp. 79–88.
33. Yannas, S. and E. Maldonado (eds) (1996). *Handbook on Passive Cooling*. Vol. 1. Final product of the EC-JOULE II. PASCOOL project.
34. *CIBSE Guide A* (1980). Design data. Section A3. Thermal Properties of Building Structures. CIBSE, London.
35. Lamrani, M.A. (1987). 'Transferts Thermiques et Aerauliques à l'Interieur des Bâtiment'. Doctoral Dissertation Thesis, University of Nice.
36. Yannas, S. (ed.) (1994). *Solar Energy and Housing Design. Vol. I: Principles, Objectives, Guidelines*. Architectural Association, London.
37. Liddament, M.W. (1996). *A Guide to Energy Efficient Ventilation*. Air Infiltration and Ventilation Centre, Coventry, UK.

3

Prediction methods

Edited by M. Santamouris

The physical processes that are involved in natural ventilation are very complex and the interpretation of their role in ventilation effectiveness is a difficult task. Classical fluid dynamics has described airflow phenomena under well defined boundary conditions in a quite satisfactory way. Description of the phenomena is achieved by solving the well known Navier–Stokes equations combined with equations describing the turbulence effects, under specific boundary and initial conditions. However, taking into account the chaotic character of the wind characteristics, a full knowledge of the boundary and initial conditions is almost impossible.

Knowledge of the specific airflow characteristics in a space as well as of the global airflow rates in buildings is necessary for both comfort and energy reasons. Designers wish to know the airflow rate through large openings to size building windows appropriately, while engineers are interested in the distribution of the air velocity in a zone to size ventilation inlets and outlets. Comfort experts wish to know the air velocity values in a zone to calculate heat convection from or to the human body, while air quality experts are interested in the flow rate, the dispersion of contaminants and the ventilation efficiency.

According to the type of information requested, various models and tools may be used. Models range from very simple empirical algorithms to calculate the global airflow rate to sophisticated computerized fluid-dynamic techniques solving the Navier–Stokes equations. In general, based on the level of modelling complexity, four different approaches can be distinguished for the description of the airflow in the case of the natural ventilation of buildings.

- empirical models;
- network models;
- zonal models;
- CFD models.

Main contributors: M. Santamouris and E. Dascalaki

The above-mentioned airflow prediction methods are presented in the following sections. It is very important to note that use of deterministic methods to predict natural ventilation airflow rates in buildings is based on assumptions that often fail to describe the actual conditions with sufficient accuracy. This affects the accuracy of the results obtained, as compared to measured values.

3.1   EMPIRICAL MODELS

Simplified empirical models offer general correlations to calculate the airflow rate, or the mean air velocity in the zone. These expressions combine the airflow with the temperature difference, wind velocity and possibly a fluctuating term in order to give a bulk evaluation of the airflow rate or the air velocity in a building. These tools are useful because they offer a fast first estimation of the airflow rate or of the mean air velocity, but should always be used within the limits of their applicability. In the following sections two categories of empirical methods are presented:

- simplified empirical methods for the prediction of the airflow rates;
- simplified methodologies for the prediction of the air velocity inside a building.

The following methodologies have been deduced either from theory or from specific experimental data and cannot be considered of general validity; therefore, as already stated, they must be used within the limits of their applicability.

3.1.1   Simplified methods for the prediction of the airflow rates within naturally ventilated buildings

Several simplified procedures based on empirical data have been developed to produce estimates of ventilation rates in essentially single-zone buildings. These models may be used during the earliest design phase to obtain an approximate value of the airflow rate. Representative methods are described in the following sections.

3.1.1.1 The British Standards method [1]

The British Standards method proposes formulae for the calculation of the air infiltration and ventilation in single-sided and cross-ventilation configurations. The method assumes two-directional flow through a building and ignores all internal partitions. Tables 3.1 and 3.2 give schematically the proposed formulae for different airflow patterns and for different conditions.

Table 3.1. Formulae for single-sided ventilation [1]

(a)	Ventilation due to wind	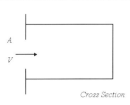

$$Q = 0.025AV$$

where A is the opening surface and V is the wind velocity.

(b) Ventilation due to temperature difference with two openings

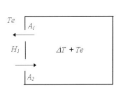

$$Q = C_d A \left[\frac{\varepsilon \sqrt{2}}{(1+\varepsilon)(1+\varepsilon^2)^{1/2}} \right] \left(\frac{\Delta T g H_1}{\overline{T}} \right)$$

$\varepsilon = A1 / A2, \ A = A1 + A2$

where C_d is the discharge coefficient

(c) Ventilation due to temperature difference with one opening:

$$Q = C_d \frac{A}{3} \sqrt{\frac{\Delta T \, g \, H_2}{\overline{T}}}$$

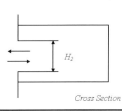

Table 3.2. Formulae for cross ventilation [1]

(a) Ventilation due to wind only:

$$Q_w = C_d A_w V \sqrt{\Delta Cp}$$

$$\frac{1}{A_w^2} = \frac{1}{(A_1 + A_2)^2} + \frac{1}{(A_3 + A_4)^2}$$

(b) Ventilation due to temperature difference only:

$$Q_b = C_d A_b \left(\frac{2\Delta T g H_1}{T} \right)^{0.5}$$

$$\frac{1}{A_b^2} = \frac{1}{(A_1 + A_3)^2} + \frac{1}{(A_2 + A_4)^2}$$

$$T = \frac{Te + Ti}{2}$$

(c) Ventilation due to wind and temperature difference:

$$Q = Q_b \text{ for } \frac{V}{\sqrt{\Delta T}} < 0.26 \sqrt{\frac{A_b}{A_w} \frac{H_1}{\Delta Cp}}$$

$$Q = Q_w \text{ for } \frac{V}{\sqrt{\Delta T}} > 0.26 \sqrt{\frac{A_b}{A_w} \frac{H_1}{\Delta Cp}}$$

$$\Delta T = Ti - Te$$

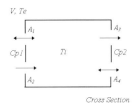

3.1.1.2 The ASHRAE method [2]

This method requires knowledge of the total effective leakage area of the building, which can either be determined using pressurization/depressurization techniques or evaluated from tables [2]. According to the method, the bulk airflow rate, Q, in a single-zone building is:

$$Q = A\sqrt{a\Delta T + bU_{met}^2} \quad (\text{m}^3 \text{ h}^{-1}) \tag{3.1}$$

where

> A is the total effective leakage area of the building (cm²);
> a is the stack coefficient (m⁶ h⁻² cm⁻⁴ K⁻¹);
> b is the wind coefficient (m⁴ s² h⁻² cm⁻⁴);
> ΔT is the average indoor–outdoor temperature difference (K);
> U_{met} is the meteorological wind speed (m s⁻¹).

The coefficient a has three different values according to the number of storeys of the building. Specifically:

> $a = 0.00188$ for one-storey buildings;
> $a = 0.00376$ for two-storey buildings;
> $a = 0.00564$ for three-storey buildings.

The coefficient b takes different values according to the number of storeys of a building, but also according to the local shielding class to which the building belongs. Values of coefficient b are given in Table 3.3 for five different shielding classes:

Table 3.3. *Coefficient* b *for various building heights and local shielding classes [2]*

Shielding class	Number of Storeys		
	1	2	3
No obstructions	0.00413	0.00544	0.00640
Light local shielding	0.00319	0.00421	0.00495
Moderate local shielding	0.00226	0.00299	0.00351
Heavy shielding	0.00135	0.00178	0.00209
Very heavy shielding	0.00041	0.00054	0.00063

3.1.1.3 The Aynsley method [3]

Aynsley [3] proposed a simple method for global airflow prediction in the case of cross ventilation. Assuming two main openings on two opposite façades of a building, the method uses the definition of the pressure coefficients Cp_1 and Cp_2 on each façade to calculate the flow rate of air through the building. Imposing mass conservation between the two openings, the following expression is derived for the global airflow rate:

$$Q = \sqrt{\frac{Cp_1 - Cp_2}{\frac{1}{A_1^2 C_{d1}^2} + \frac{1}{A_2^2 C_{d2}^2}}} V_z$$

(3.2)

where C_{d1} and C_{d2} are the discharge coefficients given as functions of the opening configuration, A_1 and A_2 are the areas of openings 1 and 2 respectively and V_z is the reference wind velocity.

The main interest of the method is its simplicity and efficiency in giving a rough estimate of the order of magnitude of the global airflow rate in a cross-ventilated building.

3.1.1.4 The De Gidds and Phaff method [4]

Most of the existing correlations for natural ventilation fail to predict the airflow observed in cases where wind or buoyant effects are absent. Experimental results have shown that the fluctuating effects are responsible for the airflow in the case of single-sided ventilation or when the wind direction is parallel to openings in two parallel façades. Fluctuating flows are attributed to the turbulence characteristics of the incoming wind and/or to turbulence induced by the building itself. Turbulence in the airflow along an opening causes simultaneous positive and negative pressure fluctuations of the inside air. An empirical correlation that integrates the turbulence effect in a more general airflow model is presented by IEA [5].

According to the De Gidds and Phaff method, a general expression is given for the ventilation rate, Q, through an open window as a function of temperature difference, wind velocity and fluctuating terms. For the case of single-sided ventilation, an effective velocity, U_{eff} is defined and refers to the flow through half a window opening. In a general form the effective velocity is defined as:

$$U_{eff} = \frac{Q}{A/2} = \sqrt{\frac{2}{g}(\Delta p_{wind} + \Delta p_{stack} + \Delta p_{turb})}$$

(3.3)

leading to the form:

$$U_{eff} = \frac{Q}{A/2} = \sqrt{C_1 U_{met}^2 + C_2 H \Delta T + C_3}$$

(3.4)

where U_{met} is the meteorological wind velocity, H is the vertical size of the opening, C_1 is a dimensionless coefficient depending on the wind, C_2 is a boundary constant and C_3 is a turbulence constant. The term C_3 is equivalent to an effective turbulence pressure that provides ventilation in the absence of stack effect or steady wind. Comparison between measured and calculated values, has led to the following values for the fitting parameters: $C_1 = 0.001$, $C_2 = 0.0035$ and $C_3 = 0.01$.

3.1.2   Simplified methods for the estimation of the air velocity inside naturally ventilated buildings

Knowledge of the characteristics of the air motion inside a building is essential for building designers. Air velocities increase the body's convective and evaporative heat loss rate and increase thermal comfort. Recent studies [6, 7], have also shown that the impact of air turbulence intensity on comfort can also be significant and it is possible for the effects of turbulence to be integrated into human thermal comfort models [8].

Assessment of the indoor air motion perceived by a building's occupants requires knowledge of the interior velocity as well as of the turbulence intensity distribution. Important research has been carried out during the past 50 years in order to develop methodologies to predict the wind-induced air motion inside buildings. According to Ernest [9], the proposed techniques can be classified into five main groups according to the methodology used:

- research based on full-scale investigations;
- research based on computerized numerical simulations;
- methods based on tabulated data obtained from parametric wind-tunnel studies;
- methods making use of wind discharge coefficients;
- methods based on direct measurements of the indoor air velocities in a scale model of the investigated building placed in a boundary-layer wind tunnel.

The main characteristics, the advantages and the disadvantages, as well as the limitations, of some of the proposed methodologies are discussed below.

3.1.2.1 *Givonni's method*
Givonni [10] has proposed a general correlation method, based on experimental data, to calculate the average indoor air velocity in rooms with a square floor plan and with identical upwind and downwind openings located in opposite walls. According to the method the average velocity inside the room is given by the following expression:

$$V_i = 0.45(1 - e^{-3.48x})V_r \qquad (3.5)$$

where V_i is the average indoor velocity, x is the ratio of the opening's area to wall area where the opening is located, and V_r the reference external wind speed.

3.1.2.2 *Methods based on tabulated data*
It is well known that the air velocity inside a building is not uniform by any means. Studies in models clearly show draughts and areas of low velocity.

However, when judging the overall efficiency of natural ventilation in a building, it is more convenient to consider an average value of the indoor air velocity, V_i.

Studies in wind tunnels have made it possible to compare indoor air velocities for naturally ventilated spaces under different wind directions and with different numbers of apertures and locations. Melaragno [11] has proposed values of the average and maximum indoor air velocity for two different ratios of the aperture width to the aperture of the wall (Table 3.4).

Table 3.4. *Indoor air velocities for naturally ventilated spaces under different wind directions and with different number of apertures and locations* [11]

Conditions	Width of aperture/ width of wall = 0.66		Width of aperture/ width of wall = 1	
	V_{avg} (%)	V_{max} (%)	V_{avg} (%)	V_{max} (%)
Single aperture in windward wall, wind direction perpendicular	13	18	16	20
Single aperture in windward wall, wind direction at an angle	15	33	23	36
Single aperture in leeward wall, wind direction at an angle	17	44	17	39
Two apertures in leeward wall, wind direction at an angle	22	56	23	50
One aperture in windward wall, another in adjacent wall, wind direction perpendicular to inlets	45	68	51	103
One aperture in windward wall, another in adjacent wall, wind direction at an angle	37	118	40	110
One aperture in windward wall, another in leeward wall, wind direction perpendicular to inlet	35	65	37	102
One aperture in windward wall, another in leeward wall, wind direction at an angle	42	83	42	94

Indoor air velocities are expressed as a percentage of the velocity of the free wind.

The same author proposes values of the mean indoor air speed for cross-ventilation configurations without internal partitions, as a function of the inlets and the outlets. For aligned inlets and outlets and for perpendicular winds (Figure 3.1), the mean indoor air speed is given in Table 3.5.

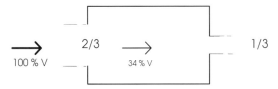

Figure 3.1. Effects on inlet and outlet sizes in cross-ventilated spaces with openings on opposite walls

Table 3.5. Effect of inlet and outlet sizes in cross-ventilated spaces; openings on opposite walls; wind perpendicular to inlet [11]

Conditions for perpendicular winds	V_{avg} (%)
Width inlet/Width of wall = 1/3 and Width outlet/Width of wall = 1/3	35
Width inlet/Width of wall = 1/3 and Width outlet/Width of wall = 2/3	39
Width inlet/Width of wall = 1/3 and Width outlet/Width of wall = 1	44
Width inlet/Width of wall = 2/3 and Width outlet/Width of wall = 1/3	34
Width inlet/Width of wall = 2/3 and Width outlet/Width of wall = 2/3	37
Width inlet/Width of wall = 2/3 and Width outlet/Width of wall = 1	35
Width inlet/Width of wall = 1 and Width outlet/Width of wall = 1/3	32
Width inlet/Width of wall = 1 and Width outlet/Width of wall = 2/3	36
Width inlet/Width of wall = 1 and Width outlet/Width of wall = 1	47

As shown, increasing the outlet size, while keeping the inlet size constant, produces very little improvement in the circulation. Therefore, the maximum efficiency is reached when both inlet and outlet have maximum size at the same time, while the minimum efficiency is attained when the inlet size is maximum and the outlet size is minimum.

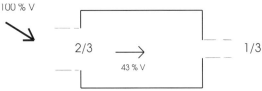

Figure 3.2. Openings on opposite walls; wind oblique to inlet

Table 3.6. Effect of inlet and outlet sizes in cross-ventilated spaces; openings on opposite walls; wind oblique to inlet [11]

Conditions for oblique to inlet winds	V_{avg} (%)
Width inlet/Width of wall = 1/3 and Width outlet/Width of wall = 1/3	42
Width inlet/Width of wall = 1/3 and Width outlet/Width of wall = 2/3	40
Width inlet/Width of wall = 1/3 and Width outlet/Width of wall = 1	44
Width inlet/Width of wall = 2/3 and Width outlet/Width of wall = 1/3	43
Width inlet/Width of wall = 2/3 and Width outlet/Width of wall = 2/3	51
Width inlet/Width of wall = 2/3 and Width outlet/Width of wall = 1	59
Width inlet/Width of wall = 1 and Width outlet/Width of wall = 1/3	41
Width inlet/Width of wall = 1 and Width outlet/Width of wall = 2/3	62
Width inlet/Width of wall = 1 and Width outlet/Width of wall = 1	65

The effect of the wind at 45° with respect to the inlet (Figure 3.2) is shown in Table 3.6. Compared with the case of perpendicular winds, it is shown that oblique winds promote more efficient ventilation in all cases.

Again, it is shown that even in the case of an oblique wind direction, the most efficient ventilation is attained when inlet and outlet are maximum. When the inlets and outlets are located in adjacent walls, the effect of the relative size is different (Figure 3.3). The average indoor velocity in cross-ventilated spaces with openings on adjacent walls and wind perpendicular to inlet and oblique to inlet is given in Tables 3.7 and 3.8 respectively.

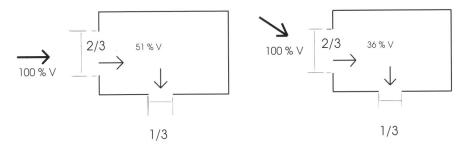

Figure 3.3. Effects of inlet and outlet sizes in cross-ventilated spaces; openings on adjacent walls, wind perpendicular and wind oblique to inlets

Table 3.7. Effect on inlet and outlet sizes in cross-ventilated spaces; openings on adjacent walls; wind perpendicular to inlet [11]

Conditions for perpendicular to inlet winds	V_{avg} (%)
Width inlet/Width of wall = 1/3 and Width outlet/Width of wall = 1/3	45
Width inlet/Width of wall = 1/3 and Width outlet/Width of wall = 2/3	39
Width inlet/Width of wall = 1/3 and Width outlet/Width of wall = 1	51
Width inlet/Width of wall = 2/3 and Width outlet/Width of wall = 1/3	51
Width inlet/Width of wall = 1 and Width outlet/Width of wall = 1/3	50

Table 3.8. Effect on inlet and outlet sizes in cross-ventilated spaces; openings on adjacent walls; wind oblique to inlet [11]

Conditions for oblique to inlet winds	V_{avg} (%)
Width inlet/Width of wall = 1/3 and Width outlet/Width of wall = 1/3	37
Width inlet/Width of wall = 1/3 and Width outlet/Width of wall = 2/3	40
Width inlet/Width of wall = 1/3 and Width outlet/Width of wall = 1	45
Width inlet/Width of wall = 2/3 and Width outlet/Width of wall = 1/3	36
Width inlet/Width of wall = 1 and Width outlet/Width of wall = 1/3	37

For perpendicular winds the minimum efficiency occurs when the inlet to wall ratio is 1/3 and the outlet size is 2/3.

For the case of a wind orientation of 45° with respect to the inlet, the highest efficiency is obtained when the inlet ratio is 1/3 and the outlet ratio is equal to 1. On the other hand, the minimum efficiency occurs for inlet ratio 2/3 and outlet ratio 1/3.

3.1.2.3 The CSTB methodology [12]

The methodology proposed by CSTB is based on data obtained from architectural scale models in a wind tunnel for the prediction of the wind-induced indoor air motion. The method is based on the evaluation of a 'Global Ventilation Coefficient', C_G, defined as the ratio of the mean indoor velocity, V, of the air at a height of 1.5 m to the outdoor air velocity, $V_{1.5}$, at the same height. According to the method, the ventilation coefficient depends directly on:

- the characteristics of the site;
- the orientation of the building and of the wind;
- the exterior characteristics of the building;
- the interior architecture and the interior aerodynamics of the building.

The method therefore proposes the evaluation of four corresponding coefficients, C_{site}, $C_{orientation}$, $C_{Arch. Exter.}$, $C_{Aero. Inter.}$. Then, the global ventilation coefficient, C_G, of a given space is equal to the minimum of the four previously defined coefficients:

$$C_G = min(C_{site}, C_{orientation}, C_{Arch. Exter.}, C_{Aero. Inter.}) \qquad (3.6)$$

For the evaluation of each coefficient, a specific, rather complex but complete, methodology is proposed, based on and relative to the ventilation performance of a reference cell, C_0, i.e. $C_x = f(C_0)$, which is measured in a wind tunnel and found as $C_0 = 0.6$. The reference cell is a 30 m² single-zone construction of a 3 to 4 m in height with a ceiling sloping (10°) towards the main direction of the wind. Inlet and outlet openings are about 30% of the corresponding windward and leeward façades, while the axis of the building is parallel to the main axis of the dominant wind. Finally, it is considered that the cell is located on flat land, free of obstructions.

THE IMPACT OF THE SITE: EVALUATION OF c_{SITE}

The impact of the site on the ventilation performance of the building depends on the following parameters:

- The topography of the site, which can be favourable or unfavourable for the natural ventilation of the building. To account for the effects of the topography, a coefficient C_{TP} is used.
- The characteristics of the surrounding environment (the presence of plantations, neighbouring buildings, etc.). To take account of these effects, a coefficient C_{EP} is used.
- The urban plan of the site. To take account of the effects of the relative position of the buildings, a coefficient C_{PM} is proposed.

To evaluate C_{site}, the coefficients C_{TP}, C_{EP} and C_{PM} must first be estimated. Details on the methods for evaluating these coefficients are given in the following paragraphs.

THE INFLUENCE OF THE TOPOGRAPHY – EVALUATION OF C_{TP}. The method makes a distinction between favourable and unfavourable sites. Unfavourable sites are considered as:

- windward zones located at the lower level of a hill; $C_{TP} = 0.6C_0$;
- leeward zones located at the lower level of a hill; $C_{TP} = 0.5C_0$;
- valleys poorly oriented to the local winds; $C_{TP} = 0.3C_0$;
- cliffs; $C_{TP} = 0.7C_0$.

Favourable zones are:

- zones between two hills with appropriate orientation to the local winds; $C_{TP} = 1.1C_0$ (Figure 3.4a);
- zones on the top of hills with a windward tilted roof; $C_{TP} = 1.2C_0$ – if the tilt of the roof is much higher than the tilt of the hill see the following cases (Figure 3.4b);
- zones on the top of hills with a tilted roof parallel to the tilt of the hill; $C_{TP} = C_0$ (Figure 3.4c);
- zones on the top of hills with a windward-oriented tilted roof with a tilt 20° greater than that of the hill; $C_{TP} = 1.3C_0$ (Figure 3.4d).

The method examines the case of buildings located in rural sites or sites with a low or medium urban density. It is considered that natural ventilation is not

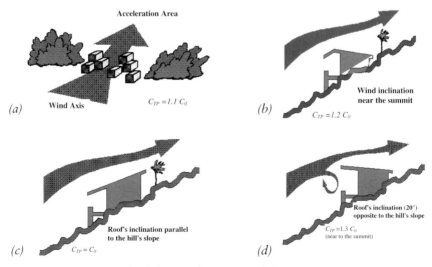

Figure 3.4. *CSTB methodology – the impact of the site: the influence of the topography*

an effective technique for sites that have very dense urban characteristics. For rural or low-urban-density sites, the presence of high trees or other obstructions, 5 to 10 m in height, in front of the windward façade of the building significantly reduces the potential for natural ventilation. In such a case the building should be placed sufficiently far from the obstruction. The method proposes the following:

- If the obstruction is parallel to the axis of the wind, the building should be placed at a minimum distance equal to 12 times the height of the obstruction (Figure 3.5a).
- If the obstruction is normal to the wind axis, the building should be at a distance equal to four times the height of the obstruction (Figure 3.5b).
- If both the above conditions are fulfilled, then $C_{EP} = C_0$; otherwise C_{EP} takes values between $0.1C_0$ and $0.5C_0$ (Figure 3.5c).

As previously mentioned the method only treats buildings located in rural or low-urban-density environments. For an isolated building it is considered that $C_{PM} = C_0$. The method examines two types of relative organization of the buildings:

- organization of the buildings in parallel lines (Figure 3.6a–c);
- a Π-shaped organization of the buildings (Figure 3.6d).

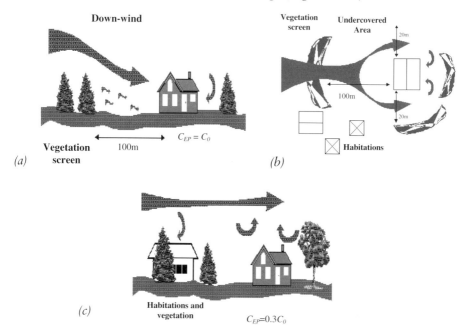

Figure 3.5. CSTB methodology – the impact of the site: the influence of the surrounding environment

The organization of the buildings in parallel lines is characterized by the number of lines, n, the distance, a, between the buildings of the same line and the distance, b, between successive lines. If the angle of incidence of the wind is parallel to the axis of the openings, $\theta = 0$, for the buildings of the first line the coefficient C_{PM} can be obtained as a function of the distance a, from Figure 3.6a. As shown, for $a = 3$ m, $C_{PM} = 1.3C_0$. For the buildings located on the other lines and for the same incidence angle, the coefficient C_{PM} can be obtained as a function of the distances a and b, from Figure 3.6b. As shown for $a = 2$ m and $b > 30$ m, or $a = 7$ to 8 m and $b > 15$ m, $C_{PM} = C_0$. According to the method, the same results are obtained for an incidence angle $\pm 20°$. If the incidence angle is between $\pm 45°$ (Figure 3.6c), then:

$$C_{PM(\phi=\pm45°)} = 0.75C_{PM(\phi=0)}$$

The method proposes $C_{PM} = 1.2C_0$ for a Π-shaped organization (Figure 3.6d) and $C_{PM} = 0.6$ to $0.7C_0$ if the wind incidence is parallel to the axis of the building openings.

When C_{TP}, C_{EP} and C_{PM} have been calculated, the coefficient C_{site} is calculated according to the following methodology:

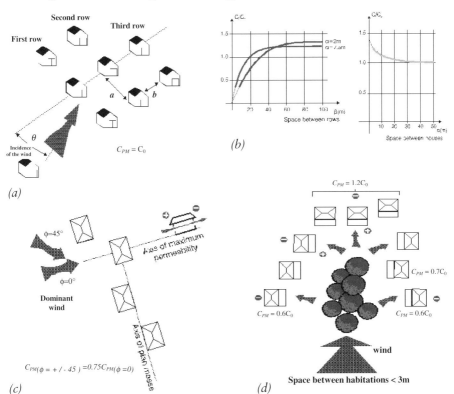

Figure 3.6. CSTB methodology – the impact of the site: the influence of the relative position of the buildings

1. If the conditions for the distance from neighbouring obstacles, previously discussed, are fulfilled then $C_{site} = C_{EP} = C_0$. If these conditions are not fulfilled then it is evident that C_{EP} has a very small value, $C_{EP} = 0.1$ to $0.5C_0$ and the potential for natural ventilation is very low. If the above condition is fulfilled, and C_{TP} is higher or equal to C_0, while the distances a and b between neighbouring buildings are appropriate, then $C_{site} = (C_{PM} + C_{TP})/2$.
2. If the first condition is fulfilled and C_{TP} is lower than C_0, then $C_{site} = C_{TP}$.
3. If the building is in a zone on the top of a hill with a windward-oriented tilted roof with a tilt 20° greater than that of the hill, and the distances from neighbouring buildings are appropriate, while the incidence angle of the wind is parallel to the axis of the openings $C_{site} = 1.5C_0$.
4. If the building is in a zone on the top of a hill with a windward-oriented tilted roof parallel to the tilt of the hill, and the distances from the neighbouring buildings are appropriate, while the incidence angle of the wind is parallel to the axis of the openings $C_{site} = 1.3C_0$.

An example describing the application of the above methodology is given at the end of this chapter.

THE IMPACT OF THE ANGLE OF INCIDENCE: EVALUATION OF $C_{ORIENTATION}$. The impact of the angle of incidence of the wind on the building depends on the following parameters:

- the angle θ between the axis of the openings and the axis of the wind (Figure 3.7a);
- the angle ϕ between the orientation of the urban plan and the axis of the wind (Figure 3.7b);
- the nature and the characteristics of the urban plan.

To estimate the coefficient, $C_{orientation}$, the following methodology is proposed:

1. If $\theta = 0$ or θ is equal or less than $\pm 20°$, then $C_{orientation} = C_0$.
2. If $\theta = \pm 45°$, then $C_{orientation} = 0.75C_0$.
3. If $\theta = 90$ degrees, then $C_{orientation} = 0.5C_0$.

THE IMPACT OF THE EXTERIOR CHARACTERISTICS OF THE BUILDING: EVALUATION OF C_{ARCHI}. The effect of the exterior characteristics of the building depends on the following parameters:

- the nature and the characteristics of the openings, to account for the impact of which a coefficient, C_p, is introduced by the method;
- the architecture of the roof, to account the impact of which a coefficient, C_T, is introduced by the method;
- the existence of an open roof, to account the impact of which a coefficient, C_{ET}, is introduced by the method;

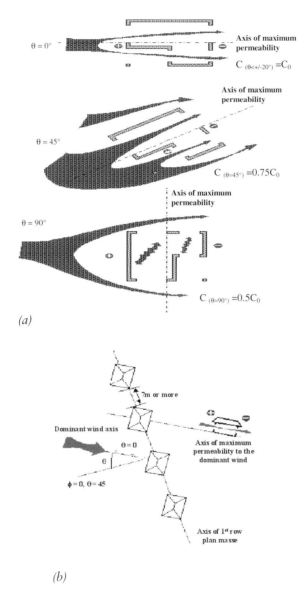

Figure 3.7. CSTB methodology – the impact of the angle of incidence

- the existence of concrete stilts, to account the impact of which a coefficient, C_{PL}, is introduced by the method;
- the presence of wing walls, to account the impact of which a coefficient, C_J, is introduced by the method.

In the following paragraphs, the procedure proposed by the present method to estimate the coefficients, C_P, C_T, C_{ET}, C_{PL} and C_J, and then C_{archi}, is described.

THE EFFECT OF THE ROOF: EVALUATION OF C_T. The coefficient C_T, is given by the method for constructions located on flat or tilted ground. For constructions on flat ground the following cases are examined (Figure 3.8):

- an extended flat terrace, $C_T = 0.6C_0$;
- a tilted roof, with the highest part towards the direction of the wind, $C_T = 0.65C_0$;
- a roof with four slopes, $C_T = 0.7C_0$;
- a simple flat terrace, $C_T = 0.8C_0$;
- a roof with two slopes, $C_T = 0.9C_0$;
- a sloped roof, with the lowest part towards the direction of the wind, $C_T = C_0$;
- a building raised by 1.5 m above the ground, with a sloped roof, where the lowest part is oriented towards the direction of the wind, $C_T = 1.1C_0$.

For buildings constructed on hillsides where the slope of the roof is opposite to the slope of the hill, the method proposes $C_T = 1.3C_0$.

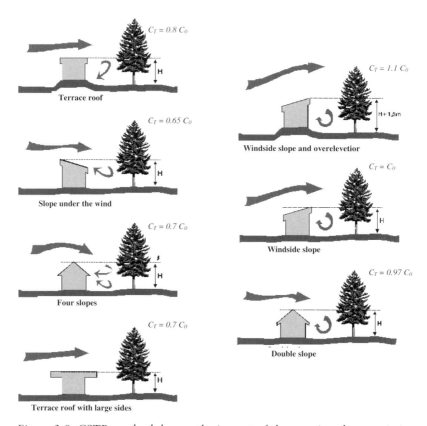

Figure 3.8. CSTB methodology – the impact of the exterior characteristics of the building: the effect of the roof

THE EFFECT OF AN OPEN ROOF, C_{ET}. An open roof is efficient if part of the opening is placed in the windward façade and the other part in the upwind facade. The total surface of the openings should be sufficiently large, 2–3 m² per room.

The method examines two cases, as shown in Figure 3.9. For the first case, where the highest part of the roof openings is located in the upwind facade, the method proposes $C_{ET} = 1.4C_0$, while for the second case, where the highest part of the roof openings is located in the windward facade, the method proposes $C_{ET} = 1.15C_0$.

EFFECTS DUE TO THE NATURE AND THE CHARACTERISTICS OF THE OPENINGS: EVALUATION OF C_p. To improve the performance of natural ventilation, the axis of the main openings of the building should be parallel to the axis of the prevailing wind. As discussed previously, there is a serious reduction of the corresponding C coefficient for high wind incidence angles.

The ratio of the surface of the openings in a façade to the surface of the façade is defined by the method as the 'porosity' of a specific facade. According to the method, the porosity of a façade should be higher than 15%. The following values of the C_p coefficient are proposed as a function of the 'porosities' of the windward and leeward façades (Figure 3.10):

- porosity of the windward and of leeward façades equal to 15%, then $C_p = 0.7C_0$;
- porosity of the windward and of leeward façades equal to 30%, then $C_p = C_0$;
- porosity of the windward and of leeward façades equal to 40%, then $C_p = 1.2C_0$.

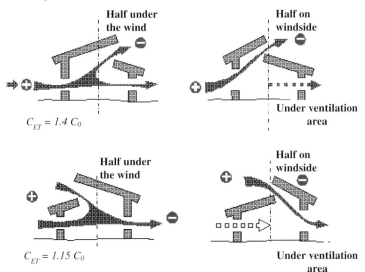

Figure 3.9. CSTB methodology – the impact of the exterior characteristics of the building: the effect of an open roof

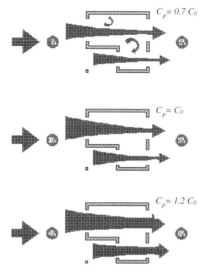

$C_p = 0.7\, C_0$

$C_p = C_0$

$C_p = 1.2\, C_0$

Figure 3.10. CSTB methodology – the impact of the exterior characteristics of the building: the effect of the nature and characteristics of the openings

If the porosities of the windward and leeward façades are not the same, then the porosity of the leeward façade should the higher. If, for example, the porosity of the windward and leeward façades are 40% and 30% respectively, then $C_p = 1.1\,C_0$, while for the adverse case, $C_p = 1.3\,C_0$.

The effect of side openings is always positive. For example, for a building with porosity of the windward and leeward façades equal to 30% and a porosity of 10% for the side openings, $C_p = 1.2\,C_0$. If the porosity of the leeward façade is zero, then possible side openings compensate, though not totally, for the lack of upwind openings. For example, if the porosities of the windward and leeward façades are 30% and 0% respectively and the porosity of the side façades is 20%, then $C_p = 0.7\,C_0$.

THE EFFECT OF A CONCRETE STILT: EVALUATION OF C_{PL}. The existence of a concrete stilt, provided that its height is greater than 1 m and the passage of the wind is free, increases the ventilation efficiency. The method proposes $C_{PL} = 1.2\,C_0$.

THE EFFECT OF WING WALLS: EVALUATION OF C_J. Wing walls, when placed appropriately, increase the pressure difference and facilitate the motion of the air through the building openings. According to the method, the height of a wing wall should be at least 2.5 m and its minimum length 2 m. If such a wing wall exists, then the method proposes $C_J = 1.1\,C_0$.

If all coefficients C_P, C_J, C_{ET}, C_{PL} and C_T are determined, then a precise methodology is proposed in order to estimate C_{archi}. The methodology has been developed for two configurations:

- a monozone building with windward or leeward openings;
- a multizone building with windward or leeward openings coupled with roof openings.

For the first case the methodology consists of the following steps:

1. The porosity of the windward and leeward openings should be higher than 15%. If the porosity of the leeward opening is zero, i.e. no openings, the porosity of the side openings should be at least 20%. In this case and if conditions 2–4 are not fulfilled, then $C_{archi} = C_p$. If this absolute condition is not fulfilled, the method considers that the architecture of the building is not suitable for natural ventilation.
2. If the above absolute condition 1 is fulfilled, and the zone is equipped with well designed roof openings, then $C_{archi} = (C_P + C_{ET})/2$.
3. If the building is equipped with concrete stilts or wing walls, then $C_{archi} = (C_P + C_{PL} + C_T)/3$ or $C_{archi} = (C_P + C_J + C_T)/3$. Note that for buildings that are raised up $C_T = C_0$.
4. If the porosity of the windward and leeward façades is 30% and the building is constructed on a hillside where the slope of the roof is opposite to the slope of the hill, the method proposes $C_{archi} = 1.3C_0$.

For the second case, the methodology consists of the following steps:

1. If there are no wing walls and no piloti, then $C_{archi} = C_{ET}$.
2. If the building is equipped with wing walls or stilts, then $C_{archi} = (C_{ET} + C_J)/2$ or $C_{archi} = (C_{ET} + C_{PL})/2$

THE IMPACT OF THE INTERIOR CHARACTERISTICS OF THE BUILDING: EVALUATION OF $C_{AERO. INTER.}$ The interior characteristics of the building should permit the flow of the air through the building and keep a relative homogeneity inside the building. The parameters that should be taken into account, according to the method, are the following:

- The internal partitions, to take into account the effects of which the method proposes to use a coefficient C_C.
- The furniture, for the effects of which the method does not propose any specific methodology.

THE ROLE OF THE INTERNAL PARTITIONS: EVALUATION OF C_C. In order to facilitate the airflow through the building, the internal partitions should be parallel to the airflow (Figure 3.11a). In this case $C_C = C_0$. If the internal partitions, doors and other internal openings are parallel to the airflow and present a porosity higher than 50%, then $C_C = 0.9C_0$.

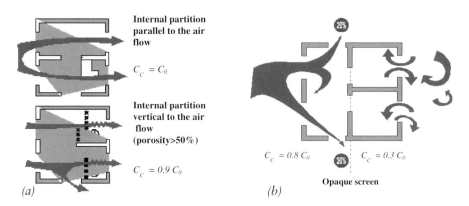

Figure 3.11. CSTB methodology – the impact of the interior characteristics of the building: the role of the internal partitions

If the internal partitions are normal to the airflow (Figure 3.11b) and their porosity is very low, lower than 20%, or the partitions are opaque, then for the leeward zones $C_C = 0.3C_0$. In this case the windward zones are ventilated only if there are side openings with a porosity higher than 20% in the zone. In this case and for the windward openings $C_C = 0.8C_0$.

Based on the above, the method proposes: $C_{\text{Aero. Inter.}} = C_C$.

EXAMPLE

Consider a four-zone building as shown in Figure 3.12. The building is on a hillside and the incidence angle of the wind is $\theta = 30°$. The porosity of the windward, leeward and side façades are 40%, 30% and 20% respectively. The building is equipped with concrete stilts and zones 3 and 4 are equipped with openings on the roof. Calculate the coefficient C_G for each zone and the ratio of the indoor to the outdoor air velocity.

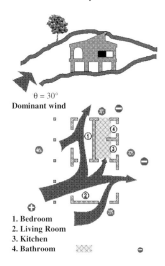

Figure 3.12. CSTB methodology – example

1. Calculation of C_{site}: As there are no obstructions we obtain that $C_{EP} = C_0$. Also, the building is isolated and so $C_{PM} = C_0$. Finally, the slope of the roof is not very favourable and $C_{TP} = C_0$. Therefore $C_{site} = C_0$.
2. Calculation of $C_{orientation}$: Taking into account that for $\theta = 20°$ $C_{orientation} = C_0$, and for $\theta = 45°$ $C_{orientation} = 0.75C_0$, by interpolation it is obtained that for $\theta = 30°$ $C_{orientation} = 0.85C_0$.
3. Calculation of C_{archi}:
   Zone 2: Because there are concrete stilts present $C_{PL} = 1.2C_0$. Also, as the porosity of the windward and leeward façades is 30% and there are side openings, $C_p = 1.2C_0$. Therefore, $C_{archi} = (1.2 + 1.2)C_0/2 = 1.2C_0$.
   Zone 1: As the porosity of the leeward façade is not higher than 15% and the porosity of the side openings is 20%, then $C_p = 0.7C_0$. In this case the effect of the stilts cannot be taken into account, so that $C_{archi} = C_p = 0.7C_0$.
   Zones 3 and 4: The presence of the stilts gives $C_{PL} = 1.2C_0$. In addition, the roof openings give $C_{ET} = 0.9C_0$. Therefore, $C_{archi} = (0.9 + 1.2)C_0/2 = 1.05C_0$.
4. Calculation of $C_{Aero.\ Inter.}$:
   Zone 2: As the internal partitions are parallel to the airflow, $C_{Aero.\ Inter.} = C_0$.
   Zone 1: As the internal partitions are opaque and the zone is equipped with side openings, $C_{Aero.\ Inter.} = 0.8C_0$.
   Zones 3 and 4: Due to the presence of roof openings, together with the side and leeward openings, $C_{Aero.\ Inter.} = C_0$.

Therefore, because $C_G = \min(C_{site}, C_{orientation}, C_{Arch.\ Exter.}, C_{Aero.\ Inter.})$, we obtain that:

- Zone 1: $C_G = \min(C_0, 0.85C_0, 0.7C_0, 0.8C_0) = 0.7C_0$ or 0.42.
- Zone 2: $C_G = \min(C_0, 0.85C_0, 1.2C_0, C_0) = 0.85C_0$ or 0.51.
- Zones 3 and 4: $C_G = \min(C_0, 0.85C_0, 1.05C_0, C_0) = 0.85C_0$

3.1.2.4 The Ernest methodology [9]

Ernest [9], using data obtained from architectural scale models in a boundary-layer wind tunnel, proposed a simple empirical model for the prediction of wind-induced indoor air motion. The model requires climatic inputs, such as the wind direction and the pressure distribution around the building, as well as building related data, such as the size and characteristics of the windows and the interior partition configurations. The method predicts an average indoor velocity coefficient, C_v, defined as the ratio of the mean interior velocity to the mean outdoor reference free-stream velocity at eaves height, which represents the measure of the relative strength of the interior movement in the horizontal plane representative of the occupied space of the room. Then the method determines the local indoor velocity distributions based on the cumulative percentage of the floor area over which a certain velocity is exceeded, without however determining the specific local indoor velocity in the space. For this purpose the method proposes the calculation of a coefficient of spatial variation, C_{sv}, defined as:

$$C_{sv} = \sigma_s(V_i)/(V_e C_v) \tag{3.7}$$

where $\sigma_s(V_i)$ is the standard deviation of the n mean interior velocities, V_e is the mean outdoor reference free stream velocity at eaves height and C_v is the average velocity coefficient defined previously. It is clear that C_{sv} is a measure of the relative spatial uniformity of the flow. A low C_{sv} indicates a rather uniform flow, while a high value represents a greater spatial unevenness for the interior velocity distribution. Finally the method proposes the calculation of an average turbulence coefficient C_t representing a measure of the turbulence level in the room defined as:

$$C_t = 1/N \sum_{i=1,N} \sigma_t(V_i)/(V_e C_v) \tag{3.8}$$

where $\sigma_t(V_i)$ is the standard deviation of the fluctuating component of the mean velocity at interior location i. The model can be applied for configurations inside the range of parameters used to generate it (Table 3.9).

To calculate the average indoor velocity coefficient, C_v, the following formula is proposed:

$$C_v = f_1(C_p, \theta) f_2(\varphi) f_3(p_n, \theta) f_4 \tag{3.9}$$

where

C_p is the pressure coefficient;
θ is the wind direction;
φ is the building porosity;
p_n is the interior partition type;
$f_1(C_p, \theta)$ is the coefficient for the effect of pressure distribution and wind direction;
$f_2(\varphi)$ is the coefficient for the effect of the window size;
$f_3(p_n, \theta)$ is the coefficient for the effect of interior partitions;
f_4 is the coefficient for the effect of window accessories.

To calculate the coefficient $f_1(C_p, \theta)$, the following empirical expression is proposed:

$$f_1(C_p, \theta) = [A\Delta C_p + BC_{p,i} \cos\theta + CC_{p,o} \cos\theta + D\cos\theta + E]^{0.5} \tag{3.10}$$

where $C_{p,i}$ is the average pressure coefficient for the upwind opening area, $C_{p,o}$ is the average pressure coefficient for the downwind area, and $\Delta C_p = |C_{p,i} - C_{p,o}|$.

Table 3.9. Range of parameters used to generate the Ernest model [9]

Upwind terrain roughness	Three different surrounding terrain roughness were investigated corresponding to (a) farmland, (b) villages and (c) suburban configurations.
Wind direction	For each building configuration, seven wind directions were measured, corresponding to wind incidence of 0°, 15°, 30°, 45°, 60°, 75° and 90° from the normal of the building.
Immediate upwind obstructions	An obstruction consisted of a long row placed at ten different spacings upwind of the building was used.
Building height and roof geometry	A two-storey building and three types of sloped roof were investigated.
Building shapes	A total of five building geometries were investigated: rectangular, (two kinds), L-shaped, U-shaped and Z-shaped.
External building projections	Two types of wing walls and two building overhangs were tested. In addition, a building with end walls and extended eaves was studied.
Window size	The range of the window size investigated was such that the porosity of the wall varied from 6% to 25% of the wall area.
Window location	Both inlet and outlet locations were examined. The location of the openings was either centred or shifted to the side of the building.
Interior room partitions	Two types of interior partitions were analysed for three different positions within the room and two different heights. The exact configuration of the tested interior partitions is given below in the text.

The empirical coefficients for this equation are: $A = 0.0203$, $B = 0.0296$, $C = -0.0651$, $D = -0.0178$, $E = 0.0054$

To calculate the coefficient $f_2(\varphi)$, the proposed expression is:

$$f_2(\varphi) = A\varphi + B \qquad (3.11)$$

where $A = 3.48$ and $B = 0.42$. It is proposed that the porosity of the building (φ) ($0.06 < \varphi < 0.25$) be calculated with the following expression:

$$\varphi = 2A_i A_o / [A_w (2A_i^2 + 2A_o^2)^{0.5}] \qquad (3.12)$$

where A_i is the open inlet area, A_o is the open outlet area, and A_w is the interior area of the wall containing the inlet.

To calculate the effect of interior partitions, f_3, the user has to select one of the configurations given in Figure 3.13 and a value for the partition position, height and wind direction within the ranges as follows, where:

Dip   is the distance between the inlet and the partition;
Lir   is the distance between the inlet and the outlet in the room;

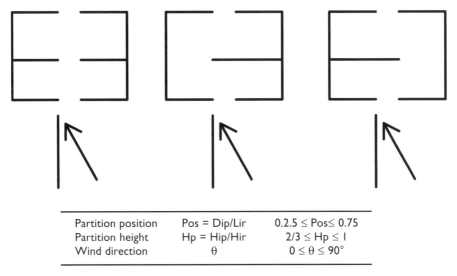

Partition position	Pos = Dip/Lir	$0.2.5 \leq Pos \leq 0.75$
Partition height	Hp = Hip/Hir	$2/3 \leq Hp \leq 1$
Wind direction	θ	$0 \leq \theta \leq 90°$

Figure 3.13. Internal partition types [9]

Hip   is the height of the interior partition;
Hir   is the interior height of the room (ceiling height).

Given these configurations, four different empirical functions have been proposed and are summarized in Table 3.10.

Table 3.10. Coefficient f_3 [9]

Partition type	$f_3(P_n, \theta)$	A	B	C	D
Type 1	$A + B\,Hp\,Pos + C \cos 6\theta$	0.770	0.287	0.045	–
Type 2, Hp = 1	$A + B \sin \theta$	0.882	0057	–	–
Type 2, Hp = 2/3	$A + B\,Pos + C \sin \theta +$ $D\,Pos \sin \theta$	0.646	0.381	0.442	–0.699
Type 2, Hp = 1	$A + B\,Pos + C \sin \theta +$ $D \cos 6\theta$	0.628	0.300	0.064	0.042

For the calculation of the f_4 coefficient the method proposes the values given in Table 3.11 as suggested by Swami and Chandra [13].

Table 3.11. Coefficient f_4 [13]

Window type	f_4
Open window with 60% porosity insect screen	0.85
Fully open awning window, no screen	0.75
Awning window with 60% porosity insect screen	0.65

EXAMPLE A. Calculate the overall average indoor velocity coefficient for a room with interior partition Type 1, Hp = 0.75, Pos = 0.33 and $\theta = 30°$. Assume that $C_{p,i} = -0.04$, $C_{p,o} = -0.51$, while the window has a 60% porosity insect screen and the building has a porosity of 20%.

Using equation (3.10), we calculate $f_1(C_p, \theta)$:

$$f_1(C_p, \theta) = [A\Delta C_p + BC_{p,i}\cos\theta + CC_{p,o}\cos\theta + D\cos\theta + E]^{0.5}$$

$$= [(0.0203)(0.47) + (0.0296)(-0.04)(0.866)$$

$$+ (-0.0651)(-0.51)(0.866) + (-0.0178)(0.866) + (0.0054)]^{0.5}$$

$$= 0.165$$

Using equation (3.11), we get:

$$f_2(\varphi) = A\varphi + B = (3.48)(0.20) + 0.42 = 1.116$$

Also, from Table 3.10 we get:

$$f_3(p_n, \theta) = A + B\,\text{HpPos} + C\cos 6\theta$$

$$= (0.770) + (0.287)(0.75)(0.33) + (0.045)(-1)$$

$$= 0.796$$

Finally from Table 3.11 we obtain that $f_4 = 0.85$. Therefore, from equation (3.9) we get:

$$C_v = f_1(C_p, \theta)f_2(\varphi)f_3(p_n, \theta)f_4$$

$$= (0.165)(1.116)(0.796)(0.85) = 0.125$$

DETERMINATION OF THE COEFFICIENT OF SPATIAL VARIATION: C_{sv}. For building types within the configurations studied by Ernest, the following expression is proposed to calculate the coefficient of spatial variation, C_{sv}:

$$C_{sv} = A + Bf_1(C_p, \theta) + C\sin\theta + D\sin 4\theta \qquad (3.13)$$

where the empirical coefficients are: $A = 0.252$, $B = 0.958$, $C = 0.080$, $D = -0.056$

EXAMPLE B. What is the value of C_{sv} for an L-shaped building and for $\theta = 30°$?
    Using equation (3.10), we get $f_1(C_p, \theta) = 0.165$. Then from equation (3.13) we get:

$$C_{sv} = A + Bf_1(C_p, \theta) + C\sin\theta + D\sin 4\theta$$

$$= 0.252 + (0.958)(0.165) + (0.08)(0.5) + (-0.056)(0.866) = 0.402$$

DETERMINATION OF LOCAL INDOOR VELOCITY DISTRIBUTION. To determine the local indoor velocity distribution, the following expression is proposed:

$$V(p) / V_e = (1 + \Omega(p)C_{sv})C_v \qquad (3.14)$$

where:

> p is the percentage of floor area $(0.05 \le p \le 1)$;
>
> $V(p)$ is the mean velocity exceeded for $p\%$ of the floor area;
>
> V_e is the mean outdoor reference free-stream velocity at eaves height;
>
> $\Omega(p)$ is the reduced mean velocity exceeded for $p\%$ of the floor area;
>
> C_{sv} is the coefficient of spatial variation $(0.20 \le C_{sv} \le 0.70)$, and
>
> C_v is the average velocity coefficient $(0.050 \le C_v \le 0.35)$.

The reduced velocity distribution is given by:

$$\Omega(p) = A \ln(p) + B \qquad (3.15)$$

The coefficients for this equation are: $A = -1.262$, $B = -1.109$

EXAMPLE C. What is the velocity exceeded for 33% of the floor area in an L-shaped building and for $\theta = 30°$, $C_v = 0.125$ and $C_{sv} = 0.495$?
   Using equation (3.15), we get:

$$\Omega(p) = A \ln(p) + B = (-1.262)(-1.11) - 1.109 = 0.290$$

Then, from equation (3.14) we get:

$$V(p) / V_e = (1 + \Omega(p)C_{sv})C_v$$

$$= [1 + (0.290)(0.495)](0.125) = 0.143$$

This value means that local indoor velocities in the room will be greater than or equal to 0.71 m s^{-1} over 33% of the floor area.

EXAMPLE D. What is the percentage of the floor area (p) over which indoor velocities exceed a target velocity of 1 m s^{-1}, $(V(p)/V_e = 0.2)$ in an L-shaped building and $\theta = 30°$, $C_v = 0.125$ and $C_{sv} = 0.495$?
   Solving equation 3.14 for $\Omega(p)$, we get:

$$V(p) / V_e = (1 + \Omega(p)C_{sv})C_v$$

$$\Rightarrow \Omega(p) = V(p) / (V_e C_v) - 1) / C_{sv}$$

$$= ((0.2 / 0.125) - 1) / 0.495 = 1.212$$

Solving for p in equation (3.15), we get:

$$\Omega(p) = A \ln(p) + B$$

$$\Rightarrow p = \exp[(\Omega(p) - B) / A]$$

$$= \exp[(1.212) + (1.109) / (-1.262)] = 0.159$$

This value means that under these conditions, indoor velocities exceed the target velocity of 1 m s^{-1} over approximately 15% of the floor area.

3.2   NETWORK MODELS

3.2.1   Introduction

Empirical models are based on simplified formulae and they must be carefully applied within the limits of their validity. Additionally, because of the simple assumptions on which they are based, they can only be expected to provide estimates of the bulk airflow rates in a building that can be regarded as single zone. However, under real conditions, the approximation of a building by a single-zone volume is of little value, since the interaction of various zones through internal openings is of great importance. In this case, a multizone airflow network analysis is required.

According to the concept of airflow network modelling, a building is represented by a grid that is formed by a number of nodes that stand for the simulated zones and the exterior environment. Interaction between various zones is denoted by flow paths linking their respective nodes. Thus, the rooms of a building are represented by nodes and the openings are represented by linking flow paths. Interaction with the outdoor environment is represented by flow paths linking interior with exterior nodes. All nodes, interior and exterior, are attributed a pressure value.

As will be analysed in the following sections, the airflow rate through a building opening is directly related to the pressure difference across the opening. Pressures at exterior nodes are known. Following the concept of network modelling the pressure values of interior nodes have to be determined in order to finally deduce the airflow rates.

The mathematical interpretation of the phenomena involved in natural ventilation, used in network modelling, is presented in the following sections.

3.2.2   Interpretation of physical mechanisms involved in natural ventilation

In all cases of natural ventilation, the driving forces are attributed to pressure differences that are created across all kinds of openings in the building structure. Pressure differences result from the combined action of two mechanisms, the wind and the temperature difference.

3.2.2.1 *The effect of the wind*
Positive pressure is created on the sides of the building that face the wind (windward sides), whereas suction regions are formed on the opposite sides (leeward sides) and on the sidewalls. This results in a negative pressure inside the building, which is sufficient to introduce large flows through the building openings. In a general case, an inflow of air is induced on the windward side and an outflow on the leeward side.

The contribution of the wind to the pressure difference across an exterior opening is calculated with the following expression:

$$\Delta P_w = 0.5 Cp \rho U^2 \qquad (3.16)$$

where ΔP_w is the wind-induced pressure (Pa), Cp is the pressure coefficient, ρ is the air density (kg m^{-3}) and U is the wind speed at a reference height, usually taken as the building height (m s^{-1}).

The wind speed is calculated as a function of available wind velocity measurements from typical meteorological data. Wind velocity measurements are made available at a fixed height, usually 10 m above the ground level. As a result, the actual wind speed (U) must be properly adjusted for a specific height and must take into account the building's orientation, the topography of the location and the roughness of the surrounding terrain in the direction of the wind. This can be calculated using three wind profiles:

- The power law wind profile [14]
  The actual wind speed U_1 is evaluated by the following expression:

$$\frac{U_1}{U_{10}} = K\, z_1^a \qquad (3.17)$$

  where the coefficient K and the exponent a are constants that depend on terrain roughness. Typical values for K and a are given in Table 3.12.
- The logarithmic wind profile, mentioned in Chapter 2, according to which the wind speed is a logarithmic function of height:

$$\frac{U_l}{U_m} = \frac{U_{*,l}}{U_{*,m}} \left[\frac{\ln \dfrac{z_{ll} - d_l}{z_{0,l}}}{\ln \dfrac{z_m - d_m}{z_{0,m}}} \right] \qquad (3.18)$$

where

$$\frac{U_{*,l}}{U_{*,m}} = \left[\frac{z_{0,l}}{z_{0,m}}\right]^{0.1} \tag{3.19}$$

where U_m is the wind speed from meteorological data (m s^{-1}), U_* is the atmospheric friction speed (m s^{-1}), z_0 is the terrain roughness (m) and d is the terrain displacement length (m). Typical values for z_0 and d are given in Table 3.12.

- An alternative power-law wind profile, developed at the Laurence Berkeley Laboratory [14]:

$$\frac{U_l}{U_m} = \frac{\alpha(z/10)^g}{\alpha_m(z_m/10)^{g_m}} \tag{3.20}$$

where α, g are terrain dependent constants, typical values of which are given in Table 3.12.

Table 3.12. Typical values for terrain dependent parameters
(h = building height) [14]

Terrain	K	a	z_0	d	α	g
Open flat country	0.68	0.17	0.03	0.0	1.00	0.15
Country with scattered wind breaks	0.52	0.20	0.1	0.0	1.00	0.15
Rural			0.5	0.7 h	0.85	0.20
Urban	0.35	0.25	1.0	0.8 h	0.67	0.25
City	0.21	0.33	> 2.0	0.8 h	0.47	0.35

The dimensionless pressure coefficient Cp is an empirically derived parameter that accounts for the changes in wind-induced pressure caused by the influence of surrounding obstructions on the prevailing local wind characteristics. Its value changes according to the wind direction, the building surface orientation and the topography and roughness of the terrain in the direction of the wind. Typical design data sets based on experimental results are given in Table 3.13 [15].

Each data set comprises Cp values for 16 different wind directions (angle of wind with the normal to the surface: 0°, 22.5°, 45°, 67.5°, 90°, 112.5°, 135°, 157.5°, 180°, 202.5°, 225°, 247.5°, 270°, 292.5°, 315°, 337.5°, progressing clockwise as seen from above).

Table 3.13 comprises 29 pressure coefficient data sets corresponding to an equal number of different façade configurations in terms of surface aspect, dimensions and exposure. The Cp values given in the table may be used for low-rise buildings of up to three storeys and they express an average value for each external building surface.

Local (not wall-averaged) evaluation of the Cp parameter is one of the most difficult aspects of air-infiltration modelling. In the following section a recently developed Cp calculation model is presented.

Table 3.13. Pressure coefficient sets [15]

No.	Facade description	AR*	Exp†	Cp sets
1	Wall	1:1	E	0.7, 0.525, 0.35, −0.075, −0.5, −0.45, −0.4, −0.3, −0.2, −0.3, −4, −0.45, −0.5, −0.075, 0.35, 0.525
2	Roof, pitch > 10°	1:1	E	−0.8, −0.75, −0.7, −0.65, −0.6, −0.55, −0.5, −0.45, −0.4, −0.45, −0.5, −0.55, −0.6, −0.65, −0.7, −0.75
3	Roof, pitch > 10–30°	1:1	E	−0.4, −0.45, −0.5, −0.55, −0.6, −0.55, −0.5, −0.45, −0.4, −0.45, −0.5, −0.55, −0.6, −0.55, −0.5, −0.45
4	Roof, pitch > 30°	1:1	E	−0.3, −0.35, −0.4, −0.5, −0.6, −0.5, −0.4, −0.45, −0.5, −0.45, −0.4, −0.5, −0.6, −0.5, −0.4, −0.35
5	Wall	1:1	SE	0.4, 0.25, 0.1, −0.1, −0.3, −0.325, −0.35, 0.275, −0.2, −0.275, −0.35, −0.325, −0.3, −0.1, 0.1, 0.25
6	Roof, pitch < 10°	1:1	SE	−0.6, −0.55, −0.5, −0.45, −,4, −0.45, −0.5, −0.55, −0.6, − 0.55, −0.5, −0.45, −0.4, −0.45, −0.5, −0.55
7	Roof, pitch 10–30°	1:1	SE	−0.35, −0.4, −0.45, −0.5, −0.55, −0.5, −0.45, −0.4, −0.35, −0.4, −0.45, −0.5, −0.55, −0.5, −0.45, −0.4
8	Roof, pitch > 30°	1:1	SE	−0.3, −0.4, −0.5, −0.55, −0.6, −0.55, −0.5, −0.5, −0.5, −0.5, −0.5, −0.55, −0.6, −0.55, −0.5, −0.4
9	Wall	1:1	S	0.2, 0.125, 0.05, 0.1, −0.25, −0.275, −0.3, −0.275, −0.25, −0.275, −0.3, −0.275, −0.25, −0.1, 0.05, 0.125
10	Roof, pitch < 10 deg	1:1	S	−0.5, −0.5, −0.5, −0.45, −0.4, −0.45, −0.5, −0.5, −0.5, −0.5, −0.5, −0.45, −0.4, −0.45, −0.5, −0.5
11	Roof, pitch 10–30°	1:1	S	−0.3, −0.35, −0.4, −0.45, −0.5, −0.45, −0.4, −0.35, −0.3, −0.35, −0.4, −0.45, −0.5, −0.45, −0.4, −0.35
12	Roof, pitch > 30°	1:1	S	0.25, −0.025, −0.3, −0.4, −0.5, −0.4, −0.3, −0.35, −0.4, −0.35, −0.3, −0.4, −0.5, −0.4, −0.3, −0.025
13	Long wall	2:1	E	0.5, 0.375, 0.25, −0.125, −0.5, −0.65, −0.8, −0.75, −0.7, −0.75, −0.8, −0.65, −0.5, −0.125, −0.25, −0.375
14	Short wall	1:2	E	−0.9, −0.35, 0.2, 0.4, 0.6, 0.4, 0.2, −0.35, −0.9, −0.75, −0.6, −0.475, −0.35, −0.475, −0.6, −0.75
15	Roof, pitch < 10°	2:1	E	−0.7, −0.7, −0.7, −0.75, −0.8, −0.75, −0.7, −0.7, −0.7, −0.7, −0.7, −0.75, −0.8, −0.75, −0.7, −0.7
16	Roof, pitch 10–30°	2:1	E	−0.7, −0.7, −0.7, −0.7, −0.7, −0.65, −0.6, −0.55, −0.5, −0.55, −0.6, −0.65, −0.7, −0.7, −7, −0.7
17	Roof, pitch > 30°	2:1	E	0.25, 0.125, 0, −0.3, −0.6, −0.75, −0.9, −0.85, −0.8, −0.85, −0.9, −0.75, −0.6, −0.3, 0, 0.125
18	Long Wall	2:1	SE	0.5, 0.375, 0.25, 0.−125, −0.5, −0.65, −0.8, −0.75, −0.7, −0.75, −0.8, −0.65, −0.5, −0.125, 0.25, 0.375
19	Short Wall	1:2	SE	−0.9, −0.35, 0.2, 0.4, 0.6, 0.4, 0.2, −0.35, −0.9, −0.75, −0.6, −0.475, −0.35, −0.475, −0.6, −0.75
20	Roof, pitch < 10°	2:1	SE	−0.7, −0.7, −0.7, −0.75, −0.8, −0.75, −0.7, −0.7, −0.7, −0.7, −0.7, −0.75, −0.8, −0.75, −0.7, −0.7
21	Roof, pitch 10–30°	2:1	SE	−0.7, −0.7, −0.7, −0.7, −0.7, −0.65, −0.6, −0.55. −0.5, −0.55, −0.6, −0.65, −0.7, −0.7, −0.7, −0.7
22	Roof, pitch > 30°	2:1	SE	0.25, 0.125, 0, −0.3, −0.6, −0.75, −0.9, −0.85, −0.8, −0.85, −0.9, −0.75, −0.6, −0.3, 0, 0.125
23	Long wall	2:1	S	0.06, −0.03, −0.12, −0.16, −0.2, −0.29, −0.38, −0.34, −0.3, −0.34, −0.38, −0.29, −0.2, −0.16, −0.12, −0.03
24	Short wall	1:2	S	−0.3, −0.075, 0.15, 0.165, 0.18, 0.165, 0.15, −0.075, −0.3, −0.31, −0.32, −0.32, −0.26, −0.2, −0.26, −0.32
25	Roof, pitch < 10°	2:1	S	−0.49, −0.475, −0.46, −0.435, −0.41, −0.435, −0.46, −0.475, −0.49, −0.475, −0.46, −0.435, −0.41, −0.435, −0.46, −0.475
26	Roof, pitch 10–30°	2:1	S	−0.49, −0.475, −0.46, −0.435, −0.41, −0.435, −0.46, −0.43, −0.4, −0.43, −0.46, −0.435, −0.41, −0.435, −0.46, −0.475
27	Roof, pitch > 30°	2:1	S	0.06, −0.045, −0.15, −0.19, −0.23, −0.42, −0.6, −0.51, −0.42, −0.51, −0.6, −0.42, −0.23, −0.19, −0.15, −0.045
28	Wall	1:1	E	0.9, 0.7, 0.5, 0.2, −0.1, −0.1, −0.2, −0.2, −0.2, −0.2, −0.2, −0.1, −0.1, 0.2, 0.5, 0.7
29	Roof, no pitch	1:1	E	−0.1, −0.1, −0.1, −0.1, −0.1 −0.1 −0.1 −0.1, −0.1, −0.1, −0.1, −0.1, −0.1, −0.1, −0.1, −0.1

*AR aspect ratio (length-to-width ratio)   † Exp exposure: E exposed; SE Semi-exposed; S Sheltered

A PARAMETRICAL MODEL FOR THE CALCULATION OF THE PRESSURE
COEFFICIENT [16]

The model (Grosso [16]) is based on a parametrical analysis of results from two wind-tunnel tests, carried out by Hussein and Lee [17] and Akins and Cermak [18]. The model consists of a number of relations between the pressure coefficient on a rectangular-shaped building model and various influencing parameters, grouped in three categories:

- *Climate parameters*, involving wind velocity profile exponent (*a*) and wind incidence angle (*anw*). Figure 3.14 shows the wind incidence angle for a building facade. The parameter *anw* is defined as the absolute value of the wind incidence angle. Windward façades have 0° <*anw*< 90° and leeward façades have 90° < *anw* < 180°.
- *Environmental parameters*, involving the plan area density (pad) and the relative building height (rbh). Plan area density is defined as the ratio of built area to total area. This ratio has to be calculated within a radius ranging from 10 to 25 times the height of the considered building. Figure 3.15 illustrates the plan area density for a building with length *L* and width *W*. Relative building height is the ratio of the building height to the height of the surrounding buildings, the latter assumed to be regular boxes, all of the same height.
- *Building parameters*, involving the frontal aspect ratio (far), the side aspect ratio (sar), the relative vertical position (zh) and the relative horizontal position (xl). The aspect ratio is defined as the ratio of the length to the height of a building facade. The frontal aspect ratio is related to the façade under consideration and the side aspect ratio to its adjacent facade, regardless of the angle the wind direction relative to the façades themselves. The relative horizontal and vertical position of a façade element is defined with respect to a reference point on the facade, as illustrated in Figure 3.16.

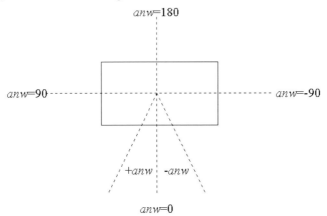

Figure 3.14. Wind incidence angle (°) in relation to the front facade (plan view)

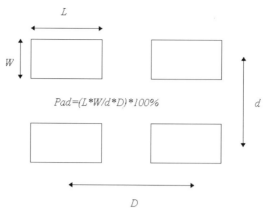

Figure 3.15. Calculation of the plan area density

The range of parameters common to both of the wind-tunnel tests mentioned above was used as a reference. It corresponds to the profile of Cp on the vertical centreline of the windward and leeward façades of a model with the approaching wind normal to the facades, in a boundary layer typical of a suburban area. The model assumes that the reference horizontal distribution of Cp does not change with plan area density, relative building height, aspect ratio and wind velocity profile exponent.

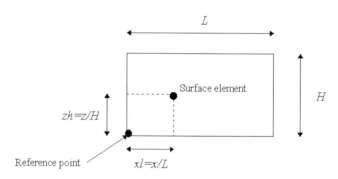

Figure 3.16. Facade element positioning

The reference profiles, as functions of the relative vertical position zh, are third or fifth degree polynomials:

$$\mathrm{Cp}_{\mathrm{ref}}(\mathrm{zh}) = a_0 + a_1(\mathrm{zh}) + a_2(\mathrm{zh})^2 + \ldots + a_n(\mathrm{zh})^n \qquad (3.21)$$

where $n = 3$ for the windward façade and $n = 5$ for the leeward facade.
    The reference profiles were defined for the following parameters:

$a = 0.22$; pad $= 0.0$; rbh $= 1.0$; far $= 1.0$; sar $= 1.0$; *anw* $= 0°$ (windward facade); *anw* $= 180°$ (leeward facade).

The rest of the Cp data were normalized for each parameter, with respect to the Cp corresponding to the reference value of the parameter. Thus, the normalized *Cp* value for the *n*, *m* and *t* values of the parameters *i*, *j* and **d** respectively, is:

$$Cp_{\text{norm } i_n, j_m, d_t} = \frac{Cp_{i_n, j_m(d_t)}}{Cp_{i_n, j_m(d_{\text{ref}})}}$$

(3.22)

The normalized Cp values are given as functions of the various parameters by first- to fifth-degree polynomials for the leeward side and by first- to third-degree polynomials for the windward side. Polynomial coefficients are given in Tables 3.A1–6 (Appendix A at the end of the chapter) for the windward façades (0° < *anw* < 90°) and in Tables 3.A9–14 (Appendix A) for the leeward side (90° < *anw* < 180°). Non-polynomial functions relate the normalized Cp values to the parameters far and sar, for far > 1.0 and sar > 1.0 (Tables 3.A7–8, 3.A15–16 in Appendix A at the end of the chapter).

The pressure coefficient of an element *k* with coordinates xl and zh on a façade of a building with shape defined by specific values of far and sar and in environmental conditions defined by specific values of *a*, pad, rbh and anw is calculated by:

$$Cp_k = Cp_{\text{ref}}(\text{zh}) \times CF$$

(3.23)

where CF is the global correction factor defined as:

$$CF = Cf_{\text{zh}}(a).Cf_{\text{zh}}(\text{pad}).Cf_{\text{zh, pad}}(\text{rbh})$$
$$\times Cf_{\text{zh, pad}}(\text{far}).Cf_{\text{zh, pad}}(\text{sar}).Cf_{\text{zh, pad}}(\text{xl})$$

(3.24)

where

$$Cf_{i_n, j_m(d_t)} = Cp_{\text{norm } i_n, j_m, d_t}$$

(3.25)

If *n* and *m* values of the *i* and *j* parameters are different from those given in the tables, then the correction factor is calculated for the closest lower and higher values and the results are linearly interpolated.

Application of the above-described method is restricted because of the variation range defined for each parameter. In particular, the model cannot be applied to:

- high terrain roughness (*a* > 0.33) and/or high density of the immediate surrounding buildings (pad > 50);
- immediate surrounding buildings with a staggered or irregular pattern layout;
- immediate surrounding buildings with pad > 12.5, when the considered building has a different height from its surroundings or a shape other than a cube,

- buildings four times higher than of the surroundings or lower than half the height of the surroundings;
- buildings with irregular shape or overhangs;
- regular block-shaped buildings with aspect ratios less than 0.5 or greater than 4.

A case study of the method is presented in Appendix A at the end of the chapter.

3.2.2.2 The stack effect

Air movement by the stack effect occurs when temperature differences between a zone and the environment adjacent to it, be it another zone or the exterior, cause light warm air to rise and flow out of the warm zone, while cooler airflows in (Figure 3.17). The stack effect occurs in tall buildings, particularly at places with vertical passages such as stairwells, elevators or shafts. In this case the airflow grows with increasing temperature difference.

If P_0 is the static pressure at the bottom of a zone, then the pressure, due to the stack effect only, at a height z of the zone is given by:

$$P_s = P_0 - \rho g z \ \text{(Pa)} \tag{3.26}$$

where P_0 and P_s are the pressures at the bottom of the zone and at a height z respectively (Pa), g is the gravitational acceleration (m s^{-2}) and ρ is the air density at a temperature T equal to the indoor air temperature (kg m^{-3}).

Assuming that the air behaves as an ideal gas, the density can be calculated by the following expression:

$$\rho = \rho_0 \frac{T_0}{T} \ \text{(kg m}^{-3}\text{)} \tag{3.27}$$

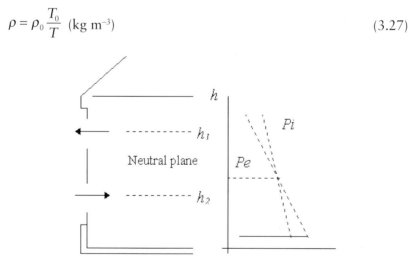

Figure 3.17. Buoyancy-driven airflow through two vertical openings

where T is the absolute temperature (K) and ρ_0 and T_0 are the reference density and temperature of the air (i.e. for $T_0 = 273.15$ K, $\rho_0 = 1.29$ kg m^{-3}).

From equation (3.27) it is clear that the stack pressure decreases with height. In the case of two isothermal zones that are interconnected by a component (door or window), the pressure difference at a height z (m), across the component will be:

$$\Delta P_s = P_{1,0} - P_{2,0} + (\rho_1 - \rho_2)gz \quad \text{(Pa)} \tag{3.28}$$

where $P_{1,0}$ and $P_{2,0}$ are the static pressures at a reference height (i.e. the bottom of the zones), and ρ_1 and ρ_2 are the air densities in zones 1 and 2 respectively.

This theory assumes that the temperature inside the zones does not change with height (isothermal zones). A more complex model has been proposed [19] to represent, in more detail, the behaviour of large openings. The model accounts for temperature stratification and turbulence effects by assuming:

- steady flow of an inviscid and incompressible fluid;
- linear density stratification on both sides of the opening;
- turbulence effects represented by an equivalent pressure-difference profile.

Thus, on each side of the opening, a linear density stratification is assumed:

$$\rho_i(z) = \rho_{0i} + b_i z \quad \text{(kg m}^{-3}\text{)} \tag{3.29}$$

and a linear pressure difference is introduced, to simulate the turbulence effect:

$$\Delta P_t = P_{t0} + b_t(z) \quad \text{(Pa)} \tag{3.30}$$

Introducing these terms into equation (3.28) for the case of gravitational flow (no wind effect):

$$\Delta P_s = P_{1,0} - P_{2,0} - g[(\rho_{01}z + \frac{b_1 z^2}{2}) - (\rho_{02} z + \frac{b_2 z^2}{2})] + (P_{t0} + b_t z) \quad \text{(Pa)} \tag{3.31}$$

3.2.2.3 Combined action of wind and temperature difference

For the calculation of the total pressure difference across the opening, the terms of the dynamic pressure must be added to those representing the stack effect. Thus, combining equations (3.16) and (3.28) gives:

$$\Delta P = P_{1,0} - P_{2,0} + \frac{\rho_1 C_p U_1^2}{2} - \frac{\rho_2 C_p U_2^2}{2} + (\rho_1 - \rho_2)gz \quad \text{(Pa)} \tag{3.32}$$

where U_1 and U_2 are the wind speeds at the two sides of the opening (m s^{-1}) and ρ_1 and ρ_2 are the air densities of the interconnected zones (kg m^{-3}).

For exterior openings, $U_2 = 0$ and U_1 is taken equal to the wind speed, U, at the building height, while ρ_1 is the indoor air density, ρ_i and ρ_2 is the density of the outdoor air, ρ_o. P_0 is the reference pressure of the zone to which the opening belongs. Thus, equation (3.32) for exterior openings can be written as:

$$\Delta P_{ext} = P_0 - \frac{\rho_i C_p U^2}{2} + (\rho_i - \rho_o)gz \ \ (Pa) \tag{3.33}$$

For interior openings, $V_1 = V_2 = 0$. If no density gradients are considered in the interconnected zones, equation (3.32) for interior openings, becomes:

$$\Delta P_{int} = P_{1,0} - P_{2,0} + (\rho_{i,1} - \rho_{i,2})gz \ \ (Pa) \tag{3.34}$$

If temperature stratification is to be taken into account, the resulting pressure difference at a height z is derived by combining equations (3.26) and (3.31):

$$\Delta P = P_{1,0} - P_{2,0} - g[(\rho_{01} \ z + \frac{b_1 z^2}{2}) - (\rho_{02} \ z + \frac{b_2 z^2}{2})] + (P_{t0} + b_t z) \ \ (Pa) \tag{3.35}$$

3.2.3   Airflow through large openings and cracks

Depending on their dimensions, two distinct categories of openings can be defined:

- large openings, with typical dimensions larger than 10 mm;
- cracks, with typical dimensions smaller than 10 mm.

Consequently, windows and doors fall within the category of large openings, while any other small-sized opening in the building structure is considered to be a crack.

Network modelling is based on two assumptions:

- The airflow through an opening is inviscid and incompressible.
- The air temperature field in the studied zone(s) is uniform.

The relation of the airflow rate to the pressure difference across an opening is generally expressed by a power-law equation of the form:

$$Q = K(\Delta P)^n \ (m^3 \ s^{-1}) \tag{3.36}$$

where K is the flow coefficient and n the flow exponent.

The flow coefficient K is a function of the geometry of the opening, while the flow exponent n depends on the flow characteristics and varies in the range 0.5–1.0. A value of n equal to 0.5 corresponds to fully turbulent flow and a value equal to 1.0 corresponds to laminar flow.

The flow equations for each of the two categories of opening mentioned above are given in the following sections.

3.2.3.1 Crack flow
If the flow equation (equation 3.36) is used directly, the coefficients K and n can be derived from the following expressions [20]:

$$K = L_{cr} 9.7(0.0092)^n / 1000 \ (m^3 \ s^{-1} \ Pa^{-n}) \tag{3.37}$$

$$n = 0.5 + 0.5 \exp(-500 W_{cr}) \tag{3.38}$$

Another form of the same equation for openings with typical dimensions smaller than 10 mm, is:

$$Q = k L_{cr} (\Delta P)^n \tag{3.39}$$

where the coefficient n ranges from 0.6 to 0.7. Table 3.14 summarizes the ranges of variation of the coefficient k for cracks with $n = 0.67$ formed around closed windows.

Table 3.14. Typical flow coefficient (K) values for cracks formed around windows (n = 0.67) [14]

Window type	Average	Range
Sliding	8	2–30
Pivoted	21	6–80
Pivoted (weatherstripped)	8	0.5–20

3.2.3.2 Large openings – the common orifice equation
Assuming steady, inviscid and incompressible flow across an opening, the Bernoulli equation gives for the points (1) and (2) of the flow (Figure 3.18):

$$p_1 + \frac{1}{2}\rho V_1^2 = p_2 + \frac{1}{2}\rho V_2^2 \tag{3.40}$$

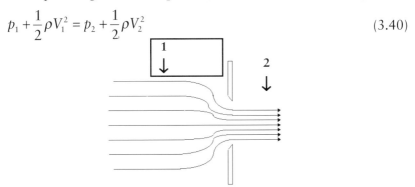

Figure 3.18. Flow modification in the presence of an opening

Assuming that the velocity profiles are uniform at sections (1) and (2) of the flow, the continuity equation gives:

$$Q = A_1 V_1 = A_2 V_2 \ (\text{m}^3/\text{s}) \tag{3.41}$$

where A_2 is small compared to A_1. Combination of the two equations results in the following theoretical air velocity:

$$V = \sqrt{\frac{2(p_1 - p_2)}{\rho[1 - (A_2 / A_1)^2]}} \ (\text{m/s}) \tag{3.42}$$

Since in the case of large openings in buildings $A_2 \ll A_1$ the term A_2/A_1 is negligible and therefore the resulting equation for the orifice flow is:

$$V = \sqrt{\frac{2(p_1 - p_2)}{\rho}} \ (\text{m/s}) \tag{3.43}$$

This equation describes the ideal situation, where the effect of viscosity is neglected. In reality, the area A_2 is less than the opening area by an unknown amount, owing to the effect of contraction. Additionally, the swirling flow and turbulent motion near the orifice introduce a non-ideal effect. To account for these 'real world' effects, a coefficient is introduced, called the discharge coefficient C_d, and equation (3.43) becomes:

$$V = C_d \sqrt{\frac{2(p_1 - p_2)}{\rho}} \ (\text{m/s}) \tag{3.44}$$

The airflow rate dQ through a small area dA of a large opening is:

$$dQ = V \, dA = VW \, dz \ (\text{m}^3 \ \text{s}^{-1}) \tag{3.45}$$

where W is the width of the opening (m).

If V is substituted from equation (3.44), equation (3.45) becomes:

$$dQ = C_d \sqrt{\frac{2(p_1 - p_2)}{\rho}} W \, dz \ (\text{m}^3/\text{s}) \tag{3.46}$$

The discharge coefficient is a function of the temperature difference, wind speed and opening geometry. A number of expressions have been proposed for its calculation, especially for internal openings. Interzonal heat and mass flow measurements in a real building [21] have given the following expression for the discharge coefficient, in the case of internal openings:

$$C_d = 0.0835(\Delta T/T)^{-0.3} \tag{3.47}$$

For steady-state and buoyancy-driven flow, the discharge coefficient for internal openings can be calculated from the following expression [22]:

$$C_d = (0.4 + 0.0075\Delta T) \tag{3.48}$$

Experimental results have been analysed in order to express the discharge coefficient in internal openings as a function of the temperature difference, air speed and opening height [23]. It was proved that the value of C_d is a strong function of the dimensions of the opening. For small internal openings, a representative value for the discharge coefficient is 0.65. For large internal openings C_d has a value close to unity. A proposed mean value for a standard opening is $C_d = 0.78$.

An evaluation of the discharge coefficient as a function of the height of the opening is attempted by Pelletret et al. [24]. For opening heights $1.5 < H5 < 2$ m, the proposed relation is $C_d = 0.21H$. According to Limam et al. [25], the values of C_d can be selected with reasonable accuracy within the range of 0.6–0.75.

Darliel and Lane Serff [26] have carried out experiments in a $18.6 \times 60 \times 40$ cm box and in a 199×9.4 cm channel using water. They have measured a C_d coefficient close to 0.311.

Measurements of airflow through large openings separating two zones in a test cell [25] have shown that the coefficient of discharge (C_d) varies between 0.67 and 0.73. This experiment was carried out using cold and hot vertical plates situated at the ends of each zone as a result of which a significant boundary-layer flow should have developed.

Khord Mneimne [27] found in a full-scale experiment using an electrical heater as a heating source that, for openings between 0.9 and 2 m, a mean C_d value equal to 0.87 should be used.

3.2.3.3 The neutral level

In network modelling the airflow through large openings is considered to be bi-directional. In the absence of wind, warm, light airflows through the upper part of an opening, while cool airflows through the lower part in the opposite direction. Thus, a level can be defined at which no air movement is observed, that is, no pressure difference occurs. This is called the 'neutral level' and is located at a height H_{NL} from the floor of the zone that can be derived from one of the equations (3.32), (3.33), (3.34), (3.35) with $\Delta P = 0$. If the chosen equation is equation (3.32) or (3.33) or (3.34), H_{NL} may be found to lie in one of the following positions (Figure 3.19):

- above the opening (H_{NL} > top of the opening);
- below the opening (H_{NL} < bottom of the opening);
- between the top and the bottom of the opening.

In the first two cases, the resulting flow is one-directional, while in the third the flow is bi-directional. If equation (3.35) is used, two possible positions of the neutral level may be derived (Figure 3.20), since equation (3.35) is a second-order polynomial.

Once the height of the neutral level, H_N, has been calculated, the rates for the various parts of the flow can be derived by integrating equation (3.49). In the general case:

$$Q_{lower} = \int_{HB}^{H_{NL_1}} C_d \sqrt{\frac{2(p_1 - p_2)}{\rho}} W \, dz$$

$$Q_{lower} = \int_{H_{NL_1}}^{H_{NL_2}} C_d \sqrt{\frac{2(p_1 - p_2)}{\rho}} W \, dz$$

$$Q_{lower} = \int_{H_{NL_2}}^{HT} C_d \sqrt{\frac{2(p_1 - p_2)}{\rho}} W \, dz \tag{3.49}$$

3.2.4   Mathematical approach

Network modelling is based on the concept that each zone of a building can be represented by a pressure node. Boundary nodes are also used to represent the environment outside the building. Nodes are interconnected by flow paths, such as cracks, windows, doors and shafts, to form a network. Figure 3.21 shows a network representation of a multizone building.

According to the network approach, a building with N zones is represented by a network of N pressure nodes. Some of them communicate with exterior nodes of known pressure, while others are only connected to interior nodes. Interior node pressures are unknown. Airflow paths can be either cracks, or windows and doors. Calculation of unknown pressures is derived by application of mass balance equations at each node.

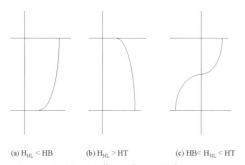

(a) $H_{NL} < HB$ (b) $H_{NL} > HT$ (c) $HB < H_{NL} < HT$

Figure 3.19. Airflow through large openings (no density gradient)

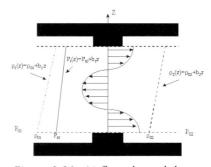

Figure 3.20. Airflow through large openings (density gradient)

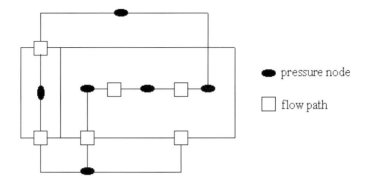

Figure 3.21. Network representation of a multizone building

Application of the mass balance equation to a zone *i* with *j* flow paths gives:

$$\sum_{k=1}^{j} \rho_i \, Q_{ik} = 0 \qquad (3.50)$$

where Q_{ik} is the volumetric flow from zone *i* to zone *k* (m³ s⁻¹) and ρ_i is the air density in the direction of the flow (kg s⁻¹).

Application of mass balance at each internal node of the network leads to a set of simultaneous non-linear equations, the solution of which gives the internal node pressures. Thus, by application of equation (3.50) to each node, a non-linear system of N equations is formed. Solution of this system is based on the Newton–Raphson iterative method. According to the method, a set of initial pressures is attributed to the unknown pressures. Until convergence is reached, the right-hand sides of the equations in the system expressed by equation (3.50) are different from zero. To minimize these values (residuals), at each iteration a new estimate of the pressure at each node is computed. For iteration *k* the new set of pressures is derived from:

$$P_n^{k+1} = P_n^k - X_n^k \qquad (3.51)$$

where the matrix of the pressure corrections [X] is defined for each iteration by the equation:

$$[J]\,[X] = [F] \qquad (3.52)$$

where [J] is the Jacobian matrix (N × N) for the simulated building, and [F] is a matrix (N × 1) containing the residuals from application of equation (3.50) to each zone. Each element of this matrix is calculated according to equation (3.50):

$$f(P_n) = \sum_{m=1}^{N} \rho_{nm} Q_{nm} \qquad (3.53)$$

The flow Q_{nm} is a function of the pressure difference, ΔP_{nm}, across the opening and can be positive or negative according to the sign of ΔP_{nm}:

$$\Delta P_{nm} = P_n - P_m \qquad (3.54)$$

If $\Delta P_{nm} > 0$ then $Q_{nm} > 0$, $\rho_{nm} = \rho_n$ and the air flows from node n to node m (outflow), while, if $\Delta P_{nm} < 0$ then $Q_{nm} < 0$, $\rho_{nm} = \rho_m$ and the air flows from node m to node n (inflow).

To take the sign of the flow into consideration, PASSPORT-AIR [28] uses the following formula for the calculation of $f(P_n)$:

$$f(P_n) = \sum_{m=1}^{N} \rho_{nm} Q_{nm} [|Q_{nm}|/Q_{nm}] \qquad (3.55)$$

The Jacobian matrix is symmetrical [19]. The elements of the matrix are calculated from the following derivatives, applied to each node n communicating with a node m:

Diagonal elements: $J(n, n) = \partial f(P_n)/\partial P_n$ $\qquad (3.56)$

Off-diagonal elements: $J(n, m) = J(m, n) = \partial f(P_n)\partial P_m$ $\qquad (3.57)$

According to the complexity of the application, a predefined value for the maximum acceptable residual (MAXRES) is defined (usually, this value is set to 0.001). Calculation of the Jacobian elements is done at each iteration and the worst (highest) residual is chosen among the elements of matrix [F]. If the absolute value of this residual is greater than MAXRES, then a new set of corrections is calculated with equation (3.51) and the derived new set of pressures is attributed to the unknown pressure nodes. Iterations continue until convergence is reached.

To accelerate convergence, various techniques have been introduced. According to Walton [29], a relaxation factor, RF(n), can be calculated at each iteration and for each node as follows:

$$RF_n = 1/(1 - r) \qquad (3.58)$$

where:

$$r = X_n(\text{current iteration}) / X_n(\text{previous iteration}) \qquad (3.59)$$

Thus, equation (3.51) is modified as follows:

$$P_n^{k+1} = P_n^k - RF_n^k X_n^k \qquad (3.60)$$

Computational tools based on the concept of the network modelling are fast and easy to use. The output comprises airflow predictions for user-specified

building structures and instantaneous climatic conditions. A recent comparative study of five existing computational tools (AIRNET [29], BREEZE [31],
ESP [15], PASSPORT-AIR [28] and COMIS [19]) has shown that their
predictions are in good agreement for a large number of configurations tested
[31]. A representative example of this comparison follows.

Figure 3.22 shows a plan view of the building that was simulated. Only three
zones were used in the simulation, namely zone A, zone B and zone C. The
dimensions of each zone are shown in the figure (zone height is 4.5m).

The case of ventilation with all windows and doors open was simulated
using five computational tools. The angle of wind incidence on window W_1 is
292.5° (clockwise from the north) and the wind speed is 1.5 m s^{-1}. The ambient
temperature is equal to 26.8°C while indoor temperatures are: 26.4°C for zone
A, 25.8°C for zone B and 25°C for zone C. Simulation results for each of the
computational tools are given in Tables 3.15 and 3.16.

3.2.5   Intermodel comparison using experimental data

3.2.5.1 *Simulations of single-sided natural ventilation experiments*

Twenty-two single-sided natural ventilation experiments were held in Athens,
Greece during the summer of 1993. The experiments were carried out in the

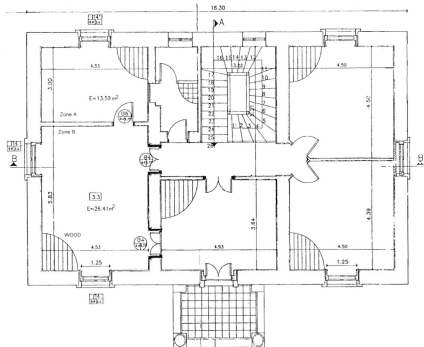

*Figure 3.22. Plan View of the Institute of Meteorology and Atmospheric
Physics (1st floor) of the National Observatory in Athens, Greece*

Table 3.15. Flow characteristics of internal and external openings; values in kg s⁻¹

	W_1	W_2	W_3	W_4 inflow	W_4 outflow	P_1	P_2
AIRNET	2.54	1.32	2.21	0.24	1.90	2.54	1.66
ESP	2.48	1.18	2.30	0.33	1.77	2.50	1.43
BREEZE	2.23	1.01	1.93	0.10	1.40	2.23	1.30
PASSPORT	2.19	1.24	2.00	0.22	1.65	2.18	1.43
COMIS	2.38	1.04	2.06	0.82	1.95	2.38	1.14
Standard deviation	0.15	0.13	0.15	0.28	0.22	0.16	0.19
Standard error	0.07	0.06	0.07	0.12	0.10	0.07	0.09

Table 3.16. Flow characteristics of zones, in kg s⁻¹. The maximum difference is defined as the ratio of the difference between the maximum and minimum value divided by the maximum value (%)

	Zone A (outflow)	Zone B (outflow)	Zone C (outflow)
AIRNET	2.54	3.87	1.89
ESP	2.50	3.73	1.77
BREEZE	2.23	3.23	1.40
PASSPORT	2.19	3.42	1.65
COMIS	2.38	3.43	1.95
Max. difference (%)	13.9	16.5	28.2

National Observatory of Athens and in a PASSYS Test Cell. Table 3.17 summarizes the prevailing climatic conditions for each experiment, the opening configurations tested and the flow rates found experimentally. Climatic data from each experiment were used as simulation inputs for five airflow computational tools, namely, ESP, BREEZE, AIRNET, COMIS and PASS-PORT-AIR. The results obtained from the simulations are summarized in Table 3.18.

Very similar airflow rates have been predicted by all tools for each experiment. The observed differences could be attributed to the various numerical solvers adopted by each tool. Airflow predictions of a network model (PASS-PORT-AIR) have been compared with experimental values and the 'simple model' predictions were not in good agreement with experimental values. Further investigation has shown that the above experiments were characterized by important wind speeds and small indoor–outdoor temperature differences. These are common characteristics in naturally ventilated buildings in hot climates. However, network modelling practically neglects the effect of the wind in the case of single-sided ventilation. In order to improve the accuracy of network models in predicting the airflow rates in the case of inertia dominated single sided ventilation, a recently developed algorithm [32] was incorporated in one of the above models (PASSPORT-AIR) and the resulting, improved model was used in order to simulate the above experiments. The algorithm is the outcome of an attempt to study whether the observed

Table 3.17. *Climatic data, opening sizes and measured airflow rates during single-sided natural ventilation experiments in the National Observatory of Athens, Greece (zone volume: 61 m³)*

Experiment no.	Opening area (m²)	Mean ambient temp. (°C)	Mean indoor temperature (°C)	Mean wind speed at 10 m (m/s)	Mean measured airflow rate (m³ h⁻¹)
1	2.02	24.1	23.4	3.3	198 ± 27
2	2.02	24.7	24.3	2.5	202 ± 39
3	2.02	25.7	26.2	3.8	245 ± 65
4	2.02	25.6	26.6	3.6	322 ± 62
5	0.68	31.3	31.4	6.8	123 ± 1
6	1.20	32.6	31.8	3.0	174 ± 4
7	0.66	30.6	32.1	5.0	193 ± 3
8	0.94	32.5	31.8	6.7	182 ± 1
9	1.88	30.5	31.5	1.7	216 ± 13
10	1.86	28.8	29.2	1.6	317 ± 10
11	2.40	30.2	31.0	3.6	482 ± 20
12	1.94	29.6	31.0	3.1	279 ± 8
13	1.94	28.2	31.0	3.4	431 ± 33
14	1.00	31.2	31.7	5.4	336 ± 15
15	1.86	30.7	31.8	4.9	379 ± 7
16	1.34	30.8	31.0	4.2	332 ± 14
17	1.60	27.6	28.8	2.0	253 ± 15
18	1.60	30.1	31.6	5.0	390 ± 18
19	2.40	27.0	31.2	3.7	434 ± 32
20	1.86	31.2	31.8	4.1	427 ± 28
21	2.40	30.8	31.4	4.0	503 ± 24
22	2.40	30.8	31.3	3.6	449 ± 18

Table 3.18. *Airflow simulation results from five computational tools (m³ h⁻¹)*

Experiment No.	ESP	PASSPORT-AIR	COMIS	AIRNET	BREEZE
1	609	632	646	620	626
2	454	467	463	459	438
3	535	539	522	526	423
4	733	762	766	766	689
5	30	28	34	34	35
6	240	193	229	229	242
7	138	116	135	135	136
8	205	171	211	205	209
9	499	413	499	499	507
10	354	296	360	360	364
11	657	560	669	669	674
12	597	664	682	874	634
13	842	898	1061	804	1093
14	220	182	220	168	182
15	391	324	321	269	376
16	193	224	270	190	224
17	533	451	437	401	541
18	607	516	507	440	631
19	1624	1355	1594	1606	1612
20	428	344	414	415	423
21	595	508	598	598	606
22	578	473	557	555	562

differences between experimental and predicted values can be correlated with indices describing the relative importance of the inertia and gravitational forces. Accordingly, a 'correction factor', CF, is used in order to multiply the initial predictions of the 'simple' network model, producing higher accuracy results in single-sided ventilation simulations:

$$Q_{predicted} = CF Q_{network(Cd=1)} \qquad (3.61)$$

The correction factor, CF, is given by the following expression:

$$CF = 0.08(Gr / Re_D^2)^{-0.38} \qquad (3.62)$$

where $Gr = g\Delta TH^3/Tv^2$ is the Grashof number and $Re_D = VD/v$ the Reynolds number with characteristic lengths H and D the opening height and the room 'depth' respectively. The room depth is defined as the distance between the wall where the opening(s) is(are) and the wall opposite to it in the single-side ventilated zone.

Table 3.19 summarizes the flow values predicted by the network model with and without the correction factor and the experimental results for single-sided ventilation experiments.

Table 3.19. Simulation results of a network model for single-sided ventilation experiments

Experiment no.	'Simple' network model ($m^3\ h^{-1}$)	Network model using CF ($m^3\ h^{-1}$)	Experimental results ($m^3\ h^{-1}$)
1	632	354	123
2	467	297	174
3	539	391	193
4	762	318	182
5	28	227	216
6	193	208	316
7	116	449	482
8	171	366	279
9	413	413	431
10	296	226	336
11	560	373	379
12	664	284	332
13	898	190	253
14	182	402	390
15	324	413	198
16	224	311	202
17	451	440	245
18	516	454	322
19	1355	568	434
20	344	429	427
21	508	476	503
22	473	429	449

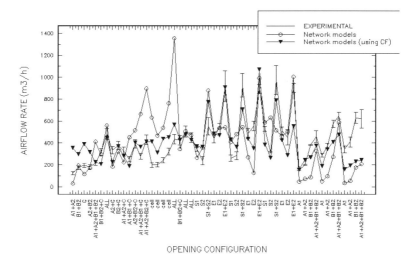

Figure 3.23. Comparison of the predictions of a network model with experimental results.

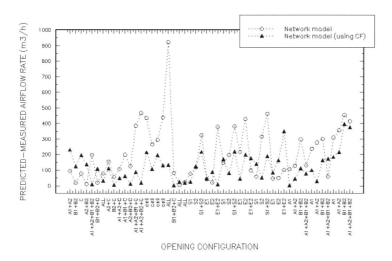

Figure 3.24. Difference between the experimental measurements and network model predictions

Results from the comparison are given in Figure 3.23. The observed differences between the 'simple network model' predictions and the experimental values are attributed to the inaccuracy of this type of modelling when simulating wind-dominated single-sided natural ventilation experiments. As shown in Figure 3.23, use of the correction factor improves the accuracy of network model predictions. Figure 3.24 gives the difference between the experimental measurements and the predictions of a network model, simple or using the correction factor, CF. By simulation of more experiments and comparison with experimental results, it was found that the correlation coefficient between the experimental set of data and the model predictions is close to 0.75 when the correction factor is used.

3.2.5.2 Cross-ventilation simulation experiments

Six different cross-ventilation experiments were carried out in two zones of a full-scale building, located on the campus of the Ecole Nationale des Travaux Publics de l'Etat – ENTPE, in Lyon, France. This is a one-storey naturally ventilated building housing the medical centre of the ENTPE campus and is located in a semi-urban environment.

Two zones in this building, having the same volume (34.32 m³) and a height of 2.6 m, were selected for the experiments. Each zone has one sliding window, 2.1 m wide and 1.1 m high. The lower edges of the windows are at 1.05 m from the floor. The maximum effective window area for ventilation purposes is 1.155 m².

The windows are located on opposite sides, on two sheltered facades. The two zones are connected through one door, with a surface area of 1.6 m². Internal doors connecting the zones to other adjacent zones were kept closed and sealed throughout the experiments. A total of six different experiments were finally performed, as shown in Table 3.20.

The experimental conditions were the same for all the experiments apart from the windows' opening areas. Three of them had exactly the same conditions, but were performed on three different days, with different outdoor conditions.

The meteorological data and the measured indoor temperatures in the two zones, for each sequence and each experiment, are shown in Table 3.21. During the experiments, the outdoor wind speed was rather low, with a maximum value of about 3.0 m s^{-1}.

Simulations of the above experiments were carried out using the COMIS network model.

For the windows, the value of the discharge coefficient, Cd, was set at 0.85, while for the internal door Cd was set at 0.65. The corresponding pressure coefficients were calculated using a simplified model valid for low-rise buildings [33], corresponding to a long sheltered wall. The wind speed at the level

Table 3.20. Characteristics of cross-ventilation experiments

Experiment No.	Opening area Zone 1 (m²)	Opening area Zone 2 (m²)	Total number of analysed opening sequences
1	1.155	1.155	3
2	1.155	1.155	5
3	0.506	0.583	3
4	0.891	0.891	2
5	0.275	0.275	1
6	1.155	1.155	4

Table 3.21. Measured meteorological and indoor temperatures during the experiments

Experiment opening sequence	Wind Direction (°)	Wind Speed (m s⁻¹)	Temperature Outdoor (°C)	Temperature Zone 1 (°C)	Temperature Zone 2 (°C)
1, 1	203	2.12	11.33	22.95	20.64
1, 2	200	1.74	11.20	23.20	20.50
1, 3	223	2.13	11.16	23.37	20.58
2, 1	116	0.00	7.28	22.85	19.85
2, 2	176	0.62	7.89	23.12	19.93
2, 3	161	0.58	8.08	22.76	19.94
2, 4	202	0.95	8.16	23.12	20.01
2, 5	245	0.21	8.20	22.98	19.85
3, 1	177	1.14	11.80	24.83	20.84
3, 2	197	2.04	11.88	24.39	20.71
3, 3	166	1.56	11.91	24.04	20.54
4, 1	137	1.82	12.60	23.46	20.09
4, 2	170	3.00	12.62	23.61	20.67
5, 1	176	3.69	12.64	24.85	20.53
6, 1	150	1.46	12.16	24.08	20.21
6, 2	187	1.41	11.30	23.89	20.54
6, 3	186	2.33	11.05	24.40	20.76
6, 4	210	2.02	11.06	23.75	20.65

of the windows was calculated using the measured wind speed from the meteorological station, modified according to the Lawrence Berkeley Laboratory (LBL) air-infiltration model wind profile [33]. The dependent parameters were evaluated for urban terrain, which resulted in a local wind-speed reduction factor of 0.6804.

The results for the total airflow rate coming into or going out of each zone and the total outdoor air entering each zone are listed in Table 3.22. This table includes for each sequence of each experiment, the maximum, average and minimum measured values of the four measuring points in each zone, along with the corresponding values calculated using COMIS.

The cross-flow experiments were performed with rather low prevailing outdoor wind speeds. Under this type of meteorological conditions, global flows were found to be reasonably well estimated by COMIS. Inaccuracies in pressure and discharge coefficients were found to cause significant errors in estimating the specific airflows at each opening between the zones and outdoors.

3.2.5.3 Simulating buoyancy dominated natural ventilation experiments

Natural ventilation experiments were carried out in the LESO building (Figure 3.25) in Lausanne, Switzerland. This is an office building with a structure that

Table 3.22. Measured and calculated airflow rates for cross-flow natural ventilation experiments

Exp. no.	Airflow in Zone 1 (kg h^{-1}) Measured			COMIS	Airflow in Zone 2 (kg h^{-1}) Measured			COMIS	Outdoor airflow (kg h^{-1}) Measured			COMIS
	Max	Avg	Min		Max	Avg	Min		Max	Avg	Min	
1, 1	1179	1037	966	1547	1418	989	590	1453	1054	771	505	1710
1, 2	1943	1646	1041	1566	1465	1348	1072	1454	1152	1027	759	1692
1, 3	2670	2033	1569	1645	1579	1436	1391	1536	1682	1541	1430	1761
2, 1	1343	1281	1218	1712	1376	1349	1324	1602	1509	1445	1383	1967
2, 2	1551	1464	1384	1719	2133	1936	1823	1601	2466	2214	1984	1931
2, 3	2016	1749	1488	1654	1784	1632	1502	1547	2188	1953	1722	1897
2, 4	2277	2192	2133	1719	1589	1578	1567	1605	2498	2390	2288	1926
2, 5	2563	2060	1963	1695	1507	1506	1177	1599	2357	2295	2231	1894
3, 1	1077	1061	1047	1178	1192	1060	932	1154	870	574	379	794
3, 2	1316	1298	1280	1014	1254	1178	1102	1142	714	670	625	795
3, 3	1420	1408	1407	1114	1627	1540	1446	1095	912	871	833	765
4, 1	918	824	735	1349	996	923	851	1222	849	742	638	1154
4, 2	2139	2024	1914	1342	1914	1876	1836	1240	1298	1235	1171	1222
5, 1	1217	1198	1180	1040	1119	1094	1071	1003	439	418	397	1003
6, 1	2006	1793	1602	1647	1740	1662	1610	1472	2187	2178	2167	1586
6, 2	1767	1763	1721	1635	1345	1325	1307	1495	1695	1624	1567	1737
6, 3	1299	1281	1264	1726	1130	1122	1094	1580	1535	1474	409	1769
6, 4	1805	1714	1649	1683	1903	1899	1895	1561	2304	2127	1955	1776

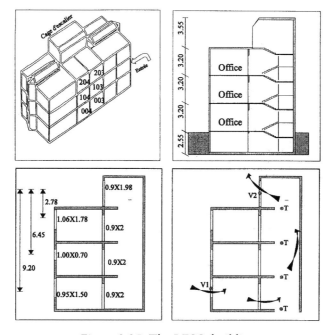

Figure 3.25. The LESO building

permits a study of the stack effect. A staircase extends from level −1 (basement) to level +3 (sunspace at roof level) and this acts as a 12 m high chimney, giving the opportunity to work with openings at different levels above ground. Two series of experiments carried out in this building and characterized by no-wind conditions were simulated using PASSPORT-AIR. This permitted a test of the accuracy of Bernoulli theory in predicting the airflow rate in the absence of wind.

The first series of experiments (B_3, B_6, B_7) was carried out using one top and one bottom opening. The experiments were carried out for three different locations and sizes of the bottom opening, as well as for three different indoor–outdoor air temperature differences. The reference height was the centre of the bottom opening. The second series of experiments (C_2, C_3, C_4) was carried out in an office on the first floor. In experiments C_3 and C_4 the two openings were opened in series, while in the last experiment they were opened in parallel. In both cases the interior door connecting the office with the staircase was wide open. Table 3.23 summarizes the input data for the simulations. The discharge coefficient was taken to be equal to 0.7 for all simulations.

The predictions of PASSPORT-AIR for the above experiments are given in Tables 3.23 and 3.24. As shown in Figure 3.26, there is good agreement between the two sets of data.

Table 3.23. Characteristics of experiments in the LESO building

Experiment	B_3	B_6	B_7	C_2	C_3	C_4
H_{total} (m)	9.2	6.45	2.76	6.45	6.45	6.45
S_1 (m²)	1.43	0.70	1.68	0.70	0.70	0.70+0.70
S_2 (m²)	1.78	1.78	1.78	1.78	1.78	1.78
T_i (°C)	18.9	18.9	18.5	19.2	19.2	19.2
T_a (°C)	9.1	9.1	10.0	9.1	9.1	9.1

Table 3.24. Predicted (PASSPORT-AIR) and measured airflow rates in the LESO building

LESO building experiment	Measured (kg s⁻¹)		Predicted (kg s⁻¹)	
	Inflow	Outflow	Inflow	Outflow
B_3	2.03	1.90	1.91	1.92
B_6	1.10	1.16	1.07	1.07
B_7	1.39	1.41	1.09	1.09
C_2	1.00	1.16	0.91	0.92
C_3	1.01	1.13	0.82	0.83
C_4	1.64	1.76	1.66	1.68

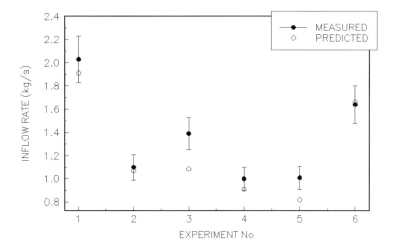

Figure 3.26. Buoyancy-dominated ventilation experiments in the LESO building – comparison of predicted and measured airflow rates.

3.3   ZONAL MODELLING AND CFD MODELLING

3.3.1   Introduction

The modelling approaches that have been discussed so far are based on the hypothesis of fully mixed zones. Although this assumption is not true in certain situations (i.e. large stratification in heated rooms), the predictions of these models fit well to the real behaviour of buildings from an overall viewpoint.

In recent years, however, new building aspects have grown in importance. For instance, comfort conditions inside buildings depend strongly on the indoor distribution of temperature, humidity and air movement, as well as on the concentration of pollutants for an adequate indoor air quality. New concepts and strategies related to these topics impose the necessity of new methods to predict both temperature and airflow patterns.

In an attempt to cope with the above requirements, two new modelling approaches have been developed: the zonal and the CFD (computational fluid dynamics) modelling approach. Both approaches are based on the discretization of the building volume into small subvolumes and application of mass, energy and momentum conservation equations to each subvolume, in order to derive temperature and air velocity fields. These modelling approaches are discussed in the following sections.

3.3.2   Zonal modelling

The basic principles of all kinds of simplified zonal models for predicting indoor patterns of temperature and air velocity are:

- splitting the studied enclosure into several macroscopic subzones;
- establishing the mass and energy conservation equations, together with either momentum equations or identification of the main flows.

In a primary approach, momentum equations are not formulated. Thus, only mass and energy conservation equations are established in each subzone. Since all subzones are related by interzonal airflow rates, the number of unknowns significantly exceeds the number of equations. To solve this problem, two approaches can be distinguished, the temperature and the pressure models.

With the temperature models, an air movement pattern inside a building is imposed. Experimental studies or results from more detailed models are necessary in order to define this pattern appropriately. Therefore, temperature models cannot be applied to any kind of geometrical configuration.

With the pressure models, simple formulations of the missing momentum equations are added as additional equations. A common approach is to introduce Bernoulli-like airflow equations. Thus, these models are more general than temperature models, as there is no need for an *a priori* definition of the airflow pattern.

Zonal modelling is an intermediate approach between network and CFD modelling. It has the advantage of providing detailed results regarding temperature and air velocity fields with relatively less complexity than CFD modelling.

A recently developed zonal model is presented in the following section.

3.3.2.1 A stratification predictive model [34]

This model is based on the division of zones into smaller parallelepipedic subvolumes with vertical and horizontal boundaries. The subvolumes are of two types:

- plume zones: zones influenced by the buoyancy effect of an internal heat source;
- normal zones: the remaining zones.

The unknowns of the problem are the normal fluxes (or velocities) on each rectangular boundary between subvolumes and two scalar variables for each subvolume: static pressure and temperature.

The basis of the model relies on the establishment of the mass, enthalpy and momentum balance equations along each of the three space coordinates, in each zone under the following assumptions:

- Each normal zone is assumed to be static, at a uniform temperature T and at a hydrostatic pressure profile P.
- The boundaries between zones are considered as totally permeable surfaces.

- The airflow between two normal zones (i, j) is modelled by a power law function (Bernoulli's equation), relating the differential mass flow rate dm_{ij} non-linearly to the static local pressure difference between both sides of the separating boundary:

$$dm_{ij} = K_{ij}\rho_i \Delta P_{ij}^n \, dA \qquad\qquad (3.64)$$

where K_{ij} is the permeability of the boundary and n is the flow exponent.

The ascendant flow rates in the plume zones are modelled through an integral form of the vertical momentum equation, supposing a parabolic velocity profile. The zones in contact with solid walls exchange heat (q) by convection:

$$q = h(T_i - T_s) \qquad\qquad (3.65)$$

where the heat transfer coefficient, h, is calculated using natural convection correlations for a flat plate in different orientations.

The mass-balance equation establishes that, for each subvolume, the sum of all airflows in the subvolume is zero under steady state conditions. The enthalpy balance establishes that the sum of all heat fluxes in the subvolume equals zero. These comprise:

- enthalpy convected by the airflows entering the subvolume;
- surface heat flux from a wall or an adjacent subvolume at a different temperature;
- the convective part of the point heat sources inside the subvolume.

The momentum balance equations are expressed along each one of the three coordinates and include balance of the following terms:

- Net flux of entering momentum in the subvolume.
- Body (mainly gravitational) forces acting on the subvolume.
- Pressure forces normal to the faces.
- Friction forces caused by different parallel velocities at both sides of the face. These forces are modelled as proportional to the kinetic energy based on the relative velocity between the two sides of the face. The proportionality constant is the friction coefficient, which is obtained from standard flat-plate correlations through the Reynolds number, based on the relative velocity mentioned. In the case of a wall face, the absolute velocity of the subvolume parallel to the surface is used to calculate the friction force. The sign of this force is opposite in each subvolume and tends to decelerate both velocities (if they are opposite) or the larger one (if they are parallel).

Finally, the following boundary conditions are imposed to close the problem:

- The presence of walls is implied by zero normal velocity.
- Large openings have prescribed surface conditions of either pressure or normal velocity (depending on the unknown of the problem).
- Cracks are treated by expressing the airflow rate as a function of the pressure difference across the opening. The effect of this difference is considered only in the mass and enthalpy balances and neglected in the momentum equations.
- Pressure forces placed in the interface between two subvolumes (i.e. fans) are included in the momentum balances.

Results obtained with this model were qualitatively compared with the predictions of a CFD program.

The first test was a simple case with a well known stratification pattern: a square cavity with two adiabatic horizontal walls and two isothermal vertical walls (a hot and a cold wall). Figure 3.27 illustrates the results obtained using a coarse grid (4 × 4) and a finer grid (6 × 10). Comparison with CFD results for this case has shown that similar tendencies were observed in the temperature distribution. Although the finer grid gave improved results, the coarse grid is preferable because it predicted more or less the same behaviour with no unreasonably increased number of nodes. The order of magnitude of the discretization subvolumes in the studied enclosures must be set between the excessively small grid size of CFDs and the fully mixed zone assumption of network modelling. A typical size of one metre is generally appropriate.

The model was further tested for the case of cross ventilation: a two-dimensional 3 m × 3 m cell with two centred 0.5 m high openings in opposite

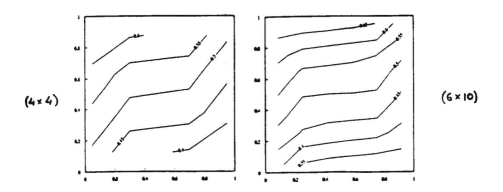

Figure 3.27. Predictions of the zonal model for the simple case

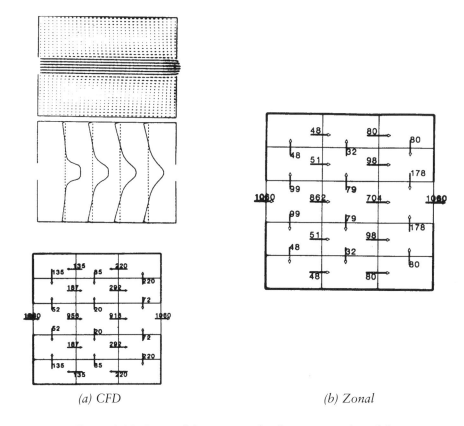

(a) CFD   *(b) Zonal*

Figure 3.28. Successful test using the dynamic zonal model

vertical façades. A uniform overpressure was fixed at the left opening and a de-pressure was set at the right one, in order to force a uniform inlet air velocity of 0.5 m s⁻¹. The CFD results gave a stream tube in the centre of the cell with recirculating flows in the adjacent zones close to the horizontal boundaries. As shown in Figure 3.28, these results were also identified by the zonal model, for a number of cross-ventilation cases, with openings on opposite sides and at the same height.

The model needs improvement in order to give realistic flow patterns in the case of cross ventilation with two openings at different heights located in opposite façades. Ongoing and future research activities involve:

- improvement of the zonal model in order to guarantee realistic results in all possible configurations;
- comparison with experimental results or with results of a numerical solution using more detailed models (CFD);
- integration of the model within a thermal simulation tool.

3.3.3   Computational fluid dynamics (CFD)

During the last few years much effort has been put into the development of computational fluid dynamics (CFD) for the prediction of the airflow in buildings. CFD programs are based on the solution of the Navier–Stokes equations, namely, the mass, momentum and energy conservation equations. CFD models are mainly used for steady-state problems to predict the temperature and velocity fields inside and the pressure field outside a building. The fundamental theory of the equations on which CFD modelling is based is presented in Appendix B at the end of the chapter.

3.3.3.1 Summary of the governing equations
The governing equations of motion on which CFD modelling is based are the Navier–Stokes equations and these are analytically presented in Appendix B. This section summarizes these equations in the conservation form, for inviscid and incompressible flow [35]:

Continuity equation:

$$\frac{\partial \rho}{\partial t} + \nabla.(\rho \mathbf{V}) = 0$$

(3.66)

Momentum equations:

$$x \text{ component} \quad \frac{\partial(\rho u)}{\partial t} + \nabla.(\rho u \mathbf{V}) = -\frac{\partial p}{\partial x} + \rho f_x$$

(3.67)

$$y \text{ component} \quad \frac{\partial(\rho v)}{\partial t} + \nabla.(\rho v \mathbf{V}) = -\frac{\partial p}{\partial y} + \rho f_y$$

(3.68)

$$z \text{ component} \quad \frac{\partial(\rho w)}{\partial t} + \nabla.(\rho w \mathbf{V}) = -\frac{\partial p}{\partial z} + \rho f_z$$

(3.69)

Energy equation:

$$\frac{\partial}{\partial t}\left[\rho\left(e + \frac{V^2}{2}\right)\right] + \nabla.\left[\rho\left(e + \frac{V^2}{2}\right)\mathbf{V}\right]$$

$$= \rho \dot{q} - \frac{\partial(up)}{\partial x} - \frac{\partial(vp)}{\partial y} - \frac{\partial(wp)}{\partial z} + \rho \, \mathbf{f}.\mathbf{V}$$

(3.70)

The above equations are solved at all points of a two- or three-dimensional grid that represents the building under investigation and its surroundings. The unknown pressure and velocity components are determined for given boundary and initial conditions.

3.3.3.2 Boundary conditions

The accuracy of results provided by CFD models strongly depends on the accuracy with which the physical quantities are defined at the boundaries of the flow domain, as well as on the methods of linking these quantities to the bulk of the flows. Flow conditions must be defined at solid boundaries as well as at other boundaries, such as the inlets and outlets of the flow.

CFD models have been applied to many airflow problems with encouraging results. However, the accuracy of the results depends on the user's experience and numerical simulation skills. Additionally, the accuracy of results is also affected by the density of the grid that represents the simulated space. Computational meshes of sufficient refinement are required in order to resolve local solution gradients. Thus, not only an experienced researcher, but also a large computer is required for a successful application of CFD programs.

The quality of results provided by CFD models, as well as their present-state requirements from the user, makes this kind of modelling more appropriate as a research tool and less suitable for building design purposes

3.3.3.3 Application of CFD modelling in simulating airflow through large openings

Schaelin et al. [36] have used CFD modelling to simulate airflow in a room with a heater inside and a large opening to the outdoors, with emphasis on the representation of the main flow, without considering the details of near-wall flow, heat transfer, etc. In this case, warm air leaves the room through the upper part of the opening and cold air enters through the lower part. The warm air rises outside as a thermal plume due to buoyancy. The calculations were done without wind (free convection) and with a wind of 1m s^{-1} normally incident to the opening. The room is 4.2 m long, 3 m high and 4 m wide, with a door 2.2 m high and 1 m wide. A heater at 50°C, 0.6 m high and 3 m wide, in the corner opposite to the door drives the airflow in the room.

A computer program developed by Rosten and Spalding [37] was used in conjunction with a standard k–ε turbulence model to solve the conservation equations in finite-volume form for pressure p, velocity components u, v and w; energy h; turbulent energy k and dissipation of turbulent energy ε.

The values of the variables u, v, w and T were compared with both analytical predictions and experimental data, whereas the computed fields of k and ε were used to verify that the plumes were turbulent. Figure 3.29 gives a schematic representation of the calculation domain with the boundaries.

At the floor, ceiling and walls of the building (inside and outside), wall friction and logarithmic wall functions for the velocity boundary layer were supplied. These surfaces (1, 5) were treated as adiabatic. The heater was modelled as a heated air volume, held either at a constant temperature or heated at a constant heat rate. Near the open-air boundaries (2–4) the normal derivative must be zero. This was imposed by a numerical boundary condition: $p = p_o = 0$ at the open boundaries. The calculation domain was taken large enough to ensure that $\mathrm{d}p/\mathrm{d}n = 0$ at the open-air boundaries. The 2D calculation

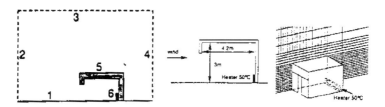

Figure 3.29. Calculation domain and boundaries: 1 ground; 2, 3, 4 open air space; 5 building walls (blocked for airflow); 6 heated air volume (not blocked for airflow)

domain was formed by a 46 x 46 cells grid and spanned 34m × 72.2m horizontally and vertically. A 41 × 31 × 31 cells grid, which spanned 34 m × 25 m × 18.7 m in the x, y, z directions respectively, was used to form the 3D calculation domain. For the case with wind, the wind speed was set uniformly to 1 m s^{-1} at the left boundary, without taking into account a wind profile. Friction at the ground causes a more realistic profile after about 10 m.

Figure 3.30 illustrates the calculated air velocity and temperature values for the 3D simulations of the case without wind (Figure 3.30a) and for the case with wind (Figure 3.30b). In the second case, the thermal plume is shown as being blown away by the wind.

Data from single-sided ventilation experiments [38] were used in order to compare the predictions of the 2D and 3D models with measured values. Figure 3.31 shows the calculated and measured air velocity profiles. For comparison reasons the velocity values from Mahajan [38] were scaled by a constant. The shape of the 3D simulation profile was in better agreement with the experimental results.

Three-dimensional CFD calculations give more accurate results, but with higher computation expense. To save computation expense, Schaelin *et al.* [36] concluded that excellent results can be obtained for cases with large openings in buildings for a computation domain that is extended only a little to the outside of the room. In free-convection cases, the length of the extra domain can be set to

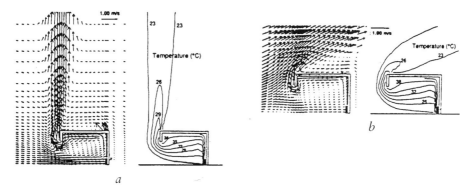

Figure 3.30. Air velocity and temperature fields derived by 3D CFD simulations: (a) no wind; (b) wind 1 m s^{-1}

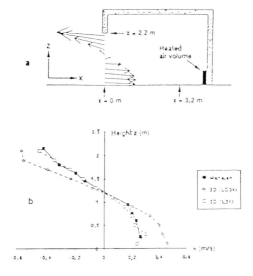

Figure 3.31. CFD predictions (case without wind)
and measured air velocity profile at the opening

about half the opening height. In wind cases, the extra domain necessary depends
on the building height or on knowledge of the local wind velocity profile.

3.3.3.4 Conclusions

In conclusion, it is clear that CFD simulations have the potential to make
predictions of the air velocity patterns and the temperature distribution in
cases of summer cooling. However, as indicated elsewhere in this chapter,
natural ventilation for summer cooling is a non-steady-state problem with
complex boundary conditions. Given the long calculation time for accurate
predictions, it is at present not feasible to study practical cases using CFD.

3.4   METHODOLOGIES FOR SIZING OPENINGS

3.4.1   Introduction

Air movement through a building may be caused by either wind or thermal
forces – or by the combination of the two forces. To estimate the area and
distribution of openings in order to achieve a certain value of airflow, data
related to the climatic conditions, local obstructions and window characteristics are necessary. Several sizing methods have been proposed to calculate the
surface areas of the openings, especially for cross-ventilation configurations.
Existing methods can be classified into two main categories:

- simplified empirical methodologies;
- computerized iterative methods.

Simplified empirical methodologies are based on simple analytical expressions for calculating the inlet and outlet areas for cross-ventilation configurations in a room or a monozone building. With some exceptions, these methods consider only the wind forces and neglect phenomena related to the temperature difference between the indoor and the outdoor environments. These methods are simple to apply and can be used easily during the pre-design phase of a building.

Computerized iterative methods are based on network models already presented in Section 3.2. Network airflow models combine the effect of wind and temperature difference and do not have the limitations of the simplified empirical methods. Also, if advantage is taken of their computerized form, these tools may be used to perform fast calculations for a wide spectrum of input data, providing the user with a sensitivity analysis on the relative impact of design characteristics in the ventilation performance of a building.

Six of the more important empirical simplified models are presented in the following chapters, together with computerized tools. A comparative analysis, presented at the end of the chapter, shows the differences observed among the methods presented in predicting the required surface area of the openings.

It should be clear to designers that all of the above methods should be used within the limits of their applicability. Climatic data used to perform calculations should be as representative as possible. If the purpose of the design is to size openings for cooling purposes, climatic data for the month presenting the highest cooling load should be used.

However, it is clear that, for some of the input data and especially for the pressure distribution around the buildings, there is a degree of uncertainty and fuzziness. Thus, these methodologies may be seen as tools to size inlets and outlets approximately and not as precise methods for precise calculation of the airflow in naturally cross-ventilated buildings.

Finally, to size openings in multizone buildings with internal partitions obstructing the air circulation, multizone computerized network models, presented in Section 3.2, should be used instead.

3.4.2 Simplified empirical methodologies

Table 3.25 summarizes the main characteristics and limitations of six simplified empirical opening sizing methodologies.

3.4.2.1 The Florida Solar Energy Method – I
The window-sizing methodology developed by the Florida Solar Energy Centre [39] assumes that the inlet and outlet areas are equal. The method can be used for slight differences, e.g. inlet = 40% of the total area. The method does not account for airflows due to temperature difference. For a two-storey building the calculations should be done for each floor. For widely different inlet and outlet areas, it is proposed that another method, developed by the same authors [40], be used.

Table 3.25. Characteristics of six simplified empirical methodologies to design openings for natural cross ventilation of buildings

Method	Opening characteristics	Flow forces
The Florida Solar Energy Centre Method – I	Considers equal inlets and outlets. Calculates the gross opening area. Consider a screen with a porosity factor equal to 0.6.	Considers only the wind forces. Proposes correction factors for the orientation of the wind, terrain type, neighbouring buildings and height of openings.
The Florida Solar Energy Centre Method – II	Considers non-equal inlets and outlets. Calculates an effective window area. Proposes a methodology to account for screens and window porosity.	Considers only the wind forces. Takes into account the pressure coefficients due to wind. Proposes correction factors for the neighbouring buildings and the height of openings.
The ASHRAE Method	Considers non-equal inlets and outlets. Proposes a coefficient to account the effectiveness of the opening as a function of the incidence angle of the wind.	Considers wind or temperature difference effects. Does not consider combined effects of wind and temperature difference.
The Simplified Method of the University of Athens	Considers non-equal inlets and outlets. Valid for Inlets/Outlets ratios lower than 2.	Considers only the wind forces. Takes into account the pressure coefficients due to wind.
The Aynsley Method	Considers non-equal inlets and outlets.	Considers only the wind forces. Takes into account the pressure coefficients due to wind.
The British Standards Institution Method	Considers non-equal inlets and outlets	Considers both the effect of the wind and temperature difference. Proposes criteria for combined effects.

According to the method, the required gross total opening area, TOA, inlets plus outlets, in order to achieve a certain number of air changes per hour, ach, can be calculated from the following expression:

$$TOA = 0.00079\,V(ach)\,/\,(Wf_1f_2f_1f_4) \tag{3.71}$$

where:

TOA is the total opening area (ft^2).

V is the volume of the building (ft^3).

ach is the design air change rate per hour.

W is the wind speed (mph), as measured by the nearest meteorological station.

f_1 is the inlet-to-site 10 m wind speed ratio. This coefficient is a function of the wind incidence angle and is given in Table 3.26. Data are mainly obtained from the wind tunnel data of Vickery and Baddour [41]. The incidence angle is zero when winds are perpendicular to a building face.

f_2 is the terrain correction factor. This factor is a function of the building location and the ventilation strategy. It can be obtained from Table 3.27.

f_3 is the neighbourhood correction factor. This coefficient is a function of the wall height of the upwind building, h, as well as of the gap between the building and the adjacent upwind building, g. Values of f_3 are given in Table 3.28 as a function of the ratio g/h and are extrapolated data from wind-tunnel results [41].

f_4 is a height multiplication factor. If sizing windows for the second floor or for house on stilts, f_4 is equal to 1.15. Otherwise, use $f_4 = 1$.

Equation (3.71) assumes a screening with a porosity of 0.6. If there is no screening, the results of this equation should be divided by 1.67. Equation 3.71 also considers that door or window framing is about 20% of the gross area, and, therefore, to calculate the net opening area, the result should be divided by 1.25.

EXAMPLE. For a given location $W = 8.8$ mph. Also, $V = 10{,}672$ ft^3, ACH = 30, while the incidence angle is 10°. The building is located in a suburban area and is ventilated on a 24-hour basis. The wall height of the upwind building $h = 8$ ft, while $g = 24$ ft. Use $f_4 = 1$. Determine the total opening area.

Table 3.26. Inlet-to-site 10 m
wind speed ratios, f_1 [40]

Wind incidence angle (°)	f_1
0–40	0.35
50	0.30
60	0.25
70	0.20
80	0.14
90	0.08

Table 3.27. Terrain correction factor, f_2 [40]

Terrain type	f_2: 24-hour ventilation	f_2: Night-only ventilation
Oceanfront or > 3 miles water in front	1.30	0.98
Airports, or flatlands with buildings separated by isolated walls	1.00	0.75
Rural	0.85	0.64
Suburban or industrial	0.67	0.50
Centre of a large city	0.47	0.35

Table 3.28. f₃, neighbourhood
correction factor [40]

Ratio g/h	Neighbourhood correction factor f_3
0	0.00
I	0.4I
2	0.63
3	0.77
4	0.85
5	0.93
6	I.00

From Tables 3.26–3.28, we get: $f_1 = 0.35$, $f_2 = 0.67$, $f_3 = 0.77$. Then from equation (3.71):

$$\text{TOA} = 0.00079\,V(\text{ach})\,/\,(Wf_1 f_2 f_1 f_4)$$

$$= 0.00079 \times (10672 \times 30)\,/\,[8.8 \times 0.35 \times 0.67 \times 0.77 \times 1] = 159.1\,\text{ft}^2$$

3.4.2.2 *The Florida Solar Energy Method – II*

This method, developed by Chandra *et al.* [40], is a simple procedure for sizing inlet and outlet window areas in cross-ventilated rooms. The method is based on the pressure difference coefficient across the inlet and outlet and permits the calculation of an effective window area, A, which is a combination of the open inlet and outlet areas. The method does not account for the airflow due to temperature difference between indoors and outdoors. The proposed procedure is for rooms with one effective inlet and one effective outlet; all the inlet windows are assumed to experience identical positive pressures and all outlet windows to experience identical negative pressures.

The effective window area, A, is defined by the following expression:

$$A = A_o A_i\,/\,(A_o^2 + A_i^2)^{0.5}\ (\text{ft}^2) \tag{3.72}$$

where A_o and A_i are the open outlet and inlet respectively.

To calculate A, the method proposes the following expression:

$$A = 0.000296\,V\,\text{ach}\,/\,[W(f_3 f_4 \text{PD})^{0.5}] \tag{3.73}$$

where V, ach, W, f_3, f_4 are as previously defined. The parameter PD is the pressure difference coefficient acting across the inlet and outlet and given by:

$$\text{PD} = \text{WPC} - \text{LPC} \tag{3.74}$$

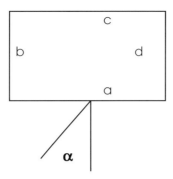

Figure 3.32. Wind incidence angle on the four façades of a building

where WPC is the windward pressure coefficient and LPC the leeward pressure coefficient. The method proposes using the pressure coefficients given in Table 3.29 [42, 43] for the four facades of a residential building, Figure 3.32.

To account for the effect of blockage due to insect screens, partially open windows, etc., a porosity factor, PF, defined as the product of an insect screening porosity factor, IPF, with a window porosity factor, WPF, is proposed:

$$PF = IPF \times WPF \tag{3.75}$$

Values of IPF and WPF for various type of screens and windows are given in Tables 3.30 and 3.31. Then, the total, not open, inlet and outlet areas, TA_i, TA_o, are given by the expressions:

$$TA_i = A_i/PF \tag{3.76}$$

$$TA_o = A_o/PF \tag{3.77}$$

Recommended pressure coefficient, PC, values for other apertures are:

- inlet with wing-wall assist, PC = 0.40;
- outlet with wing-wall assist, PC = −0.25;
- roof outlets, e.g. Venturi type, PC = −0.30.

Table 3.29. Pressure coefficients, PC, as a function of the wind incidence angle[40]

Wind incidence angle, φ (°)	Pressure coefficient, PC, at surface a	Pressure coefficient, PC, at surface b	Pressure coefficient, PC, at surface c	Pressure coefficient, PC, at surface d
0.0	0.40	−0.40	−0.25	−0.40
22.5	0.40	−0.06	−0.40	−0.60
45.0	0.25	0.25	−0.45	−0.45
67.5	−0.06	0.30	−0.55	−0.40
90.0	−0.4	0.40	−0.40	−0.25

Table 3.30. Insect screening porosity factors, IPF [40]

Screen type	Typical IPF
No screen	1.00
Bronze, 14 wires/inch	0.80
Fibreglass, 18 wires/inch	0.60

Table 3.31. Window porosity factors, WPF, [40]; these assume that interior curtains or shades will not be blocking any wind

Window type	Typical WPF
Single or double hung	0.40
Awning, hopper, jalousie or projection, which swivel open on a horizontal hinge	0.60
Casement	Varies, depending on fixed sash amount. Need to measure porosity.

EXAMPLE. The volume of a building is 1536 ft³, the required air changes per hour are 30, the wind speed is 8.8 mph, and the incidence angle on windward face, φ, is 45°, while there is a wing-wall-assisted outlet in surface d. The building is in an urban area. The ratio g/h is equal to 3 (see previous example). Calculate: (a) The required open effective area, A; (b) the inlet and outlet surface, if equal inlet and outlets are desired; (c) the total, not open, inlet and outlet window areas if fibreglass screen and awning windows are considered.

(a) From Table 3.28 we get $f_3 = 0.59$, $f_4 = 1$. From Table 3.29 we obtain that WPC = 0.25 and LPC = −0.25, then PD = 0.5. Then, using expression (3.73):

$$A = 0.000296 \, V \, \text{ACH} / [W(f_3 f_4 \text{PD})^{0.5}]$$

$$= 0.000296 \times (1536 \times 30) / [18.8 \times (0.59)^{0.5} \times (0.5)^{0.5}]$$

$$= 2.85 \, \text{ft}^2$$

(b) If $A_o = A_i$ then $A_i = 1.41A$. Therefore, $A_i = A_o = 4.01$ ft².

(c) From Table 3.30 we get IPF = 0.8 and WPF = 0.60, then PF = 0.48. Therefore, $TA_i = TA_o = 4.01/0.48 = 8.37$ ft².

3.4.2.3 The ASHRAE Method

A very simple methodology to calculate the surface of the openings in natural ventilated buildings is proposed by ASHRAE [44]. According to this method, and if the flow is mainly due to wind, the free area of inlet openings, A, in a building with equal inlet and outlet openings, can be calculated with the following expression:

$$A = Q/(EW) \tag{3.78}$$

where Q is the design airflow rate, W is the wind speed and E the effectiveness of the opening. Parameter E should be taken as 0.5 to 0.6 for perpendicular winds and 0.25 to 0.35 for diagonal winds.

According to the method, the greatest flow per unit area of openings is obtained when inlets and outlets are equal. If inlet and outlet openings cannot be equal then equation (3.78) may be used to calculate the minimum of the openings. The final flow is then obtained from Figure 3.33 as a function of the ratio of the highest to the lowest of the openings.

The procedure to calculate the openings is therefore the following. For a given ratio of inlet to outlet openings, the percentage of the flow increase, x, is taken from Figure 3.33. Then the designed airflow Q is divided by x and the resulting flow is used in equation (3.78) to calculate the minimum area of the openings.

If the local wind speed is not important and the airflow is mainly due to the temperature difference between the indoor and the outdoor environment, ASHRAE proposes another formula to calculate the area of the openings.

If the inlets and outlets are equal, then the surface of the inlet or outlet opening, A, can be calculated from the following equation:

$$A = Q / \left[116 \sqrt{h(T_i - T_o)} \right] \tag{3.79}$$

where Q is the design airflow rate (litre s^{-1}), h the height from inlets to outlets, m, and T_i and T_o are the average indoor and outdoor temperatures respectively (°C).

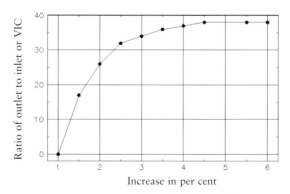

Figure 3.33. *Increased in flow caused by excess of one opening over another*

If the inlets and outlets are not equal, then for a given ratio of outlet to inlet or vice versa, the percentage of the flow increase, x, is taken from Figure 3.33. The design airflow rate Q is divided by x and the resulting flow is used in equation (3.79) to calculate the minimum area of the openings.

EXAMPLE. For a given place the design wind velocity is equal to 2 m s^{-1} and is perpendicular to the openings of a naturally ventilated building. The volume of the zone to calculate is 200 m^3 and the required air exchange rate is equal to eight air changes per hour. Also, as a result of constructional limitations, the ratio of the outlets to inlets is equal to 1.5. Calculate the area of the inlets and outlets.

The designed airflow is 1600 m^3 h^{-1} or 0.444 m^3 s^{-1}. From Figure 3.33 the expected increase of the airflow due to the non-equality of the openings is equal to 17.5%. Therefore, the flow that corresponds to the lower of the openings is equal to 0.444/1.175 = 0.38 m^3 s^{-1}. From equation (3.78), the area of the inlets should be equal to $A_i = 0.38/(0.5 \times 2) = 0.38$ m^2, while the area of the outlets A_o should be equal to $A_o = 0.38 \times 1.5 = 0.57$ m^2.

EXAMPLE. For the previous example consider that the flow is mainly due to the temperature difference between the indoor and outdoor environments. The difference of height between the inlets and the outlets is 4 m. The design temperature difference between the indoor and the indoor environment is 4°C. Calculate the necessary inlets and outlets for an airflow of eight air changes per hour.

As calculated from the previous example the flow that corresponds to the lower of the openings is equal to 0.38 m^3 s^{-1}. From equation (3.79), the area of the inlets should be equal to $A_i = 380/[11616] = 0.82$ m^2, while the area of the outlets A_o should be equal to $A_{oi} = 0.82 \times 1.5 = 1.22$ m^2.

3.4.2.4 The Aynsley Method

The method proposed by Aynsley[3] has already been presented in Section 3.2. The method calculates the airflow due to wind and neglects phenomena due to temperature difference between the inside and the outside of the building.

For a simple case of a cross-ventilated building, with a windward opening A_1 and an upwind opening A_2, the airflow rate, Q (m^3 s^{-1}), is calculated from the following formula:

$$Q = W[(Cp_1 - Cp_2)/(1/A_1^2Cd_1^2 + 1/A_2^2Cd_2^2)]^{0.5} \qquad (3.80)$$

where W is the reference wind velocity used for the pressure coefficient definition. Also Cp_1 and Cp_2 are the pressure coefficients on the two façades and Cd_1 and Cd_2 are the discharge coefficients for the two openings.

For a defined surface of the windward or upwind opening A_i, the surface of the second opening A_{ii}, can be calculated from equation (3.82). In this case and with $Cd_i = Cd_{ii}$, it is obtained that:

$$A_{ii} = A_i B[1/(A_i^2 - B^2)]^{0.5} \tag{3.81}$$

where

$$B = [1/(Cp_1 - Cp_2)]^{1/2}[Q/(WCd)] \tag{3.82}$$

EXAMPLE. For a given place the design wind velocity is equal to 2 m s⁻¹ and is perpendicular to the inlet openings of a naturally ventilated building. The outlets are located on the opposite façade to the inlets. The volume of the zone for which the calculation will be carried out is 600 m³ and the required air exchange rate is equal to eight air changes per hour. Also, as a result of constructional limitations, the surface of the upwind opening is equal to 3 m². Calculate the area of the windward opening if the discharge coefficient (Cd) for each opening is equal to 0.6 .

From Table 3.29 the pressure coefficients for the inlets and outlets are 0.4 and −0.25 respectively, therefore ΔCp = 0.65. Also Q = 1.33 m³ s⁻¹. Thus it is calculated that:

$$B = [1/(Cp_1 - Cp_2)]^{1/2}[Q/(WCd)]$$

$$= [1/0.65]^{1/2}[1.33/(2 \times 0.6)] = 1.37$$

Then:

$$A_1 = BA_2[1/(A_2^2 - B^2)]^{0.5}$$

$$= 1.37 \times 3[1(9 - 1.89)^{0.5} = 1.53 \, m^2$$

Exactly the same method is proposed by the British Standard Institution [1] for cross-ventilated configurations where the flow is due to wind.

3.4.2.5 The British Standard Method
The British Standard Method [1] proposes different expressions to calculate the airflow in natural ventilation configurations due to wind and the temperature difference between the indoor and the outdoor environments. It also proposes criteria for combining the effect of the wind and that of the temperature difference. The method has been presented in detail in Section 3.2. As already mentioned, the method that refers to the effect of the wind is exactly the same as the Aynsley method and thus the reader can refer to the previous section.

For the cases where the flow is mainly due to the temperature difference between indoors and outdoors, the method proposes the following formula to calculate the airflow Q (m³ s⁻¹).

$$Q = Cd\,A_b[2\Delta T\,gH/T]^{0.5} \tag{3.83}$$

where Cd is the discharge coefficient, ΔT is the mean temperature difference between indoors and outdoors, H is the height between the mean level of the lower and upper windows, T is the mean value of the indoor and outdoor temperatures (K) and A_b is defined by the following expression:

$$\frac{1}{A_b^2} = \frac{1}{A_1^2} + \frac{1}{A_2^2} \tag{3.84}$$

where A_1 and A_2 are the inlet and outlet openings respectively (lower and higher openings).

Based on the above, the surface of the inlet or outlet openings, A_p, necessary to achieve an airflow, Q, can be calculated from the following expression for a given value of the outlet or inlet surface, A_{ii}, respectively:

$$A_i = DA_{ii}(1/(A_{ii}^2 - D^2)^{0.5}) \tag{3.85}$$

where:

$$D = Q/[Cd(2\Delta T Hg/T)]^{0.5} \tag{3.86}$$

The criteria to define whether the flow is mainly due to temperature difference or to the wind have already been discussed in Section 3.2. However, these criteria can only be used in calculation procedures where the opening area is defined and the airflow has to be calculated.

EXAMPLE. For a given place the design indoor temperature is 27°C while the mean outdoor temperature is 31°C. The volume of the zone for which the calculation is to be carried out is 600 m³ and the required air exchange rate is equal to eight air changes per hour. Also, as a result of constructional limitations, the surface of the outlet openings is equal to 3 m³ and the vertical distance between the inlet and the outlets is equal to 6 m. Calculate the area of the inlet openings if the discharge coefficient for each opening is equal to 0.6.

It is obtained that $Q = 1.33$ m³ s⁻¹. Then:

$$D = Q/[Cd(2\Delta T Hg/T)]^{0.5}$$

$$= 1.33/[0.6(2\times4\times9.81\times6)/302]^{0.5} = 1.76$$

Thus:

$$A_i = DA_{ii}(1/(A_{ii}^2 - D^2)^{0.5})$$

$$= 1.76\times3\times(1/9 - 3.9)^{0.5} = 2.17 \text{ m}^2$$

3.4.3 Computerized network methods

Computerized methods, based on the network approach discussed in Section 3.2, can be used to define the area and the orientation of the openings of a building in order to achieve the required airflow. Network airflow models combine the effect of wind and temperature difference and do not present the limitations of the simplified methods previously presented. Also, because of their computerized character, these methods can be used to perform fast calculations for a wide spectrum of input data and thus provide the user with a sensitivity analysis of the relative impact of the design characteristics.

Calculations of opening surfaces should be performed for local prevailing wind speed and direction and also for the mean expected indoor–outdoor temperature difference. One-zone or multizone models can be used. One-zone models are simplest in their use and may be used during the pre-design phase.

EXAMPLE. Consider a monozone industrial zone having a volume of 700 m³. The height of the room is 3.5 m. Openings should be placed at the midheight of the walls. The prevailing wind direction during summer is north and the mean wind speed is 3 m s⁻¹. The design temperature difference between the outdoor and the indoor environments is equal to 3°. As a result of design restrictions, openings can be designed only in the north and south façades. Calculate the area of the north windward openings, A_1, as well as that of the south upwind opening, A_2, in order to achieve 15 air changes per hour during summer.

Using the monozone network airflow model NORMA [45], a sensitivity analysis regarding the windward opening A_1 and the upwind opening A_2 has been performed. The results of the calculation are given in Table 3.32. A discharge coefficient equal to 0.6 has been used for both the openings. Taking into account that the required airflow rate is equal to 10,500 m³ h⁻¹, it can be concluded that the possible solutions are the following:

- A_1 greater than 2 and less than 3 m² and A_2 equal to 3 m²;
- A_1 greater than 2 and less than 3 m² and A_2 equal to 4 m².

It is evident that the sensitivity analysis can provide some further solutions (Figure 3.34).

3.4.4 Comparative analysis

To compare the predictions of all above methods, calculations have been performed for a number of building configurations. As the different methods are characterized by various types of limitations concerning the effects of wind and temperature difference, as well as the ratios of the openings, the cases to be considered must be simple enough to satisfy the limitations of all methods.

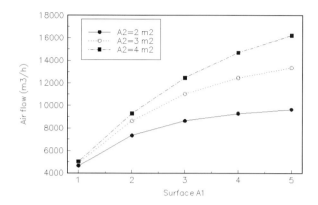

Figure 3.34. Results of the sensitivity analysis

3.4.4.1 Example 1 – A simple case

Calculate the net surface of the inlets and outlets for a naturally ventilated building of 700 m³. The required airflow is equal to six air changes per hour. The mean wind speed during the design season is 2 m s⁻¹ and is parallel to the main axis of the building. The temperature difference between the indoor and the outdoor environments is negligible. Consider that the wind speed is measured close to the building and that there is no need for correction due to terrain modifications. Furthermore, the effect of the neighbouring buildings is negligible. Finally, consider that inlet and outlet openings are equal, are located in two opposite walls of the ground floor, normal to the main axis of the building, and there is no screen.

THE FLORIDA I METHOD

This method considers almost equal inlets and outlets and does not account for the effects of the temperature difference. It uses four coefficients f_1, f_2, f_3, f_4, to account for the wind orientation, terrain correction, neighbouring buildings and the height of openings. Taking into account the assumptions of the example it is evident that $f_2 = f_3 = f_4 = 1$.

The total area of the openings, in ft², is predicted by the following formula:

$$TOA = 0.00079 V(ach) / (W f_1 f_2 f_1 f_4)$$

This equation assumes a screening with a porosity of 0.6. As there is no screening the results of the above equation should be divided by 1.67. Also, this equation considers that door or window framing is about 20% of the gross area and therefore to calculate the net opening the result should be divided by 1.25.

Substitution of the data gives that TOA = 6.88 m² and therefore the gross surface of the inlets or outlets is equal to 3.44 m². If it is taken into account that there is no screen and the method calculates the gross surface area, the net surface of inlet and outlets is equal to $A_o = A_i = 3.44/1.67/1.25 = 1.64$ m².

THE FLORIDA II METHOD
This method does not consider equal inlets and outlets and proposes the calculation of an effective window opening. It does not account for the effects of the temperature difference. It uses two coefficients f_3 and f_4, to account for the neighbouring buildings and the height of openings. If the assumptions of the example are taken into account, it is evident that $f_3 = f_4 = 1$. The total area of the openings, in ft², is predicted by equation (3.73):

$$A = 0.000296\,V\,\text{ach}\,/\,[W(f_3 f_4 \text{PD})^{0.5}]$$

From Table 3.29 WPC = 0.4, and LPC = −0.25. Then:

$$\text{PD} = \text{WPC} - \text{LPC} = 0.65$$

Substitution of the data produces $A = 1.12$ m² and therefore the surface of the inlets or outlets is $A_o = A_i = 1.41A = 1.58$ m².

THE ASHRAE METHOD
This method considers wind or temperature difference effects, but does not consider the combined effects of wind and temperature difference. It does not consider equal inlets and outlets. It proposes a coefficient, E, to account for the effectiveness of the opening as a function of the incidence angle of the wind. Based on the data of the example, E is taken as 0.5. Therefore:

$$A = Q/(EW) = 1.16 \text{ m}^2.$$

THE AYNSLEY METHOD
This method permits the calculation of the area of the inlets and outlets in natural ventilation configurations where the airflow is due to wind forces. It does not consider equal inlets and outlets. For a defined surface of the windward or upwind opening, A_p, the surface of the second opening, A_{ii}, can be calculated from the equation (3.80). In this case and if the discharge coefficients of the inlets and outlets are the same, then:

$$Q = W[(\text{Cp}_1 - \text{Cp}_2)/(1/\,A_i^2\text{Cd}_1^2 + 1/\,A_o^2\text{Cd}_2^2)]^{0.5}$$

If $\text{Cp}_1 = 0.4$ and $\text{Cp}_2 = -0.25$, and $\text{Cd}_1 = \text{Cd}_2 = 1$, then $A_o = A_i = 1.01$ m².

THE BRITISH STANDARD METHOD
As already mentioned, this method predicts the same result as the Aynsley method for configurations where the temperature difference between the

Table 3.32. Results obtained from network models

A_i (m²)	A_o (m²)	Q (m³ h⁻¹) – ach
1.0	1.0	4103 – 5.86
1.2	1.2	4965 – 7.09
1.1	1.1	4513 – 6.45
1.05	1.05	4308 – 6.15
1.02	1.02	4185 – 5.98

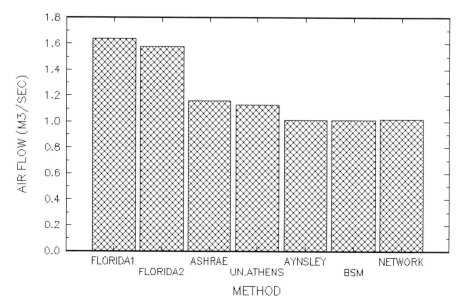

Figure 3.35. Predicted values of the airflow for the first example

indoor and the outdoor environments can be neglected. Thus, $A_o = A_i = 1.01$ m².

COMPUTERIZED METHODS

A network computerized method has been used to calculate the airflow for the example building and for different inlet and outlet opening surfaces. The results obtained are given in Table 3.32.

Therefore, $A_i = A_o = 1.02$ m².

The results obtained from all the methods are given in Figure 3.35. The calculated standard deviation is 0.27.

3.4.4.2 *Example 2 – The effect of the temperature difference*

This second example is the same as the previous one, but with a temperature difference of 3°C between indoors and outdoors. Therefore, the example is the following:

EXAMPLE. Calculate the net surface of the inlets and outlets for a naturally ventilated building of 700 m³. The required airflow is equal to six air changes per hour. The mean wind speed during the design season is 2 m s⁻¹ and is parallel to the main axis of the building. The temperature difference between the indoor and the outdoor environments is 3°C. Consider that the wind speed is measured close to the building and that there is no need for correction due to terrain modifications. Furthermore, the effect of the neighbouring buildings is negligible. Finally, consider that inlet and outlet openings are equal, are located in two opposite walls of the ground floor, normal to the main axis of the building, and there is no screen. The vertical difference between the two openings is equal to 2 m.

As already mentioned, the Florida I and II methods as well as the University of Athens and the Aynsley methods, do not take into account the effects of the temperature difference. Therefore, the predicted airflow by these methods is exactly the same as in first example.

The ASHRAE method proposes two expressions to calculate the required openings for a certain airflow. The first refers to the wind effects and the second to the effects of the temperature difference. It does not propose an expression for combined effects. As previously calculated, when only the wind effect is taken into account the required input/output area is equal to 1.16 m². If only the temperature difference is taken into account, then from equation 3.79, the necessary inlet – outlet surface is obtained as 8.5 m².

The British Standard Method proposes a method for phenomena dominated by the wind effects and another dominated by the temperature difference effects. It also proposes criteria for deciding which formula should be selected. Using these criteria, presented in Section 3.2, it is determined that wind effects dominate and thus $A_o = A_i = 1.01$ m².

Using the computerized method, it is obtained that the required inlet–outlet surface is equal to 0.97 m².

APPENDIX A

Parametrical model for the calculation of the pressure coefficient

A case study

The pressure coefficient is to be calculated for two points of the building envelope: point (1) on facade (1) and point (2) on facade (2) (Figure 3.A1).

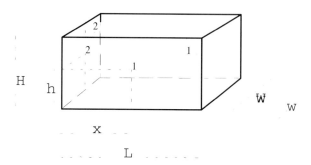

Figure 3.A1. Schematic view of the building facade

The environmental and geometrical parameters have the following values:

pad = 0.0, rbh = 1, a = 0.22, L = 6 m, H = 3 m, W = 3 m,
x = 3 m, w = 1.5 m, h = 1.5 m, $anw(1)$ = −45°, $anw(2)$ = −135°

The frontal aspect ratio for facades (1) and (2) is:

far(1) = L/H = 2, far(2) = W/H = 1

The side aspect ratio for facades (1) and (2) is:

sar(1) = W/H = 2, sar(2) = L/H = 2

The relative position of points (1) and (2) is:

xl(1) = x/L = 0.5, xl(2) = w/W = 0.5

zh(1) = zh(2) = h/H = 0.5

SIDE 1 − WINDWARD SIDE

$Cp_{ref}(zh = 0.5) = 1.21$ (from equation 3.21)

$Cp_{norm0.5}(a = 0.22) = 0.999$ (from Table 3.A1)

$$Cp_{norm0.5}(pad = 0) = 0.979 \qquad \text{(from Table 3.A2)}$$

$$Cp_{norm0.5,0}(rbh = 1) = 0.957 \qquad \text{(from Table 3.A3)}$$

$$Cp_{norm0,0.5}(far = 2) = 0.874 \qquad \text{(from Table 3.A7,}$$
$$\text{by linear interpolation}$$
$$\text{between: } Cp_{norm0,0.4}(far = 2)$$
$$\text{and } Cp_{norm0,0.6}(far = 2))$$

$$Cp_{norm0,0.5}(sar = 1) = 1 \qquad \text{(from Table 3.A8)}$$

$$Cp_{norm0.5,45}(xl = 0.5) = 0.464 \qquad \text{(from Table 3.A6)}$$

$$Cp(1) = Cp_{ref}(zh = 0.5) \times Cp_{norm0.5}(a = 0.22) \times Cp_{norm0.5}(pad = 0)$$
$$\times Cp_{norm0.5,0}(rbh = 1) \times Cp_{norm0,0.5}(far = 2)$$
$$\times Cp_{norm0,0.5}(sar = 1) \times Cp_{norm0.5,45}(xl = 0.5) = 0.459$$

Thus, $Cp(1) = 0.459$.

SIDE 2 – LEEWARD SIDE

$$Cp_{ref}(zh = 0.5) = -0.454 \qquad \text{(from equation 3.21)}$$

$$Cp_{norm0.5}(a = 0.22) = 0.954 \qquad \text{(from Table 3.A9)}$$

$$Cp_{norm0.5}(pad = 0) = 1.034 \qquad \text{(from Table 3.A10)}$$

$$Cp_{norm0.5,0}(rbh = 1) = 0.998 \qquad \text{(from Table 3.A11)}$$

$$Cp_{norm0,0.5}(far = 1) = 1 \qquad \text{(from Table 3.A15)}$$

$$Cp_{norm0,0.5}(sar = 2) = 0.645 \qquad \text{(from Table 3.A6, by linear}$$
$$\text{interpolation between:}$$
$$Cp_{norm0,0.4}(sar = 2)$$
$$\text{and } Cp_{norm0,0.6}(sar = 2))$$

$$Cp_{norm0.5,135}(xl = 0.5) = 1.707 \qquad \text{(from Table 3.A14)}$$

$$Cp(2) = Cp_{ref}(zh = 0.5) \times Cp_{norm0.5}(a = 0.22) \times Cp_{norm0.5}(pad = 0)$$
$$\times Cp_{norm0.5,0}(rbh = 1) \times Cp_{norm0,0.5}(far = 1)$$
$$\times Cp_{norm0,0.5}(sar = 2) \times Cp_{norm0.5,135}(xl = 0.5) = -0.492$$

Thus, $Cp(2) = -0.492$.

Coefficients for the curve-fitting equations

Polynomial function for the reference Cp.

$$Cp_{ref}(zh) = -2.381082(zh)^3 + 2.89756(zh)^2 - 0.774649(zh) + 0.745543$$

Coefficients for the equations of the normalized Cp as a function of environmental and geometrical parameters as given in Tables 3.A1 to 3.A8.

Table 3.A1. Coefficients for the equations of the normalized Cp as a function of terrain roughness: $Cp_{normzh}(a) = a_0 + a_1(a) + a_2(a)^2$

zh	a_2	a_1	a_0
0.1	−10.820106	+2.312434	+1.014958
0.3	−10.42328	+1.268783	+1.225354
0.5	−8.531746	+0.688492	+1.261468
0.7	−0.939153	−1.691138	+1.417505
0.9	5.10582	−3.350529	+1.489995

Table 3.A2. Coefficients for the equations of the normalized Cp as a function of density of surrounding buildings: $Cp_{normzh}(pad) = a_0 + a_1(pad) + a_2(pad)^2 + a_3(pad)^3$

zh	a_3	a_2	a_1	a_0
0.0–0.65	−2.14966e−05	+2.37444e−03	−0.089797	+0.979603
0.66–0.75	−1.775637e−05	+2.034996e−03	−0.081741	+0.995399
0.76–0.85	−1.523628e−05	+1.788998e−03	−0.074881	+1.00378
0.86–0.95	−1.571837e−05	+1.693211e−03	−0.06647	+0.994355
0.96–1.0	−1.987115e−05	+1.968606e−03	−0.067063	+0.966038

Table 3.A3. Coefficients for the equations of the normalized Cp as a function of height of surrounding buildings: $Cp_{normzh,\,pad}(rbh) = a_0 + a_1(rbh) + a_2(rbh)^2 + a_3(rbh)^3$

zh	pad	a_3	a_2	a_1	a_0
0.07	0.0	0.0	0.0	0.111687	0.848151
	5.5	0.0	0.0	0.303608	0.693641
	12.5	0.0	0.0	0.665827	0.450229
	25.0	−0.354662	1.416299	3.925792	−3.814382
0.20	0.0	0.0	0.0	0.152862	0.78183
	5.5	0.0	0.0	0.35057	0.60962
	12.5	0.0	0.0	0.691757	0.407027
	25.0	0.0	1.534332	−17.32797	14.40045
0.50	0.0	0.0	0.0	0.251497	0.705467
	5.5	0.0	0.0	0.661656	0.348851
	12.5	0.0	0.0	1.601127	−0.4244487
	25.0	2.743878	−18.09787	13.731616	2.08857
0.70	0.0	0.0	0.0	0.280233	0.697339
	5.5	0.0	0.0	0.693236	0.3469922
	12.5	0.0	0.0	1.566717	−0.325088
	25.0	−1.2113787	6.301881	4.370901	−6.988637

Table 3.A3 (cont.)

zh	pad	a_3	a_2	a_1	a_0
0.80	0.0	0.0	0.0	0.338131	0.637794
	5.5	0.0	0.0	0.719554	0.349286
	12.5	0.0	0.0	1.373569	−0.175915
	25.5	−0.403791	1.579764	5.205654	−4.533334
0.90	0.0	0.0	0.0	0.436478	0.555708
	5.5	0.0	−0.155809	1.523391	−0.266623
	12.5	0.0	−0.217166	2.2467	−0.855572
	25.0	0.0	−0.733177	6.203364	−3.94136
0.93	0.0	0.0	0.0	0.464299	0.535423
	5.5	0.0	−0.17031	1.579231	−0.294406
	12.5	0.0	−0.235091	2.28368	−0.853961
	25.0	0.0	−0.62338	5.154261	−3.165345

Table 3.A4. Coefficients for the equations of the normalized Cp as a function of frontal aspect ratio far < 1.0: $Cp_{normpad, zh}(far) = a_0 + a_1(far)$

pad	zh	a_1	a_0
0.0	0.07	0.21	0.79
	0.20	0.166	0.834
	0.40	0.102	0.898
	0.60	0.066	0.934
	0.80	−0.04	1.04
	0.93	−0.292	1.292
5.0	0.07	0.286	0.714
	0.20	0.21	0.79
	0.40	0.148	0.852
	0.60	0.156	0.844
	0.80	0.028	0.972
	0.93	−0.364	1.364
7.5	0.07	0.134	0.866
	0.20	0.12	0.88
	0.40	0.054	0.946
	0.60	0.6245004e−17	1.0
	0.80	0.038	0.962
	0.93	−0.352	1.352
10.0	0.07	0.182	0.818
	0.20	0.046	0.954
	0.40	−0.12	1.12
	0.60	−0.166	1.166
	0.80	−0.052	1.052
	0.93	−0.428	1.428
12.5	0.07	0.1	0.9
	0.20	−0.068	1.068
	0.40	−0.058	1.058
	0.60	−0.044	1.044
	0.80	0.032	0.968
	0.93	−0.334	1.334

Table 3.A5, Coefficients for the equations of the normalized Cp as a function of side aspect ratio sar < 1.0: $Cp_{normpad, zh}(sar) = a_0 + a_1(sar)$

pad	zh	a_1	a_0
0.0	0.07	−0.022	1.022
	0.20	0.056	0.944
	0.40	−0.03	1.03
	0.6	6.245004e−17	0.1
	0.80	−0.02	1.02
	0.93	−0.166	1.166
5.0	0.07	0.172	0.828
	0.20	0.19	0.81
	0.40	0.334	0.666
	0.60	0.438	0.562
	0.80	0.31	0.69
	0.93	−0.09	1.09
7.5	0.07	0.266	0.734
	0.20	0.298	0.702
	0.40	0.46	0.54
	0.60	0.436	0.564
	0.80	0.324	0.676
	0.93	−0.118	1.118
10.0	0.07	0.328	0.672
	0.20	0.318	0.682
	0.40	0.8	0.2
	0.60	0.66	0.334
	0.80	0.206	0.794
	0.93	−0.286	1.286
12.5	0.07	0.75	0.25
	0.20	1.104	−0.104
	0.40	1.428	−0.428
	0.60	1.2	−0.2
	0.80	0.634	0.366
	0.93	6.245004e−17	1.0

Table 3.A6. Coefficients for the equations of the normalized Cp: horizontal distribution vs. wind direction: $Cp_{normzb, anw}(rbh) = a_0 + a_1(xl) + a_2(xl)^2 + a_3(xl)^3$

zh	anw (°)	a_3	a_2	a_1	a_0
0.50	0.0	0.0	−3.04662	3.04662	0.268462
	10.0	0.0	−3.142447	2.873329	0.38632
	20.0	0.0	−2.001162	1.398438	0.693916
	30.0	0.0	−1.275862	0.278803	0.935081
	40.0	0.0	−1.058275	−0.01627	0.871259
	50.0	0.0	−0.891626	0.247508	0.428414
	60.0	0.0	−1.560755	1.496049	−0.257573
	70.0	0.0	−1.990676	2.614312	−0.994965
	80.0	0.0	−1.651067	2.530479	−1.359928
	90.0	−5.984848	10.036713	−3.883683	−0.778811
0.70	0.0	0.0	−2.501166	2.501166	0.401189
	10.0	0.0	−2.665435	2.355141	0.523287
	20.0	0.0	−1.674825	1.008462	0.802867

Table 3.A6 (cont.)

zh	anw (°)	a_3	a_2	a_1	a_0
	30.0	0.0	−0.869048	−0.176541	1.051723
	40.0	0.0	−0.635198	−0.467520	0.973357
	50.0	0.0	−0.667077	3.841881e−03	0.485571
	60.0	0.0	−1.415846	1.367316	−0.231142
	70.0	0.0	−2.064103	2.719557	−1.005524
	80.0	0.0	−1.842775	2.788363	−1.37687
	90.0	−4.015152	6.670746	−2.319231	−0.836434
0.90	0.0	0.0	−2.456876	2.456876	0.451469
	10.0	0.0	−2.681034	2.335446	0.581156
	20.0	0.0	−1.724942	0.981305	0.888531
	30.0	0.0	−0.832512	−0.270429	1.118564
	40.0	0.0	−0.547786	−0.547786	0.992378
	50.0	0.0	−0.88711	0.279757	0.426546
	60.0	0.0	−1.85509	1.935973	−0.375921
	70.0	0.0	−2.815851	3.659487	−1.236923
	80.0	0.0	−2.449507	3.577449	−1.585214
	90.0	−6.959984	10.745338	−3.502826	−0.877273

Table 3.A7. Coefficients for the equations of the normalized Cp as a function of frontal aspect ratios far > 1.0: $Cp_{normpad, zh}(far) = [a_1 far + a_2/far + a_3]^{1/2}$

pad	zh	a_1	a_2	a_3
0.0	0.07	−0.070887	0.335565	0.741492
	0.20	−0.061746	0.39232	0.670057
	0.40	−0.071734	0.370249	0.700161
	0.60	−0.075213	0.280472	0.799646
	0.80	−0.081452	0.261036	0.821341
	0.93	−0.05991	0.441293	0.620374
5.0	0.07	−0.625867	−3.31499	4.938818
	0.20	−0.700802	−3.691923	5.39902
	0.40	−0.551417	−2.657088	4.2088561
	0.60	−0.394759	−1.857109	3.243966
	0.80	−0.384892	−1.582766	2.964682
	0.93	−0.471534	−1.938719	3.408053
7.5	0.07	−0.464735	−4.370468	5.827134
	0.20	−0.484764	−4.700937	6.175447
	0.40	−0.357666	−3.421083	4.761667
	0.60	−0.430568	−3.272576	4.686477
	0.80	−0.538978	−3.080677	4.608249
	0.93	−0.295157	−2.106807	3.39147
10.0	0.07	−0.445623	−5.965503	7.414155
	0.20	−0.562911	−8.352512	9.919405
	0.40	−0.303556	−5.104654	6.409214
	0.60	−0.396287	−4.685712	6.096834
	0.80	−0.326486	−3.146084	4.485651
	0.93	−0.491857	−3.607476	5.109896
12.5	0.07	0.39952	−6.357705	6.938206
	0.20	0.560605	−10.512008	10.939653
	0.40	0.460531	−5.146305	5.668398
	0.60	0.052937	−4.346084	5.273574
	0.80	−0.17023	−3.285382	4.448491
	0.93	−0.489256	−4.363034	5.840238

Table 3.A8. Coefficients for the equations of the normalized Cp as a function of side aspect ratio sar > 1.0: $Cp_{normpad,\ zh}(sar) = [a_1 sar + a_2/sar + a_3]^{1/2}$

pad	zh	a_1	a_2	a_3
0.0	0.07	0.102648	0.307944	0.589408
	0.20	−0.044242	−0.132726	1.176968
	0.40	−0.02005	−0.06025	1.0802
	0.60	−2.751206e−10	−5.399712e−10	1.0
	0.80	−0.127266	−0.101574	1.22884
	0.93	0.175931	0.527814	0.296255
5.0	0.07	−0.61983	−2.745612	4.364542
	0.20	−0.455586	−2.714454	4.17004
	0.40	0.01539	−1.522998	2.507608
	0.60	8.495999e−03	−1.108008	2.099512
	0.80	0.03363	−0.665862	1.632232
	0.93	−0.83599	−2.639028	4.475018
7.5	0.07	−0.672534	−4.465068	6.137602
	0.20	−0.589638	−4.571604	6.161242
	0.40	0.44127	−2.377428	2.935258
	0.60	0.313214	−2.334822	3.021608
	0.80	0.53643	−1.011222	1.474792
	0.93	−0.32829	−2.984262	4.312552
10.0	0.07	−1.31805	−7.924662	10.242712
	0.20	−2.14576	−11.416512	14.562272
	0.40	0.0608	−6.2016	7.1408
	0.60	0.699422	−3.950934	4.251512
	0.80	0.51795	−2.521878	3.003928
	0.93	−1.627836	−6.191754	8.81959
12.5	0.07	1.15625	−5.8125	5.65625
	0.20	0.811914	−10.848372	11.036458
	0.40	3.144588	−2.954106	0.809518
	0.60	3.525422	−0.048534	−2.476888
	0.80	1.802288	−0.832296	0.030008
	0.93	−0.384444	−4.326666	5.71111

LEEWARD SIDE

Polynomial function for the reference Cp.

$$Cp_{ref}(zh) = -0.079239(zh)^3 + 0.542317(zh)^2 - 0.496769(zh) + 0.331533$$

Coefficients for the equations of the normalized Cp as a function of environmental and geometrical parameters as given in Tables 3.A9 to 3.A16.

Table 3.A9. Coefficients for the equations of the normalized Cp as a function of terrain roughness: $Cp_{normzh}(a) = a_0 + a_1(a) + a_2(a)^2$

zh	a_2	a_1	a_0
0.1	−14.368685	4.520431	0.0667639
0.3	−13.490491	4.101437	0.706052
0.5	−8.775919	1.322245	1.088822
0.7	−4.662405	−0.929782	1.395398
0.9	2.382908	−4.837467	1.940878

Table 3.A10. Coefficients for the equations of the normalized Cp as a function of density of surrounding buildings: $Cp_{normzh}(pad) = a_0 + a_1(pad) + a_2(pad)^2 + a_3(pad)^3 + a_4(pad)^4 + a_5(pad)^5$

zh	a_5	a_4	a_3	a_2	a_1	a_0
0.07	9.118209e−08	−1.050363e−05	3.932533e−04	−4.734698e−03	−0.015304	1.047295
0.20	5.934754e−08	−6.708652e−06	2.340744e−04	−1.943067e−03	−0.031483	1.043295
0.40	5.052791e−08	−5.537346e−06	1.722449e−04	−3.926684e−04	−0.046517	1.034663
0.60	5.595808e−08	−6.121612e−06	1.8897e−04	−3.177597e−04	−0.051446	1.032759
0.80	5.553558e−08	−5.931215e−06	1.719758e−04	3.013991e−04	−0.059971	1.037969
0.93	6.211419e−08	−6.759794e−06	2.024378e−04	1.182029e−04	−0.065764	1.033975

Table 3.A11. Coefficients for the equations of the normalized Cp as a function of height of surrounding buildings: $Cp_{normzh,pad}(rbh) = a_0 + a_1(rbh) + a_2(rbh)^2$

zh	pad	a_2	a_1	a_0
0.07	0.00	0.0	0.547959	0.465538
	5.00	0.0	0.625743	0.308268
	6.25	0.0	0.859533	0.107587
	12.50	0.0	1.710552	−0.681624
0.20	0.00	0.0	0.473757	0.527487
	5.00	0.0	0.636732	0.294108
	6.25	0.123639	0.432008	0.44064
	12.50	0.080203	1.471191	−0.547645
0.40	0.00	−0.043739	0.599345	0.427938
	5.00	0.054539	0.299349	0.645489
	6.25	0.100427	0.35117	0.483096
	12.50	0.175853	0.568029	0.223168
0.60	0.00	−0.069086	0.793503	0.287883
	5.00	0.029377	0.402683	0.594877
	6.25	0.066082	0.524015	0.376383
	12.50	0.145046	0.567979	0.264523
0.80	0.00	−0.036376	0.781825	0.258777
	5.00	0.011009	0.55164	0.435343
	6.25	−1.58012e-03	1.127839	−0.084281
	12.50	0.09395	1.114736	−0.111437
0.93	0.00	2.138076e-03	0.655048	0.38064
	5.00	0.03126	0.526521	0.418668
	6.25	0.102993	0.946754	−0.122071
	12.50	0.202243	1.119405	−0.353569

Table 3.A12 Coefficients for the equations of the normalized Cp as a function of frontal aspect ratio far < 1.0: $Cp_{normpad, zh}(far) = a_0 + a_1(far)$

pad	zh	a_1	a_0
0.0	0.07	0.77	0.23
	0.20	0.694	0.306
	0.40	0.624	0.376
	0.60	0.6	0.4
	0.80	0.666	0.334
	0.93	0.55	0.45
5.0	0.07	1.31	−0.31
	0.20	1.096	−0.096
	0.40	1.048	−0.048
	0.60	1.096	−0.096
	0.80	1.142	−0.142
	0.93	1.042	−0.042
7.5	0.07	1.32	−0.32
	0.20	1.17	−0.17
	0.40	1.142	−0.142
	0.60	1.17	−0.17
	0.80	1.292	−0.292
	0.93	1.25	−0.25
10.0	0.07	1.302	−0.302
	0.20	1.166	−0.166
	0.40	1.12	−0.12
	0.60	1.25	−0.25
	0.80	1.428	−0.428
	0.93	1.428	−0.428
12.5	0.07	1.336	−0.366
	0.20	1.174	−0.174
	0.40	1.166	−0.166
	0.60	1.244	−0.244
	0.80	1.4	−0.4
	0.93	1.412	−0.412

Table 3.A13. Coefficients for the equations of the normalized Cp as a function of side aspect ratio sar < 1.0: $Cp_{normpad, zh}(sar) = a_0 + a_1(sar)$

pad	zh	a_1	a_0
0.0	0.07	−0.462	1.462
	0.20	−0.444	1.444
	0.40	−0.5	1.5
	0.60	−0.6	1.6
	0.80	−0.666	1.666
	0.93	−0.986	1.986

Table 3.A13 (cont.)

pad	zh	a_1	a_0
5.0	0.07	0.62	0.38
	0.20	0.484	0.516
	0.40	0.286	0.714
	0.60	0.322	0.678
	0.80	0.358	0.642
	0.93	0.124	0.876
7.5	0.07	0.56	0.44
	0.20	0.416	0.584
	0.40	0.358	0.642
	0.60	0.378	0.622
	0.80	0.416	0.584
	0.93	6.245004e-17	1.0
10.0	0.07	0.418	0.582
	0.20	0.374	0.626
	0.40	0.28	0.72
	0.60	0.334	0.666
	0.80	0.286	0.714
	0.93	0.058	0.942
12.5	0.07	0.586	0.414
	0.20	0.392	0.608
	0.40	0.208	0.792
	0.60	0.088	0.912
	0.80	0.2	0.8
	0.93	−0.118	1.118

Table 3.A14 Coefficients for the equations of the normalized Cp: horizontal distribution vs. wind direction: $Cp_{normzh,anw}(xl) = a_0 + a_1(xl) + a_2(xl)^2 + a_3(xl)^3 + a_4(xl)^4$

zh	anw (°)	a_4	a_3	a_2	a_1	a_0
0.50	90.0	0.0	9.325952	−16.031002	6.08061	2.162909
	110.0	0.0	2.526807	−5.145221	3.28289	1.400238
	130.0	0.0	0.200855	−1.520047	1.734472	1.275364
	160.0	0.0	0.861888	−1.966841	1.561282	0.923007
	180.0	0.0	4.145989e-16	−0.107692	0.107692	0.975846
0.70	90.0	0.0	11.862859	−19.086364	6.79763	2.204853
	110.0	0.0	1.79934	−2.526981	1.326103	1.631755
	130.0	0.0	−0.069542	0.404196	0.124611	1.506259
	160.0	0.0	1.003108	−0.873077	0.398465	1.093671
	180.0	0.0	3.88578e-16	0.449883	−0.449883	1.102028
0.90	90.0	−13.234266	47.482906	−48.637238	13.933178	2.493133
	110.0	−18.269231	38.486402	−24.083741	4.338003	1.973497
	130.0	−9.985431	17.831974	−8.056789	0.346156	1.844014
	160.0	−8.458625	17.902681	−10.191521	1.433689	1.232881
	180.0	−6.555944	13.106061	−7.364394	0.809767	1.244049

Table 3.A15. Coefficients for the equations of the normalized Cp as a function of frontal aspect ratios far > 1.0:
$$Cp_{normpad,zh}(far) = [a_1 far + a_2/far + a_3]^{1/2}$$

pad	zh	a_1	a_2	a_3
0.0	0.07	0.391319	0.275277	0.305879
	0.20	0.208852	0.045117	0.727577
	0.40	0.176644	0.135403	0.657545
	0.60	0.222872	0.219437	0.5177
	0.80	0.352525	0.51124	0.095033
	0.93	0.409298	0.101415	0.461285
5.0	0.07	0.313066	1.29096	−0.679717
	0.20	0.262845	1.187068	−0.511316
	0.40	0.198393	0.852449	−0.107538
	0.60	0.202255	0.824728	−0.109405
	0.80	0.266436	0.989084	−0.34636
	0.93	0.378433	0.831703	−0.27258
7.5	0.07	0.355636	1.865418	−1.293254
	0.20	0.256393	1.501845	−0.83996
	0.40	0.195066	1.248485	−0.513001
	0.60	0.179345	1.132885	−0.406631
	0.80	0.248347	1.426085	−0.79038
	0.93	0.286457	1.200878	−0.562477
10.0	0.07	0.162696	1.401255	−0.650645
	0.20	0.14259	1.382313	−0.611037
	0.40	0.072493	1.036706	−0.199349
	0.60	0.062272	0.956828	−0.131138
	0.80	0.116832	1.191314	−0.445541
	0.93	0.111723	0.959598	−0.190495
12.5	0.07	0.187639	1.532033	−0.830662
	0.20	0.113114	1.30869	−0.518821
	0.40	0.090391	1.096843	−0.281639
	0.60	0.058215	0.921987	−0.086177
	0.80	0.138563	1.304438	−0.561468
	0.93	0.115601	1.108345	−0.337801

Table 3.A16. Coefficients for the equations of the normalized Cp as a function of side aspect ratio sar > 1.0:
$$Cp_{normpad,\ zh}(sar) = [a_1 sar + a_2/sar + a_3]^{1/2}$$

pad	zh	a_1	a_2	a_3
0.0	0.07	1.549121	4.008955	−4.558076
	0.20	1.293432	3.376296	−3.669728
	0.40	0.818276	2.757414	−2.575691
	0.60	0.622491	2.463733	−2.086225
	0.80	0.431822	2.206986	−1.638808
	0.93	1.15475	3.567738	−3.722488

Table 3.A16 (cont.)

pad	zh	a_1	a_2	a_3
5.0	0.07	1.234668	3.821814	−4.056482
	0.20	1.086419	3.381557	−3.467976
	0.40	1.110227	3.330677	−3.440903
	0.60	1.248462	3.745386	−3.993848
	0.80	1.158504	3.817008	−3.975512
	0.93	0.924129	3.214321	−3.13845
7.5	0.07	1.6176	4.7352	−5.352801
	0.20	1.405914	4.082196	−4.48811
	0.40	1.39227	4.047642	−4.439912
	0.60	1.446764	4.209078	−4.655842
	0.80	1.541118	4.623354	−5.164472
	0.93	1.395	4.185	−4.58
10.0	0.07	1.728091	5.065453	−5.793544
	0.20	1.675056	4.762584	−5.437641
	0.40	1.632	4.6368	−5.2688
	0.60	1.623354	4.746708	−5.370063
	0.80	2.133661	5.767382	−6.900996
	0.93	2.099225	5.670099	−6.769291
12.5	0.07	2.249115	6.239501	−7.488376
	0.20	2.121972	5.826368	−6.948252
	0.40	1.99874	5.578012	−6.576709
	0.60	2.373076	6.268238	−7.641063
	0.80	2.133851	5.94792	−7.081692
	0.93	2.204859	6.021059	−7.225708

APPENDIX B

Computational fluid dynamics – fundamental equations

Conservation of mass – the continuity equation
Mass conservation imposes the condition that the net rate of density increase in a control volume dxdydz is equal to the net rate of mass influx to the control volume:

$$\frac{\partial \rho}{\partial t} + \frac{\partial}{\partial x}(\rho U) + \frac{\partial}{\partial y}(\rho V) + \frac{\partial}{\partial z}(\rho W) = 0 \tag{3A2.1}$$

where U, V and W are the air velocity components in the x, y and z directions respectively and ρ is the air density (kg/m³), expressed as a function of pressure and temperature ($\rho = f(p, T)$).

To take the effect of turbulence into account, the air velocity components can be written as:

$$U = u + u', V = v + v' \text{ and } W = w + w' \tag{3A2.2}$$

where u, v, w are the time-mean components and u', v' and w' are the fluctuating terms.

Taking into account that u', v' and w' occur over a much shorter time interval than dt, it follows that: $u \approx U$, $v \approx V$ and $w \approx W$. Substitution in equation (3A2.1) gives:

$$\frac{\partial \rho}{\partial t} + \frac{\partial}{\partial x}(\rho u) + \frac{\partial}{\partial y}(\rho v) + \frac{\partial}{\partial z}(\rho w) = 0 \tag{3A2.3}$$

Conservation of momentum

According to the law of conservation of momentum, the net force on the control volume in any direction is equal to the outlet momentum flux minus the inlet momentum flux in the same direction. This is summarized in the following equations:

x direction:

$$\frac{\partial}{\partial t}(\rho U) + \frac{\partial}{\partial x}(\rho UU) + \frac{\partial}{\partial y}(\rho UV) + \frac{\partial}{\partial z}(\rho UW)$$

$$= -\frac{\partial P}{\partial x} + \frac{\partial}{\partial x}(\mu \frac{\partial U}{\partial x}) + \frac{\partial}{\partial y}(\mu \frac{\partial U}{\partial y}) \tag{3A2.4}$$

$$+ \frac{\partial}{\partial z}(\mu \frac{\partial U}{\partial z}) + \frac{1}{3}\frac{\partial}{\partial x}[\mu(\frac{\partial U}{\partial x} + \frac{\partial V}{\partial y} + \frac{\partial W}{\partial z})] + \rho g_x$$

y direction:

$$\frac{\partial}{\partial t}(\rho V) + \frac{\partial}{\partial x}(\rho UV) + \frac{\partial}{\partial y}(\rho VV) + \frac{\partial}{\partial z}(\rho VW)$$

$$= -\frac{\partial P}{\partial y} + \frac{\partial}{\partial x}(\mu \frac{\partial V}{\partial x}) + \frac{\partial}{\partial y}(\mu \frac{\partial V}{\partial y}) + \frac{\partial}{\partial z}(\mu \frac{\partial V}{\partial z}) \tag{3A2.5}$$

$$+ \frac{1}{3}\frac{\partial}{\partial y}[\mu(\frac{\partial U}{\partial x} + \frac{\partial V}{\partial y} + \frac{\partial W}{\partial z})] + \rho g_y$$

z direction:

$$\frac{\partial}{\partial t}(\rho W) + \frac{\partial}{\partial x}(\rho UW) + \frac{\partial}{\partial y}(\rho VW) + \frac{\partial}{\partial z}(\rho WW)$$

$$= -\frac{\partial P}{\partial z} + \frac{\partial}{\partial x}(\mu \frac{\partial W}{\partial x}) + \frac{\partial}{\partial y}(\mu \frac{\partial W}{\partial y}) + \frac{\partial}{\partial z}(\mu \frac{\partial W}{\partial z}) \tag{3A2.6}$$

$$+ \frac{1}{3}\frac{\partial}{\partial z}[\mu(\frac{\partial U}{\partial x} + \frac{\partial V}{\partial y} + \frac{\partial W}{\partial z})] + \rho g_z$$

Substituting equation (3A2.2) into equations (3A2.4–3A2.6) and putting $P = p + p'$ so as to include the effect of turbulence, the momentum conservation equations become:

x direction:

$$\frac{\partial}{\partial t}(\rho u) + \frac{\partial}{\partial x}(\rho uu) + \frac{\partial}{\partial y}(\rho uv) + \frac{\partial}{\partial z}(\rho uw)$$

$$= -\frac{\partial p}{\partial x} + \frac{\partial}{\partial x}(\mu \frac{\partial u}{\partial x}) + \frac{\partial}{\partial y}(\mu \frac{\partial u}{\partial y}) + \frac{\partial}{\partial z}(\mu \frac{\partial u}{\partial z})$$

$$+ \frac{1}{3}\frac{\partial}{\partial x}[\mu(\frac{\partial u}{\partial x} + \frac{\partial v}{\partial y} + \frac{\partial w}{\partial z})] \tag{3A2.7}$$

$$+ \frac{\partial}{\partial x}(-\rho\overline{u'u'}) + \frac{\partial}{\partial y}(-\rho\overline{u'v'}) + \frac{\partial}{\partial z}(-\rho\overline{u'w'}) + \rho g_x$$

y direction:

$$\frac{\partial}{\partial t}(\rho v) + \frac{\partial}{\partial x}(\rho vu) + \frac{\partial}{\partial y}(\rho vv) + \frac{\partial}{\partial z}(\rho vw)$$

$$= -\frac{\partial p}{\partial y} + \frac{\partial}{\partial x}(\mu \frac{\partial v}{\partial x}) + \frac{\partial}{\partial y}(\mu \frac{\partial v}{\partial y}) + \frac{\partial}{\partial z}(\mu \frac{\partial v}{\partial z})$$

$$+ \frac{1}{3}\frac{\partial}{\partial y}[\mu(\frac{\partial u}{\partial x} + \frac{\partial v}{\partial y} + \frac{\partial w}{\partial z})] \tag{3A2.8}$$

$$+ \frac{\partial}{\partial x}(-\rho\overline{u'v'}) + \frac{\partial}{\partial y}(-\rho\overline{v'v'}) + \frac{\partial}{\partial z}(-\rho\overline{v'w'}) + \rho g_y$$

z direction:

$$\frac{\partial}{\partial t}(\rho w) + \frac{\partial}{\partial x}(\rho uw) + \frac{\partial}{\partial y}(\rho vw) + \frac{\partial}{\partial z}(\rho ww)$$

$$= -\frac{\partial p}{\partial z} + \frac{\partial}{\partial x}(\mu \frac{\partial w}{\partial x}) + \frac{\partial}{\partial y}(\mu \frac{\partial w}{\partial y}) + \frac{\partial}{\partial z}(\mu \frac{\partial w}{\partial z})$$

$$+ \frac{1}{3}\frac{\partial}{\partial z}[\mu(\frac{\partial u}{\partial x} + \frac{\partial v}{\partial y} + \frac{\partial w}{\partial z})] \tag{3A2.9}$$

$$+ \frac{\partial}{\partial x}(-\rho\overline{u'w'}) + \frac{\partial}{\partial y}(-\rho\overline{v'w'}) + \frac{\partial}{\partial z}(-\rho\overline{w'w'}) + \rho g_z$$

The terms: $-\overline{\rho u'u'}$, $-\overline{\rho v'v'}$, $-\overline{\rho w'w'}$, $-\overline{\rho u'v'}$, $-\overline{\rho u'w'}$, $-\overline{\rho v'w'}$ are the turbulent stresses.

Conservation of thermal energy

According to the law of conservation of thermal energy, the net increase in internal energy in a control volume is equal to the net flow of energy by convection plus the net inflow by thermal and mass diffusion. This is expressed by the following equation:

$$\frac{\partial}{\partial t}(\rho T) + \frac{\partial}{\partial x}(\rho UT) + \frac{\partial}{\partial y}(\rho VT) + \frac{\partial}{\partial z}(\rho WT)$$

$$= \frac{\partial}{\partial x}(\Gamma \frac{\partial T}{\partial x}) + \frac{\partial}{\partial y}(\Gamma \frac{\partial T}{\partial y}) + \frac{\partial}{\partial z}(\Gamma \frac{\partial T}{\partial z}) \qquad (3A2.10)$$

where Γ stands for the diffusion coefficient ($\Gamma = \mu/\sigma$). To account for turbulence, T is written: $T = T + T'$. Substituting T and U, V, W from equation (3A2.2) into equation (3A2.10) gives:

$$\frac{\partial}{\partial t}(\rho T) + \frac{\partial}{\partial x}(\rho UT) + \frac{\partial}{\partial y}(\rho VT) + \frac{\partial}{\partial z}(\rho WT)$$

$$= \frac{\partial}{\partial x}(\Gamma \frac{\partial T}{\partial x}) + \frac{\partial}{\partial y}(\Gamma \frac{\partial T}{\partial y}) + \frac{\partial}{\partial z}(\Gamma \frac{\partial T}{\partial z})$$

$$+ \frac{\partial}{\partial x}(-\overline{\rho u'T'}) + \frac{\partial}{\partial y}(-\overline{\rho v'T'}) + \frac{\partial}{\partial z}(-\overline{\rho w'T'}) + \frac{q}{C_p} \qquad (3A2.11)$$

where q is the thermal energy production rate (W m^{-3}) and C_p is the specific heat (J kg^{-1} K^{-1}). The term q/C_p represents a source term, to allow for thermal energy production. The terms $-\overline{\rho u'T'}$, $-\overline{\rho v'T'}$, and $-\overline{\rho w'T'}$ are the turbulent heat fluxes.

Transport equations

In order to replace the turbulent terms in equations (3A2.7–3A2.9) and (3A2.11) with time mean quantities of the flow, the turbulent stresses and fluxes can be written as follows:

$$-\overline{\rho u'u'} = 2\mu_t \frac{\partial u}{\partial x} - \frac{2}{3}\rho k \qquad\qquad -\overline{\rho v'v'} = 2\mu_t \frac{\partial v}{\partial y} - \frac{2}{3}\rho k$$

$$-\overline{\rho w'w'} = 2\mu_t \frac{\partial w}{\partial z} - \frac{2}{3}\rho k \qquad\qquad -\overline{\rho u'v'} = 2\mu_t(\frac{\partial u}{\partial y} + \frac{\partial v}{\partial x})$$

$$-\rho\overline{v'w'} = 2\mu_t(\frac{\partial v}{\partial z} + \frac{\partial w}{\partial y}) \qquad\qquad -\rho\overline{u'w'} = 2\mu_t(\frac{\partial u}{\partial z} + \frac{\partial w}{\partial x})$$

$$-\rho\overline{u'T'} = -\Gamma_t\frac{\partial T}{\partial x} \qquad -\rho\overline{v'T'} = -\Gamma_t\frac{\partial T}{\partial y} \qquad -\rho\overline{w'T'} = -\Gamma_t\frac{\partial T}{\partial z}$$

$$(3A2.12)$$

In equations (3A2.12) μ_t is the turbulent (eddy) viscosity and k is the kinetic energy of turbulence, defined as:

$$k = \frac{1}{2}\left[\overline{(u'^2)} + \overline{(v'^2)} + \overline{(w'^2)}\right]$$

$$(3A2.13)$$

The turbulent diffusion coefficient Γ_t is given by:

$$\Gamma_t = \mu_t/\sigma_t$$

$$(3A2.14)$$

where σ_t is the turbulent Prandtl or Schmidt number.

In order to write the general transport equations for turbulent flow, two new coefficients are introduced; namely, the effective viscosity (μ_e) and the effective diffusion coefficient (Γ_e). These are defined as the sums of the laminar and turbulent components:

$$\mu_e = \mu + \mu_t \quad \Gamma_e = \Gamma + \Gamma_t$$

$$(3A2.15)$$

Thus, the transport equations for u, v, w and T are written:

x direction:

$$\frac{\partial}{\partial t}(\rho u) + \frac{\partial}{\partial x}(\rho uu) + \frac{\partial}{\partial y}(\rho uv) + \frac{\partial}{\partial z}(\rho uw)$$

$$= -\frac{\partial p}{\partial x} + \frac{\partial}{\partial x}(\mu_e\frac{\partial u}{\partial x}) + \frac{\partial}{\partial y}(\mu_e\frac{\partial u}{\partial y}) + \frac{\partial}{\partial z}(\mu_e\frac{\partial u}{\partial z})$$

$$(3A2.16)$$

$$+ \frac{\partial}{\partial x}(\mu_e\frac{\partial u}{\partial x}) + \frac{\partial}{\partial y}(\mu_e\frac{\partial v}{\partial x}) + \frac{\partial}{\partial z}(\mu_e\frac{\partial w}{\partial x})$$

y direction:

$$\frac{\partial}{\partial t}(\rho v) + \frac{\partial}{\partial x}(\rho u v) + \frac{\partial}{\partial y}(\rho v v) + \frac{\partial}{\partial z}(\rho v w)$$

$$= -\frac{\partial p}{\partial y} + \frac{\partial}{\partial x}(\mu_e \frac{\partial v}{\partial x}) + \frac{\partial}{\partial y}(\mu_e \frac{\partial v}{\partial y}) + \frac{\partial}{\partial z}(\mu_e \frac{\partial v}{\partial z})$$

$$+ \frac{\partial}{\partial x}(\mu_e \frac{\partial u}{\partial y}) + \frac{\partial}{\partial y}(\mu_e \frac{\partial v}{\partial y}) + \frac{\partial}{\partial z}(\mu_e \frac{\partial w}{\partial y}) - g(\rho - \rho_o)$$

(3A2.17)

z direction:

$$\frac{\partial}{\partial t}(\rho w) + \frac{\partial}{\partial x}(\rho u w) + \frac{\partial}{\partial y}(\rho v w) + \frac{\partial}{\partial z}(\rho w w)$$

$$= -\frac{\partial p}{\partial z} + \frac{\partial}{\partial x}(\mu_e \frac{\partial w}{\partial x}) + \frac{\partial}{\partial y}(\mu_e \frac{\partial w}{\partial y}) + \frac{\partial}{\partial z}(\mu_e \frac{\partial w}{\partial z})$$

(3A2.18)

$$+ \frac{\partial}{\partial x}(\mu_e \frac{\partial u}{\partial z}) + \frac{\partial}{\partial y}(\mu_e \frac{\partial v}{\partial z}) + \frac{\partial}{\partial z}(\mu_e \frac{\partial w}{\partial z})$$

In equations (3A2.16–3A2.18) the terms $2/3\rho k$ were neglected and $\mu_e \cong \mu_t$, since for turbulent flow $\mu \ll \mu_t$. The terms ρg_x and ρg_z were neglected. The term $-g(\rho - \rho_0)$ represents the buoyancy force in the *y* direction, with ρ_0 the air density at a reference temperature T_0.

The transport equation for temperature is:

$$\frac{\partial}{\partial t}(\rho T) + \frac{\partial}{\partial x}(\rho u T) + \frac{\partial}{\partial y}(\rho v T) + \frac{\partial}{\partial z}(\rho w T)$$

$$= \frac{\partial}{\partial x}(\Gamma_e \frac{\partial T}{\partial x}) + \frac{\partial}{\partial y}(\Gamma_e \frac{\partial T}{\partial y}) + \frac{\partial}{\partial z}(\Gamma_e \frac{\partial T}{\partial z}) + \frac{q}{C_p}$$

(3A2.19)

To solve the transport equations (3A2.16–3A2.19), two additional transport equations need to be introduced for the quantities μ_e and Γ_e. A number of turbulence models have been developed for this purpose. The most widely used of these is the k–ε model. This model has been applied with success to a wide range of flow problems and has lower computational demands than other existing models.

The k-ε *model*

This model introduces two transport equations for the kinetic energy, k, and its dissipation rate, ε. These two quantities, k and ε, are related as follows:

$$\varepsilon = \frac{C_\mu \rho k^{1.5}}{L} \tag{3A2.20}$$

where C_μ is a constant ($\cong 0.09$) and L is a length scale. The turbulence viscosity μ_t is given by the Kolmogorov–Prandtl equation:

$$\mu_t = \rho L \sqrt{k} \tag{3A2.21}$$

Combination of equations (3A2.20) and (3A2.21) gives:

$$\mu_t = \frac{C_\mu \rho k^2}{\varepsilon} \tag{3A2.22}$$

The two transport equations introduced by the k–ε model are:
For k:

$$\frac{\partial}{\partial t}(\rho k) + \frac{\partial}{\partial x}(\rho u k) + \frac{\partial}{\partial y}(\rho v k) + \frac{\partial}{\partial z}(\rho w k)$$

$$= \frac{\partial}{\partial x}(\Gamma_k \frac{\partial k}{\partial x}) + \frac{\partial}{\partial y}(\Gamma_k \frac{\partial k}{\partial y}) + \frac{\partial}{\partial z}(\Gamma_k \frac{\partial k}{\partial z})$$

$$+\mu_t \left\{ 2\left[\left(\frac{\partial u}{\partial x}\right)^2 + \left(\frac{\partial v}{\partial y}\right)^2 + \left(\frac{\partial w}{\partial z}\right)^2 \right] \right.$$

$$\left. + \left(\frac{\partial u}{\partial y} + \frac{\partial v}{\partial x}\right)^2 + \left(\frac{\partial u}{\partial z} + \frac{\partial w}{\partial x}\right)^2 + \left(\frac{\partial w}{\partial y} + \frac{\partial v}{\partial z}\right)^2 \right\}$$

$$+C_\mu \rho \frac{k^{1.5}}{L} + \beta g \frac{\mu_t}{\sigma_t} \frac{\partial T}{\partial y} \tag{3A2.23}$$

where $\Gamma_k = \mu_e/\sigma_k$ and $\sigma_k \cong 1$, and σ_t is the turbulent Prandtl or Schmidt number ranging from 0.5 to 0.9. The last term stands for buoyancy and β is the coefficient of volumetric expansion.

For ε:

$$\frac{\partial}{\partial t}(\rho\varepsilon) + \frac{\partial}{\partial x}(\rho u\varepsilon) + \frac{\partial}{\partial y}(\rho v\varepsilon) + \frac{\partial}{\partial z}(\rho w\varepsilon)$$

$$= \frac{\partial}{\partial x}(\Gamma_\varepsilon \frac{\partial\varepsilon}{\partial x}) + \frac{\partial}{\partial y}(\Gamma_\varepsilon \frac{\partial\varepsilon}{\partial y}) + \frac{\partial}{\partial z}(\Gamma_\varepsilon \frac{\partial\varepsilon}{\partial z})$$

$$+ C_1 \frac{\varepsilon}{k}\mu_t \left\{ 2\left[\left(\frac{\partial u}{\partial x}\right)^2 + \left(\frac{\partial v}{\partial y}\right)^2 + \left(\frac{\partial w}{\partial z}\right)^2 \right] \right. \tag{3A2.24}$$

$$\left. + \left(\frac{\partial u}{\partial y} + \frac{\partial v}{\partial x}\right)^2 + \left(\frac{\partial u}{\partial z} + \frac{\partial w}{\partial x}\right)^2 + \left(\frac{\partial w}{\partial y} + \frac{\partial v}{\partial z}\right)^2 \right\}$$

$$+ C_2\rho\frac{\varepsilon^2}{k} + C_1\beta g \frac{\varepsilon}{k}\Gamma_t \frac{\partial T}{\partial y}$$

where $G_e = m_e/s_e$ and s_e is equal to 1.22, $C_1 = 1.44$ and $C_2 = 1.92$.

Equations (3A2.23) and (3A2.24) are called 'closure' equations because they complete (close) the system of equations to be solved for the determination of the air velocity and temperature fields in the investigated space.

REFERENCES

1. BS 5925 (1980). Code of Practice for Design of Buildings: Ventilation principles and designing for natural ventilation. British Standards Institution, London.
2. *ASHRAE Fundamental Handbook* (1985). Ch. 22. Natural ventilation and infiltration. American Society of Heating, Refrigeration and Air-Conditioning Engineers, Atlanta, GA.
3. Aynsley, R.M., W. Melbourn and B.J. Vickery (1977). *Architectural Aerodynamics*. Applied Science Publishers, London.
4. De Gidds, W. and H. Phaff (1982). 'Ventilation Rates and Energy Consumption due to Open Windows'. *Air Infiltration Review*, Vol.4, No. 1, pp. 4–5.
5. IEA (1992). Annex 20: Airflow Patterns within Buildings – Airflow through Large Openings in Buildings. Energy Conservation in Buildings and Community Systems Programme, International Energy Agency, Paris.
6. Mayer, E. (1987). 'Physical Causes for Draft : Some New Findings'. *ASHRAE Transactions*, Vol. 93, Part 1.
7. Fanger, P.O., A. Melikov and H. Hanzawa (1988). 'Air Turbulence and Sensation of Draft'. *Energy and Buildings*, Vol. 21, No. 1.
8. Arens, E., D. Ballanti, C. Bennett, S. Guldman and B. White. (1989). 'Developing the San Francisco Wind Ordinance and its Guidelines for Compliance'. *Building and Environment*, Vol. 24, No. 4, pp. 297–303.

9. Ernest, D.R. (1991). 'Predicting Wind-Induced Air Motion, Occupant Comfort and Cooling Loads in Naturally Ventilated Buildings'. PhD Thesis, University of California at Berkeley.

10. Givonni, B. (1978). *L'Homme, l'Architecture et le Climat*. Eyrolles, Paris (French Edition).

11. Melaragno, M. (1982). *Wind in Architectural and Environmental Design*. Van Nostrand Reinhold, New York.

12. Centre Scientifique et Technique du Batiment (CSTB) (1992). *Guide sur la climatisation naturelle de l'habitat en climat tropical humide – Methodologie de prise en compte des parametres climatiques dans l' habitat et conseils pratiques*. Tome 1 (in French). CSTB, 4 Avenue du Recteur Poincaré, 75782 Paris Cedex 16, France.

13. Swami, M.V and Chandra S. (1988). 'Correlations for Pressure Distribution on Buildings and Calculation of Natural Ventilation Airflow'. *ASHRAE Transactions*, Vol. 94, Part 1, pp. 243–266.

14. Awbi, H.B. (1991). *Ventilation of Buildings*. Chapman & Hall, London.

15. Clarke, J., J. Hand and P. Strachan. (1990). ESP – A Building and Plant Energy Simulation System. ESRU Manual U90/1, Energy Stimulation Research Unit, Dept. of Mechanical Engineering, University of Strathclyde.

16. Grosso, M. (1992). 'Wind Pressure Distribution around Buildings: A Parametrical Model'. *Energy and Buildings*, Vol.18, pp. 101–131.

17. Hussein, M. and B.E. Lee (1980). 'An Investigation of Wind Forces on Three Dimensional Roughness Elements in a Simulated Atmospheric Boundary Layer'. BS 55. Department of Building Science, University of Sheffield, UK.

18. Akins, R.E. and J.E. Cermak. (1976). 'Wind Pressures on Buildings', CER76-77EA-JEC15. Fluid Dynamic and Diffusion Laboratory, Colorado State University, CO.

19. Feustel, H.E, F. Allard, V.B. Dorer, Garcia Rodriguez, M.K. Herrlin, L. Mingsheng, H.C. Phaff, Y. Utsumi and H. Yoshino (1990). 'Fundamentals of the Multizone Airflow Model - COMIS'. International Energy Agency, AIVC, Technical Note AIVC 29, Coventry, UK.

20. Clarke, J.A. (1985). *Energy Simulation in Building Design*. Adam Hilger Ltd., Bristol, UK.

21. Riffat, S.B. (1989). 'A Study of Heat and Mass Transfer through a Doorway in a Traditionally Built House'. *ASHRAE Transactions*, pp. 584–589.

22. Kiel, D.E. and D.J. Wilson. (1989). 'Combining Door Swing Pumping with Density Driven Flow'. *ASHRAE Transactions*, pp. 590–599.

23. Santamouris, M. (1992). 'Natural Convection Heat and Mass Transfer Through Large Openings'. Internal report, PASCAL Research Program, European Commission DGX11. Available from the author.

24. Pelletret, R., F. Allard, F. Haghighat and J. van der Maas (1991). 'Modeling of Large Openings'. *Proceedings of the 12th AIVC Conference, Canada*, AIVC, University of Warwick.

25. Limam, K., C. Innard and F. Allard. (1991). 'Etude Experimentale des Transferts de masse et de chaleur a travers les grandes ouvertures verticales'. *Conference Groupe d'Etude de la Ventilation et du Renouvellement d'Air, INSA, Lyon*, pp.98–111.

26. Darliel, S.B. and G.F. Lane-Serff (1991). 'The Hydraulics of Doorway Exchange Flows'. *Building and Environment*, Vol. 26, No. 2, pp. 121–135.

27. Khodr Mneimne, H. (1990). 'Transferts Thermo-aerouliques entre Pieces à travers les grandes ouvertures'. PhD Thesis, Nice University.

28. Dascalaki E. and M. Santamouris. (1995). Manual of PASSPORT-AIR, Final Report, PASCOOL Research Program, European Commission, DGXII.

29. Walton, G.N. (1988). 'AIRNET, A Computer Program for Building Air Flow Network Modeling'. NISTR, 89-4072, National Institute of Standards and Technology.
30. Dascalaki E., P. Droutsa and M. Santamouris (1992). 'Interzonal Comparison of Five Multizone Airflow Prediction Tools'. MDS PASCOOL Meeting 22–24 May, Florence, Italy.
31. BRE (1992). Manual of Breeze. Building Research Establishment, Garston, Watford, UK.
32. Dascalaki, E., M. Santamouris, A. Argiriou, C. Helmis, D.N. Asimakopoulos, C. Papadopoulos and A. Soilemes (1995). 'Predicting Single Sided Natural Ventilation Rates in Buildings'. *International Journal of Solar Energy*, Vol. 55, No. 5, pp. 327–341.
33. Liddament, M.W. (1986). *IEA, Air infiltration calculation techniques - an applications guide*. Air Infiltration and Ventilation Centre (AIVC), University of Warwick.
34. Allard, F. (ed.) (1995). Zonal Modeling for Natural Ventilation, PASCOOL, Research Project, Ventilation-Thermal Mass Subtask Final Report, Ch. 7, EC DGXII.
35. Anderson, J.D. (1995), *Computational Fluid Dynamics – The Basics with Applications*. McGraw-Hill International Editions, Mechanical Engineering Series, New York.
36. Schaelin, A., J. van der Maas and A. Moser (1992). 'Simulation of airflow through large openings in buildings'. *ASHRAE Transactions*, Vol. 98, Part 2.
37. Rosten, H.I. and D.B. Spalding (1987). 'The PHOENICS reference manual for version 1.4'. Report No. TR/200, CHAM Ltd, London.
38. Mahajan, B.M. (1987). 'Measurement of Interzonal Heat and Mass Transfer by Natural Convection'. *Solar Energy*, Vol. 38, pp 437–446.
39. Chandra, S, P.W. Fairey and M.M. Houston (1986). 'Cooling with Ventilation'. SERI/SP-273-2966, DE86010701. Solar Energy Research Institute, 1617 Cole Boulevard, Golden, CO 80401-3393, USA.
40. Chandra S, P.W. Fairey and M.M. Houston (1983). 'A Handbook for Designing Ventilated Buildings'. Florida Solar Energy Centre, Final Report, FSEC - CR - 93-83, 300 State Road 401, Cape Canaveral, FL 32920, USA.
41. Lee, B.E , M. Hussain and B. Soliman (1980). 'Predicting Natural Ventilation Forces upon Low-Rise Buildings'. *ASHRAE Journal*, February.
42. Vickery, B. J. and R.E. Baddour (1983). 'A study of the External Pressure Distributions and Induced Internal Ventilation Flows in Low Rise Industrial and Domestic Structures'. University of Western Ontario, Boundary Layer Wind Tunnel Laboratory Report No BLWT-SS2-1983.
43. Cermak, J.E et al. (1981). 'Passive and Hybrid Cooling Developments: Natural Ventilation – A Wind Tunnel Study'. Colorado State University, Fluid Mechanics and Wind Engineering Program Report No CER81-82JEC-JAP-55A-MP24.
44. ASHRAE (1991). *Handbook of Fundamentals*. ASHRAE, Atlanta, GA.
45. Santamouris, M. (1994). *NORMA, A Tool for Passive Cooling*. Edited and published by the University College Dublin for the Zephyr Architectural Competition, European Commission, Directorate General for Research and Development.
46. Grosso, M. (1995). 'Manual of CpCalc⁺', Final Report, PASCOOL Research Program, European Commission, DGXII.

4
_____

Diagnostic techniques

Edited by P. Wouters

4.1   CONTEXT OF DIAGNOSTIC TECHNIQUES

To judge the performance of a building, a system or a particular technology,
we need a set of evaluation tools: diagnostic techniques. In the case of buildings
conceived for passive ventilation, such diagnostic techniques aim to obtain a
good understanding of the physical behaviour of the building and/or the
appreciation of its users.

Diagnostic techniques can be applied in different situations:

- in existing buildings before retrofitting, the main aim being to obtain
  a better understanding of the building performances;
- in new or retrofitted buildings, the typical aim being to evaluate to what
  extent the building functions as predicted.

Diagnostic techniques are not meant for the purpose of validation of models.
More detailed, well controlled and prepared experiments are needed for this goal.

Different levels of diagnostic techniques can be imagined. The information
in this chapter is limited to basic diagnostics and detailed studies are not
reported here. The overall context for diagnostic studies on buildings with
natural ventilation is shown in Figure 4.1.

4.2   OBJECTIVES OF DIAGNOSTIC STUDIES

Diagnostic studies may be exclusively focused on natural ventilation, but often
include other aspects as well.

There may be several reasons for carrying out diagnostic studies:

- To evaluate the performances of a range of buildings during summer.
  The sample will then be either the complete building set or a

_____
Main contributors: P. Wouters, L. Vandaele and D. Ducarme

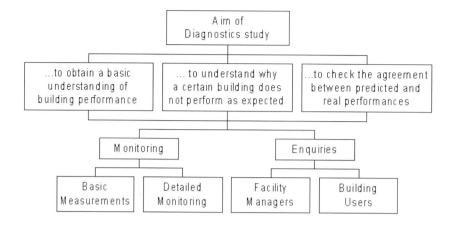

Figure 4.1. Overall context for diagnostic studies on buildings with natural ventilation

representative sample of the population of buildings. Physical parameters can be included, as well as users' views.

- To evaluate a specific building to obtain a better understanding of its performance without any specific aim of solving or improving certain aspects of the building.
- To evaluate a specific problem building with the aim of obtaining good indications of how to improve the building's performance.

The cost and complexity of a diagnostic study will (or, at least, should) vary as a function of the objectives of the study. In all cases, a distinction can be made between physical measurements ('monitoring') and information collection from the occupants and building managers ('enquiries'). This chapter is not intended to deal with the detailed monitoring activities or to go into detail about enquiry studies. The key objectives are:

- to give an overview of typical monitoring possibilities;
- to give an indication of the possibilities and potential problems of the various measurements;
- to give some hints about a correct interpretation of the monitored data.

4.3   PHYSICAL PARAMETERS AND MONITORING EQUIPMENT

4.3.1   Temperature recordings

An evaluation of the temperatures in passively ventilated buildings is an essential measurement for assessing the level of thermal comfort reached in such buildings under varying climatic conditions.

*Figure 4.2. Stand-alone temperature
recorder*

The equipment requirements for this type of measurement include:

- good measurement accuracy (of the order of 1°C);
- easy to install, preferably with no wiring;
- relatively cheap;
- the possibility of recording over a period of several weeks with a measurement frequency of at least once an hour.

Several measurement systems are available on the market. An example of stand-alone equipment with a single temperature measurement per unit is shown in Figure 4.2. Other data loggers exist which simultaneously record measurements from several sensors to which they are connected. A significant inconvenience of such systems is the need for wiring inside the building.

The use of reliable and practical data loggers is an essential requirement; it is also important that these sensors be installed correctly. This may appear to be self-evident, but it is not. Sensor locations should be identified which do not hinder users, while, at the same time, giving representative temperatures. This means that:

- the sensor should not be exposed to direct solar radiation;
- during the heating season, the location should not be too affected by the heating system (i.e. a sensor should not be sited above a radiator).

In case of studies on night-time ventilation, one may be interested in the difference between the air temperatures and the surface temperatures of walls and floors. An example of such temperature measurements is given in Figure 4.3, which shows that the air and wall temperatures are not homogeneous and that a single recording of air and wall temperature is not necessarily a reliable

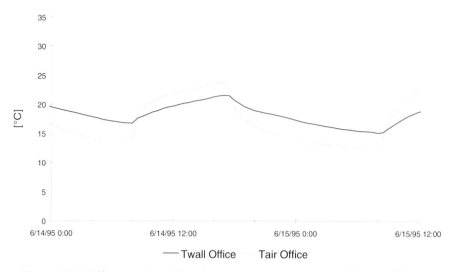

Figure 4.3. Differences in wall and air temperatures measured in an office room

indication of the temperature difference. Installing more sensors is recommended but not always obvious.

4.3.2   Ventilation measurements

A reasonable-to-good understanding of the airflow processes in the building is very important in the evaluation of passive ventilation concepts [1]. Unfortunately, the available monitoring techniques are often expensive and are difficult to apply in occupied buildings. In the context of this chapter, three techniques are presented (Figure 4.4)

All measurement techniques are based on the monitoring of the concentration of a certain gas (the 'tracer' gas).

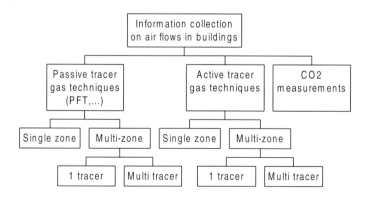

Figure 4.4. Methods for collecting information on ventilation

For practical purposes, the methods can be subdivided in three groups [2]:

- *Active tracer gas measurements*, requiring the injection of a tracer gas. In most cases, the tracer gas concentration is continuously monitored with a gas analyser. Sometimes, the injection rate of the tracer gas must also be monitored continuously.
- *Passive tracer gas measurements*, in which a tracer gas is injected by a continuous passive release at a more or less constant rate. Only the average concentration over the measurement period is determined.
- *CO_2 measurement technique*, based on the monitoring of the CO_2 concentration with the occupants in the space as the only (or at least the main) source for release of CO_2.

4.3.2.1 Active tracer gas techniques
The measurement of the airflow rate into and out of a space involves the release and the monitoring of a tracer gas (SF_6, N_2O, etc.) within the enclosure.

The general mass balance equation of this tracer gas is:

$$V \frac{dC}{dt} = Q[C_e - C] + F \tag{4.1}$$

where V is the effective volume of the enclosure (m^3), Q is the specific airflow rate through the enclosure ($m^3 s^{-1}$), C_e is the external tracer gas concentration ($m^3 m^{-3}$), C is the internal concentration of tracer gas ($m^3 m^{-3}$) and F is the production of tracer gas by all sources in the enclosure ($m^3 s^{-1}$). (See Figure 4.5.)

Tracer gas methods use this equation to derive the airflow rate from the monitored data. Various techniques are used depending on the way the tracer is injected. Table 4.1 gives an overview of the three main techniques.

All techniques require the pseudo-continuous measurement of the tracer gas concentration in the investigated space. The minimum monitoring frequency depends on the technique employed and on the experimental conditions (air change rate, etc.) but generally one concentration measurement is taken every 1 to 30 minutes.

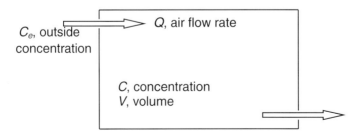

Figure 4.5. Measurement of the airflow rate in an enclosure using active tracer gas techniques

Table 4.1. Overview of various techniques for active tracer gas measurement of ventilation rate

	Tracer injection	Result
Concentration decay	One-time injection. The amount of tracer injected must not be known	Average air change rate during the measurement period (typically 30 min–2 h)
Constant emission rate	Continuous injection at a known rate	Continuous airflow rate
Constant concentration	Continuous injection controlled to maintain a defined tracer concentration in the space	Continuous airflow rate

CONCENTRATION DECAY METHOD

This method involves the release of a tracer gas before the measurement period and no injection of tracer gas ($F = 0$) during the measurement period. In the event that the airflow rate Q is constant during the measurement period, equation (4.1) yields:

$$C = C_0 \exp(-\frac{Q}{V}t) = C_0 \exp(-Nt) \qquad (4.2)$$

where t is the time (s), C_0 is the tracer gas concentration at time $= 0$, and N ($= Q/V$) is the air change rate (s^{-1}).

The air change rate (N) can be easily derived from the monitored concentrations using equation (4.2).

CONSTANT INJECTION METHOD

The tracer gas is injected at a known constant rate in the investigated space and the time varying concentration response is recorded. This method allows us to calculate the airflow rate for each measured concentration from equation (4.1).

CONSTANT CONCENTRATION METHOD

This method is aimed at adapting the injection rate of tracer gas in order to keep the tracer gas concentration constant in the measured spaces. This technique is the most complicated and requires an accurate measurement of the injection rate of tracer gas and an intelligent algorithm for controlling the injection rate of tracer gas.

The idea behind the constant concentration method is to hide interzonal flows. This allows measurement of the outside airflow rates into several spaces using a single tracer gas. This technique is also useful for measurements in occupied buildings, because the tracer gas concentration is pre-set and therefore there is no risk of exceeding the maximal acceptable concentration level for health safety.

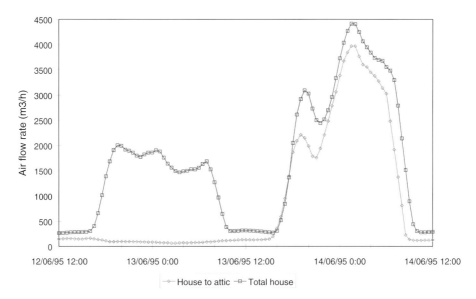

Figure 4.6. Results of tracer gas measurements in a row (terraced) house with night-time ventilation applied

Using the monitored injection rate and tracer gas concentration, equation (4.1) yields the airflow rate for each data point.

MULTITRACER GAS TECHNIQUE
A further distinction can be made between so-called single-zone ventilation measurements and multizone measurements. In the latter case, there is not only air exchange with outside but in most cases also airflows between the different zones. The use of several tracer gases can allow the determination, with rather good accuracy, of all airflow rates between the different zones.

An example of active tracer gas measurements in summertime, using the constant concentration technique, is given in Figure 4.6. The figure shows measurements in a row (also called terraced) house where night-time ventilation for cooling is applied. Very large differences between daytime and night-time airflow rates can be observed.

The use of active tracer gas measurements is not often seen in practice: the equipment is very expensive (up to 50,000 ECU for a commercial system), gas bottles have to be used, together with a lot of tubing, etc. In general, this type of technique is not applicable for the first stage of a diagnostic study, but is more applicable for detailed studies.

4.3.2.2 Passive tracer gas methods
Passive tracer gas techniques also make use of the injection of a tracer gas, but the hardware aspects are completely different from those used with an active tracer gas.

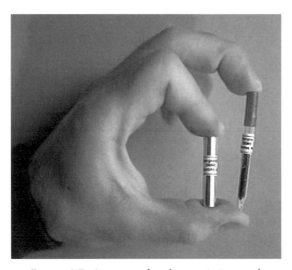

Figure 4.7. An example of an emission and absorption set for passive tracer gas measurements

Perfluorocarbon tracers (PFT) are released at a constant rate by diffusion from liquid tracer compound in miniature containers. Air sampling is also done passively by diffusion into an adsorbent of activated charcoal contained in a narrow glass tube.

Various concepts of passive tracer gas measurements have been developed by various organizations. In principle, passive tracer gas methods are very appropriate for diagnostic studies; they are very easy to install, they provide reasonable measurement accuracy in many circumstances, and the cost is reasonable. The monitoring campaign starts with the distribution of passive gas sources (Figure 4.7) in the building to be investigated where they will be left for a period ranging from a few days to several weeks. The samplers are then collected and analysed by gas chromatography in a specialized laboratory. This measurement technique gives an estimation of the average air change rate during the whole measurement period. In the case of night-time ventilation, very large variations in the air change rate may occur and this can result in large measurement errors. Moreover, no information on the variation in air change rate will be collected.

4.3.2.3 CO_2 recordings

All persons emit a certain amount of CO_2 as a result of their metabolism. A typical value is 18 litre h^{-1} per person. The CO_2 emission is not constant but depends on the type of person and on the activity level. An example of CO_2 measurements recorded in a dwelling is given in Figure 4.8.

There are situations for which the recording of the CO_2 concentrations can give useful information on the order of magnitude of the air change rates:

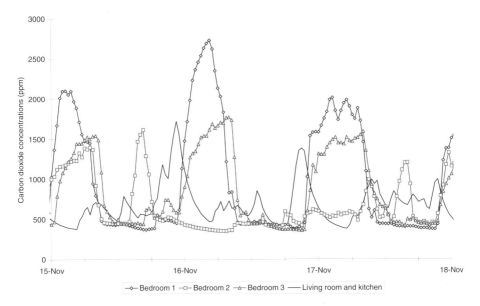

Figure 4.8. Measured CO$_2$ concentrations in a dwelling

- In cases where the number of occupants in the space is known (classrooms, auditoria, theatre, offices): knowing the number of people allows analysis of the measured concentration in the same way as a constant injection measurement;
- In periods with no occupancy, but following a period of rather intensive occupation: the monitored concentrations can be analysed in the same way as for a decay method (no injection of tracer gas during the monitoring period).

The advantage of the CO$_2$ technique is the rather simple equipment required for the monitoring: a CO$_2$ analyser and preferably a recorder. However, there are several constraints:

- the number of occupants must be known approximately;
- in the case of night-time ventilation without occupancy, the CO$_2$ concentration will very quickly drop to zero and measurements are only possible during the first hour(s) of non-occupancy.

4.3.3   Air velocity measurements

Intensive ventilation is often used as part of a passive cooling strategy. This can increase the risk of creating draught problems. Measurement of the air velocity at representative locations may be appropriate. An example of such measurement is given in Figure 4.9 overleaf.

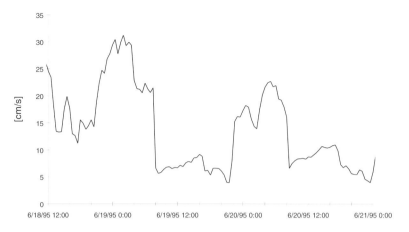

Figure 4.9. Results of airflow measurements in a dwelling with night-time ventilation

4.3.4   External climate

The measurement of external temperature and solar radiation can give very relevant information. The temperature recordings can be done using the same equipment as for indoor measurements (Section 4.3.1).

Specific attention is needed with respect to the protection of the sensors from solar radiation. Measurement errors of the order of 5–10°C may occur if the sensor is not protected from direct solar radiation. To reduce the measurement error, the sensors can be installed at a shaded location with no direct solar radiation, or can be protected with an appropriate shielding device. In the latter case, the inner part of the shield must be sufficiently ventilated. The better method uses a ventilated air temperature sensor [3]; see Figure 4.10.

Figure 4.10. Ventilated air temperature sensor

Figure 4.11. ESTI reference sensor for solar radiation

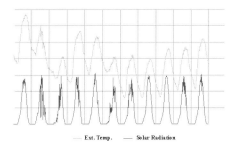

— Ext. Temp.   — Solar Radiation

Figure 4.12. Example of recording of external temperature and solar radiation

For the measurement of solar radiation, classical solarimeters (pyranometers) can be used but these are very expensive (more than 1000 ECU). An attractive alternative is the use of the ESTI [4] reference sensor, which consists of a calibrated photovoltaic cell (Figure 4.11).

As result of such monitoring, data sets are obtained which indicate the variation in time and space of the variables (Figure 4.12).

4.3.5   Enquiries

Physical measurements are important to obtain a good understanding of the functioning of a building. In addition, enquiries can also give very reliable information on how the building is operated and especially on how the occupants appreciate the indoor climate. Such enquiries can be carried out in different ways:

- by more or less random oral discussions with the building users and building operators, querying their appreciation of the functioning of the building. A simple checklist with indications of points of concern can be of help . The information given in Chapter 5 regarding critical barriers, as well as the case studies, can be very useful to the interviewers;
- in the form of structured oral discussions based on a pre-defined questionnaire. Such an approach was used in the EC JOULE project NATVENT™ [5];
- in the form of structured written interviews.

Permission to carry out such enquiries in non-domestic buildings may require some discussion.

4.4   INTERPRETATION OF THE DIAGNOSTIC RESULTS

The outcome of both physical measurements and enquiries is a large amount of data. The analysis can include various aspects. In this report four levels of analysis are briefly described:

- evaluation of the indoor climate condition;
- evaluation of the energy performances;
- evaluation of whether the building performs as predicted in the design phase;
- evaluation of possibilities for improving the building's performance.

EVALUATION OF THE INDOOR CLIMATE CONDITIONS

The physical measurements regarding temperature, parameters related to air quality and airflow rates allow comparison of the recorded values with reference values (from standards, building regulations) used for the assessment of thermal comfort, indoor air quality, ventilation requirements, etc. Large variations exist in the methods used for assessing thermal comfort.

Adding information obtained from enquiries or interviews allows one to obtain not only a quantitative assessment of the indoor climate, but also a qualitative indication of the user's satisfaction. Therefore, a combination of physical measurements and enquiries/interviews is an attractive approach.

EVALUATION OF THE ENERGY PERFORMANCES

The evaluation of the energy performance can be interesting, e.g. for comparing the annual energy data with existing databases. Such analysis is not straightforward if the monitoring period is relatively short (not more than a few weeks). Relevant data can only be obtained by combining the monitored data with some numerical work. Such an approach requires reliable models and appropriate user skills.

The importance of the natural ventilation design and operation is often not the dominant parameter in the energy consumption and, as a result, it is not possible to draw valid conclusions from such analysis with respect to the natural ventilation performance.

EVALUATION OF WHETHER THE BUILDING PERFORMS AS PREDICTED IN THE DESIGN PHASE

Monitoring of buildings can be done to check the performance of buildings with specific reference to natural ventilation. Experience shows that important differences can occur between the predicted and the measured performances. The reasons can be multiple: differences in climatic data, uncertainty in input data (e.g. wind pressure coefficients, uncertainty of thermal mass, building use, window use), measurement errors. Therefore, one should be very careful when interpreting the results and drawing conclusions.

A distinction should be made between the evaluation of the predicted performances regarding the natural ventilation and the predicted performances regarding the indoor climate and the energy use. For the latter parameter, ventilation is only one of the influencing parameters. Hence, a reliable analysis requires the analysis of a whole range of variables, including thermal insulation, solar gains, shading performances and internal gains.

In all cases, the analysis of the operation of the building should be an important aspect of such an evaluation. One often observes strong differences between the assumed operation of a building (especially in case of manual control by the users) and the real operation.

EVALUATION OF POSSIBILITIES FOR IMPROVING THE BUILDING'S PERFORMANCE

Monitoring of building performances can indicate that the indoor climate and/or energy performances are unacceptable or that there is room for improvement. Deriving reliable indications regarding the ways of achieving the required improvements from monitoring results is not evident. However, some small-scale tests (e.g. applying single-sided night ventilation in one office, external solar shading) may give useful indications. Comparing the monitored performances in adjacent rooms, with and without the improvements, may be helpful as well.

However, natural ventilation is only one out of a whole range of means for achieving/improving the thermal comfort in summer conditions. Often solutions can be found by using other improvements, e.g. improved solar shading, lowering internal gains, intelligent artificial lighting, general operation mode of the building.

4.5   CONCLUSIONS

1 The monitoring of the performances of existing buildings can be done in various ways and these can range from very simple temperature measurements or a few discussions with the users to very heavy monitoring campaigns involving multi-tracer gas measurements and extensive enquiries.

2 This chapter has only given a brief overview of the type of monitoring techniques. Especially for airflow-related measurements that make use of the tracer gas technique, the reader must be aware that this is a relatively complicated technology requiring expert knowledge in order to obtain the correct interpretation.

3 The analysis and interpretation of the information obtained from diagnostic techniques can cover a wide range of aspects. Depending on the complexity of the building, the type of analysis can range from relatively straightforward to very complex.

REFERENCES

1. Liddament, M. (1996). *A Guide to Energy Efficient Ventilation*. Air Infiltration and Ventilation Centre, Coventry, UK.
2. Roulet, C.-A. and L.Vandaele. (1991). 'Air flow patterns within buildings – measurement techniques'. Technical Note AIVC 34, Air Infiltration and Ventilation Centre, Coventry,UK.

3. Vandaele, L. and P. Wouters. (1994). The Passys Services. Summary Report of the PASSYS Project. European Commission, Belgian Building Research Institute.
4. ESTI sensor, calibrated photovoltaic cell of European Solar Test Installation, European Commission, Joint Research Centre, Institute of Advanced Materials, I-21020 Ispra (Va), Italy.
5. NATVENT™, Overcoming technical barriers to low energy natural ventilation in office-type buildings in moderate and cold climates. EC JOULE Project (1996–1998), led by Building Research Establishment, Garston, UK.

5

Critical barriers

Edited by E. Maldonado

5.1   INTRODUCTION

Natural ventilation can play a decisive and important role in the control of indoor air quality and indoor temperature in summer, contributing to the prevention of overheating when an adequate ventilation strategy is adopted. However, a successful application of natural ventilation strategies is only possible when there are no problems in many areas that are unrelated to thermal performance, at various levels from the design stage to actual operating demands placed on the building users (Figure 5.1). These potential barriers are discussed in the following sections.

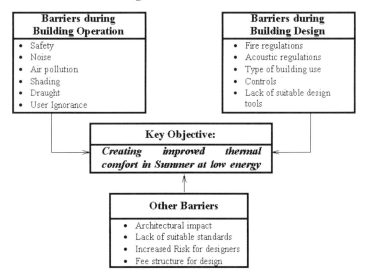

Figure 5.1. Overview of potential barriers to the application of natural ventilation in buildings

Main contributors: E. Maldonado, G. Guarracino, L. Vandaele and D. Ducarme

5.1.1   Barriers during building operations

There are many problems of user acceptability that may prevent building occupants from implementing natural ventilation in a building, even if the building was designed and prepared so that it would provide natural ventilation, which is not always the case. The most important barriers are the following:

- *Safety* concerns, i.e. preventing unauthorized entry of other people, of animals, including bugs and insects or, simply, preventing rain from damaging the furnishings.
- *Noise* from outdoors, which may interfere with normal activities and sleep or simply be unpleasant.
- *Air pollution* that must be kept out of the building, from urban pollution to dust in the countryside, from harmful chemicals to simply bad odours.
- *Shading* for solar control, or simply for privacy considerations, that may require partial or total covering of the openings provided in the outer envelope for natural ventilation.
- *Draught prevention*, stemming from comfort or from work requirements (e.g. to keep papers in place).
- Last but not the least, *ignorance on the part of the occupants* about the correct strategies that should be adopted to take the best advantage of natural ventilation.

5.1.2   Barriers during building design

Designers also face a host of objective and subjective barriers that may simply lead them not even to foresee opportunities for providing natural ventilation or, at the very least, not to count on existing opportunities for that purpose. The most important objective obstacles that designers face are the following:

- *Regulations* in general and *fire regulations* in particular, which may prevent the free flow of air to prevent smoke or odour propagation; *acoustic regulations* may also pose some restrictions, especially in noisy urban areas.
- The *pattern of use* foreseen for the building, which may be incompatible with using natural ventilation strategies appropriately, i.e. having the occupants operating suitable openings at the most appropriate times, as well as doubts designers may have about the ability of the occupants to choose suitable strategies for each operating mode.
- The need to provide *shading*, *privacy* and *daylighting*, which may require devices or solutions that seriously hamper the free flow of air.
- The unwillingness of the owner or promoter to adopt more or less sophisticated *automatic controls* that could overcome some of these

latter barriers by introducing appropriate automatic routines to optimize the operation of the building at each moment, independently of direct occupant involvement.

- The *lack of suitable, reliable design tools*, which also introduces an added degree of difficulty to the implementation of a control strategy incorporating natural ventilation.

5.1.3   Other barriers

There are other more subtle types of barrier, subjective in nature, but nevertheless posing very real obstacles to the implementation of a natural ventilation strategy in a building:

- Natural ventilation requires designing a suitable envelope, which influences *architecture* and may sometimes be incompatible with the overall design concept.
- Natural ventilation involves *acceptance of a certain degree of fluctuation of the indoor conditions*, which could be a risk for a designer, who may be held liable by a dissatisfied customer. A fully controlled, easier-to-design mechanical ventilation solution that will minimize the risk of complaints and reduce designer liability may be a safer and more common solution. The *lack of suitable regulations* does not provide the designers with the protection they have when they adopt more conventional design approaches.
- Designing a naturally ventilated building requires more work than a conventional mechanically ventilated alternative. Yet, as the naturally ventilated building is usually less costly to build than the normally mechanically cooled alternative with oversized systems, the *fee* received by the designer of the mechanical systems, normally a fixed percentage of a system's cost, is smaller. This is certainly a strong disincentive for the designer to pursue a riskier course of action.

5.1.4   Possible ways around the barriers

All these barriers have appropriate solutions and ways of getting around them, but these may not always be acceptable to everyone and for every case. Each type of barrier is discussed in the following sections and solutions are identified, with advantages and disadvantages listed. It would seem, however, that the provision of natural ventilation requires the simultaneous concurrence of two things:

- First, building designers must provide the occupants with the possibility of implementing natural ventilation when desirable (either automatically, if management control systems exist, or manually otherwise); in doing so, designers must think about all the barriers that they face in their job and those that the building occupants will later face as regular users, and find appropriate solutions for each one of them. A single unsolved problem will result in little chance of natural ventilation ever being used or, at the very least, that it will be used infrequently.

- Second, the occupant must know how to use natural ventilation and to be aware of its advantages, as well as accepting any minor inconveniences that may come along. If occupants wish to have a foolproof system that requires no interaction and is always able to create indoor conditions close to the ideal set by current ISO comfort standards [1], then natural ventilation will certainly not be the most suitable solution for them.

This shows that naturally ventilated buildings face many hurdles and that they will be the exception rather than the rule as long as most of these barriers are not overcome with good, inexpensive, common solutions. This text aims to guide designers in the search for good alternatives, as good as the current state of the art allows. Research is continuing on this topic and the interested reader should try to remain updated with the latest progress, which may be pertinent to the task at hand.

5.2   TYPES OF BARRIERS AND POSSIBLE SOLUTIONS

5.2.1   Safety

One of the most important concerns for a building occupant is safety against unauthorized intrusion. This means that any openings in the envelope must be protected to hinder intrusion, especially in the lower floors of buildings where access is easier. Typical solutions may be limiting the maximum size of the openings to the size of a child's head (15 cm) or protecting the openings with bars with a spacing not exceeding the same distance (Figure 5.2).

Not only people, but also other types of animals can enter a house through openings intended for natural ventilation: mice, cats, dogs, etc. on the lower floors, plus birds on the upper floors. Moreover, insects (bugs, mosquitoes, etc.) can enter through any opening, no matter how high or how small it may be. Thus screens may be needed to overcome this problem. Window frames with easy-to-operate screens already incorporated as an option or ventilation grilles with insect screens incorporated, readily available in many markets, may be an easy and convenient solution to this problem.

The smaller size of openings suitable for preventing intruders may cause limitations to the intensity of natural ventilation, while bars or screens are objectionable to many people if placed over windows intended for daylight and for visual contact with the outside, as well as representing an added cost. They also constitute an additional resistance to airflow that influences the intensity of natural ventilation. Moreover, bars also eliminate an alternative

Figure 5.2. Protection bars on windows can be made attractive, rather than like a prison

escape route for emergencies (e.g. as a fire escape), which may require compensating solutions imposed by applicable regulations.

Rain is also a problem. The openings in the building envelope for natural ventilation will also allow rain to enter the building if they are not closed prior to the onset of rainy periods. To prevent the damage caused by rain, openings must be manually controlled by the occupants or some kind of automatic control system must be implemented. Manual control also requires the presence of people inside the building, meaning that, during occupant absence, openings will probably stay closed for safety reasons and ventilation will be limited to infiltration, which may be at a sufficient rate for indoor air quality (IAQ) control but at an insufficient rate for summer cooling. Indeed, as night ventilation is often the chosen operating mode for providing natural cooling in summer in naturally ventilated buildings, this barrier may play a decisive role unless automatic controls are provided.

To solve these problems, alternative solutions are possible. For example, there are special windows with incorporated self-controlled openings for natural ventilation already available on the market for IAQ control (Figure 5.3), especially in winter, and similar units, with larger openings, could be developed for natural ventilation control. It is also possible to uncouple windows (for daylight and vision) from openings for natural ventilation that are well protected against intrusion, insects and rain and can be closed with an insulated shutter (Figure 5.4). Research is also continuing to produce better units and further attenuate this type of barrier [2].

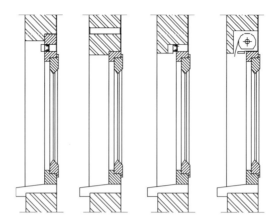

Figure 5.3. Windows with self-controlled openings for natural ventilation

Figure 5.4. Uncoupled window and ventilation grille at the BBRI building, Belgium

5.2.2   Noise

Practically all intrusive noise in a building is undesirable, whether it comes from outdoors or from other rooms in the same building. Normally, noise originating from either outdoors or other spaces in the building itself is attenuated by the physical boundaries of the room (e.g. walls and doors) and, then, whatever is transmitted is further attenuated by multiple reflections inside the room. In a naturally ventilated building, where there must be openings in the envelope to allow for airflow and indoor barriers to airflow should be as small as possible, there is less attenuation by the boundaries and problems of excessive noise transmission may arise. Traffic noise can be of particular concern and there are regulations that require minimum levels of noise attenuation for each façade in most countries (e.g. 65–70 dBA in France).

Special openings with noise-reducing baffles have been under development to overcome this difficulty, in a similar fashion to those shown in Figure 5.3 for low airflow rates. However, the noise reducing mechanisms usually involve significant resistance to airflow and a careful balance between the two opposing effects must be sought.

It should be noted, however, that mechanically ventilated buildings are not noise-free. Mechanical systems produce noise in fans and motors and this often propagates through the structural elements of the building. Aerodynamic noise produced by the movement of air in the ducts, grilles, diffusers, etc. is also transmitted into the room. These types of noise can of course be minimized through good design, including, for example, selection of low-noise equipment, installation of anti-vibration mounts for motors and fans, insertion of flexible joints between machinery and ducts, the lining of ducts with noise-absorbing materials, installation of noise attenuators where appropriate, the provision of smooth bends, the insertion of turbulence reducing vanes where sharp curves must occur, and making smooth changes between duct sections in the ductwork. These techniques can be effective in reducing most of the noise, but there is always a background noise level remaining.

Thus both naturally and mechanically ventilated buildings pose problems of noise control, which must be carefully assessed by the design teams. A naturally ventilated building, under the right circumstances, may not be noisier than the conventional mechanically ventilated alternative.

5.2.3   Air pollution

In suburbs or rural areas, concentrations of pollutants in the outdoor air do not usually reach high levels. Thus, in most cases, outdoor air entering an interior space does not cause problems of indoor air quality and natural ventilation is an acceptable passive cooling strategy in such areas. Dust or foul smells may nevertheless occur sometimes and these must be carefully evaluated on a case-by-case basis. Controls are always necessary to allow occupants to stop natural ventilation when outdoor pollution reaches undesirable levels, even in normally unpolluted areas.

Conversely, pollution of outdoor air in urban areas is a frequent and normally rather intense phenomenon, as very high concentrations of various pollutants are observed, mainly during the daytime. Consequently, outdoor air entering a zone may give rise to serious indoor air quality problems. In the majority of cases, the indoor concentrations of various contaminants will reach relatively high levels, resulting in poor indoor air quality, harmful not only for the occupants but for the building materials and the furnishings as well.

Obviously, natural ventilation is not recommended in polluted urban areas, especially during the daytime, nor in rural areas where dust or foul smells are frequent.

In order to illustrate the impact of natural ventilation upon indoor air quality in a polluted city centre, simulations were performed for a building under design, comparing indoor air quality levels for mechanically and naturally ventilated alternatives. The building is for the New Acropolis Museum, to be located in the centre of Athens, Greece. The volume of the exhibition hall was considered as a single, well-mixed zone with a volume of 127,000 m^3. Simulations were performed for five common contaminants in urban environments (NO, NO_2, SO_2, O_3 and CO_2).

The mechanical ventilation system is shown in Figure 5.5. There is no stratification and the recirculation factor is 0.7. It is also assumed that the system is well balanced, i.e. the supply airflow rate is the same as the return airflow rate and the ventilation efficiency is 1 (i.e. no direct bypass). The filters absorb the contaminants through chemical reaction (e.g. with activated carbon) with an efficiency that is assumed constant at 97.5%, a little better than stated by international regulations, which only recommend filter efficiencies greater than 85% for museums [3]. The outdoor airflow rate is assumed to be 8 litre s^{-1} per person, as also recommended by international standards [3].

In the natural ventilation alternative, there are of course no provisions for filtering of the incoming outdoor air and there is no recirculation either. In both cases, there is no generation of pollutants indoors except for CO_2 generated by people inside the museum.

The indoor concentration of each of these pollutants was calculated during a typical day of museum operation (8 a.m. to 6 p.m.) in summer (May–October) for three levels of outdoor pollution (low, medium and high pollution

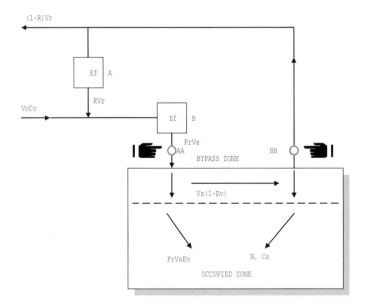

Figure 5.5. General model of ventilation system for the Acropolis Museum

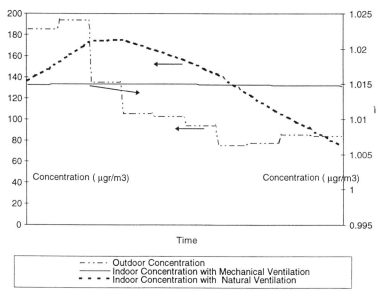

Figure 5.6. Variation of outdoor and indoor concentrations of SO₂
for high outdoor pollution, for a naturally and a mechanically
ventilated building

outdoors). The concentrations of all pollutants show the same trend. Thus, only the results for SO_2 are shown, as an example, in Figure 5.6. This figure shows that the indoor concentrations of SO_2 follow the variation of the outdoor concentration with a time lag of few hours. In all cases of mechanical ventilation, the indoor concentration is kept under the standard level of 10 $\mu g\ m^{-3}$ needed for preservation of exhibits throughout the day. Conversely, in all cases of natural ventilation, the indoor concentration is above that same level. In cases of heavy and medium outdoor pollution, the indoor concentration is above the standard level required for reasons of occupant health, set by ASHRAE at 80 $\mu g\ m^{-3}$ for exposure of one year. The maximum limit of 365 $\mu g\ m^{-3}$ proposed by ASHRAE for one hour's exposure is however never exceeded, meaning that visitors should not be much affected by this level of pollution. Conversely, the museum staff may suffer some deleterious effects after long periods of exposure.

For other contaminants, the conclusions are similar, though with nuances regarding the actual levels of contaminants relative to the maximum concentrations allowed by the existing standards. In one case (CO_2), the maximum levels allowed are never exceeded, while in most others (NO_2, NO, O_3) they are often exceeded in the naturally ventilated alternative.

These results clearly demonstrate that natural ventilation in urban polluted areas may cause significant indoor air quality problems. Thus, in these cases, mechanical and chemical filtering may be required and natural ventilation may be a difficult option to implement.

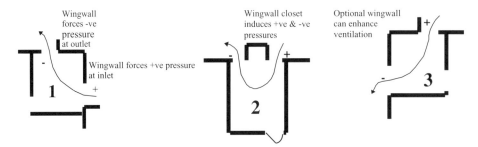

Figure 5.7. Use of outside fins to enhance natural ventilation and provide shading

5.2.4   Shading

When natural ventilation is needed during the daytime hours in clear days in summer, load-avoidance techniques require blocking of direct solar gain to avoid indoor overheating. In some cases, shading of all the openings may also be required. Privacy considerations may also dictate some means to block direct visual contact between indoors and outdoors. However, any obstructions, either external (overhangs, fins, roller shades, etc.) or internal (curtains, shades, etc.), may also represent a serious obstacle for airflow. In naturally ventilated buildings, designs must specify shading devices that, while serving their purpose (shading or privacy protection), will still allow for enough airflow, taking into account the direction of prevailing winds during the periods when conflicts may occur.

In some cases, outdoor fixed shading devices, such as vertical fins or horizontal slabs, may even be quite useful in creating larger pressure differences on the outer envelope of the building, thus creating the possibility of intensifying natural ventilation, particularly for single-sided schemes – see Figure 5.7 [4]. In these cases, shading and natural ventilation may actually coexist and lead to the same architectural solutions for the building envelope.

5.2.5   Draught

Naturally ventilated buildings must provide enough air exchange under a large variety of outdoor and indoor conditions, from favourable to very unfavourable conditions (e.g. low wind speeds, small temperature differences, etc.). Under these latter circumstances, relatively large openings may be required. Thus, unless automatic controls are provided (see Section 5.2.8), it is impossible for occupants to respond to the normal rapid fluctuations in outdoor conditions and act to limit large air exchange rates alternating with smaller ones. Even with automatic controls, the system may not be able to cope with very fast changes in outdoor conditions.

When the air exchange is large enough, air velocities indoors may become larger than desired and cause uncomfortable or simply undesirable draughts. If they are strong enough, draughts may even move papers and other light

 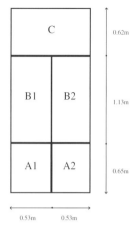

Figure 5.8. Window with multiple openings to allow control of natural ventilation at the National Observatory of Athens, Greece

objects from their desired positions, something that is usually unacceptable, both in residences and in offices. Thus, designers must provide the means to avoid draughts when the occupants so wish but, at the same time, still provide enough air exchange. This is an exercise in compromise and careful design, requiring some experience and knowledge of physics on the part of the designer. A typical solution in traditional buildings is the use of windows with multiple openings, i.e. windows that can be opened only partially according to variable geometry (see Figure 5.8).

5.2.6   User ignorance and patterns of use

Natural ventilation can take place for various reasons: to control overheating, to promote comfort (ventilative body cooling) or to improve indoor air quality. This means that it must take place under very precise conditions: either when the outdoor air is cooler than the indoor air (to cool the temperature indoors); or when the indoor temperature becomes too hot and higher air velocities are needed, even if outdoor temperatures are higher than those indoors; or simply when the indoor air quality is unacceptable, no matter what the conditions may be outdoors, cold or warm.

This means that the onset and end of natural ventilation should be controlled, meaning either occupant intervention or some form of automatic system. When human intervention is needed, it is necessary that occupants are willing to perform the needed tasks. It is also necessary that the activities performed indoors be compatible with either higher air velocities typical of intensive natural ventilation or that the air exchange rates can be controlled in such a way that the air velocity stays within acceptable levels.

Controlling natural ventilation requires opening and closing windows, doors or specific openings in response to changes in the indoor and outdoor conditions. As wind direction and intensity change, the most effective pattern of window openings may also vary. For example, the window shown in Figure 5.8 can be used for cross ventilation with increasing intensities of air exchange with increased area of opening, or it can be used for single-sided ventilation using the stack effect by opening a portion in the lower zone and another in the upper zone. Knowing which portions of the window to open and which to keep closed requires some experience that the occupants may not always possess.

Experience with thousands of passive solar buildings shows that only simple solutions work, except when occupants are specialists and, even then, only for short periods as they usually lose interest as time goes by. Complex patterns of window openings cannot be relied upon. Designers must produce buildings that are simple and intuitive to operate, suitable for the 'man in the street'. Otherwise, the possibility of adopting automatic controls must be seriously considered (see Section 5.2.8).

5.2.7   Building regulations

5.2.7.1   Introduction
An important boundary condition for the application of natural ventilation in buildings as a passive cooling strategy is the link with building regulations. They can play two major roles:

- Regulations can be a support for applying a particular technique, natural ventilation concepts in this case; if appropriate regulations do not exist, their absence, just by itself, is an important barrier to implementation of natural ventilation.
- Regulations can also be an important barrier by imposing specific requirements, e.g. fire safety and acoustics.

These barriers will be discussed next.

5.2.7.2   Absence of technical regulations
There are very few regulations that address the topic of natural ventilation. In the framework of the European Standards Organization (CEN), only one working item (WI 38) has been identified for the calculation of temperatures in summer: 'Internal temperatures in summer in a room without mechanical cooling – General criteria and calculation procedures'. The standard in preparation (prEN ISO 13791) describes the minimum requirements for dynamic simulation programmes. It also gives a few test cases. Each simulation tool must be checked against these test cases.

The modelling of ventilation is very briefly described in the proposed standard (§4.4.6). In an informative annexe H, formulae are given for natural ventilation, including airflow through large openings.

At the national level, there are no examples of significant regulations specifically dealing with natural ventilation. The reason for this absence is, no doubt, the technical complexity of the topic. Night cooling, the major

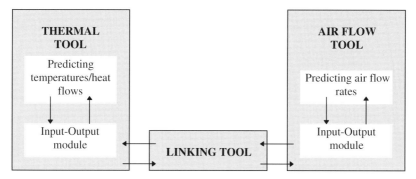

Figure 5.9. Combining thermal and airflow models

technique of interest, requires a knowledge of airflows in the different spaces of a building. These airflows depend on parameters that are very difficult to quantify, e.g. leakage distribution in the building envelope, internal and external temperatures, wind velocity and wind direction. The latter two, to compound the problem, may fluctuate rapidly, causing immediate changes in airflows. All these parameters are required inputs for codes that are able to calculate airflows and thermal energy balances, which interact with each other, making this a rather complex topic to study. This is illustrated in Figure 5.9. At present, most software tools are limited to just one part of the problem; airflow problems can be solved with programs such as COMIS or PASSPORT-AIR [5], and thermal modelling is solved with programs such as TRNSYS and DOE-2. ESP-r is capable of solving both problems in the same simulation environment. However, the use of these tools as reference tools for checking building regulations is not an evident option.

There are, however, a few national codes that favour the adoption of natural ventilation solutions in buildings insofar as they demand lower energy consumption and implementation of natural ventilation as one of the means for reaching that goal. One example is the Dutch Energy Performance Norm. This applies to domestic and non-domestic buildings and focuses on the overall energy consumption of the building. This integrated performance approach is very interesting as it stimulates the design of good buildings and related systems. Since the energy consumption for cooling is included in the evaluation of the overall energy use of the building, passive ventilation as a strategy for cooling may be a favourable strategy for meeting the global criterion of maximal energy use.

The Swiss building regulations, in the most important cantons, also favour natural ventilation for cooling since the use of air conditioning is severely restricted: obtaining a permit to install air conditioning requires that designers show that it is really unavoidable and that there are no other low-energy-consuming alternatives that will produce comfortable ambient conditions inside the building.

However, these are just special situations, not common in most countries, and political will is necessary to implement such demanding regulations elsewhere. Climatic conditions may also be more demanding in other regions with warmer climates (e.g. the southern European countries), rendering such a limitation impossible to implement except in selected cases.

5.2.7.3 Fire regulations

The concept of passive ventilation is often based on the use of large open windows and chimneys for natural ventilation. This requires the highest degree of free flow of air. Conversely, fire regulations are made to ensure the safety of the occupants and to provide assistance to fire fighters. Since air movement by ventilation is an important means of fire propagation inside a building, it follows that a building concept based on intensive ventilation for cooling must take into account these increased risks of fire spread. Permanent openings in the façades for air intake and large chimneys for air exhaust, with transfer openings between the two systems, may represent a severe problem.

Although fire regulations may differ strongly from country to country, and even within each country, depending on the personal interpretation of the local chiefs of the fire brigades, there are some general rules that must be addressed:

- *Requirements at the façade level.* External walls of a building are required to resist the spread of fire over their surfaces and from one building to another. Fire spread usually occurs through openings in the external walls, called 'unprotected areas' in the British Building Regulations. Air intake devices such as grilles, louvres, operable windows, etc. are classified as such 'unprotected areas', increasing the risk of fire spread. Therefore, they must be lockable in case of fire to prevent fresh oxygen from being supplied to fuel the fire, like, for example, the thermally-fused fire dampers that are inserted in the duct systems in HVAC systems. Moreover, in closed position, these devices must not decrease the fire resistance performance of the façade or wall of which they are a part .
- *Requirements regarding zoning.* In case of fire, and in order to limit the spread of the fire through the whole building, many fire regulations are based on the concept of zoning and subdividing the building into fire-resisting compartments. The idea is to isolate the fire for a certain time (for example, from 30 minutes to a few hours) at the source in order to allow the safe evacuation of the remainder of the building and to minimize fire damage. For example, the Belgian fire regulations (1 December 1996) establish requirements as a function of the height of the building (the lowest requirements for buildings of less than 10 m and the highest requirements for buildings taller than 25 m).

It is, of course, possible to design naturally ventilated buildings that meet these stringent requirements. For example, the IVEG building, in Belgium, is a three-storey naturally ventilated building less than 10 m tall where fire regulations require a minimum of two zones. Therefore, the designers decided to separate

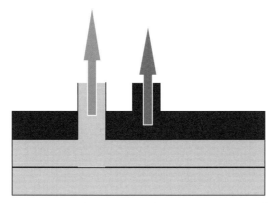

*Figure 5.10. The concept of a two-zone, naturally
ventilated building that meets fire regulations*

the upper floor from the lower two floors, as illustrated in Figure 5.10. The
implementation of night ventilation is thus independently controlled for each
of the two zones.

5.2.7.4 *Acoustic regulations*

Most acoustic regulations establish requirements for sound attenuation between indoors and outdoors. As already discussed in Section 5.2.2, openings
in the envelope for natural ventilation are clear paths for noise to enter a
building. Wherever applicable, thus, openings must have noise attenuators or
special locations to meet those requirements.

5.2.7.5 *Conclusions*

Barriers imposed by existing fire and acoustic regulations pose serious constraints that must be carefully addressed. There are technical solutions to meet
the requirements, both at the component and at the conceptual design levels,
but this integration requires a special effort by designers.

The complexity associated with the physical modelling of natural ventilation, requiring interaction between airflow and thermal models, coupled to the
rapidly varying nature of the driving mechanisms of natural ventilation, make
it very unlikely that performance standards will soon become available to help
designers in their task of designing naturally ventilated buildings. Attention is
being devoted to the topic in CEN and in various European countries, but the
level of scientific development in the area does not allow any reason for
optimism in the medium term.

5.2.8   Controls

5.2.8.1 *Introduction*

As explained in previous chapters, natural ventilation induced airflows depend
on wind pressures and temperature differences. These are, of course, not

constant in time and, as a result, airflows in buildings vary over a large range and can possibly even become uncomfortable, e.g. when winds are strong, if openings are maintained at a constant position during the day. Some kind of control is therefore necessary in order to adjust window openings, vents, etc. according to indoor requirements (air quality, thermal comfort, etc.). Control can be either manual or automatic. Both have advantages and drawbacks that will be discussed in the following paragraphs.

Other problems that also have to be solved by control techniques when natural ventilation is implemented are as follows:

- How can airflow intensity and direction be controlled in the whole building? This is especially a problem when the building has internal partitions.
- How can the risk of draught be avoided and the stability of the controlled equipment (operation of the window or the vents) ensured?
- How can incoming fresh air be preheated in winter or precooled in summer?
- How can the use of natural ventilation be integrated with auxiliary cooling or heating systems?
- How can rain be prevented from penetrating through ventilation openings?

All these topics will also be discussed in the following sections. Practical solutions to some of the critical barriers will be discussed at the end.

5.2.8.2 Automatic or manual control?

Selecting the right control strategy for natural ventilation is a difficult task. The final choice depends on many independent parameters such as the type of building (home, office, public building, etc.), the other parameters and equipment controlled (heating, cooling, etc.), the building architecture (internal partitions), the capability of the occupants to choose the most appropriate actions and to implement them at the best times, and, of course, total cost.

An automatic control system is composed of one or more sensors to measure the parameters required for the implementation of any control strategy, e.g. indoor and outdoor temperatures, CO_2 (or air-quality) sensors, wind velocity and direction and rain detectors; one or more actuators to operate the openings (windows or grilles); and a controller/supervisor, to instruct the actuators based on programmed algorithms and in response to the measurements [6]. An effective automatic control system is difficult to design and implement and, of course, relatively expensive.

Manual control requires only actuators or human intervention, i.e., having the building occupants operate windows, vents, doors, etc. at any time and at any desired position. The resulting control strategy is therefore based on purely subjective criteria, such as indoor air quality perception and/or thermal comfort sensation. Occupants usually accept wider comfort bands when they can have control of their environment [7]. An example is the combined management of shading devices and natural ventilation. Occupants will set priorities and decide whether opening the windows is more important than closing the blinds or not, according to their personal feelings. Therefore, from a psychological point of view, pure manual control can be considered the most suitable type of control. Besides, manual control is cheap and easy to implement.

However, this does not mean that manual control is the most efficient solution to natural ventilation control. Relying on occupant behaviour will not always result in improved comfort levels [8], nor in energy savings. As an example, for the control of shading devices and vents in a sunspace, simulations have shown that manual control could result in severe discomfort (indoor temperatures up to 5°C higher) and/or increased energy consumption when compared to the same space automatically controlled [9]. Generally speaking, manual control cannot be used as an effective global control strategy, even if the occupants are knowledgeable and able to choose the best possible courses of action demanded by each situation. Although this is not a major problem in small and low-rise buildings (such as homes), it can be the source of major problems in high-rise buildings such as offices or public buildings, where the complexity increases substantially. For example, in case of fire, there are no means to close the vents that could cause serious problems. On the other hand, in most buildings, occupants will keep openings closed at night; building safety will thus be satisfied, but night cooling will become impossible.

Another major problem is also found in spaces with more than one occupant. Who will be in charge of controlling the equipment and according to which criteria?

Automatic control is a way to overcome these difficulties. But, as occupants like to keep control of their environment, if an automatic control strategy is ever to be selected, it may be desirable to provide a manual override whenever possible. These types of systems are thus expensive and technically complex.

5.2.8.3 Synthesis

In order to summarize the advantages and drawbacks of both manual and automatic control options, Table 5.1 lists the impact of the control mode on various parameters and for various types of buildings. A minus sign (−) indicates a negative aspect of the considered control mode on the specific criterion, while a plus sign (+) indicates a positive aspect. This table shows that automatic control will usually not be well suited to homes, but will in most cases be appropriate in public buildings and offices.

Moreover, researchers in the UK have proposed selecting the type of control to be used according to maximum heat gains in the room [10]. Their conclusion was that, below 25 W m^{-2}, manual control was satisfactory, while automatic control could be used with internal heat gains up to 40 W m^{-2}. They also agreed that, in public buildings, automatic control was more suitable.

Table 5.1. Comparison between automatic and manual control

Criterion	Home		Office		Public building	
	Automatic	Manual	Automatic	Manual	Automatic	Manual
Cost	− −	++	−	++	−	++
Impact on occupant;	+	−	+	−	+	−
draught risk psychology	−	+	−	(−)*	+	−
Impact on air quality and thermal comfort	++	+	++	+	++	−
Impact on fire safety	0	0	+	−	+	−
Impact on people and building safety	−	−	−	−	−	− −
	+†	+†	+†	+†	+†	+†
Impact on noise	− −	−	− −	−	− −	−
Effect of outdoor pollution	+	−	+	−	+	−

*If more than one occupant in the same office   †If night cooling is not implemented

5.2.9   Lack of suitable design tools

During the design process, proposed architectural and engineering solutions must be evaluated to check how they perform under normal and extreme conditions. For this task, designers need to have at their disposal the best tools available. Tools must be accurate and reliable, providing objective assessments of each possible solution. Ideally, they should also allow sensitivity studies on the main parameters so as to allow a search for the optimum solution.

Natural ventilation has been an area where reliable tools have been conspicuously scarce. The highly variable character of the mechanisms that cause natural ventilation, namely the wind, makes simulations very difficult and complex. Interaction with thermal aspects – see Section 5.2.7.2 – further complicates modelling this phenomenon. There are a few tools that are able to predict average conditions under precise wind and temperature conditions, but they are not able to simulate natural ventilation as it constantly fluctuates in real time in response to changes in wind direction and intensity. Moreover, to study fully how a building behaves, it would be necessary to simulate a large number of conditions (wind direction and intensity as well as indoor–outdoor temperature differences), and natural ventilation rates will cover a large range of conditions. There will be cases when natural ventilation is satisfactory, others when it is insufficient and others where it may be excessive. This range of solutions will require flexible controls for natural ventilation, with the possibility of changing the locations and areas of the active openings for each situation.

To perform all the tasks described in the previous sections, there are no user-friendly design tools. The tools that are available require a reasonable degree of user training and a good ability to interpret the results. Thus, most designers will not feel too comfortable using them and may even feel distrustful and confused by the often contradictory recommendations for different wind patterns. This difficulty is a major obstacle to the adoption of solutions based on natural ventilation, as only expert designers or consultants will be able to advise the architect on the best solutions to be implemented. This difficulty still has to be overcome with the development of new software packages.

5.2.10 Architectural impact

Naturally ventilated buildings may need special features, e.g. windows and openings strategically placed in the envelope, draft-enhancing chimneys in the roof, envelopes designed with features such as extensions or fins to augment pressure differentials on the various windows, specially designed windows for manual or automatic control of natural ventilation (Figures 5.3, 5.4 and 5.8), etc. Although, in most cases, natural ventilation can be implemented in buildings that look perfectly conventional, with no distinctive features, as demonstrated by the vast majority of naturally ventilated buildings in southern European countries, there are some examples of buildings that incorporate more advanced features and may have an appearance that may look out of the ordinary to many people. Examples of such cases are shown in Figures 5.11 and 5.12.

The integration of the components required for natural ventilation are the ultimate responsibility of the architect, whose ability is critical for the quality of the final design. In many cases, the designer, the building owner or both, may find the aesthetics of the building objectionable or, at least, not the solution that they would prefer and natural ventilation may be discarded as an option. Of course, this is not an exclusive problem of natural ventilation; it is just one item among many that contribute to defining the final design for a building. It is not a problem that should be hidden, but it should be realized that there are acceptable solutions to every problem.

Figure 5.11. The Wood Green Community Mental Health Centre, UK (MacCormac Jamieson Prichard, Architect)

*Figure 5.12. The new office building for the
UK Parliament (Michael Hopkins, architect)*

5.2.11   Increased risk for designers

The different barriers to implementation of natural ventilation as the main (or sole) operation strategy for a building, namely the uncertainty about the ability to be able to control the indoor environment to give ideal conditions under many circumstances, certainly means that there is a risk of the building owners and users being dissatisfied. In extreme cases, litigation may ensue, even if the options are explained and accepted beforehand, thus raising the possibility of liability. Certainly, the easiest and most comfortable solution for the designer is to opt for a conventional mechanical ventilation scheme, where all the variables can be controlled by well established principles that, if applied well, will, in the end, produce a risk-free product that will guarantee customer satisfaction. Running costs for the building will be higher, but most building owners will not even complain because they lack the knowledge to realize this.

So, in accepting this risk, the designer must have other forms of compensation. Money is not usually the reason (see Section 5.2.12). Satisfaction from a job well done, of accepting a challenge and succeeding, could be a reason. By using natural ventilation, the designer produces a more environmentally friendly building, with a lower energy consumption and, thus, a lower running cost. On a life-cycle basis, the natural ventilation alternative is usually less expensive and, thus, must be considered by designers and not used only if some insurmountable barrier is identified (and, of course, there are many possibilities for that to happen, as described in this chapter).

5.2.12   Fee structure for design

Building designers usually receive a fee based on a percentage of the cost of the building, or of the systems they design for a building (e.g. mechanical systems, electrical and lighting systems, structural design, etc.). This type of fee schedule is not very encouraging when a search for a less costly solution to a problem is required, as more work is needed and, in the end, the designer's fee may even be reduced. Even if the building cost is about the same and the architect's fee remains unchanged, the engineering fees will certainly often be reduced. The honesty and the ethics of the designer are the only guarantees that the search for the best solution will indeed be performed.

Naturally ventilated solutions are just one more example of how a designer will have to do significantly more work to produce a good design and, on the basis of the same fee structure, get paid less for the job. This fact, combined with an increased risk of liability, as discussed in the previous section, results in a serious disincentive.

To overcome this, designers of naturally ventilated buildings can agree with the building owner or promoter a fixed fee that is based on time really spent in developing the solution and producing the design, or on what they would receive for designing the conventional mechanically ventilated alternative or some other equivalent amount. This requires a change in mentality, although nothing that has not already been done quite often in many cases by consultants in design firms.

5.3   CONCLUSIONS

The list of barriers to the implementation of natural ventilation schemes is impressive and somewhat discouraging. There are so many barriers that one has to wonder how natural ventilation is still used in any building. However, although the percentage of new or retrofitted buildings with mechanical ventilation is ever increasing, the vast majority of the existing building stock is still naturally ventilated. Indeed, all the barriers that have been identified and discussed also have solutions. They are merely difficulties to solve, not impossibilities. The skill and technical knowledge of good designers is usually adequate to get around them and find solutions that will work.

Occupants of naturally ventilated buildings are usually happier with their indoor environments than when they have little control over them. Running costs are lower and first costs are also usually lower. So, there is every reason to expect that natural ventilation will continue to be a viable alternative, and designers, building owners, promoters and occupants alike should merely consider these barriers as challenges to be overcome, just like many others that always occur in every new building design.

REFERENCES

1. ISO Standard 7730-1993. Moderate Thermal Environments.
2. Kolokotroni, M., V. Kukadia and E. Perera (1996). European Project on Overcoming Technical Barriers to Low-Energy Natural Ventilation'. *Proceedings of the CIBSE/ASHRAE Joint National Conference, Harrogate, UK, September 1996.* Vol. 1, pp. 36–41.
3. ASHRAE Standard 62-1989. Ventilation for Indoor Air Quality. ASHRAE, Atlanta, USA.
4. Chandra, S., P. Fairey and M. Houston. (1986). *Cooling with Ventilation.* Solar Energy Research Institute, Boulder, CO.
5. Dascalaki, E., M. Santamouris and F. Allard. (1995). 'PASSPORT-AIR, a Network Air Ventilation Tool'. In *Proceedings of the Passive Cooling Workshop*, ed. M. Santamouris, pp. 183–192. University of Athens.
6. Levermore, G. J. (1989). *Staff Reaction to Building Energy Management Systems.* BSRIA, Bracknell, UK.
7. Baker, N. and M. Standeven (eds.). (1995). 'PASCOOL – Comfort Group – Final Report'. European Commission, Brussels.
8. Kelly, K., M. Brien and R. Stemp. (1993). 'Occupant Use of Ventilation Controls and Humidifiers during Cold Seasons', O. Seppänen (ed.), *Proceedings of Indoor Air 93*, Vol. 5, pp. 69–72, Helsinki University of Technology.
9. Bruant, M., G. Guarracino, P. Michel, M. Santamouris and A. Voeltzel. (1996). 'Impact of a Global Control of Bioclimatic Buildings in terms of Energy Consumption and Buildings' Performance'. *Proceedings of the Fourth European Conference on Architecture, Berlin*, pp. 537–540. H.S. Stephens & Associates, Bedford, UK.
10. Martin, A. J. (1995). *Control of Natural Ventilation.* Technical Note TN11/95, BSRIA, Bracknell, UK.

6

Design guidelines and technical solutions for natural ventilation

Edited by C. Priolo

The effectiveness of natural ventilation, i.e. its ability to ensure indoor air quality and passive cooling in a building, depends greatly on the design process.

Mechanical ventilation systems can be designed separately from the design of the buildings in which they are installed; they can also be installed in existing buildings after a few modifications. In contrast, ventilation systems using only natural forces such as wind and thermal buoyancy need to be designed together with the building, since the building itself and its components are the elements that can reduce or increase air movement as well as influence the air content (dust, pollution, etc.).

Architects and engineers need to acquire qualitative and quantitative information about the interactions between building characteristics and natural ventilation in order to design buildings and systems consistent with a passive low-energy approach. Qualitative information includes design context background, design concepts and design criteria; quantitative information includes calculation techniques for defining climate parameters, sizing openings and estimating airflow rate, and evaluation methods so that proper technologies can be chosen.

This chapter gives the basic information needed by a building designer in order to implement natural ventilation concepts and techniques, as well as examples of technical solutions implementing natural ventilation strategies. References to other chapters of the book are made to link the physical fundamentals and theoretical models of ventilation to building design practice.

6.1   DESIGN GUIDELINES

Design guidelines and criteria for natural ventilation include recommendations and rules of thumb on:

Main contributors: M. Grosso, S. Sciuto, C. Priolo, G. Guarracino and M. Bruant

- *site design* aspects regarding the location, orientation and layout of buildings as well as landscaping;
- *design programme* aspects related to indoor air quality and ventilative cooling requirements;
- *building design* aspects related to the building form, the vertical and plan distribution of spaces, and the location and sizing of openings;
- *opening design* aspects concerning the selection of the types of opening and screen, as well as their operational features.

6.1.1   Site design

The following main objectives should be taken into account when selecting and designing the site for a building project suitable for natural ventilation:

- the best exploitation of the airflow pattern due to topography and surrounding buildings, in order to increase the potential ventilation rate within the interior spaces;
- the best compromise between summer and winter comfort conditions;
- the avoidance of permanent unwanted wind sheltering situations;
- the avoidance of discomfort due to outdoor conditions or caused by high wind velocities;
- the avoidance of airflow paths transporting dust and pollutants.

The location, layout, general form and orientation of the buildings, as well as landscaping of the site, are the principal aspects to be considered.

6.1.1.1 Building location and layout

If the site is *not in an urban area*, a building should be located in a way that takes advantage of local gradient winds. In mountain and hill sites, the best location is generally at the middle of a slope along the contour lines (Figure 6.1). In this position, temperate slope winds can drive cross ventilation through the shortest section of the building. A down-valley location would expose the

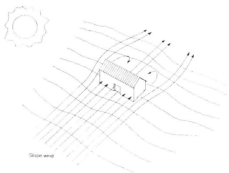

Figure 6.1. The best location for a building on a hill site

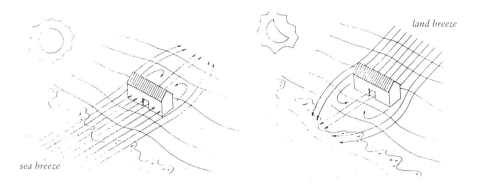

Figure 6.2. The best location for a building on a site near a shore

building to colder and damper winds. A ridge location would expose the building to much higher wind velocities.

Similarly, by the sea, a lake or a large river, a building should be positioned fairly close to the shore and with the longitudinal axis parallel to the line of the coast or the bank in order to make use of day water and night land breezes (Figure 6.2). However, constraints posed by danger of flooding, as well as environment and wildlife protection regulations, should take priority over natural ventilation criteria when a building near a shore line is designed.

If a building is designed for an urban site, its location should be at a distance from other buildings that is greater than the depth of their wake so that they will not shelter it from summer winds. If this is not possible, the building should be positioned randomly with regard to the upwind buildings and with its longitudinal axis perpendicular to the prevalent summer wind direction in order to catch the streamline flow. If the prevailing winter wind direction is different from the summer one, as is usually the case, it is possible to optimize the location of the building in order to obtain a good summer wind exposure while sheltering the building from cold winter winds (Figure 6.3).

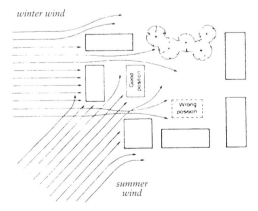

Figure 6.3. Examples of good and bad locations of a building on an urban site, with respect to wind

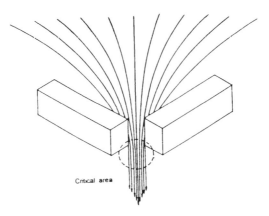

*Figure 6.4. Critical positions for pedestrian
discomfort due to wind on an urban site*

In very dense urban areas, spaces most needing ventilation should be put on the highest floors where wind flow is stronger and less turbulent than near the ground. Narrow passageways, corners of buildings too close together and arcades that go from side to side of the building should be avoided in order not to expose pedestrians to gusty acceleration of the airflow due to the Venturi effect (Figure 6.4).

When a project involves a compound with several buildings, as far as possible their *layout* should satisfy the criterion of avoiding a wake interference flow regime (see Chapter 2) in the prevailing summer wind direction in order to allow each building to be exposed to relatively streamline airflow when needed. However, the best compromise should be chosen with consideration of the winter period, during which opposite, sheltered conditions are required.

A scattered pattern layout is more appropriate to an optimum use of air movement within the buildings than a normal pattern layout, because the configuration provides less sheltering from the wakes. A similar effect can be obtained with a normal layout pattern, but with the buildings slanted with respect to the normal grid (Figure 6.5).

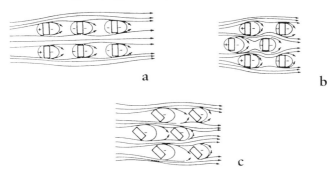

*Figure 6.5. Airflow patterns through (a) a normal,
(b) a scattered and (c) a diagonal layout of buildings*

When the density and configuration of the surrounding buildings do not allow for a proper wind exposure, a building should be designed to be high enough to overcome the wind sheltering obstructions, subject to considerations related to other requirements and building regulations.

6.1.1.2 Building form and orientation
The size of the wake, especially its depth, is not only influential on the ventilation of buildings located downwind, but is also directly related to the potential of air movement through the building itself. The deeper and higher the wake, the higher is the pressure differential across the structure and, therefore, the higher the airflow rate.

The shape and dimensions of a wake depend on the form and orientation of the building that generates it. The actual dimensions of the building are relatively unimportant, since the proportions of the building form determine the size and nature of the air movement pattern. A comprehensive wind-tunnel analysis on building models of various forms – square, rectangular, L-shaped, U-shaped, T-shaped – was carried out by Boutet [1]. From this study, the relative dimensions of the wake downwind of a building can be derived in relation to the building's size and orientation.

6.1.1.3 Landscaping design
Landscaping has an important function in controlling the air movement around buildings for optimum natural ventilation. The type and layout of vegetation to be included in a site plan should be chosen with the airflow pattern taken into account (see Chapter 2), as well as aesthetic and environmental considerations.

The main functions of vegetation as far as air movement is concerned are: *wind sheltering*; *wind deflection*; *funnelling and acceleration of air*; *air conditioning*.

Areas of calm around a building can be required both to reduce undesirable airflow, as in winter, and to create suction zones for outlet openings. If a sheltered area is desired, it is recommended that the landscaping be designed to allow for reduced air velocities without large scale turbulence. To achieve this, windbreaks should be at least 35% porous [2]. A windbreak is most effective when the building to be protected is located within a distance of 1.5 to 5 times the height of the windbreak.

Dense hedges can be placed near a building to create positive and negative pressure zones in order to enhance the airflow through the building. Although less efficient than solid wingwalls in producing an increase of the pressure differential, hedges can be more cost effective and have a more pleasant appearance. Their position (Figure 6.6), and their distance from the opening (Figure 6.7, left) have to be properly chosen since they affect the airflow pattern through the building interior.

When the placement of trees on a site is being designed, their distance from buildings should be determined in relation to the area of the wake as well as

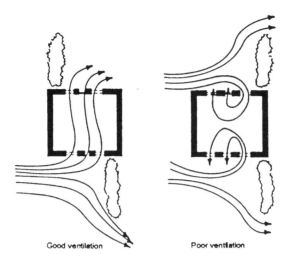

Good ventilation   Poor ventilation

Figure 6.6. The effect of hedge positioning on the airflow pattern through a building, in the case of wind parallel to the wall containing windows (a similar pattern can be foreseen for a wind direction with an incidence angle of 30°) [3]

to the cross-sectional airflow pattern, which is characterized by the proportion between canopy and stem. A high-stem tree with a large base canopy, such as a horse chestnut tree, would decrease the air velocity at canopy level within a large area downstream while letting through the airflow and accelerating it near the ground. This could affect the vertical displacement of the indoor airflow in relation to the position of the openings (Figure 6.7, right).

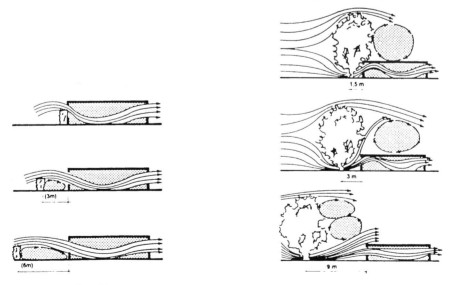

Figure 6.7. The effect of a hedge (left) and a tree with large base canopy (right) on the airflow pattern through a building in relation to their distance from the windward opening [3]

Rows of trees and hedges can be placed to direct air towards or away from a building (Figure 6.8). Vegetation can create areas of higher wind velocities by deflecting winds or funnelling air through a narrow passage (Venturi effect) (Figure 6.9). Reducing the spacing of the trees used to funnel air can increase the airflow up to 25% above that of the upwind velocity [2]. A similar effect occurs at the side edge of a windbreak.

The zones of accelerated airflow are the zones where the highest negative pressures and, therefore, the highest suction effects occur. This should be taken into account when designing the openings on the walls facing those areas. Only outlet openings are appropriate in those walls.

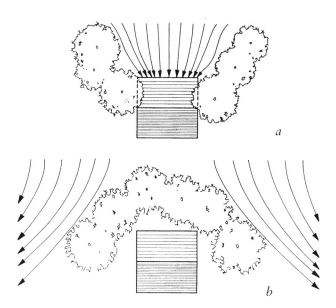

Figure 6.8. Funnelling of air to direct air (a) towards (b) or away from a building

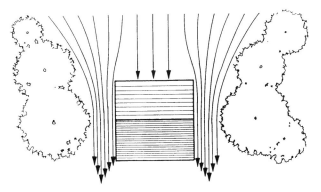

Figure 6.9. Narrowing of spacing between windbreaks and a building to accelerate the airflow

Not only the air movement, but also the *quality of air*, is affected by vegetation. As air travels beneath canopies of vegetation, especially trees, it is conditioned with respect to both psychometric and environmental characteristics.

Through the effects of shading and transpiration, the heat content of the ambient air crossing a vegetation barrier decreases, while the humidity of the air increases. This process induces an air cooling effect. In addition, vegetation reduces noise, removes dust particles, absorbs carbon dioxide and introduces oxygen into the air.

6.1.2   Design programme

The information needed during the design programme phase in order to define proper requirements for natural ventilation, related both to the building under design as a whole and to the various spaces which constitute the building, include:

1 the type of building (residential, commercial, tertiary, industrial, etc.);
2 the type of space (living room, bedroom, bathroom, office, drafting, etc.);
3 the schedule of use for each space;
4 the climate of the location during the hottest period of the year, usually represented by the maximum monthly average daily dry-bulb air temperature and relative humidity ranges;
5 within that hottest period of the year, the hours of the day in which heat gains within the space induce discomfort (DCH, degree cooling hours);
6 the quantity of heat to be removed in such a periods;
7 the type of structure and, particularly, the dimensions of the exposed thermal mass.

Items 1, 2 and 3 are useful in order to determine:

• the amount of fresh air needed hourly in each space at all times for occupants' health and well-being;
• the upper limit of the indoor air velocity related to physiological comfort as well as to other factors, such as objects and the transport of pollutants.

Item 4, represented on a building bioclimatic chart or psychometric chart, allows for evaluation of the natural ventilation potential of the site to cool air to the levels required by items 5 and 6. The possibility of using night ventilation structural cooling is evaluated through items 5–7.

6.1.2.1 The ventilation rate

The ventilation rate in buildings can be expressed in terms of air changes per hour (ach), i.e. the number of times in an hour that a volume of air equal to the volume of a room or building is renewed with fresh outdoor air; this can also be given in litres per second (litre s^{-1}), or cubic metres per hour ($m^3\ h^{-1}$).

The minimum ventilation rate is required to dilute odours and the concentration of CO_2 to an acceptable level, and to provide oxygen for occupant needs. The amount of fresh air needed to satisfy these requirements can vary greatly as a function of occupation and occupant activity; these determine the rate of production of occupant-related pollutants (cigarette smoke, body odours, carbon dioxide and water vapour). A typical range is from a minimum of 5 litre s^{-1} (18 $m^3\ h^{-1}$) per person for non-smokers up to 18 litre s^{-1} (90 $m^3\ h^{-1}$) per person for heavy smokers.

The indoor air quality varies over time as a function of the ventilation rate and the rate of pollutant production. Hence, the ventilation effectiveness is not only a function of the average ventilation rate over a given period, but also a function of the ratio of air change to the pollutant concentration. This is particularly important in spaces, such as in classrooms, with a concentration of occupants for some period of the day.

Minimum ventilation rates for hygiene requirements are usually set by national building codes and environmental standards; recommended ventilation rates for thermal comfort need to be calculated through one of the methods described in Chapter 3. Minimum and recommended ventilation rates are also indicated in the European Prestandard 1762: 1994 for 'Ventilation of buildings' [4].

Quantitative air change requirements are currently set for spaces supplied with mechanical ventilation systems, whereby a fixed air change rate can be provided over a given period of time. When natural ventilation is the only air change system applied in a building, a fixed air change rate cannot be achieved. A variable daily profile for air change requirements would fit better with the characteristics of natural ventilation. Standard air change requirements should then be considered in terms of average values, obtainable for the whole day (or for a considered period), when natural ventilation is applied.

6.1.3   Building design

Designing a building for optimum natural ventilation means paying much more attention to the various aspects related to the airflow movement around and within the building than is generally paid by professionals in current practice.

The aspects of building design related to air movement can be grouped according to their relation to:

- the form of the building envelope;
- the internal distribution of spaces and functions;
- the dimensions and location of openings;
- the characteristics and dimensions of the exposed thermal mass;
- the interactions with the HVAC system.

6.1.3.1 The form of the building envelope

The wind velocity and pressure fields around a building are greatly affected by the form of the building envelope and in particular by:

- the height of the building;
- the roof form;
- the aspect ratios, i.e. the ratios of the height of the building to its length and width;
- the corrugation of the building envelope (overhangs, wingwalls and recessed spaces).

THE BUILDING HEIGHT

Changing the height of a building, while keeping length and width unchanged, will produce an increase in depth of the downwind wake without variation of shape. In addition, the wind velocity increases at higher levels inducing an increased airflow rate through the windward openings of the top floors and higher suction at the side walls.

As the building is increased in height, the distribution of the airflow paths around and within it changes. The amount of air passing around the sides of the building increases in proportion to the amount of air travelling over it. This causes less upward air movement through the openings placed on the lower two-thirds of the building windward façade, with a direct influence on the airflow within the spaces inside. The top one-third of the windward façade of a building will always experience upward airflow, regardless of the height of the building.

Increasing the height of a multistorey building causes an additional strengthening of the stack airflow through stairwells and other shafts. This effect can be used for ventilation purposes when the wind flow is weak (see Chapter 3). However, above a certain height, stratification of air density and temperature may cause an excess in temperature differential between the bottom and top of the building, which may not be easily eliminated by passive means.

THE ROOF FORM

The form of the roof of a building affects the shape and size of the downwind eddy, as well as the wind pressure distribution on the roof and on the upper parts of the façades. Consequently, the airflow beneath the roof, through attic spaces and rooms located on the upper floor, is modified.

A flat roof, a single-slope roof with a pitch up to 15° or a single-slope roof facing downwind has negative pressures over all the surface at any angle of the oncoming wind. Any opening located in one of these types of roof experiences suction and therefore has the function of an airflow outlet. Above a 15° pitch, when the wind angle is perpendicular to the eaves line, the pressure becomes positive: at a tilt angle of about 15°, in the middle of the slope; at a tilt angle of about 25°, also on the area near the ridge; at a tilt angle of about 35° over all the surface of the slope.

Both slopes of a double-slope roof are under negative pressure over all their surfaces up to a pitch of 21°, regardless of wind direction. The leeward slope of a double-slope roof is always under negative pressure, regardless of roof pitch. On the windward slope, with wind perpendicular to the eaves line, pressures become positive: at a pitch of about 21°, in the middle of the slope, and at a pitch of about 33°, also near the eaves. Near the ridge, pressure is positive for pitches of between 30° and 41° and negative above 41°.

When the angle of incidence of the wind is 30° to the normal to the eaves line, the windward slope of a double-slope roof is under positive pressure: above a pitch of 22°, in the middle of the slope, and above a pitch of 30°, also near the eaves. Near the ridge, pressure is positive for pitches of between 35° and 50° and negative above 50°. When the angle of incidence of the wind is 60° to the normal to the eaves line, the windward slope of a double-slope roof is under positive pressure in the middle of the slope and near to the eaves, above a pitch of 30°. The area near to the ridge is under negative pressure up to pitches of over 50° [5].

ASPECT RATIOS

Quantitative values of the influence of aspect ratios on the wind pressure distribution can be drawn from the CPCALC⁺ model [6], schematically described in Section 2.1, and from the relevant correlation equations and graphs given by Grosso [7].

As a general rule, the dimension of the cross section along the prevalent summer wind direction should be kept to a functional minimum in order to enhance the use of cross ventilation. In addition, the ratio of the length to the width (the shorter plan dimension) should be not too high in order to avoid a significant decrease in the pressure on the middle of the windward façade with possible suction effects at the edges.

THE CORRUGATION OF THE BUILDING ENVELOPE

Corrugation of a box-shaped building envelope can have a significant function in enhancing natural ventilation, when the microclimate and environmental conditions of the site, i.e. sun and wind exposure, restrict the range of possible choices for the orientation of openings and the building layout.

As an example, the use of external walls as wing-walls, or the staggering of spaces, can solve problems such as a worst combination of wind and sun exposure in hot climates, where cross ventilation is required for comfort (Figure 6.10).

With wind and sun from the west, rooms with two external walls facing north and south will have little air movement, but will have protection from solar radiation (Figure 6.10a). If the building is rotated through 90°, the rooms with openings facing west and east will have cross ventilation but will have no protection from high solar radiation; this is a less desirable combination (Figure 6.10b). A proper placing of external wind-deflecting walls can be used to create high- and low-pressure zones to achieve cross ventilation, directing

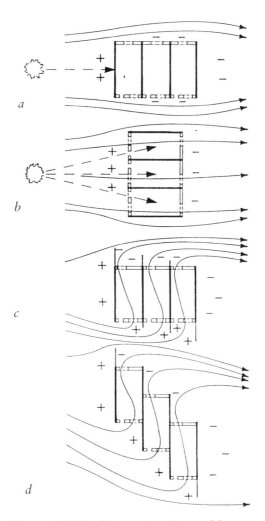

Figure 6.10. Building orientation and layout with respect to sun and wind exposure: (a) sun protection, no ventilation; (b) cross ventilation, no sun protection; (c) and (d) sun protection and ventilation. Adapted from Arens [2]

the air movement through 90° while protecting the rooms from direct solar radiation (Figure 6.10c). Alternatively, the rooms can be staggered to achieve the same results (Figure 6.10d).

Another example of the application of building forms as environmental control devices is the use of overhangs, which combine the functions of solar control and air movement control. Increasing the depth of an overhang can increase the positive pressure near an opening and thereby the interior air velocity and airflow rate, while also increasing the shading effect of the overhang (Figure 6.11).

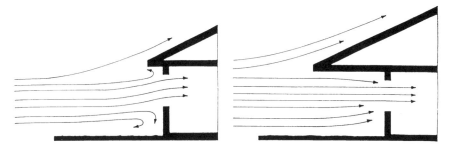

Figure 6.11. Effect on the airflow through an opening of increasing the depth of an overhang

6.1.3.2 *Distribution of internal spaces*

Interior spaces need to be properly distributed in order to achieve an effective use of natural ventilation. The function of each space, the layout and orientation of the building, and the position of the openings, all are important factors to be considered and, if possible, dealt with in an integrated way.

HORIZONTAL DISTRIBUTION

The horizontal, or plan, distribution of the internal spaces in a building should principally take cross ventilation into account.

In residential apartment buildings, the kitchen and bathroom should be placed on the leeward side of the building, with large windows functioning as outlets of an airflow coming as directly as possible from rooms located on the opposite windward side. This layout allows for good ventilation while avoiding transport of odours from kitchen and bathroom to the other rooms.

Partitions perpendicular to the airflow path should be kept at a functional minimum in order to limit the obstructions to the flow. In addition, the placement of furniture in a room should be designed in a way that reduces the possibility of hindering the air movement within and across the room.

Living rooms and studios should be placed on the windward side and well exposed to the wind, while bedrooms can be placed either on the windward or on the leeward side, but in a more protected position. An example of cross ventilation within a standard apartment of a multistorey residential building, in relation to wind direction, is shown in Figure 6.12. The airflow patterns shown in the figure are drawn from empirical estimates taking the wind pressure distribution on the façades into account; they can be assumed to be appropriate for a range of wind incidence angle between ±20° from the angles, as indicated in the figure.

In office buildings, open spaces should have windows in opposite walls. If partitions of height lower than the ceiling are present, they should be staggered in order to reduce their airflow obstruction effect. Office rooms served by a corridor should have always opening windows on the windward façade of the building to allow fresh air to entering. The corridor should be placed along the opposite external wall and have large operable windows.

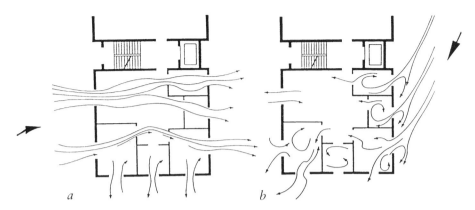

Figure 6.12. Cross-ventilation airflow patterns in an apartment with different wind directions: (a) good ventilation; (b) poor ventilation

A single-row office layout is better than a double-row layout with a central corridor, both for ventilation and for daylighting. If the central-corridor layout must be used for reasons of space economy, natural ventilation can be enhanced by combining indirect cross ventilation with stack ventilation through corridor vents (in one-storey buildings or on the top floor of multistorey buildings) or though shafts (in multistorey buildings).

VERTICAL DISTRIBUTION

The vertical distribution of the internal spaces in a building is basically influenced by the air movement created by stack ventilation.

In a two-storey single-family house, spaces generating high thermal gains, such as a kitchen or computer office, should not be placed on the upper level. Furthermore, the living spaces located on the upper level should not be in direct communication with the lower level in order to avoid warmed and polluted air from below entering the upper rooms. If the staircase connecting the two levels is open, a ventilated filter room should separate it from the rooms on the upper level.

In multistorey residential or office buildings, particular attention should be paid to the placement of stairwells and other shafts, which should function as exhaust-stack ventilation systems in order to avoid warmed air entering the top apartments or office rooms. The outlet openings of the shafts should be positioned on the leeward side of the building, significantly above the top floor level; the inlet openings of the apartment or office rooms should be placed on the windward side of the building.

In office and commercial multistorey buildings, fire safety regulations require that stairwells and shafts be separated with fire resistant walls and doors from the spaces served by the shaft. In addition, the outlet openings must have an operating mode by which they close automatically in the case of fire. More complex fire safety devices need to be apply if the building is higher than about 12 m.

6.1.3.3 *Position and size of openings*

The following recommendations should be considered when positioning and sizing the openings of a building:

- Outlet openings should be equal to or greater in size than inlet openings in order to avoid excessive air velocities with a limited airflow rate,
- For occupant cooling purposes, openings should be placed at occupant height (Figure 6.13a).
- For structural cooling requirements, the position of openings should be closer to the thermal exchange surfaces (wall, ceiling or floor) (Figures 6.13b and 6.14).
- The vertical position of inlet openings in two-storey dwellings or high spaces should be lower than the position of outlet openings in order to avoid a conflict between cross ventilation and the stack effect.
- In single-sided ventilation, more than one opening should be provided to a room; these openings should be placed far apart so that a better use of skewed winds can be made; wind deflectors can be used to enhance ventilation within the room.
- When stack ventilation is used in multistorey buildings, outlet openings should be located in the leeward side of the building; the height of their position and the size of the overall opening area should be chosen as a means of controlling the neutral pressure level and thereby enhancing the ventilation of the spaces.

When structural cooling is foreseen, the building should be relatively massive and a large surface area of the thermal mass should be exposed to the indoor air. This means that suspended ceilings cannot be installed if the ceiling is night ventilated, and similarly elevated (secondary) floors cannot be used if the floor is night ventilated.

Cooling of the ceiling works better than cooling of the floor because of the higher absorbed heat. Flush-to-ceiling windows, such as basement, awning or hopper windows, may be used for ceiling ventilation. Operable vents are recommended for night ventilation of floor surfaces.

Figure 6.13. Position of an opening for (a) optimum body cooling and (b) structural cooling

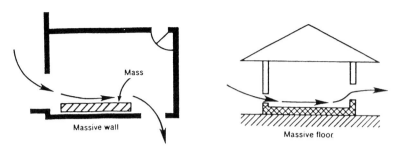

Figure 6.14. Night flushing of exposed surfaces of thermal mass

6.1.3.4 *Interaction with the HVAC system*

In complex multifunctional tertiary buildings, zoning ventilation can be applied in relation to the distribution of spaces and functions. Mechanical ventilation, air conditioning and natural ventilation can be all present in these cases. A detailed analysis of the interzonal airflow patterns and the pressure distribution has to be carried out using appropriate simulation tools, such as Network models or CFD models (see Chapter 3).

An interesting aspect of the interaction between mechanical and natural ventilation is the integration of passive heating and cooling systems.

6.1.3.5 *Control strategies for naturally ventilated buildings*

Manual control of natural ventilation does not require any specification (apart from the type of actuators to use) and its implementation is relatively straightforward. We will therefore not discuss solutions based on this control mode.

On the other hand, as explained in Chapter 5, automatic control of natural ventilation is a recently developing field. Examples of buildings implementing this technology are thus not very numerous and there is still a lack of guidelines on this topic. In particular, there is no general rule that would help to design the control system for any naturally ventilated building. However, various solutions have been proposed in order to solve this problem for a specific set of buildings. We will therefore describe the techniques implemented in these buildings and investigate, when possible, their efficiency. We will focus on examples taken from office or public buildings rather than homes, since manual control is usually more suitable for the latter.

CONTROL SYSTEMS

Before starting the presentation of any specific control strategy, we will describe how control systems in buildings work. As explained earlier, they are composed of sensors, actuators, controllers and usually a supervisor (especially in large buildings). The current needs of and technology for natural ventilation control are described next.

SENSORS. Many sensors are usually required for natural ventilation control. The main types are:

- *Temperature sensors*. These are the basic components of a control system, used for measuring indoor and outdoor temperatures. The difference between indoor and outdoor temperatures indicates whether fresh air should be introduced as a means of cooling. Most temperature sensors used in control systems are resistance thermometer devices (RTDs), which are based on a simple principle, the variation of the electrical resistance of a metal (usually platinum or nickel) with temperature. The accuracy of such sensors varies from 0.1°C to 0.5°C. Indoor sensors should be placed several metres away from the window at a position where incoming air has mixed. They should also be protected from direct solar radiation.

- *Carbon dioxide (CO_2) sensors*. These are used in order to evaluate indoor pollution caused only by the occupants. Most of these sensors are based on infrared absorption spectrometry. The main problems with these sensors are their accuracy (from 50 to 100 ppm, while set points are typically around 800 ppm) and their cost. Furthermore, these sensors have to be recalibrated every 6 to 12 months.

- *Mixed gas sensors (air quality sensors)*. These are newly developed sensors, used to estimate indoor air quality. Unlike CO_2 sensors, they are based on multigas sensing. Their sensitivity can be adjusted by the system manager. Their advantage lies in the fact that, unlike CO_2 sensors, they are sensitive to pollutants other than those produced by people (such as cigarette smoke). There is, however, a lack of validation on the correlation between the output of these sensors and actual indoor air pollution. They also require frequent recalibration.

- *Wind speed and wind direction sensors*. Wind speed and direction sensors are essential when natural ventilation is implemented. Wind direction is measured so that a decision can be made on which openings in which façades should be opened, while wind speed is mostly used in order to determine the adjustment of the position of the openings and to close them if the wind is too strong.
  The three-cup anemometer is most commonly used to measure the horizontal component of the wind speed, while a vane anemometer is used to determine wind direction. The three-cup anemometer is rather cheap and does not require much maintenance. However, it is not very sensitive to very low wind speeds. Such sensors are usually placed on top of the roof.

- *Rain detectors*. These should also be placed on top of the roof. They are absolutely necessary to avoid water ingress into the building. They are often combined with wind speed and direction sensors so that vents are shut only when both factors introduce a risk. One sensor is usually sufficient. However, if the building is long, it is advisable to have more than one sensor. The most commonly used rain detector works by a change of capacitance as the area of moisture on the detector increases. Such sensors are heated in order to dry the detector quickly and to melt, and thus detect, snow.

Other sensors are also commonly found in such control systems. These include:

- *Window security sensors.* These are needed for the detection of intrusion or breaking glass.
- *Solar gain sensors.* The role of these sensors for natural ventilation control could be to increase ventilation rates in the case of high solar radiation.
- *Humidity sensors.* These are sometimes necessary in order to control specific room ventilation rates (especially bathrooms). However, in-door relative humidity cannot easily be controlled with natural ventilation and humidity sensors will thus not often be used.

ACTUATORS. Natural ventilation can be controlled in different ways: using windows, casement vents, louvres or dampers. Louvres are not used for natural ventilation only, but mostly for daylighting purposes. Extra costs are thus not very important, but effects on comfort are sometimes not positive. Dampers, on the other hand, are used to open or close specific inlets and outlets designed only for ventilation purposes. They can, for example, be used to supply air under floors or to extract air to top of the roof or into specific ventilation shafts. Various actuators are required to operate such equipment. The sizing of the actuators (in terms of the necessary driving force) depends not only on the window's weight, but also on its position and type (horizontal or vertical) and on the wind load. This last parameter should never be neglected.

The main types of actuators used in buildings are:

- *Window actuators.* There are three main types of window actuators:
  - *Electric chain actuators* (Figure 6.15). This type of actuator is generally used on casement vents, top-hung and bottom-hung windows. They are usually supplied with an adjustable stroke.
  - *Electric linear actuators (piston actuators)* (Figure 6.16). These are very convenient for operating sliding and louvre windows, but can be used with almost any type of window. Unlike electric chain actuators, they are not very compact and thus can be unsightly. Furthermore, the stroke is not always adjustable. They are, however, not very noisy.
  - *Spindle actuator.* Window actuators should include 'overload' protection, so that in the event of an obstruction preventing normal operation (for example, somebody's hand), the actuator will cut off.
- *Damper actuators.* These are required in order to rotate the damper to a specified position. They can be either electric or pneumatic. Pneumatic

actuators are sometimes cheaper than electric ones and they are always faster. The choice of either of these actuators will, however, depend on availability.

Actuators should also incorporate spring returns when dampers are used for fire safety and smoke venting.

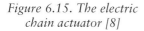

Figure 6.15. The electric chain actuator [8]   *Figure 6.16. The electric linear actuator [8]*

CONTROLLERS. Current controllers available on the market provide huge possibilities in terms of control strategies. They are similar to personal computers (they use the same kind of microprocessors) with specific operating software. This software includes a library of control functions such as: ON–OFF control loops, PID loops, arithmetic and mathematical operators, Boolean operators (AND, OR, etc.), comparators (>, <, =, etc.), time programming functions ... (see Levermore [9] for details on basic control functions). A specific program dedicated to the control of natural ventilation (and other equipment such as heating and lighting) and implementing any control strategy can then easily be created by using and combining these functions.

One of the important advantages of modern controllers is their ability to implement 'logic control'. The principle of logic control is extremely simple. It is comparable to a simplified expert system dedicated to control and based on 'logic rules' such as:

IF ambient temperature is less than 15°C THEN implement control strategy number 1.

Another classic rule, if we consider the example of natural ventilation control, could be:

IF ambient temperature is lower than indoor temperature AND indoor temperature is higher than 26°C THEN open ventilation vents (i.e. use natural ventilation as cooling means).

These rules have Boolean conclusions (either true or false) and, organized in a hierarchical way, they can be used to control very complex systems.

Though most manufacturers offer very comparable products, some controllers are limited by the number of rules or control functions that can be implemented (for example, no more than 99 AND modules can be implemented in the same program of most controllers distributed by a well-known manufacturer). This restriction will in most cases not be a major problem, but should be considered when complex control strategies have to be implemented.

CONTROL STRATEGIES

As explained in previous chapters, one of the main problems in the control of natural ventilation is the instability of climatic parameters, especially wind speed and direction. It is therefore sometimes very difficult to control airflow direction and intensity within the buildings. Different solutions can be found for solving this problem:

- The easiest one consists of implementing single-sided ventilation only.
- A second solution consists of taking advantage of the stack effect in atria.
- A third solution consists of using extractor fans in order to force the direction of the airflow
- The last solution, the most difficult, consists of monitoring outdoor parameters and assessing which openings have to be operated in order to provide optimum ventilation. A very good knowledge of airflow variations as a function of wind speed, wind direction and window opening configuration will be necessary. This means that reliable simulation tools, based on reliable data (pressure coefficients, wind direction, discharge coefficients, etc.) are required.

Whichever solution is chosen, an important parameter to take into account in order to improve the stability of vent opening is the sample time for wind speed and direction. As far as possible. averaged rather than instantaneous values should be considered (typically every 1 to 3 minutes). Using instantaneous values (particularly for wind direction) would result in sudden changes in vent opening ratios.

Another important point to raise here is the positioning of windows. Though not specific to control requirements, some configurations will contribute to an efficient design of control strategies. When possible, two openings on the same façade of a room (each controlled separately) should be supplied: one at the top and one at the bottom. Figure 6.17 presents such a solution

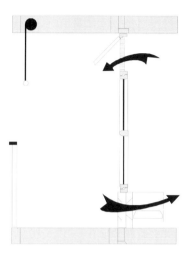

*Figure 6.17. Example of
bottom and top openings on
the same façade*

implemented in a low energy building in the Netherlands [10]. In this specific
solution, the bottom opening will usually be an air inlet and can be coupled to
a fan coil, thus allowing preheating (precooling) of supply air in the winter
period (summer period). The top part will be operated in the summer period
only either as an inlet (if air is extracted to an atrium for instance) or as an outlet
(in a single-sided ventilation case) in order to increase ventilation rates. This
solution is also more suitable in terms of comfort, since the effect of possible
draughts in the room will be reduced.

GENERAL CONTROL STRATEGIES. Although defining a general control strategy for
buildings is almost impossible, there are some common rules and common
principles that can be applied to any building. Three basic control strategies
can thus be defined as follows:

- *Control based on indoor pollution*. This strategy consists of monitoring an air quality index (i.e. CO_2 or air quality sensor) and opening or
  closing windows and vents as follows:

  - if measured CO_2 concentration is above the set point, open vents;
  - if measured CO_2 concentration is below the set point, close vents.

  The number of vents to open and/or the opening ratio of each vent (if
  control is not restricted to simple on–off control) cannot be defined for
  a general strategy. This will depend on wind conditions, the building's
  shape, rain and differences from one zone to another; logic control will
  have to be implemented in order to define these parameters.

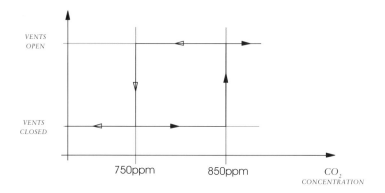

Figure 6.18. The role of the dead band for an indoor pollution-based natural ventilation control

CO_2 concentration should be measured in each room. However, this is expensive and, if this solution is not possible, at least one CO_2 sensor should be placed on each façade in a representative room (representative for number of occupants, volume, etc.), although unnecessary ventilation may occur in unoccupied or partly occupied rooms.

In order to avoid constant operation of windows (excess CO_2 concentration can be prevented very quickly if the wind outside is significant), it is necessary to introduce a 'dead band' in the control process in which no change is performed (unless the wind becomes too strong or rain falls). Figure 6.18 presents such a case for a CO_2 concentration set point at 800 ppm with a 100 ppm dead band. The exact width of this dead band should be set after a trial-and-error procedure on site, indicating the exact rate of change of CO_2 concentration with various wind speeds and directions.

Using this strategy is equivalent to the replacement of a demand control-based ventilation (DCV) system implemented with mechanical ventilation. Ventilation is supplied only when required for indoor air quality purposes and its potential as a cooling technique is not used. PID control is usually not suitable for such techniques since it introduces the risk of constant operation.

- *Control based on indoor and outdoor temperatures.* This strategy is a 'free cooling strategy'. The aim of such a strategy is to determine whether outdoor air can be used as cooling means or not. There are various ways of achieving this. The problem is to know which action to take when internal temperature is lower than external temperature. At night, when the building is not occupied, vents should be closed if external temperature is greater than internal. During the day, however, the increase in relative velocity could compensate the relative increase of indoor temperature due to ventilation. This is difficult to assess. However, when outdoor temperature exceeds indoor temperature by more than 2–3°C, vents should be closed [11].

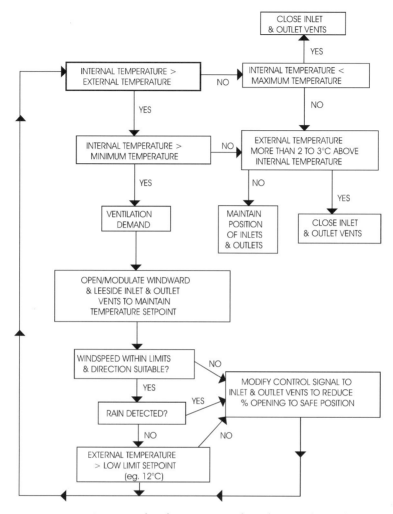

Figure 6.19. Example of temperature-based natural ventilation control strategy [8]

Figure 6.19 presents a flowchart of temperature-based natural ventilation control. In this example, two internal temperature limits are specified (maximum and minimum). These are supposed to be the bounds of the thermal comfort band. Vents and windows are opened according to indoor–outdoor temperature difference and the value of the internal temperature.

Each separate zone should be equipped with a temperature sensor and individually controlled. In this regard, it is sometimes necessary to modulate openings according to the number of open vents in adjacent zones, wind conditions and rain detection (see practical examples below for a better understanding).

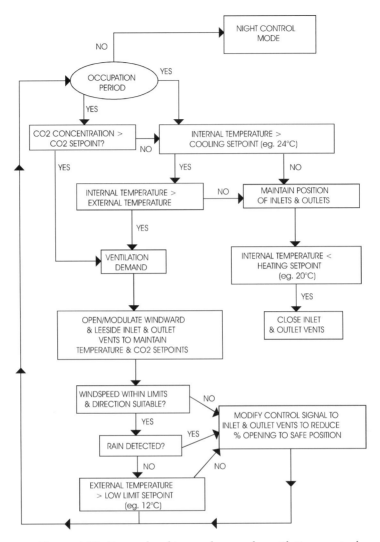

Figure 6.20. Example of integral natural ventilation control strategy [8]

As for the previous control strategy, the number of vents to open and/ or the opening ratio of each vent (if control is not restricted to simple on–off control) will depend on wind conditions, the building's shape, rain and differences from one zone to another; logic control will have to be implemented in order to define these parameters. PI or PID controllers could also be implemented for the determination of each window opening ratio. This could, however, result in constant operation of windows and should thus be used with care.

When such strategies are implemented, background ventilation has to be provided in order to satisfy indoor air quality standards. This can

be achieved by means of either mechanical ventilation or specific natural ventilation obtained through air bricks (see the third example below, 'Natural ventilation control in buildings with atria').
Equivalent strategies are typically implemented for night cooling ventilation control (see the night ventilation example below).

- *Integral control strategy.* In this case, both indoor air quality indices and temperatures are taken into account in the control strategy. Vents, windows or dampers are operated according to the most demanding of the two criteria. An example of such a strategy is given by Martin [8] and its flow chart is presented in Figure 6.20. This strategy is quite similar to the temperature-based strategy. The numeric values (given as examples only) and the settings of the control strategy depend strongly on the shape, function and organization of the building. This strategy is the most suitable type of control strategy, though the most difficult to implement, since it integrates both aspects of ventilation functions: cooling and maintaining indoor air quality.

MIXED-MODE CONTROL STRATEGIES. In many buildings, natural ventilation will not be sufficient for achieving thermal comfort throughout the year. Mechanical cooling systems are thus necessary. Specific control strategies need to be developed in order to integrate control of passive and active systems. These control strategies are defined as 'mixed-mode control strategies' [12]. They can easily be integrated into the temperature-based or integral control strategies. The main rules to follow when implementing this strategy are the following:

- Set two temperature set points: one at which heating is required (e.g. 21°C) and one at which cooling is required (e.g. 24°C).
- Avoid implementing heating and cooling on the same day;
- Define priorities:
  - if the temperature is between heating and cooling set points, use natural ventilation only;
  - if the temperature is above the cooling set point, then, according to the difference between this cooling set point and the actual temperature (error) and that between indoor and outdoor temperatures, first implement natural ventilation (e.g. up to an error equalling 1°C) and then auxiliary cooling;
  - if the temperature is lower than the heating set point (minus a specified dead band), start auxiliary heating (auxiliary heating should always be started at errors lower than for auxiliary cooling, since occupants are usually more sensitive to environments that are too cold than to environments that are too hot).

Again however, settings will strongly depend on the shape and organization of the building and on its equipment (*Air Handling Units*, local fan coil units, etc.).

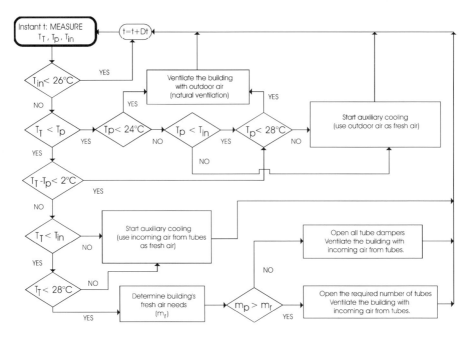

Figure 6.21. Flow chart of the control strategy designed for the coupled control of buried pipes, ventilation and auxiliary cooling

A specific example can be found in the optimum use of buried pipes, ventilation and auxiliary cooling during the cooling season [13]. The strategy is based on sensing indoor temperature (T_{in}), outdoor temperature (T_p) and air temperature in the tubes (T_T). The mass flow rate (m_p) in the tubes is also measured and compared to a 'required' mass flow rate (m_r). The flow chart for this specific strategy is presented in Figure 6.21.

Various set points have to be defined: the cooling set point (e.g. 26°C in this example), the minimum and maximum outdoor temperatures (e.g. 24°C and 28°C respectively here) and the maximum temperature in the tubes (28°C in this example).

The difference between tube and outdoor temperatures is also required in order to decide whether the energy required to activate the fans in the tubes is compensated by the cooling power difference between air from the tubes and outdoor air. This case focuses more on the use and efficiency of buried pipes than on the natural ventilation, but provides an example of the combination of different systems implemented through control logic.

PRACTICAL EXAMPLES

NIGHT VENTILATION CONTROL. Night ventilation is the main application of natural ventilation strategies in buildings. It has thus been the focus of much study and this 'free cooling' technique is incorporated in many buildings, by means of either mechanical ventilation or natural ventilation, or by a combination of the two.

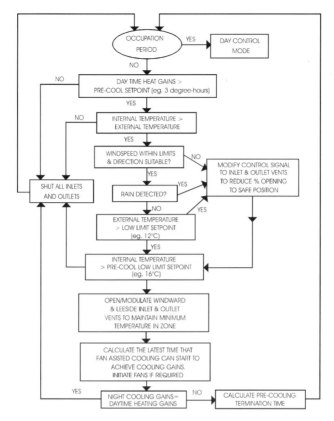

Figure 6.22. Flowchart of the advanced night cooling control strategy based on calculation of heat gains (from [8]).

In most cases, the temperature-based control strategy described above will be satisfactorily implemented. There is no need for pollution-based control for two reasons:

• The building is not occupied and there is almost no pollution source.
• Ventilation rates required for cooling will be far more important than those required for indoor air quality.

More advanced strategies have, however, been developed (just as advanced strategies have been developed for optimum start-up of heating in office buildings). One of these is based on calculating the degree-hours during the day [14]. The flow chart presented in Figure 6.22 describes this specific strategy for a free-running building. The heat gains stored during the day are first calculated in degree-hours, which are the sum of the difference between the hourly averaged indoor temperature and its set point for the number of daytime hours for which the cooling set point was exceeded.

If these heat gains exceed a specified value (e.g. 3 degree-hours) and the outdoor temperature is lower than the indoor temperature, then natural ventilation is activated until the indoor temperature reaches a minimum (e.g. 16°C) or outdoor conditions are no longer favourable to use of natural ventilation (rain, strong wind or very low outdoor temperature).

When natural ventilation is associated with mechanical ventilation (for example, using specific extractor fans), the optimum use of these fans should also be determined (accounting for different electricity tariffs at night).

SINGLE-SIDED VENTILATION CONTROL. As explained earlier, single-sided ventilation makes control much easier, since there is no coupling between different zones. Air entering the room cannot be anything else but outdoor air. Opening windows (or vents) on the façade will thus result in immediate variations in indoor air quality and temperature. The risk is that single-sided ventilation will not actually occur (for example, if a door is kept open).

One of the general control strategies described above or one of the specific control strategies for night-ventilation cooling can be implemented for single-sided ventilation control. The opening ratio will then be selected using the following procedure:

- If the building is not occupied (and there is no security or rain risk), windows can be fully opened in the summer time for 'free cooling'.
- if the building is occupied, then:
  - during the heating season, windows will be open at their minimum position;
  - during the cooling season, vents can be opened step by step (for example by steps of 25% of the opening) according to wind velocity in order to avoid draughts within the building. A minimum period between two changes of opening position should be set in order to avoid constant operation of the window. However, in case of rain, windows should be closed immediately and kept at this position for a minimum period after the last detection of rain.

Van Paassen proposed another solution for the temperature-based control of single-sided ventilation [15]. The controlled windows are composed of two casements (one pivoting inward, the other outward) (Figure 6.23).

The control technique implemented here is derived from a PI controller. A cooling requirement is first computed in the following way :

$$q_w(k) = q_w(k-1) + (k_p + k_i)(\theta_{SH}(k) - \theta_i(k))$$

$$-k_p .(\theta_{SH}(k-1) - \theta_i(k-1)) \tag{6.1}$$

where $q_w(k)$ is the cooling requirement at temperature k, k_p and k_i are the control parameters (proportional and integral gains respectively), $\theta_{SH}(k)$ is the cooling set-point at temperature k (°C) and $\theta_i(k)$ is the operative temperature

Figure 6.23. Example of single-side ventilation control [15]

at temperature k (°C), an average of the indoor temperature and the mean radiant temperature.

If the outdoor temperature is lower than the operating temperature, the window position (e_w) is than determined as follows, in order to maintain a constant cooling effect despite temperature variations:

$$X_w(k) = \frac{q_w(k)}{\theta_0(k) - \theta_i(k)}$$

(6.2)

where $q_w(k)$ is the outdoor temperature at temperature k (°C).

In order to avoid both heating and cooling occurring on the same day, a few additional rules have been added:

- 'If during office hours the control system has put the windows in maximum position, then the next night, pre-cooling is allowed.' In this case the night cooling set point is reduced to 21°C (instead of 24°C during occupancy) for optimum efficiency.
- In addition, if the outside air temperature is lower than 15°C, the lower window is kept closed in order to avoid draughts.

NATURAL VENTILATION CONTROL IN BUILDINGS WITH ATRIA. Atria are particularly suitable for the implementation of naturally ventilation in buildings. The stack effect created in these solar-heated spaces forces air to rise. This air can thus be drawn from adjacent zones and removed from the side of the atrium's roof (Figure 6.24). The atrium's roof should have openings on different sides. Then, in the case of strong wind, only leeward (rather than windward) openings should be opened, thus reducing the risk of these openings becoming air inlets rather than outlets and the flow within the building being reversed.

This solution was implemented at the Anglia Polytechnic University in the UK [16]. This four-storey building has a total area of 6000 m² and includes two atria. The control strategy is based on both CO_2 concentrations and

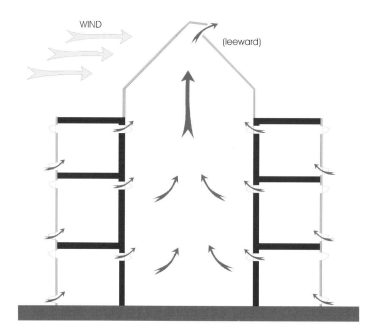

Figure 6.24. Typical natural ventilation control strategy in a building with an atrium

temperature differences, as described above in the section on 'General control strategies'. The building is split into three zones per atrium and per floor with one temperature sensor in each zone. Each zone is controlled separately.

A background ventilation of approximately 0.25 ach is provided through air bricks at floor level. Additional ventilation is provided through the automatic operation of clerestory windows and atria roof vents. Windows can be open in steps of 25%. A step change cannot occur within 15 minutes of the previous change (unless rain makes it necessary for the windows to be closed to a 25% opening ratio, which is maintained up to 30 minutes after the end of any detected rain).

Clerestory windows on the top floors open wider than those on lower floors in order to compensate the relative decrease in stack effect due to different stack heights (and thus avoid warm air rising up the atrium to the top floors). Another way to avoid this would be to build the atrium much taller than it is (more than one extra floor taller).

The number (and ratio) of vents to open on both atria roofs is selected according to the number of clerestory windows open on the four floors.

6.1.4   Opening design

In relation to their functions and location on the building envelope, openings can be grouped in the following categories:

- *Windows*, which have multiple integrated functions such as viewing, daylighting, solar gain control and ventilation; windows are divided into various categories in relation to:
  - the plane of placement (vertical plane windows and non-vertical-plane windows, horizontal or tilted);
  - the position on the building envelope (walls or roof);
  - the opening system (hanging, swinging, pivoting).
- *Screens*, which function basically as shading devices, but can also be designed for ventilation purposes, as in traditional Arabic architecture; however, even if used as shading devices only, screens alter the opening size and the aerodynamic performance of the windows on which they are installed.
- *Doors*, with the basic functions of interconnection between spaces and maintaining the privacy of a room, and with additional functions depending on the material (e.g. glazing for solar transmittance) and location (interzonal airflow control for interior doors).
- *Vents and ventilators*, functioning only as means to enhance and direct the air movement.

6.1.4.1 Windows

The effectiveness of windows in controlling air movement depends not only on the opening size but also on the type of window (only operable windows are considered as airflow control devices).

The wide variety of wall window styles, regardless of their plane of placement or position on the building envelope, can be classified as one or a combination of three primary window types [1]:

- *Simple opening*, defined as any window that opens by sliding in a single plane and including single-hung, double-hung, and horizontal sliding windows (Figure 6.25).

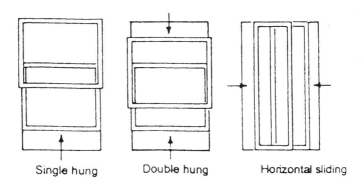

Figure 6.25. Simple opening windows

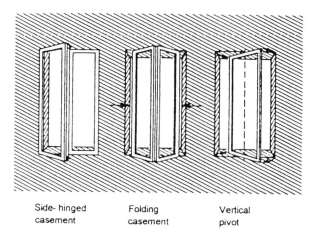

Side- hinged   Folding   Vertical
casement   casement   pivot

Figure 6.26. Vertical-vane opening windows

- *Vertical-vane opening*, defined as any window that opens by pivoting on a vertical axis such as the side-hinged casement (single-sash or double-sash), folding casement, and vertical-pivot windows (Figure 6.26).
- *Horizontal-vane opening*, defined as any window that opens by pivoting on a horizontal axis and including the projected sash, awning, basement, hopper, horizontal-pivot, and jalousie windows (Figure 6.27).

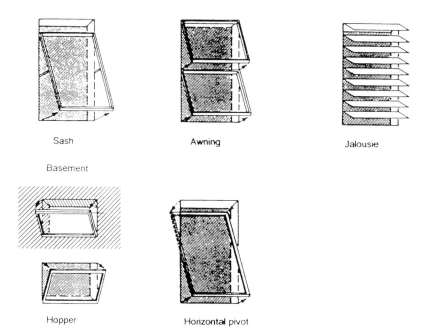

Sash   Awning   Jalousie

Basement

Hopper   Horizontal pivot

Figure 6.27. Horizontal-vane opening windows

However, a particular window style may fit into two or three classifications. For example, some window manufacturers produce an awning window that switches to a single-sash side-hinged casement opening.

All the above types of windows are usually installed on *walls*, but all or some of them can be installed on *roof monitors* as well. Roof monitors include dormers, clerestories, skylights, belvederes and cupolas. Dormers and clerestories have openings in a vertical plane; skylights have openings on a horizontal or tilted plane; belvederes and cupolas can have windows in both vertical and non-vertical planes.

All or some of the above types of window may be installed on roof monitors with vertical-plane openings, in relation to the type of monitor: all types of window on belvederes and cupolas; side-hinged casement on dormers; awning, basement and hopper windows on clerestories.

On roof monitors with horizontal or tilted-plane openings, such as skylights, horizontal-vane opening windows can be installed. The most common types are: awning, basement, hopper and horizontal-pivot windows.

A wide variety of airflow patterns is generated by the various types of windows in relation to their operational condition. This is defined by: the effective open area, i.e. the open area as projected perpendicularly onto the flow; the tilt angle between flow direction and displacement plane of the sash (or sashes); the degree of symmetry of the sashes relative to the axis of the window and the flow direction.

AIRFLOW PATTERNS THROUGH WINDOWS ON WALLS
Graphs representing various airflow patterns for different opening conditions of each type of window, are shown in Boutet [1]. The following synthetic considerations are drawn from those graphs.

- *Simple openings* do not generally affect the pattern or velocity of airflow except near the window as the airstream squeezes through the opening. The direction of the flow path is not influenced by projecting sashes. A double-hung window allows selection of the height of the airflow, while a horizontal sliding window designates the placement of the airstream within the interior space.
- *Vertical-vane openings* exert a wide variety of influences on both the pattern and velocity of the airflow with a particular effect on the horizontal airflow pattern. The most common window of this type, the side-hinged casement window, has a great versatility with regard to airflow control.
  The side-hinged casement window can be installed as a one-sash (single casement window) or two-sash (double casement window) unit; the sashes can be inswinging, i.e., opening towards the inside of the space, or outswinging, i.e. opening towards the outside of the space. The opening type mostly used in Europe is the inswinging type. The airflow patterns depend on the type of unit, the type of opening and the

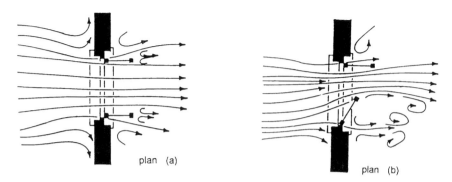

Figure 6.28. Airflow patterns through (a) a fully open and (b) a partially open inswinging double casement window

operational position of the sashes. An example of the airflow pattern through an inswinging double side-hinged casement window is shown in Figure 6.28.

• *Horizontal-vane openings* influence the velocity and pattern of air movement mainly on the vertical direction, although their versatility is limited. Projected sash, basement and horizontal-pivot windows direct the airflow upward; hopper windows and horizontal-pivot windows installed in reverse direct the airflow downward. Jalousie windows have the possibility of directing the airflow in either direction according to the position of the sashes.

AIRFLOW PATTERNS THROUGH WINDOWS ON ROOF MONITORS

Roof monitors are usually employed as daylighting devices rather than for air movement control. However, a proper design and handling of windows on roof monitors can have a significant effect on the ventilative cooling of the space under the roof. Roof-monitor windows as air-movement control devices can be divided according to their plane of placement: vertical or non-vertical.

The airflow pattern through the *vertical-plane window* of a roof monitor, such as a dormer or clerestory, is greatly affected by the roof slope adjacent to the window, though the air movement near the window panes may be similar to the air movement of the same type of window placed on a wall.

Unless the roof monitor is close to one of the eaves, airflow would enter the windward monitor's window angled to the horizontal plane and, usually, from below up the roof slope (Figure 6.29). If the roof has a low pitch, the zone near the monitor may be highly turbulent and the airflow can enter at any angle. In such a case, even a windward monitor could become an airflow outlet.

The airflow pattern through a *non-vertical-plane window* of a roof monitor, such as a skylight, is even more influenced by the roof pitch, since it lies in the plane of the roof slope (Figure 6.30). A skylight is usually located in the middle of the slope of a gable-roof building. It will be in a suction zone, thus functioning as an airflow outlet for pitches up to 21° and for any wind angle

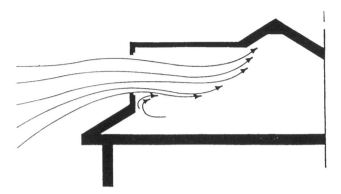

Figure 6.29. Cross-sectional airflow patterns through the
windward window of a dormer (single-sided ventilation)

with the normal to the roof edge. On the windward side, i.e. at a wind angle
between 0° and 90°, the roof pitch at which the skylight position changes from
negative to positive pressure, and thus from a suction to an airflow inlet

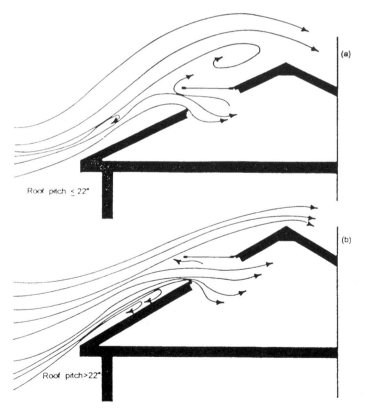

Figure 6.30. Cross-sectional airflow patterns through a skylight
(single-sided ventilation), at wind angles between 0° and 30°:
(a) low-pitch roof (< 22°), (b) high-pitch roof (> 22°)

function, shifts in relation to the wind angle: a pitch of 22° at a wind angle of 30°, and a pitch of 30° at a wind angle of 60°.

6.1.4.2 Screens

Two main categories of screens are considered in terms of their operational features:

- *Fixed screens*, either externally attached to windows, such as insect screens, safety grilles or *brise soleil*, or separated screens, such as the Arabic *mashrabiya*.
- *Operable screens*, such as the various types installed externally or internally on a window, as shading and night-insulating devices, in all European Countries.

The most common types of operable screens are:

- *Exterior screens*:
  - rolling blinds, which can be full-plane or hung-slat and operate on a vertical-vane or awning frame;
  - sliding-sash shutter, single or double, with or without slats;
  - side-hinged casement shutter, with or without slats.
- *Interior screens*:
  - venetian blinds;
  - vertically operating curtains;
  - horizontally operating curtains;
  - louvres.

AIRFLOW THROUGH EXTERIOR SCREENS

Fixed exterior screens have the characteristic of reducing the approaching airflow in a uniform way over the entire surface, without changing the direction of the flow.

Operable exterior screens such as vertical-vane rolling blinds affect the airflow pattern similarly to hung windows, but with a wider range of opening positions (Figure 6.31a). Hung-slat rolling blinds, down but not fully closed, have the effect on air movement of a low porosity fixed screen. The air can flow uniformly through the narrow slots distributed uniformly over the entire surface. Awning-frame rolling blinds combine this behaviour with the airflow patterns of an awning window; they have the optimum integrated performance of all screens, in terms of shading and ventilation (Figure 6.31b).

Operable exterior screens, such as sliding-sash shutters and side-hinged casement shutters, behave, with respect to air movement, like horizontal-sliding and side-hinged casement windows respectively, but outswinging instead of inswinging. Sliding-sash shutters perform better than casement shutters for airflow control owing to their rigidity in countering the wind flow (Figure 6.32).

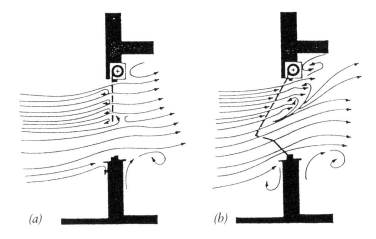

Figure 6.31. Airflow patterns through (a) a vertical-vane and
(b) an awning-frame rolling blind

AIRFLOW THROUGH INTERIOR SCREENS

Interior screens, made generally of fabric (curtains), plastic (curtains, louvres, venetian blinds) or light metal (venetian blinds), have less airflow deflection potential and more wind energy absorption power than exterior screens owing to their relative lightness and softness. The airflow is greatly reduced before entering the room, the degree of reduction is a function of the screen coverage of the window opening area, and the direction of the unsheltered flow is a function of the screen position. Vertical-operating screens tend to lower the airflow; horizontal-operating screens tend to move the flow horizontally.

Venetian blinds and louvres are more versatile in controlling the air movement. Compared to the other interior screens, they absorb the airflow less

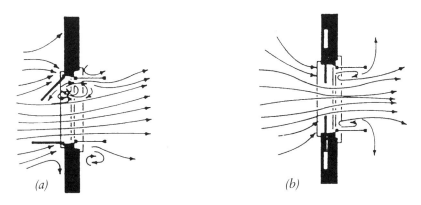

Figure 6.32. Airflow patterns through (a) side-hinged casement and (b)
sliding-sash shutters on a fully open double casement window

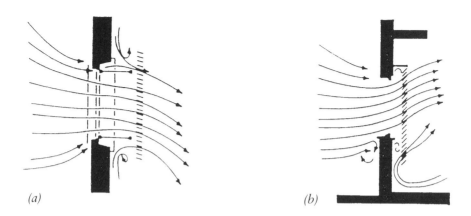

Figure 6.33. Airflow patterns through (a) louvres and (b) venetian blinds on a fully open double casement window

but can redirect it better and more uniformly through the operation of the slats. Louvres can induce horizontal flow deflection (Figure 6.33a), while venetian blinds can direct the flow vertically in the same way as jalousie windows (Figure 6.33b).

6.1.4.3 Doors

Doors are much less significant as airflow control devices than windows. External entrance doors may have the function of inlet openings, occasionally, in single-family houses, and more often in commercial buildings in relation to the rate of entry of customers. When cooling requirements are high in single-family houses, a door grille or door screen is often placed on a door opening to let air, but not insects or intruders, through while the door is open. Door vents have a similar function but with higher security.

Exterior entrance doors in residential buildings are, basically, of the type opening by pivoting on a vertical axis as a one-panel unit (single door) or two-panel unit (double door). They are usually inswinging, although they may also open towards the outside of the space (outswinging). The airflow through a double door has similar patterns to the airflow through a double casement window (see Figure 6.28). An example of the airflow patterns through a single door is shown in Figure 6.34.

In addition to the above mentioned single and double doors, tertiary buildings may have doors of different types, such as folding doors, fire-safety doors, automatic-opening doors and rotating doors. The airflow pattern through these types of door has to be evaluated in relation to the operation schedule and the configuration of the whole building, including HVAC systems.

Interior doors can be of a variety of types. In residential buildings, single and double doors, and sometimes folding doors, are usually used, while in tertiary buildings, fire-safety doors and automatic-opening doors can be used as well.

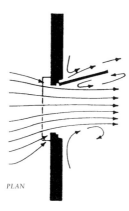

Figure 6.34. Airflow
patterns through an
inswinging single door

The main function of interior doors, as far as air movement is concerned, is the control of interzonal airflow.

6.1.4.4 Vents and ventilators
Vents and ventilators are devices used to provide ventilation to spaces without windows, such as attic spaces, service rooms and inner bathrooms.

Vents can be divided into various types in relation to their function and position in a building:

- attic vents, such as gable louvres, soffit vents and ridge vents;
- wall-to-floor vents, for night structural cooling of commercial and office buildings;
- door vents, for interzonal air change.

As part of mechanical ventilators, ventilators include:

- stationary ventilators, such as the gravity ventilator, low-pitch slant roof ventilator, and roof mushroom ventilator;
- rotary ventilators, such as the roof turbine, free-flow ventilator and revolving ventilator.

ATTIC VENTILATION
Attic spaces are common in residential buildings, although modern construc-tions tend to use the space underneath the roof as a living space, providing the roof is well insulated. However, an efficient ventilation of attic spaces is essential to provide thermal comfort conditions to the spaces or apartments located underneath the attic. In addition to releasing heat from the attic space, attic ventilation prevents condensation during the winter.

Gable louvres are triangular vents located at the two gable ends of a house. When the wind angle is almost perpendicular to the louvre surfaces, cross ventilation occurs, mainly in the upper part of the attic space. When the wind is normal to the eaves, the gable louvres are in a negative-pressure zone, so minute air movement is created at each vent and no cross ventilation occurs.

Soffit vents are located in the eaves and bring air movement only along the attic floor. As for the gable louvres, airflow through the soffit vents is influenced by wind direction. Cross ventilation through the attic floor occurs when the wind angle is almost perpendicular to the eaves. Separate airflows through each venting system occur when the wind blows parallel to the eaves.

Ridge vents are openings located along the roof ridge. They function basically as an airflow outlet and do not provide air movement if used by themselves.

An efficient ventilation of attic spaces can be provided only by a combination of these venting systems. Although it would increase the volume of the air changed by cross ventilation, a combination of soffit vents and gable louvres is still an inadequate method since the two sets of vents tend to act independently.

The *ridge-and-soffit vent system* is the most efficient since it combines the wind and buoyancy effects. An excellent quantity and uniformity of airflow throughout the entire attic space is secured by this system, regardless of wind direction and wind speed. In order to achieve optimum performance, the net free area of the ridge vents should be equal to the net free area of the soffit vents.

Ventilators are installed on the roof, usually in combination with soffit vents or fans, to enhance attic ventilation when ridge vents cannot be installed.

STRUCTURAL NIGHT VENTILATION

For night structural cooling purposes, venting grilles are installed on the external walls, flush with the floor or the ceiling of the space to be cooled, usually a commercial or office building.

Ceiling ventilation is more efficient than floor ventilation since more free surface is available for ventilation on the ceiling than on the corresponding floor of equal area. In addition, venting grilles positioned on the upper part of a wall pose fewer problems for furniture placement than grilles close to the floor. A drawback of ceiling ventilation is that no suspended ceiling can be installed and, therefore, service cables and pipes need to be placed under the floor.

Venting grilles for structural cooling are not as simple as attic vents; they have to provide inlet–outlet night airflow without conflicting with other important requirements, such as protection against intruders and insects, and winter thermal insulation. However, several types of multifunctional grilles are produced for mechanical and air-conditioning systems and these can be applied to night structural cooling as well.

SERVICE ROOM VENTILATION

When cross ventilation or single-sided ventilation cannot be provided either through windows or through vents, such as in bathrooms and other service rooms (laundry rooms, storage spaces, etc.) located far from external walls or in the basement, ventilators and door grilles are installed to provide stack exhaust ventilation.

Ventilators, either stationary or rotary, are usually installed on the roof and connected through pipes to the service room. In a multistorey building, each room should be served by a separate pipe-ventilator system to avoid mixing of polluted air between rooms. A venting grille placed at the bottom of the room door functions as an air inlet from the adjacent room.

A stationary ventilator is usually sufficient for ventilating bathrooms in multistorey residential buildings, providing the room adjacent to the bathroom is well ventilated and exposed to the wind or if the ventilator distance from the room is long enough to produce the necessary pressure head.

Rotary ventilators work better than stationary ventilators if the site of the building is not too sheltered from the wind, as it might be in a densely built-up urban area. However, mechanical ventilators may have to be installed to provide the necessary air change to the service room if the site or the building layout and structure do not allow the use of passive means.

6.2 TECHNICAL SOLUTIONS

In most European countries, building codes prescribe a minimum window-to-floor ratio in order to ensure sufficient daylighting as well as air changes in residential buildings. This prescription may be enough to provide ventilation when microclimate conditions are within the comfort range, but is far from satisfying more stringent requirements. A performance-based ventilation standard would respond better to the need to provide a space with indoor air quality and comfort in relation to variable specific climate conditions.

On the other hand, in regions with temperate and hot climates, technical solutions for natural ventilation have long been applied to traditional architecture in order to cope with weather conditions outside the comfort range.

In recent years, a new trend emphasizing the use of hybrid mechanical ventilation systems has characterized the design of tertiary buildings. It is probably related to an increasing awareness of the need for an energy-conscious and environmentally-sound approach to architecture. However, this new trend involves only a few well known professionals and, thus, is far from offering a substantial contribution to the decrease of the world energy consumption for ventilation and cooling. Nevertheless, it represents a reference pattern for the newest generation of architects.

Examples of technical solutions for natural ventilation in traditional architecture, in current residential buildings and in designs for contemporary non-residential buildings are presented in the following sections.

6.2.1 Natural ventilation techniques in traditional architecture

6.2.1.1 *Wind-driven comfort ventilation*

The most archetypal model of the use of natural ventilation in traditional dwellings is probably the Native American *tipi*. Its envelope is a membrane of sewn buffalo skins, or canvas in more recent years, with large flaps at the top providing an opening for smoke. This envelope is conceived as a skin with variable climate-adaptive modes:

- When there is heavy rain, the flaps are closed to protect the inside from water infiltration.
- In temperate weather conditions, the envelope is closed except at the top, where an opening has the function of letting out the smoke generated inside; the variable position of the flaps allows for inducing wind negative pressure at the opening to increase stack exhaustion of the smoke.
- In hot weather, the perimeter of the *tipi* can be rolled up to allow maximum comfort ventilation, i.e. body cooling, inside.
- In cold weather, an inner liner can be added to create a dead air space or allow limited ventilation required for smoke exhaustion while shielding the occupants from direct draughts; when chilly winds blow, a windbreak of dead branches is positioned around the *tipi* to protect the inside.

Similar climate-responsive skin patterns can be found in traditional dwelling types of very different regions. Examples are the *ma'dam* house from Iraq and the Mongolian *yurt*.

The *ma'dam house*, a 6000 year old design, is built of 6 m tall local swamp reeds set into the ground with the ends bent over to form the ribs of a barrel vault which is then infilled with overlapping layers of reed matting. The matting on the sides can be opened or closed depending on weather.

The *Mongolian yurt* is a nomadic structure with walls formed in a circle by a set of collapsible 'pantograph-type' lightweight willow panels with a single entry door. The roof is either a dome or a conical structure composed of radial beams spanning from the outside wall to a central compression ring, which is left open for smoke and ventilation. The frame is covered with one or more – depending on the weather – layers of thick felt mats and held in place with a pattern of ropes. The sides may be rolled up to provide ventilation on warm days.

6.2.1.2 *Wind-stack driven ventilation*

Building components and technical solutions providing ventilation, both for body and structural cooling, in hot climates were already used in ancient times. For example, in Iran, *curved-roof air vent* systems were incorporated in buildings as early as 3000 BC, while *wind-tower* systems, the *cistern* and the *ice*

Figure 6.35. Wind towers in the Iranian city of Yazd [19]

maker, may not have appeared until about 900 AD [17]. The *malkaf*, or wind-catch, was used by ancient Egyptians in the houses of Tal Al-Amarna and is represented in wall paintings of the tombs of Thebes, among which is, for example, the tomb of Pharao Neb-Amun of the Nineteenth Dynasty (1300 BC) [18]. Some of the most significant, and most studied, examples of traditional building systems employing both wind and the stack effect to induce ventilation and cooling are schematically depicted below.

WIND-TOWER SYSTEMS
The Iranian passive cooling wind-tower system (Figure 6.35), both in its basic configuration and associated with evaporative cooling, using a domed roof air vent or linked to a cistern, has been thoroughly described by Bahadori [17].

A wind tower (Figure 6.36) operates as a ventilation-inducing device as a result of the combination of three types of physical mechanisms:

- *Downdraught*. In the absence of wind, hot ambient air enters the tower in the morning through the openings in the sides and is cooled when it comes in contact with the tower walls, which have enough thermal inertia to release at night the heat absorbed during the day. A downdraught is thus created when cooled air, which is denser than the warmer air inside, sinks down through the tower.
- *The wind effect*. Wind makes air cool more effectively and flow faster through the tower and then through the doors, which can be opened

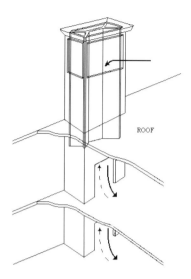

ROOF

*Figure 6.36. Airflow patterns
through a wind tower (daytime:
solid line, night-time: dashed line)*

into the central hall and basement of the building. When these doors are open, the cooled air from the tower is pushed through the building and out of the windows and other doors, taking room air with it. Ventilation and cooling are more effective if the outlet openings are located on the leeward side of the building. Wind at night has a lower cooling effect than during the day since the tower walls warm night air before it enters the building.

• *The stack effect.* When there is no wind at night, heat released by the tower walls warms up the air, thus creating an air density differential and a reduced pressure zone at the top of the tower, causing an updraught.

A wind tower system can be associated with ground cooling by separating the wind tower from the building (Figure 6.37) and connecting them through an underground tunnel which keeps the air cool before it enters the rooms [17].

In addition to these ventilation mechanisms, wind-tower systems use evaporative cooling by moving air through fountains or over underground streams. However, this aspect is not treated in this book.

The top of the Iranian wind towers, called *badgir*, had a four-shaft cross section and openings on the four sides to allow the wind to enter from all directions (Figure 6.38).

Dust, insects, and birds can enter the wind tower with the air. To cope with this problem, newer towers are equipped with screens to keep out at least insects and birds. Ways of keeping the dust out are:

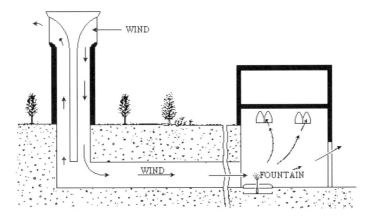

Figure 6.37. A wind-tower system associated with ground cooling

Figure 6.38. A badgir: *the top of a
wind tower in Yazd (Iran) [19]*

- taller towers, expensive to build and maintain;
- a larger cross sectional area of the airflow, which reduces the wind velocity at the bottom of the tower allowing the dust to settle on shelves called dust pockets;
- placing the opening at the top of the tower as a function of the direction of wind, in areas where dusty winds and dust-free winds blow in different directions.

WIND ESCAPES AND AIR VENTS

Wind escapes and air vents are outlet openings located at the top of a building, the former usually on a vertical vane and the latter on a domed roof. Their function as air outlets is based on Bernoulli's theorem – the pressure of a moving fluid decreases as its velocity increases – applied to a Venturi tube with a side opening and transported to building design.

A pattern example of a *wind escape* is described by Hassan Fathy [18] and is related to a pump room for an artesian well in Alexandria, Egypt. The air enters the openings on the vaulted roof of the well and exits through the wind escape positioned under a slanted roof on the leeward side of the structure.

Domed or cylindrical roof *air vents* are employed in Iran in areas where dusty winds make wind towers impractical [17]. These vents are holes cut in the apex of a domed or cylindrical roof and protected by a cap with openings that direct the wind across the vent (Figure 6.39). When air flows over a curved surface, its velocity increases and its pressure decreases at the apex of the surface. The decrease in pressure at the apex of a curved roof induces the hot air under the roof to flow out through the vent.

In this way air is kept circulating through the room under the roof, where living rooms are usually located. A pool of water is often placed directly under the vent to cool air moving through the room.

Both the wind escape and the domed roof air vent can accelerate effective ventilation and air circulation when used with other devices such as windows, doors, wind towers and the *malqaf* or wind catcher, described below. Although the wind effect is prevalent, the stack effect is also in action in both systems.

WIND CATCHERS (*MALKAF*)

The *malkaf*, or wind catcher, is a shaft rising high above the building with an opening facing the prevailing wind. It traps the air where it is cooler and at

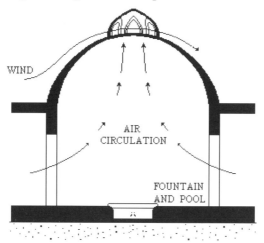

Figure 6.39. Airflow patterns through a domed roof air vent

higher velocity and channels it down into the interior of the building. This device is used in the hot arid zones of Arabia and Asia, where the three functions of an ordinary window – light, ventilation, and view – need to be separated in order to achieve comfort.

The cooling effectiveness of the *malkaf* is even higher in dense cities in warm humid climates, where thermal comfort depends mostly on air movement and the urban density reduces the wind speed at street level, making windows inadequate for ventilation. The *malkaf* is much smaller than the building façade and thus offers less surface area to screen the *malkaf* of the buildings downwind. An example of a generalized use of the *malkaf* can be seen in villages of the Sind province of Pakistan.

In addition to increased ventilation, the *malkaf* is also useful in reducing wind-borne sand and dust since the wind captured above the building contains less solid material than the wind at lower heights and much of the sand that does enter is dumped at the bottom of the shaft.

In Egypt, the *malkaf* has long been a feature of traditional architecture. A well studied example of a natural ventilation system combining a *malkaf* with a wind-escape in the *qa'a* – a central upper-storey room for receiving guests – is the house of Othman Katkhuda, Cairo. Measurements of air velocity and direction around and within the *qa'a* were made by scholars from the Architectural Association Graduate School of London in 1973 [18].

6.2.1.3   *Ground-cooling ventilation: the* Covoli

An ingenious ventilative ground-cooling system was used in a group of six sixteenth century villas in Costozza, near Longare, at the foot of the Berici hills, some 10 km south of Vicenza, Italy. One of these villas, and the relevant ground-cooling system, is mentioned in the first of the *Four Books of Architecture* by Palladio (Venice, 1570).

The system, analysed as the subject of a degree thesis submitted to the Venice School of Architecture [20], is based on the use of large underground natural, or partially artificial, sloped caverns – called *covoli* – as coolness reservoirs. In the *covoli*, the air temperature is almost constant all year long owing to the high thermal inertia of the ground above. Cracks at different heights connect the *covoli* to the outside, and thus a downdraught of denser cooler air is generated inside the cavern when the outside air temperature is higher than the air temperature in the *covolo*, as in the summer, while an updraught is generated during the winter when the temperature outside is lower than in the cavern.

The villas are built at a lower level than the *covoli* and connected to them by means of underground galleries (Figure 6.40), to make use of the cooled air during summer. The cool air is entrained from the *covoli*, or the galleries, to a basement, and from there distributed with the stack effect to the upper rooms through vents and openings.

Measurements made for the thesis work on 31 July and 1 August showed for one of the villas that, while the outside temperature was fluctuating between 21°C and 29°C and the temperature in the *covolo* was around 12°C, the

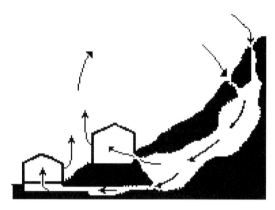

*Figure 6.40. Scheme showing the connections
and the airflow patterns between* covoli *and
villas in the ground-cooling ventilation system
of Costozza, Vicenza (Italy) [20]*

temperature in the basement ranged between 13°C and 14°C, and the temperature in the room above the vent – which was covered by a plastic foil in order not to reduce the temperature too much – fluctuated between 20.5°C and 21.5°C.

6.2.2   Natural ventilation in residential buildings

Proper technical solutions for natural ventilation in residential buildings depend on the building type, size, and form, as well as on the climate of the site. Two basic types of dwelling are the most common in Europe: the one- or two-storey single-family unit, either a single house or a unit in a terraced building, and the multistorey apartment building.

Some schematic solutions are depicted below for these two basic types of residential buildings.

6.2.2.1 Single-family residential unit

Wind-driven cross ventilation through windows placed on opposite external walls is relatively easy in single-family residential units, if a careful interior design and a proper location of the windows allow for optimal use of the differential pressure generated across the building.

When wall cross ventilation is not effective owing to low air speed caused by the low level of openings, shielding or meteorological conditions, *roof ventilation* can be added. This is based on the Bernoulli–Venturi effect that induces air to be sucked out of a roof opening at the ridge, as mentioned above in relation to wind escapes and air vents. The sucking effect is stronger if a Venturi tube is used as a roof ventilator. Based on this principle, wind-driven cross ventilation can be enhanced in both one-storey and two-storey residential units, providing ground and upper floors are connected by an open stairwell.

Even when wind is absent, roof ventilation can increase the airflow rate as a result of the stack effect. As shown in Chapter 3, stack-induced airflow rates depend on the vertical distance between openings and on the temperature difference between outside and inside. A roof ridge opening is at the greatest vertical distance from any wall window and stratification of air temperature occurs in the open space below, thus increasing the indoor–outdoor temperature difference. The higher the roof opening, the higher is the airflow rate. A way to increase further the stack airflow is the use of solar chimneys. However, such chimneys need to be placed higher above the roof ridge in order to avoid heat transfer from the solar chimney to the space underneath.

Special roof openings can be employed in order to optimize the combination of wind and stack ventilation. A double-shaft roof ridge opening lets both wind and stack airflow occur at the same time, with some possibility of conflict below the separation plane. A single-shaft roof ridge opening with mono-directional flaps against the wind functions only as a suction device combining the Bernoulli and stack effects.

6.2.2.2 Multistorey apartment buildings

Apartment buildings have, when compared to single-family units, greater height – usually, three or more storeys – all rooms on the same level and no usable roof space except, occasionally, for the top floor. These characteristics make *wind-driven wall cross ventilation* practically the only effective natural ventilation technique that can be used in multistorey apartment buildings.

Although stack ventilation is theoretically possible if the building is considered as a whole, some constraints apply for reasons of indoor air quality and economics. Stack ventilation through stairwells may cause transport of odours from an apartment to the one above. Separate purpose-made shafts serving each apartment are effective ventilation devices for windowless bathrooms, but would not be sufficient to ventilate an entire apartment unless built in a very costly way.

To allow for effective wind-driven wall cross ventilation, apartments should have external walls on the opposite sides of the building or, at least, on the windward and leeward sides, in order to avoid single-sided ventilation. For that reason, the building type with loaded stairwell plans – where single-sided units are possible but avoidable – is more effective, with regard to cross ventilation, than the type with loaded corridor plans – where all apartments have single-sided ventilation.

The building type with a double-loaded stairwell plan is far better, with regard to cross ventilation, than the type with a triple-loaded stairwell plan, where one of the apartments has single-sided exposure. Similarly, if buildings with public loaded corridor plans use transoms (windows above doors) to induce some cross ventilation, single-loaded corridor plans are far better than double-loaded corridor plans because of the reduced internal resistance to the flow.

An ingenious technical solution allowing the use of cross ventilation in an apartment building with double-loaded corridor plan is *L'Unité d'Habitation*,

Marseilles, designed by Le Corbusier. It has a corridor every third floor and each apartment is a duplex with an opening to the corridor as well as to the opposite side of the building.

6.2.3   Natural and hybrid ventilation systems in contemporary non-residential buildings

The examples shown in this section are related to non-residential building projects, only some of which have been realized, designed mainly by well-known architects and employing natural ventilation alone or combined with mechanical ventilation.

The projects are grouped into three categories in relation to the building type and form: multistorey office buildings, institutional buildings and industrial buildings. A synthetic description of the ventilation system used in each building follows. It is taken from a graduate thesis work for the School of Architecture of the University of Rome [21].

6.2.3.1 Multistorey office buildings
GATEWAY 2: LOCATION – BASINGSTOKE (UK); DESIGNERS – ARUP ASSOCIATES (1983)
This is a five-storey 14,000 m² office building with a deep width and a large atrium, 50 m long.

The central atrium is the social core of the building and has a passive climatization function as well (Figure 6.41). The warm air stored inside during winter is recirculated down the atrium to provide a partial supply to the office spaces of pre-heated air, which will be heated by radiant floors. In summer, the atrium, which is one and a half storeys higher than the roof, will act as an exhaust-stack ventilation system, sucking warmed air from the office spaces.

BUSINESS PROMOTION CENTRE: LOCATION: DUISBURG (G); DESIGNER – NORMAN FOSTER (1993)
This is one of the ten leading projects selected for the EC 'Solar House' Programme.

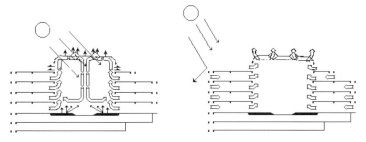

Figure 6.41. ARUP's Gateway 2 [22] - airflow patterns through the building and the atrium in winter (left) and summer (right)

With regard to ventilation, its main feature is a micro-climate air circulation system around the desk of each office. A purposely designed HVAC system, integrating photovoltaic (PV) solar collectors with TIM (transparent insulation material) captors, heats and cools water circulating through radiant panels located in the floor for heating and in the ceiling for cooling. Air, mechanically supplied from grilles in the floor, flows through both panels before reaching the desk on the floor above and is heated or cooled depending on which of the panels is active. An independent airflow is driven by the stack effect during summer within curtain wall panels with an air cavity.

Although the building cannot be considered naturally ventilated, it is worth mentioning because of its careful design in relation to comfort ventilation.

INLAND REVENUE SERVICES: LOCATION – NOTTINGHAM (UK); DESIGNER – MICHAEL HOPKINS (1993)

Hopkins's design for the Headquarters building of the British Inland Revenue Services was the winner in a competition whose participants were, among others, Richard Rogers and ARUP Associates.

Inspired by Australian termite mounds, the basic characteristics of the multiblock complex are the huge cylindrical towers located at the four corners of each block (Figure 6.42). Each tower acts only as an exhaust stack ventilation system sucking air from halls and corridors (Figure 6.43).

Figure 6.42. Hopkins's Inland Revenue Centre: perspective view (M. Hopkins & Partners, 1994) [23]

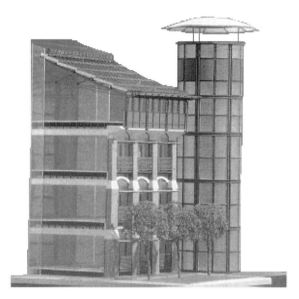

Figure 6.43 : Hopkins's Inland Revenue Centre: a wind tower (M. Hopkins & Partners, 1994) [23]

An additional exhaust stack airflow is driven through clerestories from the upper floor of each building wing.

INLAND REVENUE SERVICES: LOCATION – NOTTINGHAM (UK); DESIGNER – RICHARD ROGERS (DESIGN FOR COMPETITION) (1991)
Rogers's design for the Inland Revenue Headquarters is based on natural airflow control from several viewpoints.

First, the form itself of the building complex suggests a soft adaptation to wind flow rather than the usual sharp-edged approach. Second, landscaping, water and architecture are closely integrated to allow for improving microclimate conditions as well as ambient perception (Figure 6.44). Third, the overall conception of a reciprocal mutual function between inside and outside,

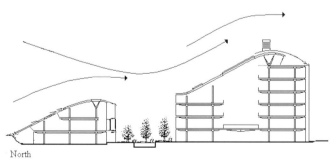

North

Figure 6.44. Rogers's design for the Inland Revenue Centre

emphasized by the extended transparent undulated roof covering the whole complex, creates a 'breezes' feeling. Fourth, technological components, such as a stack exhaust tower, double-envelope ventilated walls and exposed concrete ceilings for night ventilation, act as passive means of cooling and heating.

OFFICE BUILDING WITH A WIND-TOWER–ATRIUM SYSTEM: LOCATION – ROME (ITALY); DESIGNER – CRISTIANA PAOLETTI [21]

The subject of the thesis was the design of an office building complex on the site of a former municipal warehouse, near the river Tevere in Rome. Bioclimatic characteristics were one of the main requirements of the thesis work.

Optimal use of naturally induced ventilation is the principal criterion followed by the thesis design. The complex comprises two separated building blocks of different height, connected at the basement level. The wind-stack-driven main ventilation system works, basically, in the same way as the Iranian wind tower system discussed above.

Bow-shaped wind towers at each end of the main block (Figure 6.45) catch the cool westerly breezes high above ground, frequent in Rome on hot summer afternoons. The entering air, denser than the air inside the tower, flows down and is drawn through buried pipes, wherein it is further cooled, and then driven up through ducts placed in the north side wall of each building wing as a result

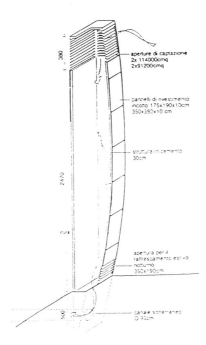

Figure 6.45. Paoletti's office building:
the wind tower [21]

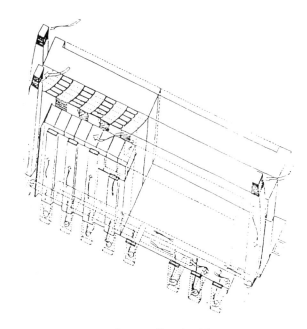

*Figure 6.46. Paoletti's office building: axonometric
view showing the airflow through the wind towers,
buried pipes and vertical ducts [21]*

of the stack effect of the atrium (Figure 6.46). In the lower building, outdoor air is taken directly from wind catchers at ground level to the buried pipes and then to the vertical ducts. From the vertical ducts the airflow enters the office spaces through grilles in suspended floors and then exhausted through the openings at the top of the atrium.

In summer, at night, an upwards airflow is generated within the towers owing to the release of the heat stored during the day. However, this flow may not be sufficient to suck air from the office spaces, so the towers are separated from the building, the buried pipes closed and the atrium openings used as exhaust vents.

On a winter day, the cold air entering the towers flows down to the buried pipes and is warmed because the ground temperature is higher than the outside ambient temperature. Air solar collectors placed on the concave atrium roof are used to heat the air pre-heated by the buried pipes. Openings at the top of the atrium let the air out to ventilate the office spaces. At night, all systems are non-operational in order to minimize heat losses.

6.2.3.2 *Institutional buildings*

CULTURAL CENTRE JEAN-MARIE TIJBAOU: LOCATION – NOUMEA (NEW CALEDONIA); DESIGNERS – RENZO PIANO BUILDING WORKSHOP

Composed of a series of seashell-like structures 9 to 24 m high, the architecture designed by Piano (Figure 6.47) is an inspiring modern interpretation of the

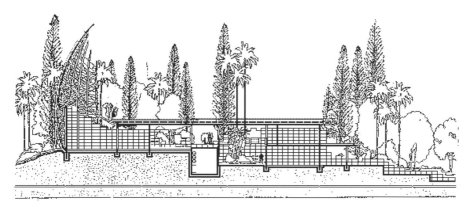

Figure 6.47. Cross section of Piano's design for the Tijbaou Centre [23]

adaptable-skin concept, on which are based traditional shelters, such as the American Indian *tipi* or the Iraqi *ma'dam* house described above.

The forms, as well as the layout, of the buildings constituting the Centre take the climate characteristics of the site and wind movements into account. The linear narrow development of the complex along a spinal path, to which are symmetrically connected the seashell structures grouped in three 'villages' separated by gardens, allows for air to be let through while protecting the inner spaces from strong hot winds.

The seashell structure has a double envelope: an external openable bent grid-like shell and an internal impermeable, but also openable, vertical wall. When the wind is weak, both the bottom part of the external envelope and the top of the inner wall, are open, so that warm air inside the building can be exhausted as a result of the stack and Venturi effects (Figure 6.48).

When the wind is of medium strength, both bottom parts are open to allow for cross ventilation. When the wind is very strong, all openings on the shell are automatically closed. A negative pressure zone is created at the top of the external shell deflecting the wind, thus increasing the stack airflow driven from the inside spaces through a roof vent.

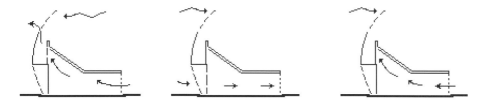

Figure 6.48. Piano's Tijbaou Centre design; schemes of the airflow patterns with wind: weak (left), medium (centre), strong (right) [21]

This project, aimed to host the first University Campus of Cyprus, was developed following the organizational principle of the oasis, integrating architecture, climate and site.

The building complex is longitudinally laid out against a stepped embankment so that the roof level is roughly at the same height as the highest ground terrace, placed on the north side of the complex, from where cooler winds blow.

Placed against the vertical wall of the highest terrace, wind towers with PV panels on the roof catch the air almost at ground level and bring it down through air canals located under the buildings, using PV-assisted fans when the wind speed is not high enough (Figure 6.49).

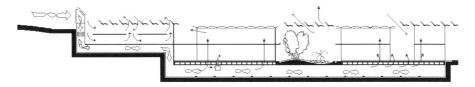

Figure 6.49. Cucinella's University of Cyprus: cross section showing the airflow patterns; in summer the ground acts as a heat sink, in winter as a heat source [25]

The air canals feed a plenum – called an air lake – positioned under the ground floor of the buildings. Grilles in the floors allow for ventilating the internal spaces with air that is cooler than the outside air during summer and is warmer in winter.

Polluted air is sucked out naturally through openings on a level roof, which covers both buildings and semi-outdoor spaces. The roof is made of 2.4 m long beams with a flying-bird-like cross section, partially tilted to reflect daylight into the buildings without direct solar gain (Figure 6.50).

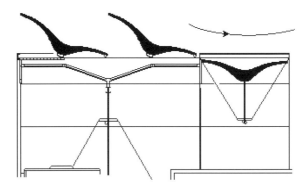

Figure 6.50. Cucinella's University of Cyprus: detail of the roof

Underneath the tilted beams, openable skylights are located to allow for both light penetration and inlet–outlet airflow. The orientation of the tilted-wing beams is such that only wind from the north can enter. When warm winds blow from the south, the cross-sectional shape of the beams induces negative pressure as a result of the Venturi effect, thus enhancing the stack flow through the roof.

SCHOOL OF ENGINEERING, DE MONTFORT UNIVERSITY: LOCATION –
LEICESTER (UK); DESIGNERS – ALAN SHORT AND BRIAN FORD
The various spaces – classrooms, studios, offices, laboratories, auditoria – are articulated around a void between two auditoria.

The natural ventilation system, which uses one of the passive energy-conservation strategies, together with solar control and optimum daylighting, is based on exhaust stack airflow through tower chimneys of square cross section, recalling the existing red ones in Leicester (Figure 6.51).

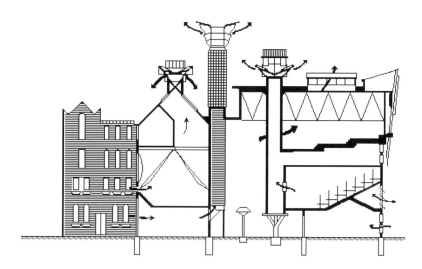

Figure 6.51, School of Engineering at Leicester: cross section showing the airflow through the chimneys [26]

NIGERIAN SOLAR ENERGY CENTRE: LOCATION: NIAMEY (NIGERIA);
DESIGNER – LAZLO MESTER DE PARAJD [27]
This building complex, designed to host a research centre, is an experimental construction itself. Several climate and energy control technologies were used in the building, mainly related to solar protection and the use of thermal inertia to take account of the local climate.

The only characteristic regarding natural ventilation is a special double-envelope external wall, which is cooled by stack airflow induced within the air cavity by bottom and top vents (Figure 6.52).

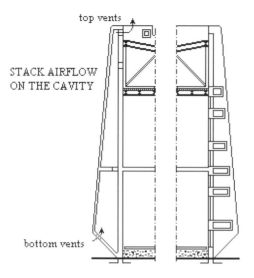

Figure 6.52. Nigerian Solar Energy Centre:
the ventilated double-envelope cavity wall

6.2.3.3 Industrial buildings

OFFICE SERVICES FOR AN ELECTROMECHANICAL FACTORY: LOCATION –
VICENZA (ITALY); DESIGNER – RENZO PIANO BUILDING WORKSHOP
(1985) [28]

The building is a large monozone volume covered by a concave curved roof and connected to the electromechanical factory by a filter corridor. Its tent-like roof based on a tensile structure seems to have been inspired by the Bedouin canvas shelter (Figure 6.53).

A narrowing space between the higher end of the roof and a curved upper wall leaning against the V-shaped tilted pillars, with a vent in between, functions as a funnel for the air rising as a result of the stack and Venturi effects.

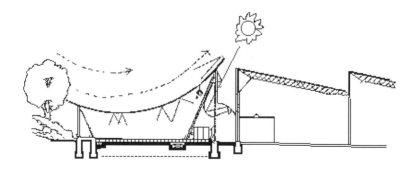

Figure 6.53. Piano's office building: cross section showing the airflow
patterns around and through the building

FARSONS BREWERY: LOCATION – MALTA; DESIGNERS – ALAN SHORT AND
BRIAN FORD

The Simmonds Farsons Building is an industrial brewery with no air conditioning, in spite of the hot climate of Malta (summer ambient temperature range
between 20°C and 35°C; mild winters with temperatures ranging from 9°C to
19°C). This is due to the highly passive design of the complex.

With regard to natural ventilative cooling, the main strategy combines
night-time convective cooling of the large exposed thermal mass with daytime
stack ventilation through shafts and chimneys (Figure 6.54).

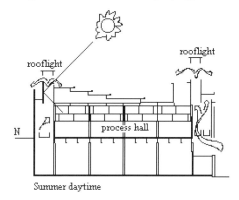

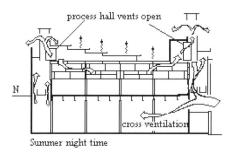

*Figure 6.54. Short and Ford's Farsons
Brewery: stack airflow patterns [29]*

REFERENCES

1. Boutet, T.S. (1987).*Controlling Air Movement: A Manual for Architects and
   Builders*. McGraw-Hill Book Company, New York.
2. Arens, E. (1984). *Natural Ventilative Cooling of Buildings*. Design Manual 11.02,
   NAVFAC, Alexandria, VA.
3. Olgyay, V. (1969). *Design with Climate*. Princeton University Press, Princeton, NJ.
4. European Prestandard 1762:1994. 'Ventilation of buildings'.
5. Grosso, M., D. Marino and E. Parisi (1994). 'Wind Pressure Distribution on Flat
   and Tilted Roofs: A Parametrical Model'. *Proceedings of the European Conference
   on Energy Performance and Indoor Climate in Buildings*, Lyon, France.

6. Grosso, M. (1995). 'CPCALC⁺: Calculation of Wind Pressure Coefficients on Buildings'. CEC-DGXII PASCOOL Programme, Final Report, Athens, Greece.
7. Grosso, M. (1992). 'Wind Pressure Distribution around Buildings – a Parametrical Model'. *Energy and Buildings*, Vol. 18, No. 2, pp. 101–131.
8. Martin, A.J. (1995). *Control of Natural Ventilation*. Technical Note TN11/95, BSRIA, Bracknell, UK.
9. Levermore, G.J. (1992). *Building Energy Management Systems, an Application to Heating and Control*. E&FN Spon, London.
10. Van Paassen, A.H.C., R.W. Kouffeld and E.J. Swinkels. (1993). 'Installations in Low Energy Houses'. *Third European Conference on Architecture*, Florence, May 1993, pp. 409–412.
11. Oseland, N. (1994). 'A Review of Thermal Comfort and its Relevance to Future Design Models and Guidance'. *Proceedings of BEPAC Conference*, York, pp. 205–216.
12. Arnold, D. (1996). 'Mixed-mode HVAC – An Alternative Philosophy'. *ASHRAE Transactions*, Vol. 102, Part 1, pp. 687–693
13. Santamouris, M. and D.N. Asimakopoulos (eds) (1994). *Passive Cooling of Buildings*. Central Institution for Energy Efficiency Education (CIENE), Athens, 1994.
14. Martin, A. J. (1995). 'Night Cooling Control Strategies'. *Proceedings of CIBSE National Conference*, Vol. 2, Eastbourne, UK, pp. 215–222.
15. Van Paassen, A.H.C. and P.J. Lute (1993). 'Energy Saving through Controlled Ventilation Windows'. *Third European Conference on Architecture*, Florence, May, pp. 208–211.
16. Evans, B. (1993). 'Integrating fabric and function'. *The Architects' Journal*, 2 June, 42–48.
17. Bahadori, M.N. (1978). 'Passive Cooling Systems in Iranian Architecture'. *Scientific American*, Vol. 238, No. 2 (February), pp. 144–154.
18. Fathy, H. (1986). *Natural Energy and Vernacular Architecture: Principles and Examples with Reference to Hot Arid Climates*. Published for The United Nations University by University of Chicago Press, Chicago, IL.
19. ENEA – IN/ARCH. *Bioclimatic Architecture* (1992). Leonardo-De Luca Editori, Rome.
20. Fanchiotti, A. (1982). 'The *Covoli*: A Natural Cooling System in Palladian Villas'. *Spazio e Società*, No. 19.
21. Paoletti, C. (1995). 'Progetto di un Edificio per Uffici a Roma: Il Comfort Attraverso la Ventilazione Naturale Integrata'. Thesis for Degree in Architecture, School of Architecture, University of Rome La Sapienza.
22. 'Gateway 2' (1984). *The ARUP Journal*, June, pp. 2–9.
23. Hopkins, M. & Partners (1994). 'Low Energy Offices – Interim Report', EC JOULE II Contract No. JOU2-CT93-0235.
24. '"Centre Culturel Kanak à Nouméa", Concours: Projet Piano' (1991). *L'Architecture d'Aujourd'hui*, Paris, No. 277, pp. 9–11.
25. Arnaboldi, M. A. (1994). '"Changes at School", Progetto: Mario Cucinella'. *L'Arca*, Milan, No. 81, pp. 50–55.
26. Hawkes (1994). 'User Control in a Passive Building'. *The Architect's Journal*, 9 March, pp. 27–29.
27. Mester de Parajd, L. 'L'architecture Exportée'. *Le Mur Vivant*, No. 92.
28. *Renzo Piano and Building Workshop: Buildings and Projects 1971–1989* (1989). Rizzoli Publisher, Milan, pp. 156–163.
29. Evans, B. (1993). 'An Alternative to Air-conditioning'. *The Architects' Journal*, 10 February, pp. 55–59.

7

Naturally ventilated buildings

Edited by E. Maldonado

To illustrate how the principles of natural ventilation can be applied in real buildings and how these operate in practice, a selection of case studies has been monitored and studied throughout Europe. The buildings that were selected covered several types of climates (Figure 7.1), from the moderate summers of the Atlantic coast in the west and the North Sea neighbourhoods in the north, to the extreme heat of the Mediterranean Coast in the south, without forgetting the warm continental climates either.

Figure 7.1. Locations of the naturally ventilated buildings studied

Main contributors: 7.1 E. Maldonado and J.L. Alexandre; 7.2 M. Grosso, S. Sciuto and C. Priolo; 7.3 E. Dascalaki and M. Santamouris; 7.4 P. Wouters, L. Vandaele and D. Ducarme; 7.5 K. Limam and M. Abadie; 7.6 G. Guarracino and V. Richalet

Several types of buildings were also studied:

- A detached single-family residence (in Porto, Portugal);
- A row-house single-family residence (in Louvain-la-Neuve, Belgium);
- Two apartments in multifamily high-rise buildings (in La Rochelle, France and in Catania, Italy);
- An office building (in Athens, Greece);
- A school building (in Lyon, France).

Most of the buildings perform quite well, providing quite comfortable conditions for their occupants. As common characteristics, all the buildings that perform well have high internal inertia, efficient window shading for control of solar gain and the possibility (and practice) of implementing natural ventilation when conditions are suitable and it is desirable to do so. The effectiveness of natural ventilation, in both cross-ventilation and single-sided ventilation cases, is demonstrated in each case by real measurements of the performance of the buildings with and without allowing natural ventilation to occur: indoor temperatures are always lower when there is natural ventilation during cool night periods.

Most of these buildings perform so well that they need no air conditioning at all and overheating is a rare occurrence. Of course, this is possible only when internal gains are small, such as in the four residential units described henceforth. In the office building, with higher internal gains, as is usually the case, air conditioning is still needed, but the required energy consumption is significantly reduced.

However, there is one case included, the School of Architecture in Lyon, where the recommended design criteria were not followed, with undesirable results for the indoor comfort of the students. Inertia is low, shading is not the most effective and the existing schemes for promoting natural ventilation are not too 'user-friendly'. Temperatures in excess of 35°C were measured indoors. This case is included because it is important to realize that not all buildings behave as well as the other five cases described in this chapter. It is also an illustration of the consequences of neglecting one or more of the critical points (high inertia, good shading and natural ventilation when desirable) in normal building design in temperate climates.

In every case, it is evident that compromises are present. Different solutions have been selected by the designers to overcome many of the difficulties that were listed in chapter 5, depending on specific circumstances and the personal preferences of either the designers themselves or the building owners. This conveys the necessary link between theory and practice, providing the lesson that every designer must translate models and principles, such as those described in the first six chapters of this book, into real (successful) buildings.

7.1   SINGLE-FAMILY RESIDENCE (PORTO, PORTUGAL)

Figure 7.2. The single-family residence in Gaia, a suburb of Porto

This is a residence that was designed using bioclimatic principles. Its main axis runs along a east–west direction, exposing one of the large façades to the southern sun (Figure 7.2). There are few openings in the north, east and west façades, mostly for daylighting and promoting natural ventilation. All glazings in the main façade are well shaded by at least one device: overhangs, internal wooden doors and outside movable metallic roller shades. The envelope is adequately insulated. The geographical location in Gaia, a suburb of Porto, is indicated in Figure 7.3.

Figure 7.3. The location of the single-family residence in Gaia, Portugal

As the basis for temperature control in summer, the building uses load-avoidance techniques (insulation of the envelope and shading), a high level of inertia (brick and concrete structure with heavy interior surfaces) and ventilative cooling whenever the outdoor air is colder than the indoor temperature. Natural ventilation plays a decisive role in ensuring occupant comfort. It can be as low as 0.3 ach when all windows are closed and as much as 20 ach when cross ventilation is allowed to take place.

The performance of the building is extremely good, with indoor temperatures reaching, at most, 27°C for a few hours in the office, where internal gains are higher. Most of the time, during the warmest periods, temperature remains between 23 and 25°C.

Occupant control is essential for starting and stopping natural ventilation, as well as for choosing the most efficient ventilation paths.

7.1.1   Site characteristics

The building is located on the top of a hill, on a site very exposed to south and westerly winds coming from the sea. Other buildings around the site are one or two stories high and thus offer little or no buffering, even from northerly winds, the direction in which nearby buildings are closer. In summer, strong north-west winds are very frequent in the afternoon. During the warmest periods of summer, winds are either calm or continental, from east or north-east. The site and wind characteristics are illustrated in Figure 7.4.

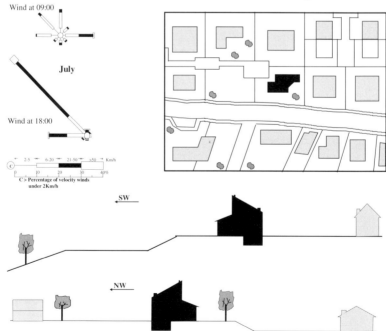

Figure 7.4. Characteristics of the site and typical summer winds

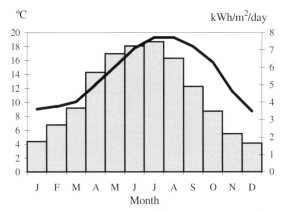

Figure 7.5. Mean monthly temperature and radiation in Porto

The local climate is quite mild, though still hot enough in summer to require special care in building design if comfort is to be attained without air-conditioning (Figure 7.5).

Large daily amplitudes in summer (about 10-11°C) mean that night temperatures are always cool (below 20°C) and thus suitable for night ventilation. During the afternoon, temperatures are normally above the comfort range.

7.1.2   Description of the building

This residence has two main floors, plus a basement (garage and storage space) and an attic (half with a room, the rest unfinished and used for storage). The main floors connect through an open staircase but are physically separated from the basement and the attic by doors that are kept permanently closed except for access of the occupants for a few seconds at a time.

The ground-floor plan (Figure 7.6, left) has a relatively complex shape, with multiple paths for ventilation possible. The top floor (Figure 7.6, right) has a more linear plan and natural ventilation is also possible in various modes. The master bedroom, however, presents the most challenges, as it only has a south

Figure 7.6. Plan of the Porto residence: left, ground floor; right, top floor

*Figure 7.7. The east and north sides of the house,
showing the lack of windows on these two sides*

Figure 7.8. The four main elevations

Figure 7.9. View showing the wrought iron movable bars

facing window and a nearby door to the rest of the house, with little interaction with most of the other spaces.

The internal doors are mostly kept open, allowing the free flow of air. However, the envelope is reasonably airtight (< 0.3 ach on average) and air movement is low unless windows are opened. There is no mechanical ventilation system.

A view of the side of the house is given in Figure 7.7, while drawings of the four elevations are given in Figure 7.8.

All the windows are double glazed, with clear glass shaded by overhangs or outdoor roller shades, and by wooden shutters indoors. For security reasons, downstairs windows are also protected outside by wrought iron movable bars that represent about a 10% shading of the windows but pose little resistance to airflow (Figure 7.9).

7.1.3   Building fabric

The building has a concrete and brick structure. The walls have two layers of hollow bricks with an internal air gap. A 3 cm layer of extruded polystyrene is glued to the external surface of the internal brick layer (Figure 7.10). All the walls are covered by a 1 cm thick layer of plaster.

The roof is covered with traditional reddish clay tiles and has 6 cm of insulation. The floor over the garage is insulated underneath with 5 cm of cork board. Ceilings are plastered and floors are covered with clay tiles except in the master bedroom, which is carpeted.

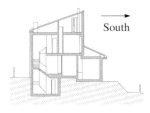

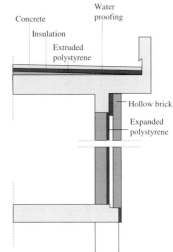

Figure 7.10. Section (above) and insulation detail (right)

Table 7.1. Heat loss coefficients

	A (m^2)	K (W m^{-2}K^{-1})	AK (WK^{-1})
External walls	402.6	0.65	261.7
Buried perimeter	60	1.2	7 2
Roof (attic)	35	0.7	24.5
Roof (rooms)	135	0.48	64.8
Floor (over garage)	55	0.57	31.4
Floor (over outdoors)	15	0.59	8.9
Windows	39.1	3.9	152.5
Air exchange:	0.3 ach		
Total			
Heating load	12.3 kW		
Cooling load	7.7 kW		

All the ends of the exposed concrete slabs, where they connect with walls, are covered with 5 cm of insulation to minimize the effects of thermal bridges.

The solid and heavy indoor finishings give a strong thermal inertia to the building and make it particularly well suited for ventilative cooling. Table 7.1 shows the heat loss coefficients.

7.1.4   Pattern of use

The building is occupied by a family of two. It is generally empty during the day and occupied after 6 pm until 8–9 in the next morning during weekdays, and 24 hours a day during weekends.

In summer, windows are kept closed during the day, the outdoor roller shutters upstairs are deployed to provide almost total shading, and the indoor wooden shutters are mostly kept half shut downstairs and in the master bedroom, to avoid excessive solar gains while still providing enough daylighting.

In the evening, windows are opened to promote natural ventilation when conditions are suitable, but they are closed during the night for security and noise protection during sleep.

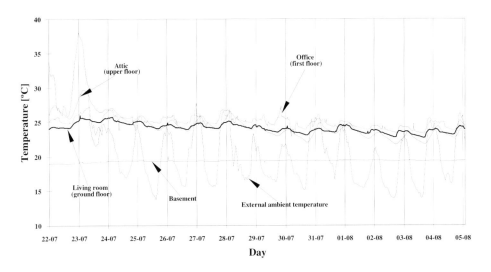

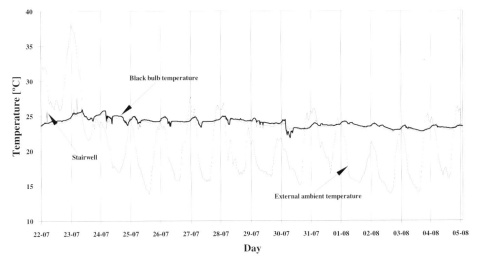

Figure 7.11. Temperature variations over the monitoring period

7.1.5   Thermal behaviour of the building during summer

The building was monitored over a two-week period during the summer of 1993. The climate was typical for the site, with a few very hot days before and at the beginning of the monitoring period, followed by average days with highs around 25°C. Despite the early hot period, the building's high inertia and careful load avoidance control by the occupants prevented serious overheating indoors; the indoor temperature upstairs never went above 27.5°C. Then, it slowly cooled down to around 25°C, with daily indoor variations of about 2°C. As surface temperatures indoors are lower than air temperatures, comfort is always possible, and black bulb temperature upstairs, where it is warmer, always stayed between 24°C and 26°C (Figure 7.11).

The temperature in the basement, which is in direct contact with the soil because it is buried on all sides but one, is constant (0.2°C variation over the two-week period) and slightly below the average outdoor air temperature, as can be predicted by theory. The ground floor is generally 1–2°C cooler than the upper floor, showing a slight stratification and confirming a low air circulation rate between the two floors.

7.1.6   Impact of ventilation strategies

The plots in Figure 7.11 are too general to show the impact of ventilation upon the thermal performance of the various spaces. However, more detailed plots show that:

- When windows are opened and natural ventilation starts, indoor temperature suddenly drops to a value closer to outdoors and remains there while the windows are opened (Figure 7.12). Then, after the windows have been closed, the temperature rises again, but to a value lower than if the natural ventilation had never taken place.

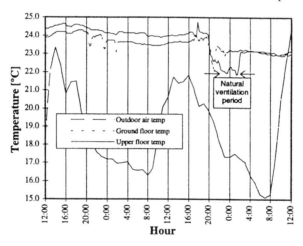

Figure 7.12. The effect of opening windows

- The same phenomenon can also be shown by comparing two similar days, with identical indoor and outdoor conditions, one with natural ventilation in the evening (airflow as in Figure 7.13) and another without. Although this cannot be taken as absolute proof, because no two days are exactly alike, the trends are visible and indicative of the potential of natural night ventilation as a cooling sink.
- For the situation shown in the Figures 7.12 and 7.13, with the window open in the bedroom (1.60 m high by 0.32 m wide) and in the bathroom (1.35 m high by 0.26 m wide), cross ventilation takes place along a relatively indirect path. The AIOLOS software predicts an

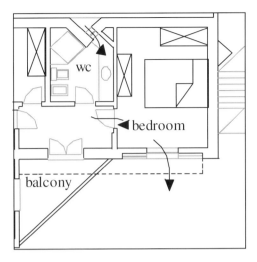

Figure 7.13. The airflow for natural ventilation

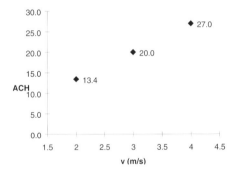

Figure 7.14. AIOLOS predictions of the airflow

average air change rate of 6 ach during the period when natural ventilation takes place (Figure 7.14).

7.1.7 Occupant response

The occupants promote natural ventilation whenever the indoor temperature is above 24°C and the temperature outdoors is cooler though not too cold. Windows are only kept open, at the latest, until bedtime, as noise from the street traffic would be uncomfortable and prevent sleep. Anyhow, there is no need for more natural ventilation than during the few hours a day when it takes place, because indoor temperatures are already quite comfortable during the night (about 23°C) and cooler temperatures would also become uncomfortable. Natural ventilation is also stopped whenever the outdoor air becomes too cold and uncomfortable.

A problem with natural ventilation is the entry of mosquitoes. Though there are not many flies, mosquitoes and other bugs in the area, one is enough to annoy the occupants. Natural ventilation is thus promoted only when it is really necessary, i.e. when indoor temperatures go above 25°C.

Natural ventilation is more common upstairs than downstairs, owing to the temperature gradient that makes upstairs warmer than downstairs.

Indoor temperatures are kept within the comfort range almost all the time, and the occupants are quite happy with the building.

7.1.8   Conclusions

This is a good example of how natural ventilation can complement good building design (gain avoidance on the basis of insulation, light colours and solar control) and, as a result of correct implementation, allow lowering of the indoor temperature of the building by 1°C to 2°C using ventilation only during a small portion of the day. The local climate is very favourable, with not too extreme outdoor temperatures but quite large daily temperature swings that make late evening and night temperatures usually colder than indoors.

7.2   APARTMENT BUILDING (CATANIA, ITALY)

Figure 7.15. The apartment building in Catania

This is an apartment building located in the promenade of Catania, Italy (Figures 7.15, 7.16). The building has an L shape and has a large east-oriented façade facing the sea. The south-oriented façade faces a large square.

The flat selected for the analysis is on the third floor and has one side oriented to the square (south) and the opposite one facing the internal

Figure 7.16. The geographical position of Catania

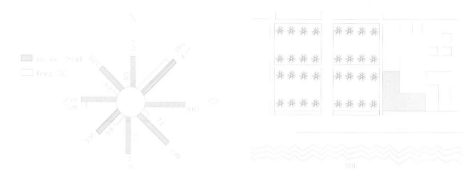

Wind distribution in July

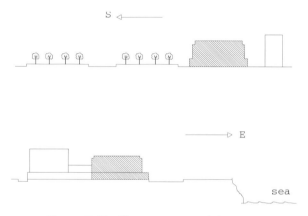

Figure 7.17. Characteristics of the site

courtyard (north). All the south-facing windows are shaded by interpane venetian blinds and also partially shaded by the balcony of the floor above.

During summer, the temperature control of the flat is achieved by solar control and natural ventilation. No mechanical system is utilized in summer for air conditioning. During afternoon and night, when the external temperature drops below the internal one, the occupants usually open the windows to provide cooling.

The performance of the building is quite good, since the presence of apertures on two opposite sides and the see breeze often make it possible to achieve a good level of ventilation.

The use of natural ventilation allows the internal temperature of building to be reduced by about 3°C, as confirmed during the short monitoring period.

7.2.1   Site characteristics

The building is located on the promenade of Catania, in a site very exposed to the see breeze and the east winds (Figure 7.17). Despite the medium built-up density of the urban zone where the building is located, no nearby building

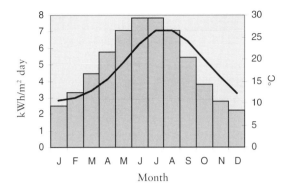

Figure 7.18. Mean monthly temperature and radiation in Catania

interferes with the one studied. In summer the wind generally comes from the east and, as consequence, reaches the building directly from the sea.

The local climate of Catania is quite hot, with a mean maximum temperature during July and August higher than 30°C (Figure 7.18).

During summer nights the temperature drops and the average difference between daily maximum and minimum temperatures is about 10°C. The mean wind speed during summer is about 2.6 m s^{-1}. These characteristics make night ventilation a very effective strategy.

7.2.2   Description of the building

The building has no bioclimatic property but has interesting architectural features and is well exposed to sea winds. It has an L shape with the main

Figure 7.19. A general view of the apartment block showing the variations in the window line

Figure 7.20. Plan of the selected flat

façades oriented to the east (the sea side) and south (the square side). The rear overlooks an open courtyard.

The building has six storeys with an attic on the upper floor. The main façades of the building show a variation created by the recession of some of the windows (Figure 7.19).

The flat selected for the analysis is situated on the third floor and has three external sides facing to north, south and west (Figure 7.20). The living room (Figure 7.21) and one bedroom are placed along the south side; two bedrooms and the kitchen are north-oriented facing the courtyard. Only one little aperture is located on the west side. A central corridor connects the rooms.

Figure 7.21. The living room

Almost all the rooms have large windows that make it possible to achieve, when required, good levels of natural ventilation. Several possible paths for cross ventilation are available to cool the apartment during the nights.

During the monitoring carried out in summer 1996 the effects of the cross ventilation between the living room and the kitchen and of the single-sided ventilation in the living room were analysed.

7.2.3   Building fabric

The building has a structure made of concrete and bricks, very common in southern Italy. The external walls have two layers of hollow bricks (outer thickness 12 cm, inner thickness 8 cm) with an internal air gap of 10 cm, without any insulation layer. The floors have a concrete structure and are finished with marble tiles.

The windows of the bedrooms and of the living room have double-pane glazing with an interpane venetian blind (Figure 7.22). The air gap of the glazing is about 30 mm.

Figure 7.22. Blinds within the double-paned glass

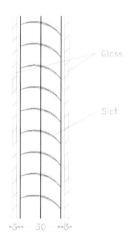

The windows of the kitchen are single-glazed without any solar protection (the kitchen is oriented to north). The air tightness is quite good. Table 7.2 shows the heat loss coefficients of the flat.

Table 7.2. Heat loss coefficients of the flat

	A (m²)	K (W m⁻²K⁻¹)	AK (WK⁻¹)
External walls	98.5	1.1	108.3
Windows:			
double pane	20.2	3.2	64.6
single pane	9.7	5.8	56.3
Air exchange:	0.5 ach		
Total	248 W°C⁻¹		

7.2.4   Pattern of use

The apartment is occupied by a family of four. In general, it is empty during the morning and almost fully occupied during the rest of the day.

During summer, temperature control is obtained by the correct use of the natural ventilation. During the morning and until the late afternoon (when the external temperature is higher than the internal temperature) the windows are kept closed and shades kept partially down. During the evening and night some windows are kept partially open according to the wind conditions.

7.2.5   Thermal behaviour and impact of ventilation strategies

The apartment was monitored over a two-week period during the summer of 1996. In order to evaluate the effect of natural ventilation, the monitoring was carried out during two periods with different patterns of use.

During the first period (three days), the windows of the living room and of the kitchen were kept open during evenings and nights, in order to promote cross ventilation. During the second period the windows were kept closed for the whole day.

Sensors of internal temperature and air velocity were placed in the kitchen and in the living room (Figure 7.23).

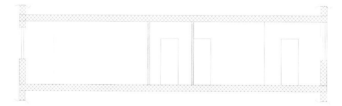

Figure 7.23. Section of the selected flat (between living-room and kitchen)

Two different procedures were utilized in order to evaluate the performance of the building under natural ventilation:

- a short monitoring period, during which measurements of indoor and outdoor temperature, air velocity and solar radiation were performed continuously for two weeks;
- tracer gas experiments, which were carried out over two nights.

7.2.5.1 The short monitoring period

During days when monitoring took place, the climatic conditions were representative of the hot season in Catania. Before the monitoring period there were three very hot days, with a maximum temperature of about 35°C. During the first days of monitoring the external temperature reached 30–31°C during

A = windows opened B = windows closed

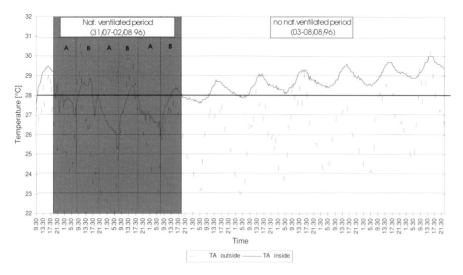

Figure 7.24. Analysis of the temperatures in the living room during the monitoring period

the day and went down to about 23°C during the night. The second period of monitoring was characterized by lower peaks of temperature, with a maximum temperature of below 29°C.

The graph in Figure 7.24 shows the comparison between the internal and external temperatures for the first three monitoring days (during which there was night ventilation) and for some of the following days (without natural ventilation). The plots show that:

- During the naturally ventilated period, the internal temperature went down during the night. Then, during the following day, it rose again, but reached lower peak values. During the third day the maximum temperature was 28.4°C and the average temperature 27.3°C.
- During the period without ventilation, the internal temperature rose steadily from day to day, even with lower outdoor ambient temperatures. After nine days the peak temperature was 30.5°C and the average temperature 30°C.
- Despite the continuous rise of the internal temperature, the building seems to have a high thermal inertia. In fact, the daily indoor temperature swings did not exceed 1°C.
- Figure 7.24 shows a demarcation line of 28°C that can be considered the separation between comfort and discomfort conditions. During the first period of monitoring the temperature exceeded this limit only for few hours in the day. During the second period, the temperature was always higher than 28°C.

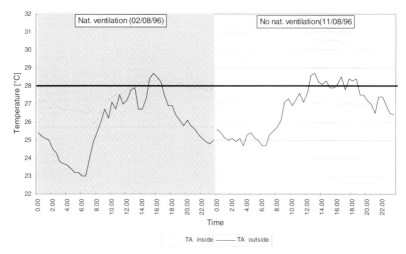

Figure 7.25. Comparison between a day with natural ventilation and one without natural ventilation

Figure 7.25 compares indoor temperatures on the third day of the naturally ventilated period with those on the ninth day of the non-ventilated period. The internal temperature during the non-ventilated day is about 2°C higher than on the ventilated day.

The internal air movement, for the living room and for the kitchen, during the first period of monitoring, is shown in Figure 7.26. When the windows are closed, the air velocity was in general lower than 0.15 m s^{-1}. During cross ventilation, the air movement reached 0.3–0.4 m s^{-1}.

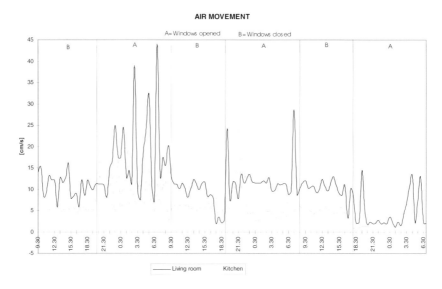

Figure 7.26. Air movement in the flat during the natural ventilation period

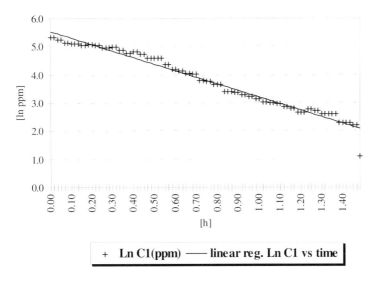

Figure 7.27. Results of the tracer gas experiments

7.2.5.2 Tracer gas experiments

Tracer gas experiments were carried out over two nights in order to investigate the single-sided ventilation in the living room.

During the experiments one hinged window in the living room, having an area of 1.0 m², was opened. Tracer-gas decay corresponds to an air change rate of 2.3 ach. Figure 7.27 shows the experimental points and the decay curve calculated by means of linear regression between the logarithm of the concentration and time.

7.2.6 Conclusions

The efficacy of natural ventilation in shared buildings without any specific bioclimatic features can be very high for meteorological conditions similar to those in Catania.

In this case study the effect of night ventilation gave very good results because of both the configuration of the flat (two opposite façades with apertures) and the climate (sea breeze, good temperature difference between day and night).

7.3   OFFICE BUILDING: MELETITIKI LTD (ATHENS, GREECE)

Figure 7.28. The office building in Athens

This is the architectural office of Meletitiki Ltd., A.N. Tombazis and Associates (Figure 7.28). It was constructed in 1995 and it is privately owned. The office occupies the right-hand wing of a complex with a Π shape, designed by the architect Alexandros Tombazis. The other spaces of the complex are used as offices by a construction company. The geographical position of Athens is shown in Figure 7.29.

Figure 7.28. The geographical position of Athens

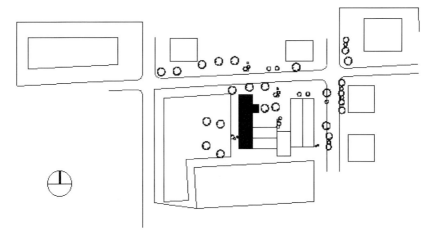

Figure 7.30. The siting of the office building

The long axis of the building runs north to south (Figure 7.30). The main entrance is on the eastern façade. The west and south façades of the building overlook an open space. A rectangular section of the east façade is adjacent to another building, which is part of the complex. The remaining part of the façade (20 m long) overlooks a paved semi-urban space. Opposite the east façade of the office there is a second building.

The envelope structure of the building is heavy, consisting of thick, well insulated exterior walls. Double-glazed window openings are mainly located on the east and west façades, providing adequate daylight conditions in the working spaces. Movable exterior roller shades above all windows are used in order to improve both visual and thermal comfort in the hot periods of the year.

Natural ventilation techniques are used in order to avoid overheating in the summer, as well as to improve thermal comfort conditions. Manual control of ceiling fans, as well as opening different windows to maintain an efficient cross ventilation of the interior spaces, help towards maintaining a thermally comfortable indoor environment. Ventilative cooling is achieved using night ventilation techniques.

The thermal performance of the building is very good. When the outdoor air temperature reaches 36°C, the mean indoor air temperature is 29°C, while night ventilation techniques lower the peak indoor air temperature by at least 2°C.

7.3.1   Site characteristics

The building is located in Polydrosso, a residential area in the northern suburbs of Athens. The local climate is mild; the heating period lasts from November to March while the cooling period lasts from June to September. During the summer period, the prevailing wind direction in the morning is north with a wind speed often exceeding 6 m s^{-1} (Figure 7.31). In the afternoon the wind blows mainly from the south or south-west with lower speeds.

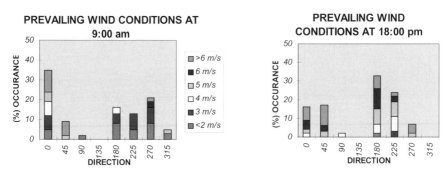

Figure 7.31. Prevailing wind conditions

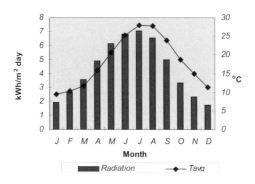

*Figure 7.32. Mean monthly temperature
and radiation in Athens*

The average ambient air temperature in the morning is 29°C and 24°C in the night (Figure 7.32), which indicates the potential for applying night ventilation as a cooling technique. Peak ambient air temperatures during the cooling period are mainly observed during the afternoon hours (12:00–16:00). During this period of the day, the prevailing wind direction is south-east and the average wind speed is 6 m s^{-1}.

7.3.2   Description of the building

The building is a unique space, in terms of interior design and space layout. It has a rectangular shape, 7 m wide, 29.6 m long and a total height of 10.60 m. The main axis runs north to south and the shallow plan of the east–west axis permits a satisfactory daylighting performance. The only internal partitions in the space are the light-weight floors and stairs. The structure of the building provides a lot of space for the drawing boards, computer-aided design offices, a meeting room and a library.

The total floor area of the building is 1000 m^2. The building consists of three floors and a basement. Figures 7.33 and 7.34 show north and west elevations respectively, while Figure 7.35 shows a cross section of the building. Each floor has an area of about 250 m^2. The height of each floor is 3.00 m. Each floor has

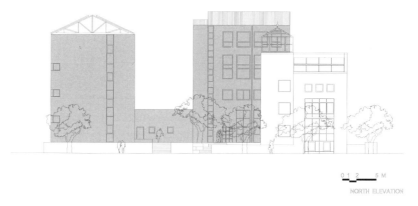

Figure 7.33. North elevation

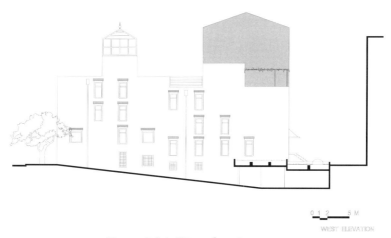

Figure 7.34. West elevation

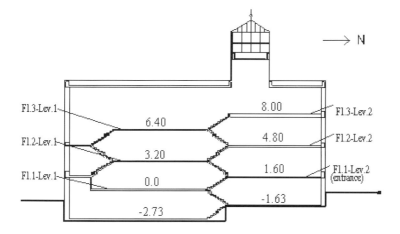

Figure 7.35. Cross section of the building, showing the different levels

*Figure 7.36. The different levels (library–meeting room,
drawing boards) composing the second floor*

a continuous layout, with no internal walls, and develops into different levels, which differ in height by 1.60 m. Each level is connected through a staircase to one level above and another one below it (Figures 7.35 and 7.36). The entrance hall (1.60 m above ground level), with service areas (lifts and WC) on one side, is a space 4.75 m long and 1.75 m wide. It is separated from the reception area by a glazed door. The reception level (level 2) is next to the entrance, but 1.60 m higher. A staircase connects the reception level with the levels above and below it. The underground basement extends from a level with one elevation at –1.60 m to a lower level at –2.73 m. The building has skylights on the top floor.

7.3.3   Building fabric

Table 7.3 gives details of the structural elements of the building, while Figure 7.37 shows aspects of the construction.

Table 7.3. The structural elements

Element	Structural details
Exterior walls	Plaster + Bricks (2 rows) + Insulation (100 mm) + Bricks (1 row)
Underground walls	Concrete (200 mm) + Aquoifine (3 mm)
Garage walls	Plaster + Concrete (200 mm) + Insulation (100 mm) + Bricks (1 row)
Floors with ground contact	Gravel + Insulation (100 mm) + Concrete (170 mm) + Mosaic (200 mm)
Interior floors	Sound insulation + Concrete (120 mm) + Mosaic (50 mm) + Oak wood
Roof	Sound insulation (50 mm)+ Concrete (150 mm)+ Roofmate + Gravel + Concrete tiles
Staircase	Metal + Oak wood

Figure 7.37. Views of the construction

The windows are positioned on the same central axis on the east and west façades. This produces high illuminance on the working plane of the drawing boards, which are placed in front of the openings. All window sills are 0.65 m above floor level. There are also four monitor windows on the third floor. All the windows are shaded by exterior blinds and the monitor windows by interior blinds. These blinds are made of a special white plastic cloth with small holes on its surface. The shading devices are adjusted by a mechanically controlled rotation mechanism in order to provide effective shading. Panels of cloth hanging from the roof are used to shade the monitor windows on the upper level.

Ventilation of the space can be controlled by the occupants by opening various windows to enhance the natural flow of the air. Ceiling fans are

Table 7.4. Heat loss coefficients

	A (m²)	K (W m⁻²K⁻¹)	AK (WK⁻¹)
Exterior walls	709.15	0.24	170.20
Roof	207.20	0.27	55.68
Basement floor	207.20	1.22	252.78
Windows	66.77	2.90	193.63

Cooling requirements (kWh)	Set-point temperature (°C)
7500	25
4500	27
2250	29

installed on all levels to improve the circulation of indoor air in cases when indoor temperature conditions exceed the acceptable levels for thermal comfort. Additionally, a system of two exhaust fans supplying $2 \times 25,000$ m³ h⁻¹, is located on the roof of the building. Both ceiling and exhaust fans are automatically turned on/off according to set-point temperature values implemented by a computer control program.

The overall heat loss coefficients are summarized in Table 7.4 for the main building elements.

7.3.4   Pattern of use

The majority of employees are in the building from 8:30 am until 5:30 pm. Occasionally, small groups remain in the building until later in the evening.

7.3.5   Building performance regarding ventilation

7.3.5.1 Natural ventilation
Four cross-ventilation experiments were carried out in order to study the performance of the building, as well as to determine the best patterns that the occupants can use to take best advantage of the building. The tracer-gas decay technique was followed, using N_2O as a tracer gas. The tested configurations are briefly discussed below.

CONFIGURATION A (FIGURE 7.38a)
The prevailing wind speed during this experiment was 4.2 m s⁻¹ coming from the south-west. The average indoor–outdoor air temperature difference was 2.8°C. Two openings of 2.25 m² each, one on the east and the other on the west façade of the building, were used to provide ventilation in the space. The openings were on the fifth and second levels respectively. Wind and temperature conditions enhanced circulation from the lower to the upper window. Cool outdoor air entered the lower level, while warm air exited from the upper

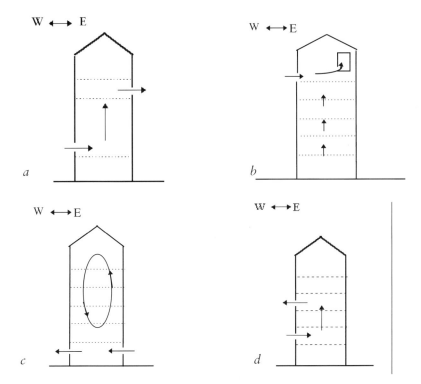

Figure 7.38. Natural ventilation configurations

level. A temperature difference of 2°C between the lower and the upper level caused an airflow acceleration, resulting in an average airflow rate equal to 6 ach.

CONFIGURATION B (FIGURE 7.38b)

The prevailing wind speed during this experiment was 2 m s^{-1} coming from the north-west. The average indoor–outdoor air temperature difference was 2.8°C. Two openings of 2.25 m^2 each, one on the west and the other on the north façade and both on the sixth level of the building, were used to provide ventilation in the space. As both windows were on the same level, on which the highest indoor–outdoor air-temperature difference was observed (3.4°C), the measured air exchange rate on this level was higher than that on lower levels. Ventilation of lower levels was due to buoyancy flow and, as the temperature difference between them was not very high (1.3°C), the observed airflow rates were small. Thus, the resulting average air exchange rate for the whole building was 1.6 ach.

CONFIGURATION C (FIGURE 7.38c)

The prevailing wind speed during this experiment was 8.2 m s^{-1} coming from the north-east. The average indoor–outdoor air temperature difference was

1.8°C. Two openings of 2.25 m² each, one on the east and the other on the west façade of the building, were used to provide ventilation in the space. Both openings were on the first level. The position of the openings towards the prevailing wind direction enhanced the flow from the window on the east to the window on the west, resulting in high air exchange rates measured on this level (10 ach). Consequently, ventilation of the upper levels was not as effective and warm air was trapped in the building. The average air renewal rate for the whole building was 4 ach.

CONFIGURATION D (FIGURE 7.38d)
D. This was a single sided ventilation experiment with openings at different heights. The prevailing wind speed during this experiment was 9.1 ms⁻¹ coming from the north-east. The average indoor–outdoor air temperature difference was 1.3°C. Two openings of 2.25 m² each, on the west façade of the building were used to provide ventilation in the space. The openings were on the first and fourth level respectively. Although the average wind speed during the experiment was high, the fact that both openings were on the leeward side of the building caused the flow to be mainly affected by buoyancy. The temperature difference between the higher and lower level was 1.8°C. This caused a stack effect from the lower to the upper level and a more homogeneous mixing of the indoor air. The average measured air exchange rate was equal to 2.4 ach.

7.3.5.2 *Mechanically assisted night ventilation*
The indoor air temperature of the building was monitored during two weeks in the summer 1995 (Table 7.5). The measurements were taken during the vacation period (26 July to 11 August 1995). During those 16 days, the building was empty of occupants (so, there were no internal gains) and the air conditioning system was off. While in this free-floating situation, the building underwent night ventilation during eight nights, from 10 pm to 6 am of the next day. During the night-ventilation period, a system of two exhaust fans was used in order to supply the building with outdoor air at a rate of $2 \times 25,000$ m³ h⁻¹. Additionally, four windows (three on the east and one on the south façade) were kept open during the same period. During the rest of the day, all windows and doors of the building were kept closed. Indoor air temperature was monitored at several levels in the building (Figure 7.39).

Table 7.5. Night ventilation
dates (1995)

26–27 July
27–28 July
30–31 July
31 July–1 August
1–2 August
2–3 August
8–9 August

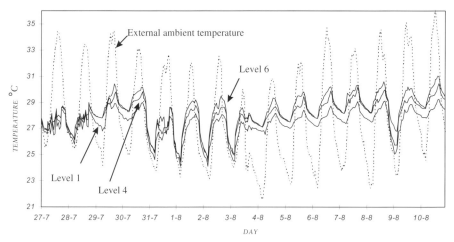

Figure 7.39. Temperature measurements during the monitoring period

During the periods without night ventilation the average indoor air temperature tended to rise. This trend stopped when night ventilation was applied. When the windows were closed, the high mass of the building caused the indoor air temperature to present a small variation (maximum − minimum ≈ 2°C) compared to the outdoor air-temperature variation (maximum − minimum ≈ 10°C). During the periods with night ventilation, the measured temperature on all floors dropped until it came very close to the ambient temperature. During the daytime, the temperature variation was similar on all floors and the existence of stratification was verified, resulting in a difference of 1–2°C between the highest and lowest measuring points in the building (levels 6 and 1 respectively).

7.3.5.3 *The impact of night ventilation on the building behaviour*

A closer look (Figure 7.40) at the plot in Figure 7.39 gives some insight into the impact of night ventilation on the performance of the building. During the night-ventilation period, the temperature in the building dropped and followed the variation of the ambient temperature. When night ventilation stopped, the temperature in the building was 2°C lower than when this strategy was not applied.

Comparison of two days with similar outdoor ambient temperature conditions (Figure 7.41) leads to the observation that the maximum indoor air temperature was reduced by 1°C when night ventilation techniques were used. In this case, the maximum indoor air temperature occurred four hours later than the maximum outdoor air temperature. In the absence of night ventilation, the peak indoor air temperature occurred three hours later than the maximum outdoor air temperature. In both cases, the peak load in the building was observed late in the afternoon, which is attributed to its high inertia.

7/ 8 - 9/ 8/ 95

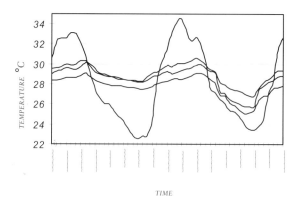

*Figure 7.40. Comparison of one day without (7/8)
and one day with (8/9) night ventilation*

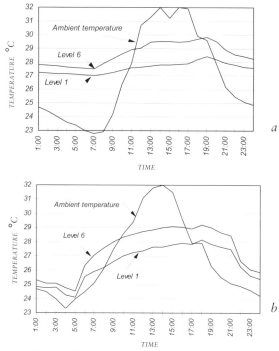

*Figure 7.41. Comparison of two days with
similar outdoor ambient temperature conditions,
without (a) or with (b) night ventilation*

These night ventilation experiments were simulated using the TRNSYS thermal simulation tool. Simulation results regarding indoor air temperature were compared with experimental values for the calibration of a model for the optimum description of the building. Simulation results using the derived model were found to be very close to the measured values.

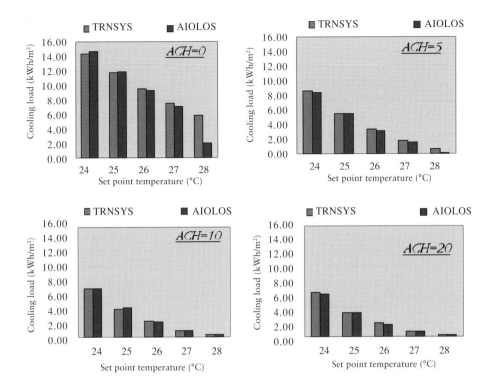

Figure 7.42. Comparison of simulations carried out with TRNSYS and the thermal model of AIOLOS

An intermodel comparison was also carried using two simulation tools: TRNSYS and the thermal model of AIOLOS. Night ventilation was applied on a daily basis from 10 pm to 6 am for the period from 1 May to 30 September, using climatic data from 1985. The two models were run for 0, 5, 10, 20 and 30 ach and set points ranging from 24°C to 28°C. For this set of simulations no internal gains were considered. Results (Figure 7.42) are given in terms of cooling loads per floor area (kWh m⁻²) for the whole period of simulation.

The graphs in Figure 7.42 show that the two models are in good agreement. When a night ventilation rate of 5 ach is achieved, a reduction of up to 50% is observed for the cooling load. A smaller reduction is observed when 10 or 20 ach are used. Exceeding 20 ach does not have any further impact on the cooling load of the building.

The building is fully operated by a building management system (BMS). The temperature set point during winter is 21°C while during summer it is 27°C. Night ventilation is applied during the cooling season from 10 pm to 6 am as long as the outdoor air temperature is at least 1°C lower than the indoor air temperature.

7.3.6   Conclusion

The architectural characteristics of this building (a tall building with an open-plan structure of the interior space) permit a vertical circulation of the air as a result of the stack effect. The most efficient opening configuration providing wide air circulation in the building is cross ventilation with openings on both the upper and the lower floors. In this case, an upward movement of the air is enhanced by the presence of vertical temperature stratification. Single-sided ventilation with openings at different levels on the same façade is not as efficient. Cross ventilation with openings on the same floor causes high local air-exchange rates and restricted airflow in the rest of the building.

The high inertia of the building makes it a good example of the possibilities of application of night ventilation to office buildings. The climate in the area where this office is located is characterized by large temperature swings, with night temperatures low enough for night ventilation to be applied. This technique was found to reduce the maximum indoor air temperature by 1–2°C. By taking advantage of the heavy mass of the building, this strategy contributes towards delaying the peak load hour by 4–5 hours.

7.4   THE PLEIADE DWELLING (LOUVAIN-LA-NEUVE, BELGIUM)

Figure 7.43. The PLEIADE dwelling: Ir. Arch. Ph. Jaspard

The PLEIADE (Passive Low Energy Innovative Architectural DEsign) dwelling is the Belgian participation in the Task XIII 'Solar Low Energy Houses' project of the International Energy Agency and is an application of intensive night ventilation, driven by the stack effect, for controlling summer thermal comfort. The PLEIADE dwelling is a two-storey row house built in the new city of Louvain-La-Neuve, 30 km south of Brussels (Figure 7.44). The dwelling is designed to house a four-person family.

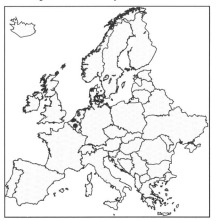

Figure 7.44. The geographical situation of the PLEIADE dwelling

The integration of the bio-climatic architectural concepts was the central point during the design stage:

- good thermal comfort during winter and summer;
- good indoor air quality;
- good visual comfort;
- low energy consumption.

In particular, special attention was paid to the following aspects:

- efficient use of solar gains;
- efficient use of daylighting;
- high insulation level;
- high thermal inertia;
- good building airtightness;
- overheating prevention;
- an adequate ventilation system;
- an efficient and well controlled heating system.

The overheating prevention strategy in the PLEIADE dwelling calls upon, on the one hand, the use of external solar screens, allowing limitation of the solar entry during periods of potential overheating and, on the other hand, the application of passive intensive ventilation to cool down the building structure at night. The night-ventilation concept is mainly based on the stack effect.

The ventilation concept in the PLEIADE dwelling can be called 'hybrid': natural ventilation plays a central role for the control of summer thermal comfort, while a mechanical ventilation system with heat recovery is used to provide a good indoor air quality for the inhabitants.

Measurements under normal occupancy showed that overheating can be avoided during summer, even during periods with very high outdoor temperatures, thanks to the combination of intensive night ventilation and external solar protections on the south façade.

The PLEIADE project is intended to be an example of design and construction of an affordable low-energy building for the years 2000–2005.

7.4.1   Site characteristics and climatic conditions

The house is built on a site with a south-west–north-east orientation. The characteristics of this site are common in Belgium: classical dimensions (9 m × 30 m), strict town-planning rules representative of the Belgian context and a row-house arrangement (Figure 7.45). Most of neighbouring buildings are single family houses and have two storeys.

Figure 7.46 shows various aspects of the local climate. The average wind velocity during the summer months (June, July, August) measured at a height of 10 m on site is about 3.5 m s^{-1} with a predominant direction from south to

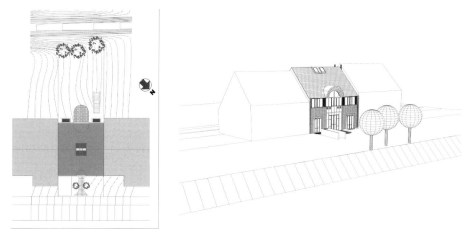

Figure 7.45. The siting of the PLEIADE dwelling

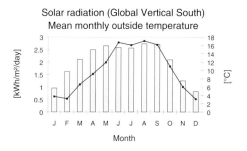

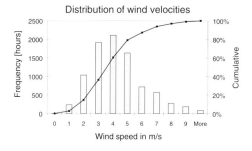

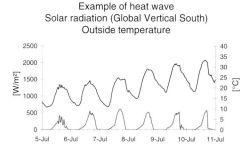

Figure 7.46. Aspects of Belgian climate

south-west. There is no strong seasonal pattern in the wind velocity distribution.

The total number of degree-days (base 15–15) during the heating season is about 2100 K day.

The average temperature during the summer months is about 17–18°C with peak values that may reach 29–32°C.

The Belgian climate shows large day–night temperature swings (6–14°C), which makes passive night ventilation a potential cooling strategy. Moreover, high-temperature periods are often characterised by low wind velocities, which makes it difficult to rely upon the wind as the driving force for natural ventilation.

7.4.2   Design of the building

7.4.2.1   General
The total net floor area of the PLEIADE dwelling is about 240 m² (Figure 7.47). The spatial organization of the rooms is quite classical. The living room (Figure 7.48), the dining room, the kitchen and the garage are located on the ground floor. On the first floor one finds the bedrooms, the bathrooms and an office. The attic space is fitted out as an additional bedroom. There is a basement under the whole area of the house.

7.4.2.2   Building envelope and structure
The internal walls are made of solid concrete blocks (Figure 7.49) and constitute the dwelling structure, while the façades are made of light prefabricated highly insulated panels. This option guarantees a high thermal inertia, which plays an important role in the prevention of overheating. The roof and the ground-level floor are highly insulated as well. The dwelling is equipped with improved double glazing (argon filling and double low-emissivity coating). Table 7.6 gives the *U*-values of the envelope elements.

The south-west façade has a higher glazed area than the north-east one in order to take advantage of the free solar gains during the heating season. Moreover, in order to limit the solar energy entry during periods of potential overheating problems, there are external solar protections on the south-west façade (Figure 7.50) which are controlled by the computer system on the basis of the solar radiation and of the inside and outside temperatures.

Table 7.6. U-values of the envelope elements

Envelope element	U-value (W m^{-2} $^{-1}$)
External walls (25 cm insulation)	0.14
Ground-level floor (12 cm insulation)	0.19
Roof (33 cm insulation)	0.12
External doors	0.7
Improved double glazing on north-east façade	1.14

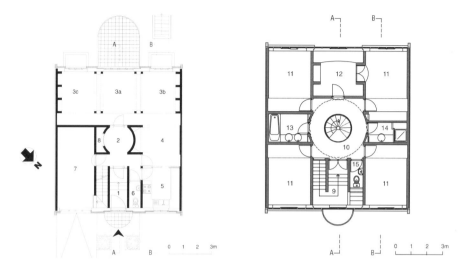

1 Entrance, 2 Hall, 3a Sitting Room, 3b Library, 3c TV corner, 4 Dining
Room, 5 Kitchen, 6 WC, 7 Garage, 8 Coat stand, 9 Staircase, 10 Hall, 11
Bedrooms, 12 Office, 13 Bathroom, 14 Shower, 15 WC

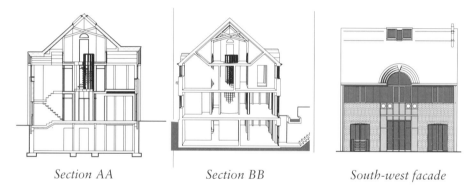

Section AA   *Section BB*   *South-west facade*

Figure 7.47. Plan and sections of the house

Figure 7.48. The living room

*Figure 7.49. Internal walls of
concrete blocks*

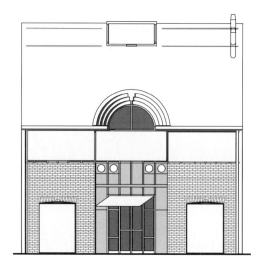

*Figure 7.50. External solar protections on
the south-west façade*

Two heating systems are installed in the house, an electrical heating system that makes use of accumulators and a warm-air gas heating system. It is not the intention to use both systems at the same time, but rather to evaluate the relative performances of the two installations.

7.4.2.3 Mechanical ventilation
A balanced mechanical ventilation system with heat recovery is installed. It supplies outside air to the bedrooms, the office and the living room, while air extraction takes place in the bathrooms, kitchen and toilets. Outside air is not directly provided to the living room, the kitchen and the entrance hall but the system supplies recycled air coming from the first-floor landing and the ground-floor hall to these spaces through the air heating system (Figure 7.51). When the electrical heating system is in use, the fan of the heat generator is still working at low speed so as to ensure the ventilation of the living room, the kitchen and the entrance hall.

7.4.2.4 Air tightness
Energy-efficient ventilation necessitates a sufficient level of air tightness. Given a balanced ventilation system, the objective was to achieve an overall air tightness corresponding with an n_{50}-value of 1 h^{-1} (the n_{50}-value is the number of air changes per hour for a pressure difference of 50 Pa across the building envelope). Such an air-tightness level is not difficult to achieve in research conditions, but the aim was to evaluate whether a building contractor could achieve such a level without specific guidance during the construction phase. Although the façade elements have a continuous vapour barrier, which should guarantee a very good air tightness, the overall air-tightness level was not

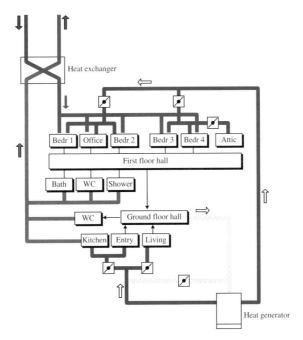

*Figure 7.51. Schematic representation of the
mechanical ventilation*

sufficient: the first measurement gave an n_{50}-value of 5 h^{-1}. After improvements (sealing of various flow paths between the inside and the outside) an
n_{50}-value of 2 h^{-1} was finally achieved (Figure 7.52).

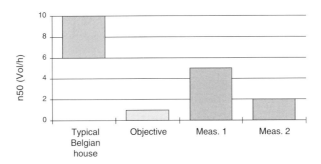

Figure 7.52. Air tightness measurements

7.4.2.5 Night cooling strategy

One of the major challenges in the design of passive solar low-energy buildings
is the prevention of overheating problems during summer. As mentioned
earlier, night cooling is a part of the strategy applied in the PLEIADE dwelling.

The natural ventilation is induced thanks to the stack effect taking place
because of the temperature difference between the inside and the outside at
night time. As illustrated in Figures 7.53 and 7.54, the air can enter the house

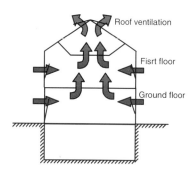

Figure 7.53. The night ventilation concept

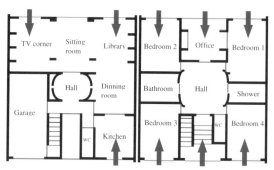

Figure 7.54. Locations of the tilt-and-turn windows used for night ventilation

Figure 7.55. A tilt-and-turn window

through the tilt-and-turn windows of the living room, the kitchen, the staircase, the office and the bedrooms (Figure 7.55). These must be manually opened by the occupants, who therefore play a central role in the application of the strategy. Two large roof windows are also opened at night by the centralized computer control system of the dwelling if the indoor temperature exceeds a predefined value.

7.4.3   Thermal behaviour of the building during summer

The PLEIADE dwelling has been the object of intensive monitoring campaigns with regard to many aspects of building physics (*U*-values, global insulation

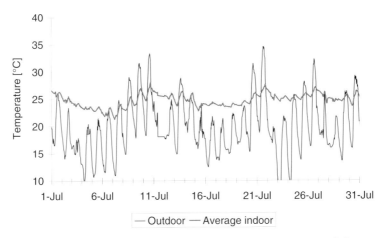

Figure 7.56. The evolution of the indoor temperature and the
outdoor temperature during July 1995

level, solar gains, energy consumption, etc.). In this book the emphasis is put
on evaluation of the performance of the intensive ventilation as a passive
cooling technique and its effect on thermal comfort during the summer.

7.4.3.1 *Summer thermal comfort*
The application of passive cooling techniques should ensure a good thermal
comfort level in the PLEIADE dwelling during summer. On the one hand, solar
protection controlled by the centralized computer management system covers
the largest part of the south-west-oriented windows, while, on the other hand,
a night-time ventilation strategy, taking advantage of the building's high
thermal mass, can be applied.

Figure 7.56 shows the evolution of the average indoor temperature and the
outdoor temperature during July 1995. As can be seen, the maximum outdoor
temperature is about 34°C, whereas the average indoor temperature never
exceeds 28°C. The efficiency of the overheating-prevention strategy and the
importance of the night ventilation are illustrated in the next section for two
specific measurement periods of summer 1995.

7.4.3.2 *The hottest days of summer 1995*
During this period of high outdoor temperatures (from 7 to 11 July) the night-
ventilation strategy was partly applied by the inhabitants, depending on their
feeling whether it was needed or not to maintain thermal comfort within
acceptable limits.

Figures 7.57 and 7.58 give the evolution of the temperatures measured in
different rooms, as well as the average indoor temperature and the outdoor
temperature.

The application of the overheating prevention strategy and the building
characteristics have allowed the indoor climate to be maintained far below the

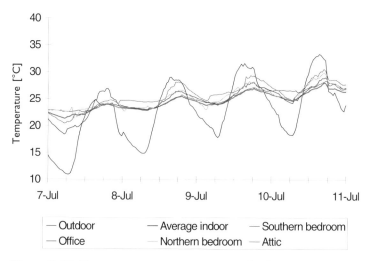

Figure 7.57. Temperature measurements in the first-floor and attic rooms on the hottest days of summer 1995

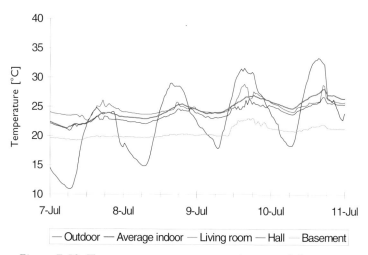

Figure 7.58. Temperature measurements in ground-floor rooms and basement on the hottest days of summer 1995

outdoor temperature peaks. However, as expected, the office and living room are more sensitive to overheating risks. Indeed, a part of the office window is not protected by external solar screens. Likewise, the infiltration of warm outside air into the living room is higher than into other rooms because it is the leakiest room of the dwelling and also because it is the room the inhabitants use the most.

In addition, the attic space presents temperatures that are higher than the dwelling average because of temperature stratification in the house. Also, very logically, the coolest place in the house is the basement. It was, however, ventilated with outside air through its door to the garden on 9 July, which explains the sudden increase in temperature.

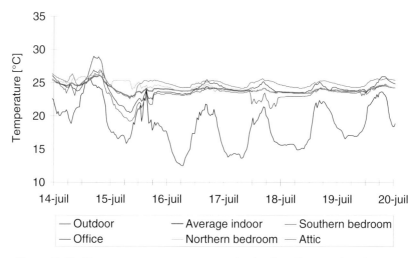

Figure 7.59. *Temperature measurements in the first-floor and attic rooms during the moderate outdoor temperature period*

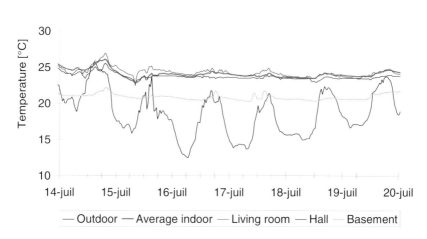

Figure 7.60. *Temperature measurements in ground-floor rooms and basement during the moderate outdoor temperature period*

7.4.3.3 Moderate outdoor temperature period

Figures 7.59 and 7.60 show the evolution of the temperatures measured in different rooms during a moderate outdoor temperature period (from 14 to 20 July), as well as the average indoor temperature and the outdoor temperature. During the daytime, the outdoor temperature stays between 20°C and 25°C.

When Figures 7.59 and 7.60 are compared with Figures 7.57 and 7.58, it is striking that the indoor temperatures remain higher than the outdoor temperature for most of the time. This means that night ventilation was never used by the occupants because they felt comfortable with indoor temperatures around 25°C.

The house behaves like a closed insulated system where the heat losses through infiltration and transmission are compensated by the solar gains.

If the night-ventilation strategy had been fully applied, the indoor temperatures would have shown values between the daily maximum temperature and the night minimum temperature, i.e. about 20°C.

The effect of intensive ventilation can clearly be seen on 17 July in the southern bedroom, where a window was opened. The temperature dropped quickly because the outside air was colder. Once the window was closed, the heat contained in the building structure and in the other rooms warmed up the air again, though to about 2°C lower level than before.

7.4.4   Performance evaluation of intensive ventilation as a passive cooling technique

Measurements were made in order to understand the building behaviour with respect to night ventilation, to measure the obtainable airflow rates and to evaluate the impact of the building configuration (roof windows and internal doors) on the efficiency of night ventilation.

Figure 7.61 shows a typical evolution of the air and wall (thermal mass) temperatures in the dwelling when passive intensive night ventilation is applied. During the day, the air is hotter than the wall and thus warms it up while, at night, the cold outside air is used to cool down the building structure.

Figure 7.62 shows the air velocity measured at a height of 25 cm above the floor of the living room. There is clearly an increased velocity when night ventilation is applied. This may be of importance for two aspects: the thermal comfort of the occupant may be affected when intensive ventilation is used (draught complaints) and the heat transfer coefficient on the surface of the thermal mass is modified.

7.4.4.1 *The impact of the roof windows*

Figure 7.63 shows continuous measurements of the total airflow rate in the dwelling and of the airflow rate through the roof windows on two consecutive nights with very similar climatic conditions with the bedroom doors closed. Even when the roof windows are closed (first night), the natural ventilation taking place in the house still provides an important airflow rate of about 2000 m³ h⁻¹ (air change rate ≈ 4 h⁻¹). The ventilation pattern is probably a mixing of *stack ventilation* (from the ground floor to the first floor) and of *cross ventilation* (from one façade to the other) as illustrated in the figure. In this respect, it is important to note that this ventilation pattern is not optimal for cooling down the building structure because a large part of the air leaving through the first floor rooms comes from the ground floor and has therefore already been warmed up.

During the next night, the roof windows were open and the ventilation reached the maximal value of 4500 m³ h⁻¹ (air change rate ≈ 9 h⁻¹). The fact that the difference between the total ventilation in the house and the ventilation through the attic space is small indicates that the stack ventilation is strongly predominant when the roof is open. This ventilation pattern is more efficient because cool outside air enters all the rooms except the attic.

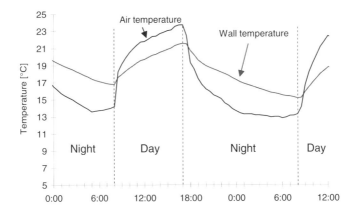

Figure 7.61. Air and wall temperature in the office

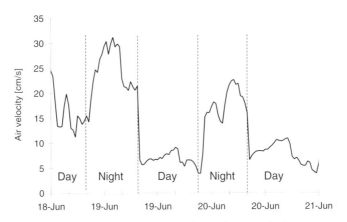

Figure 7.62. Air velocity 25 cm above floor in the living room

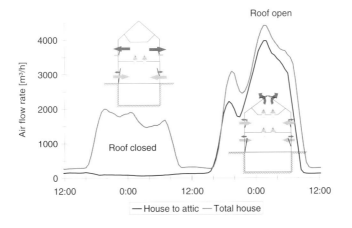

Figure 7.63. Measurements of total airflow rates

The average wind velocity at roof level was 1.5 m s⁻¹ (first night) and 1.8 m s⁻¹ (second night) and the average air temperature difference between the inside and the outside was 7.1°C and 6.8°C, respectively. These values are very representative of the climatic conditions during potential overheating periods in Belgium (see Figure 7.56).

7.4.4.2 Impact of bedroom doors

Figures 7.64 and 7.65 illustrate the impact of the bedroom doors on the distribution of the ventilation. They show continuous measurements of airflow rates in different spaces of the dwelling on two nights. During the first night all the bedroom doors were closed, whereas they were wide open on the second night. The climatic conditions were not completely similar: during the

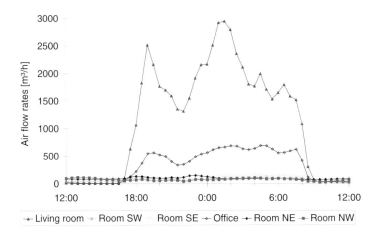

Figure 7.64. The impact of roof ventilation – bedroom doors closed

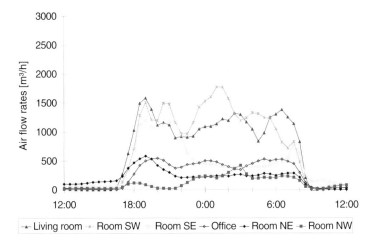

Figure 7.65. Ventilation in different rooms – roof open, bedroom doors open

first (second) night, the average wind velocity at roof level was 1.5 m s^{-1} (0.8 m s^{-1}) and the average air temperature difference between the inside and the outside was 7.1°C (5.1°C). In both cases, the total ventilation of the house reached about 4500 m^3 h^{-1} (air change rate $\approx$ 9 h^{-1}).

When the bedroom doors are closed, the ventilation rate in the living room is 15–30 times higher than the ventilation in the bedrooms. In addition, the ventilation rate in the office (door open) is about seven times higher. The orientation of the bedrooms has no great impact on the airflow rates as they are all of the same order of magnitude. When the bedroom doors are open, the distribution of airflow rates is more homogeneous. There are, however, still some differences between the different spaces (a factor of 2–3) that can be explained by their orientations: the wind was blowing from south to south-west during the test period, which indeed induced higher ventilation rates in rooms opening onto the southern façade.

7.4.4.3 *Impact of ventilation strategies*
Measurements for the whole test period were used to calculate average airflow rates for the different building configurations. These are expressed as percentages of the total airflow rate in the dwelling in order to eliminate, to some extent, the impact of the climatic conditions.

Figure 7.66 shows that when the roof is open, the cross ventilation is about 20–30% of the total airflow rate in the dwelling. Figure 7.67 shows that the living room receives the highest ventilation thanks to its two large windows. It is noticeable that a better distribution of airflow rates in the bedrooms is achieved when their doors are open. Furthermore, it can also be noted that the roof windows have a slight impact on the distribution of the ventilation among the rooms.

7.4.5   Infrared thermography

Thermography measurements were carried out in the PLEIADE dwelling to follow the evolution of the surface temperatures when intensive night ventilation was applied.

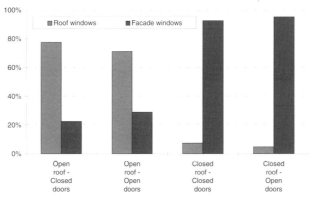

Figure 7.66. Impact of roof ventilation on the ventilation pattern

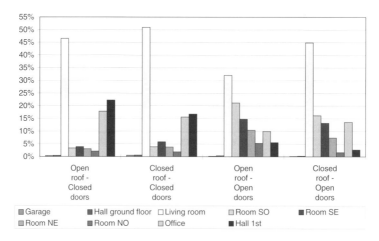

Figure 7.67. Impact of bedroom doors on the distribution of the airflow rates

Figure 7.68 shows the view that was recorded by the infrared instrument over two days and two nights. Three building materials with very different thermal masses are highlighted in the figure: A is a wooden part of the inside door, B is a light inner wall (plaster) and C is a marble floor.

Figure 7.69 shows the difference between the thermogram recorded at the end of the day before intensive night ventilation and the thermogram recorded in the morning after intensive night ventilation. The values shown on the thermogram are thus temperature differences over the night-ventilation period.

It can be seen that the temperature difference over the night is far from homogeneous: the lighter building materials show larger temperature swings (inside door, light internal wall, wooden floor). The highest

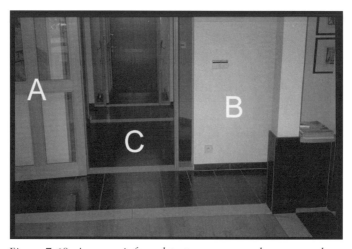

Figure 7.68. Average infrared pattern measured over two days and two nights

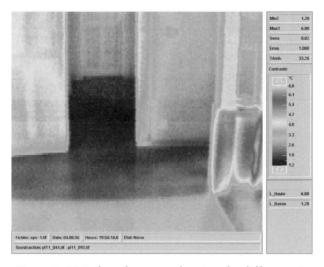

Figure 7.69. Infrared pattern showing the difference in temperature before and after night ventilation period

temperaturedifferences on the column on the left-hand side are due to solar radiation heating up the material at the end of the day.

7.4.6   Simulation with AIOLOS and comparison with experimental data

A model of the PLEIADE dwelling was run with the AIOLOS software in order to simulate the night ventilation in the dwelling. The objective of this test was to see whether AIOLOS can *qualitatively* reproduce the behaviour of the house regarding night ventilation.

The simulation was run for a period of one day for three distinct situations (See Figure 7.70):

- The tilt-and-turn windows are open but the roof windows are closed.
- All the windows are closed during the daytime.
- Both the tilt-and-turn windows and the roof windows are open.

The measured average inside and outside temperatures were taken as boundary conditions, together with the wind speed and direction at a height of 10 m.
The following assumptions were made:

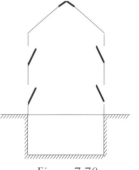

Figure 7.70

- a one-zone model;
- four large vertical openings, simulating the tilt-and-turn windows in the façades (opening ratio of 20%);
- one large horizontal opening at roof level, simulating the roof windows;

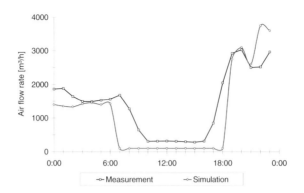

Figure 7.71. Measurement versus simulation with AIOLOS

- pressure coefficients from the literature (AIVC database);
- five cracks (one at each large opening) for daytime infiltration;
- windows open according to one of the three experimental situations listed previously.

Figure 7.71 shows the comparison between simulated and measured airflow rates. The agreement is quite good. There are still some differences of up to 25% at certain periods but, globally, the behaviour of the dwelling is well simulated.

7.4.7   Conclusions

Intensive night ventilation, in combination with external solar protection, has proved to be an efficient strategy for preventing overheating problems in the PLEIADE dwelling. Even during a period of very high outdoor temperatures, the inside climate remained acceptable.

Night ventilation driven by the stack effect makes it possible to obtain air change rates ranging from 4 to 10 h^{-1}, depending on the climatic conditions and the building operating configuration.

The opening of the roof windows ensures an optimal night ventilation pattern in the dwelling. This is possible because the stack effect strongly predominates over the wind effect in the Belgian climate.

The closing of the internal doors of the bedrooms significantly reduces the night ventilation airflow rates, but the thermal comfort seems to remain acceptable.

The AIOLOS software proved to be able to simulate the global behaviour of the house with respect to night ventilation.

7.4.8   Acknowledgements

The information in this case study was supplied by the participants in the PLEIADE project: Architecture et Climat (UCL) and BBRI, financed by the Walloon Region; ELECTRABEL and its laboratories LABORELEC and ARGB: Ir. Architect Ph. Jaspard; COMITA and BCDI.

7.5   PORTE OCEANE RESIDENCE (LA ROCHELLE, FRANCE)

Figure 7.72. The Porte Ocean Residence

Porte Oceane is a residence built just in front of the ocean (Figure 7.72), in the south-west of the city of La Rochelle. The building has a tower in the middle and two side buildings, including the large opening on the west side, from which the building takes its name. The main axis runs from west to east and the principal façade is exposed to both the southern sun and the ocean winds. The building has six floors with balconies on the southern façade, on each of the side buildings, and only small window openings on the west, north and east sides. The building is particularly interesting because its south façade of white stone and glass gives a fantastic view on the ocean to every inhabitant. The

Figure 7.73. The geographical position of La Rochelle

south façade shows the effect of openings and transparency given by the integration of large windows and balconies of glass. Although this building has not been designed especially for natural ventilation, it seems well adapted. In order to check its potential an experimental study was carried out on one apartment.

The chosen apartment (shown by an X in Figure 7.72) is situated on the fifth floor, just on the west side of the Porte Oceane opening, after which the building is named. The city of la Rochelle is on the Atlantic coast (Figure 7.73) and temperatures in summer reach between 18°C and 32°C. There is an interesting potential for natural ventilation if the building orientation and its location near the sea shore are taken into account.

7.5.1   Site characteristics

The building is located very close to the ocean and is extremely exposed to all winds coming directly from the sea, especially north or north-west winds. There are other buildings around, but all are about three-storied at the very most, so that no buffering is to be noted (Figure 7.74).

The site has a typically temperate climate. In summer, the mean temperature does not generally exceed 25°C (Figure 7.75); nevertheless, there is quite a

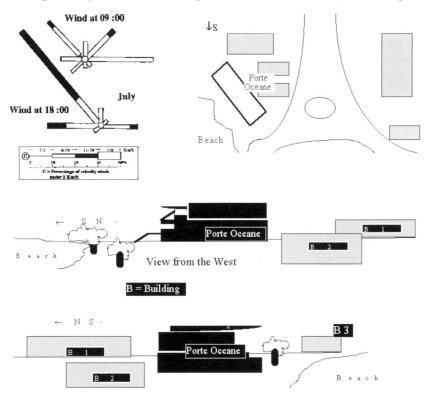

Figure 7.74. The siting of the Porte Oceane Residence

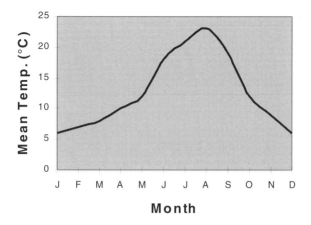

Figure 7.75. The climate of La Rochelle

large variation between night and day temperatures; for example in August there is a difference of 11–12°C.) This means that night temperatures are quite cool and therefore would be favourable to natural ventilation during the night.

7.5.2   Description of the apartment

The typical apartment consists of one room with kitchenette, bathroom, and WC (Figure 7.76a).

The apartment has the advantage of presenting a large balcony (10.20 m²) facing the ocean (Figure 7.76b). Inside the apartment there is one large room (26 m²) with a window (11.32 m²) like a loggia bay. Connecting to it, there are a bathroom (5 m²), a kitchenette (2 m²) and a WC (1.67 m²).

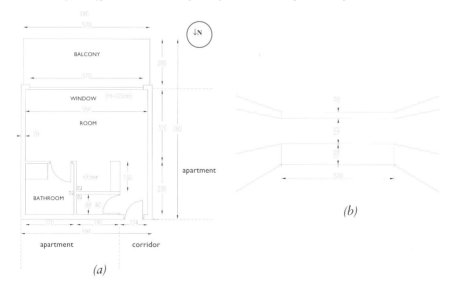

Figure 7.76. (a) plan of the apartment; (b) the balcony characteristics

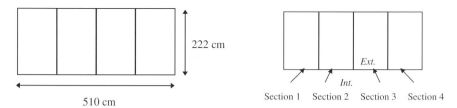

Figure 7.77. Window characteristics

Figure 7.78. The apartment on the fifth floor of the building

Figure 7.79. The glass doors to the balcony with four independent sliding sections (see Figure 7.77)

This apartment is occupied typically by one or two persons and it is generally empty during the day and occupied after 7 pm in the evening.

The window pane (Figure 7.77) has a width of 5.10 m and is divided into four sliding sections of identical area. The minimum of opening is 2.83 m² and the maximum is 5.66 m². It is striking that the window faces the ocean, and should therefore have an important impact on natural ventilation if it is opened.

Figure 7.78 shows an outside view of the apartment and Figure 7.79 a view of the outside of the windows onto the balcony.

7.5.3   Building fabric

This building has a concrete structure (Figure 7.80). The external walls consist of concrete block (20 cm), extruded polystyrene insulation and a thin layer of cement (exterior) and plaster (interior).

The internal walls are made of brick and a layer of plaster on each side. The floor and ceiling consist of a concrete slab (15 cm) and a plastic covering. The bay window is double-glazed.

Table 7.7 lists the thermal characteristics of the walls and windows. Heat loss due to temperature difference between the two sides of the wall only affects the external walls and the window; the other coefficients are just given for information as they separate spaces with identical temperatures.

7.5.4   Thermal behaviour of the building during summer

An apartment located on the fifth floor was monitored during July and August 1996. The experimental results are described below, focusing on two main points:

Table 7.7 Thermal characteristics of walls and windows

	K (W m⁻²K⁻¹)	In contact with	S (m²)	KS (W K⁻¹)
External walls	0.53	Exterior	18.2	9.646
	1.9	Apartment	24.7	46.93
	1.9	Corridor	0.7	1.33
Window	4.2	Exterior	11.3	47.46
Internal walls	2.4	Interior	15.3	36.72
Floor	0.7	Apartment	32	22.4
Ceiling	0.7	Apartment	32	22.4

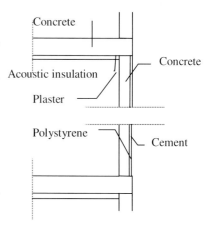

Figure 7.80. Section and insulation detail

- *The cooling effect induced by natural ventilation.* This analysis is based on the evolution of the black-bulb temperature as this is the most representative indicator for expressing the feelings of the users in evaluating the effect of cooling induced by natural ventilation.
- *The impact of ventilation strategy.* The window facing the ocean is assumed to have an important impact upon natural ventilation when it is opened. The analysis concentrates on estimating the efficiency of this natural ventilation with different window opening strategies.

7.5.4.1 *Cooling effect induced by natural ventilation*

The evolution of the black-bulb temperature measured during the month of July is shown in Figure 7.81. The top graph shows a 12-day period with similar exterior conditions. In the 18–19 July period, only section 3 was opened. The lower part of Figure 7.81 is an enlargement of part of the top half. It is striking to notice that the black-bulb temperature is lower when the window is open (about 3°C), as a direct cooling effect of natural ventilation. Another important point is that the black-bulb curve has an amplitude of 7°C, while the exterior temperature curve has an amplitude of 15°C. In addition, there is a difference in phase of about an hour. That shows the high inertial effect of the apartment, the structure of which reduces and alters the important outdoor temperature oscillations. To design a night-ventilation strategy for the apartment, this fact must be taken into account.

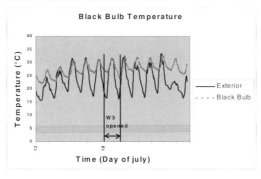

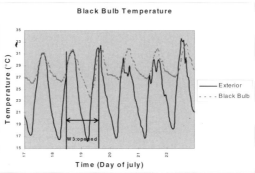

Figure 7.81. July measurements of black-bulb temperature

7.5.4.2 *The impact of ventilation strategy*

In order to evaluate the impact of various natural ventilation strategies, multi-tracer gas measurements were carried out. As can be seen in the two parts of Figure 7.82, for the same lapse of time (about 20 minutes), double the quantity of gas has disappeared when sections 1 and 4 of the window are opened (compared to the case of one open window). Moreover, opening two windows has led to better air mixing (the three curves for the ceiling, corridor and middle of the room are the same), so there was no accumulation at the ceiling (as there is in the top graph).

From these experiments it was also possible to define a natural ventilation efficiency index for each configuration as an average of the ratio of the local mean average and room mean average. Table 7.8 gives the natural ventilation efficiency coefficients averaged for various experiments. It is clear that natural single-sided ventilation can be very efficient. The comparison between cases 1

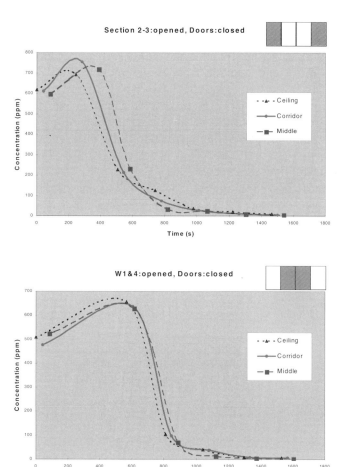

Figure 7.82. Tracer gas results for different openings

Table 7.8. Ventilation efficiencies for different window-opening patterns

			Efficiency (%)
S 1 opened		Case 1	68,3
S 2&3 opened		Case 2	71,7
S 1&4 opened		Case 3	87,5

and 2 shows that opening a double section in the middle of the window does not increase significantly the ventilation efficiency (68.3→71.7). In contrast, when the same area is open but located on the two sides of the window (case 3), the efficiency is significantly increased because the airflow pattern has completely changed.

7.5.5   Conclusions

Porte Oceane Residence has not been designed especially for natural ventilation purposes, but rather to catch the wonderful view over the sea. Nevertheless, its location and general architecture make this building a real wind catcher.

The monitoring carried out on a typical apartment clearly showed the important impact of natural ventilation on the behaviour of the building. Even with low wind and single-sided ventilation, the airflow rates obtained were typically around 10 or 12 ach. They led to very comfortable conditions in the building during the whole monitoring period.

Furthermore, the results obtained on this building show clearly how night ventilation can also be very efficient, to take advantage of the high inertia of the building. Unfortunately, the occupants usually close the windows during the night for privacy reasons, showing how, in practice, operating difficulties often prevent natural ventilation from effectively contributing to indoor cooling in summer.

7.6   SCHOOL BUILDING (LYON, FRANCE)

Figure 7.83. The School of Architecture of Lyon

The School of Architecture at Lyon (Figure 7.83), designed by the architects Jourda and Perraudin, has significant architectural features that have contributed to the building's fame. It is characteristic of modern architecture, with a combination of large glazed façades and concrete walls. The classrooms at ground level and two large studios on the upper level are distributed along a central 'street', with a south–north axis, that connects the pedagogic part of the

*Figure 7.84. The geographical
position of Lyon*

building to the administrative part, the offices of which are distributed around a hemispherical atrium on three floors. The specific techniques used to avoid overheating during summer are openable louvres and horizontal overhangs along the glazed façades of the studios, as well as the planting of trees with deciduous leaves.

Massive concrete walls for the ground-level classrooms lead to small daily swings of the indoor temperature in an acceptable range from the comfort point of view, while the large volumes of the highly glazed studios have large indoor temperature variations.

Simple passive cooling techniques, such as drawing the existing curtains, natural cross ventilation from the windows and running the mechanical ventilation either at night or both day and night are used. Occupant control is essential for assessing the use of the passive cooling techniques using the existing equipment.

7.6.1   Site characteristics

The building is located in the east suburb of Lyon and it sits in the centre of a wide plot on a flat ground (Figure 7.85). The building is oriented 25° from the south–north axis. The southern side is obstructed by adjacent low rise buildings (Figure 7.86). Trees and buildings are located at a certain distance around the school. These obstacles do not interfere with solar access of the building's other elevations except at very low altitude angles.

The site has predominant winds from the north in winter and from the south in summer. The climate of the region is fairly warm in summer, with mean daily maximum temperatures in July and August of 30°C (Figure 7.87). The mean daily temperature swing in summer is over 10°C.

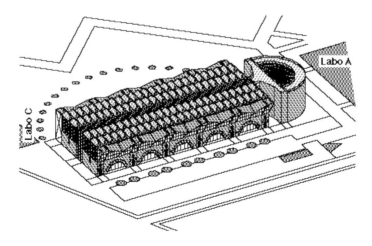

Figure 7.85. Axonometric view of the site

Figure 7.86. West and east façades of the building and adjacent low-rise buildings

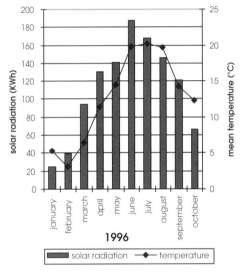

*Figure 7.87. Mean monthly temperature and
radiation in Lyon*

7.6.2   Description of the building

The building combines large glazed façades (Figures 7.88 to 7.90) with concrete walls, and is divided into the following spaces:

- The administrative part of the school is a four-storey circular building, the rooms of which are distributed around a central courtyard with a glazed roof.
- The pedagogic part of the school is distributed over two floors along an interior 'street', the roof and north wall of which are glazed. It is connected to the courtyard of the administrative part.
- Classrooms and some other specific rooms (library, arts café, workshops, etc.) are located on ground level at the east and west sides. The

*Figure 7.88. West façade – pedagogic and
administrative parts of the school*

*Figure 7.89. North façade – the pedagogic part
of the school with the central 'street'*

*Figure 7.90. South façade – the administrative
part of the school*

Figure 7.91. Central 'street' – upper part   *Figure 7.92. Central 'street' – ground floor*

Figure 7.93. The administrative part of the school, with small windows and heavy structure   *Figure 7.94. The upper floor with light structure and large glazed surfaces*

walls are made of solid concrete shaped either to form a vault (west side) or a portico (east side).

- Two large studios occupy the first floor along each side of the interior 'street'. They are separated from outside by a narrow sunspace.

The central street is 10.6 m high and has a fully glazed roof (Figures 7.91 and 7.92). It is often used for exhibitions and presentations of student work, as well as for circulation.

For classrooms, natural ventilation can only occur through the doors to the outside and to the central 'street'. Natural ventilation is limited because of the small openable area and the noise in the central street. Each office has one, two or three small windows on the outer façade and one or two glazed doors to the atrium (Figure 7.93).

On the upper floor, natural ventilation can be used to cool the studios. Louvres are located on both façades, together with 78 pairs of openable windows (Figure 7.94). In practice, several limitations occur. The windows are very difficult to open because their crank systems are not very efficient. Moreover, fresh air goes through the sun-space attached to each studio and then through to the studio only if the doors are fully open. To obtain cross ventilation, it is necessary that all windows on both façades are open, together with all the doors. Because of security and water penetration, it is not, however, possible to keep the windows open all the time.

7.6.3   The building fabric

The construction consists of concrete slabs and walls on the ground floor and a light weight timber structure on the upper floor. The outside walls of the administrative part are concrete, with small windows.

   The east and west façades are fully glazed at the upper-floor level and include a set of louvres and windows. This contributes to the poor thermal inertia of the building at this level. They are shaded by horizontal translucent awnings (Figure 7.95). These partially shade the windows of the top floor but they have no effect upon the lower level.

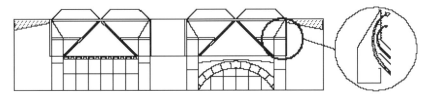

Figure 7.95. General cross section and natural ventilation of the sun spaces

Figure 7.96. The central 'street': a classroom at the ground level, composed of massive elements with large glazing elements

On the ground floor, classroom walls are made of concrete shaped either as a vault or a portico (Figure 7.96). The glazing is fitted with an internal roller shade for solar control.

7.6.4   Thermal mass

On the lower floor, the inner layer of the walls of the classrooms is made of 20 cm of concrete and the floor is made of a concrete slab. The ceiling in the east classroom is 4.3 m high and made of fibreglass. Rooms have little furniture, only five or six drawing tables. The ceiling in the west classrooms is vaulted, thanks to a thick layer of plaster, and the rooms have about 100 tables and chairs.

The resulting thermal inertia is high, but reduced by the large glazed surface on the outside façade and by the floor covering of either carpet or linoleum.

On the upper floor, the materials used are mainly glass and wood, for the frames. The ceiling is made of rubber shells filled with polyurethane. The furniture is mainly made of metal. The only massive parts are thus the floor, made of concrete but covered with linoleum, and the wooden mezzanines. The resulting thermal inertia of the studios is very low.

7.6.5   Pattern of use

The building is normally occupied from September to July, every day except Saturday and Sunday during normal class hours, i.e. 08:00–20:00.

7.6.6   Thermal behaviour of the building during summer

The building was monitored during the summer and winter of 1993 and 1994 over a period of several months (Figures 7.97 and 7.98) and in the summer of 1996 for a period of one week.

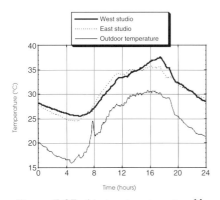

Figure 7.97. Air temperature profiles in the studios on 18 June 94

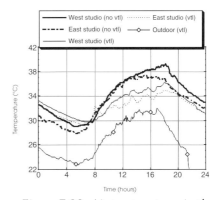

Figure 7.98. Air temperatures in the studios on 3 and 30 July 94 (without/ with natural ventilation)

The offices of the administrative part have a low daily swing of temperature, with a radiant temperature about the same as the air temperature. During the monitoring period, the temperature was in a range from 25°C to 32°C with a daily swing of about 1°C if no opening of doors or windows occurs.

The west classroom on the ground level has a daily swing of about 2°C, much smaller than the 15°C swing of the outside temperature. Its temperature varies from 25°C at the beginning of spring to 32°C on the hottest day. When the room is occupied, free heat gains lead to an increase in indoor temperature of as much as 2°C. The east classroom is more exposed to solar radiation. Thus its temperature can vary more (a daily swing of about 4°C), with a peak in the morning. The maximum recorded temperature was 34°C.

The daily temperature swing in the upper-level studios follows approximately that of the outdoor temperature, with a 5°C temperature difference. The large glazed surface and the lack of inertia of this part of the building are the cause of this phenomenon. Temperatures of 30°C are exceeded from early morning to late afternoon, with a maximum of 41°C recorded on one day when there was no natural ventilation at all. Indoor relative humidity can be as low as 20%. Strong vertical temperature gradients are recorded, especially when there is natural ventilation.

The internal 'street' is also responsible for this overheating. Because its roof is fully glazed, it acts as a solar collector and it also makes a connection between the east and west wings of the building resulting in quite a uniform temperature in the studios, in spite of their different azimuths.

7.6.7   The impact of ventilation techniques

Mechanical ventilation supplies fresh air at each extremity of the studios with an intermediate booster (Figures 7.99 and 7.100). The air goes through vents to the central street where it is extracted by depression.

Running the mechanical ventilation inside classrooms on the lower floor is not efficient because of the HVAC system itself. In fact, the amount of recycled air is too large compared to the quantity of fresh air, so that the temperature difference between the indoor temperature and the air supplied by the outlets is small, less than 2°C to 3°C. This is not enough to refresh spaces at night (Figure 7.101). Moreover, tracer gas measurements have shown that airflows between 1000 and 3000 m^3 h^{-1} or 1.5 to 4 ach are available, depending on the dirtiness of the filters.

The vertical gradient is about 3°C if natural ventilation is small or much higher if there is cross ventilation near the floor. When it is possible to open the windows of the façades (Figure 7.102), e.g. on 30 July 1994 (Figure 7.98), the temperature effect is immediate. However, it is impossible to get air temperature lower than that of the outdoor air because of the lack of inertia. The temperature of the lower part of the 'street' is about 35°C to 37°C in summer at noon, and a sensitivity analysis has shown the potential of solar shading

Figure 7.99. A view of the studios

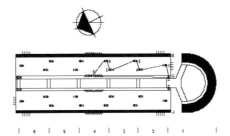

*Figure 7.100. Mechanical ventilation
scheme of the studios*

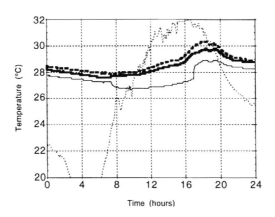

*Figure 7.101. Effect of night ventilation on
26 July 1994*

Figure 7.102. Details of the glazed façade with open louvres

devices on the glazed roof. A reduction of 4°C could be obtained in these spaces if solar control were to be applied.

7.6.8   Conclusions

This building (Figure 7.103) was not designed to satisfy summer comfort constraints. The building seriously overheats in summer and even natural

Figure 7.103. A general view of the School of Architecture

ventilation can only offer a partial solution, reducing overheating in the studios by 4°C to 5°C, although still with uncomfortable temperatures up to 34–36°C. To obtain this, all windows of the façade must be open, but this is difficult to achieve because the mechanical devices provided to work them are very awkward to use. Thus the occupants normally forgo this potentially useful cooling technique.

To reduce discomfort, blinds should be added on all vertical and horizontal glazed surfaces and openings created at roof level to increase the stack effect. Then, natural ventilation could indeed be able to add a valuable contribution for indoor climate control, although temperatures in excess of 30°C could still occur. Best of all, having a better balance between glazed and unglazed areas, together with provisions for higher inertia, would have been desirable to reduce loads in the first place.

IMPORTANT NOTICE

The software described in Chapter 8, *The Aiolos Software* and provided with this book is provided free of charge. It has been authored by E. Dascalaki, M. Santamouris, N. Klitsikas and V. Geros of University of Athens, Department of Applied Physics, Group Building Environmental Studies, Building Phys.-V, University Campus, 157-84 Athens, Greece, S. Alvarez of School of Engineering, University of Seville, Av Reina Mercedes s/n, 41012 Seville, Spain and M. Grosso of Polytechnic University of Turin, Departimento di Scienze e Techniche per i Processi di Insediamento, Viale Mattioli 39, I-10125 Torino, Italy.

The software is intended to assist in the calculation of the airflow rate in natural ventilation configurations. Based on the principles of network modeling this tool offers users simulation possibilities. It is intended solely to provide a tool to assist practitioners to think about natural ventilation in buildings and to augment the material published in the accompanying book.

The software is provided with a non-exclusive right to use the pro- gramme on a single PC only. It may not be copied, except for back-up purposes or in order to load the programme into a computer while executing the programme.

A registration card is included with the software. Support is only offered by the Authors at their discretion to those who have completed and returned the card.

8
___

The *AIOLOS* software

Edited by E. Dascalaki

AIOLOS is software for the calculation of the airflow rate in natural ventilation configurations. Based on the principles of network modelling discussed in Chapter 3, this tool offers the user many simulation possibilities, which can either be used for design purposes or simply be exploited to provide a deeper insight into the mechanisms involved in natural ventilation. In the following sections, the possibilities of the tool are presented, along with some examples of its use.

8.1   WHAT CAN *AIOLOS* DO?

The *AIOLOS* software is focused on the calculation of the airflow rates in multiroom buildings. The following possibilities are offered.

- calculation of the global airflow rates in each simulated zone;
- calculation of the airflow rates through each of the openings in the building structure;
- sensitivity analysis for the investigation of the impact of specific parameters on natural ventilation;
- an optimization process for the derivation of the appropriate opening sizes for achieving optimum airflow rates in the investigated configurations;
- a thermal model for the assessment of the impact of various natural ventilation strategies on the thermal behaviour of the building.

The above calculations can be run for a short (a number of days) or an extended (up to a year) time period. Climatic data can be treated statistically through an in-built climatic pre-processor. This feature gives the user the possibility of having a fast assessment of the prevailing climatic characteristics in the region in which the building is located. Results are reported in tabular or graphical

Main contributors: E. Dascalaki and M. Santamouris

form. For a better understanding of the results, statistical treatment is also possible.

The above features are combined in a user-friendly interface. To facilitate use, the software is provided with an on-line help facility.

8.2   REQUIREMENTS

The following minimum configuration is required for a successful installation of *AIOLOS*:

PC486/DX or Pentium (recommended)
16 MB RAM
Windows 3.1 or Windows 95 (recommended)
5 MB free on hard disk for installation
VGA monitor (640 × 480 screen resolution recommended).

In order to run the program, you should make sure that there is enough free space on the hard disk. The software uses a lot of virtual memory. Therefore, appropriate configuration of the virtual memory size is very important.

If the message 'Out of memory' appears, even though the above criteria are met, you are advised to increase the virtual memory size and free more space on the hard disk.

8.3   INSTALLATION

Before beginning the installation process, make sure that all other applications (even the OFFICE toolbar) and resident programs (e.g. any anti-virus shield) are closed.

Insert the *AIOLOS* setup diskette marked as #1 in your disk drive and run the file:

setup.exe

which is on the diskette. Continue as prompted by the installation program.

When the installation process is complete, a program group will be created, containing the *AIOLOS* icon. Click on the icon to start the program. While in the application, you can press the F1 key at any time to get on-line help.

8.4   DESCRIPTION OF THE SOFTWARE

The program is started by double-clicking on the *AIOLOS* icon. The opening screen is the main panel of the program and it consists of the following menu names:

File
Climatic
Edit
View
Calculations
Results
Sensitivity
Optimization
Thermal model
CpCalc
Help

You may enter each of these menus by clicking on the respective label. When *AIOLOS* is started for the first time, no problem has been defined. Thus, only the options *File*, *Climatic* and *Optimization* are accessible and appear highlighted in the screen. First, you have to either define a *New Project* or retrieve a previous project through the option *Open* in the *File* menu. Then, all the other menus are activated with the exception of *Results* and *Thermal Model* which become accessible only when *Calculations* are completed.

The following sections aim to guide the reader through each of the above-mentioned menus, highlighting each available option.

8.4.1   The *File* menu

Through this menu you can choose a project among existing ones through the option *Open Project* or start an entirely *New Project*. Additionally you can *Save (a) Project*, *Print (the) Project data* or *Save (the) Results* of a simulation. Furthermore, access to previous project results is achieved through the options *Load/View Previous Results* and *Previous Sensitivity Results*.

8.4.2   The *Climatic* menu

It is necessary to choose a climatic file in order to proceed with the simulation. You may choose to *Load Extended (not exceeding one year) Climatic Data* or *Load Short (not less than one day) Climatic Data*.

Extended climatic files contain hourly values for a period of a year and for the following meteorological parameters:

- diffuse horizontal solar radiation (W m^{-2});
- air temperature (°C);
- total horizontal solar radiation (W m^{-2});
- wind velocity (m s^{-1});
- wind direction (°, clockwise from the north);
- relative humidity of the air (%);
- cloud cover (tenths).

They also contain the latitude of the location where the above data have been recorded.

Short climatic files contain data for the following parameters:

- latitude (°);
- air temperature (°C);
- wind velocity (m s⁻¹);
- wind direction (ranging from 0 to 360° clockwise from the north);
- total horizontal radiation (W m⁻²).

You may create your own climatic file in the appropriate ASCII format. You may also *Edit (the existing) Climatic Data* in order to make changes in an existing file or choose a shorter period, creating thus a shorter climatic data set. The new data files are saved through the *Save Climatic Data* menu.

Note: Although extended climatic files may contain data for a period of a year, a maximum of only 30 days (720 h) can be used for the simulations.

Finally the option *Statistical Analysis* is used if a statistical treatment of the climatic data is required. In this case, the minimum, maximum and mean values of the analysed data are calculated. Then, for a user-specified number of intervals (not exceeding 2000), frequency distributions for each of the following parameters are provided (for the specified simulation period):

- air temperature;
- wind speed
- wind direction.

A frequency distribution of the air temperature or the wind velocity in relation to the wind direction is also possible. In this case the wind direction can have by default one of 16 different orientations. Statistical analysis can be run on a 24-hour basis or for user-specified time periods within a day. In the first case all the data are analysed, while in the second only data for the selected time period are analysed.

This option provides very important qualitative information regarding the prevailing climatic conditions in the area where the building is situated, which it is necessary to take into account when designing for natural ventilation.

8.4.3   The *Edit* menu

In this menu the problem description is given. You can click on of the options described in the following subsections.

GENERAL INFORMATION

In this screen the *Maximum Number of Iterations*, the *Convergence Residual* and the *Number of Zones* participating in the simulation are defined. The first two input values are used by the program's equation solver and they vary according to the complexity of the simulated problem as well as to the desired accuracy. The set of default values that appears on the screen is that recommended: *Maximum Number of Iterations*: 100, *Convergence Residual*: 0.001. These values have been tested with success for the simulation of a large number of problems. Note that the total number of zones participating in the simulation is also defined here.

DATA OF ZONES

For each zone the following information has to be given: *zone number*, *volume* (m^3), *temperature* (°C), *total number of external openings* in the zone (windows, doors) excluding the horizontal ones, *total number of external cracks* in the zone (openings with one of their dimensions smaller than 0.1 m) and the *reference height* (m) of the zone, defined as the height of the floor of the zone above ground level.

Note: total number of external openings/cracks in each zone should not exceed ten. The indoor air temperature of the zone can either be *Fixed* or *Variable*. In the first case, the user-defined air temperature of the zone is kept constant throughout the simulation period. In the second case, the zone temperature values will be read from a user-provided ASCII file with an extension '.tem'. Each '.tem' file must contain one value in each row, corresponding to the hourly value of the zone temperature. The number of rows must be equal to or greater than the *Simulation Period* (the number of hours for which the simulation will be performed). The same '.tem' file can be used for more than one zone.

EXTERNAL OPENINGS

This option permits the user to input data concerning all the external openings, except for horizontal ones, which are defined through the *Edit Horizontal Openings* option. The *External Openings* option is activated only if the total number of external openings, defined in the previous menu, is different from zero. For each external opening in each zone the following information must be input:

- Width (m).
- Height of the opening top and bottom above the zone floor (m).
- Pressure coefficient, ranging from −1 to 1 according to the position of the opening relative to the wind direction. Negative values indicate a leeward position, while positive values indicate a windward position.
- Discharge coefficient, for which you can find values in the literature. For large external openings a representative value is 0.9.

- Orientation, defined as the angle between the normal vector to the opening and due north, moving clockwise and ranging from 0 to 360°.
- Tilt, defined as the angle between the horizontal and the level of the opening and ranging from 1 to 90° (i.e. a vertical opening has a tilt of 90°). The tilt cannot be equal to 0 as this value stands for a horizontal opening. (**Note:** existing airflow algorithms can safely be used for tilt angles above 30°. While the program can handle smaller tilt angles, the accuracy of results is no longer guaranteed.)
- Operational schedule, which can take a value from 1 to 100 and defines the hourly status (open/closed) of the opening on a daily basis. Each schedule is defined through the option *Schedules* in the *Edit* menu. The user can *Review Schedules* in order to view and/or edit the operational schedules. Operational schedules from 1 to 99 are user-defined and can be edited, while schedule number 100 cannot be edited and, by default, keeps an opening closed for the whole simulation period. So if operational schedule number 100 is assigned to an opening, this means that the opening will remain constantly closed and thus will not be taken into account in the airflow calculations.

The pressure coefficient can be held *Fixed* or *Variable* throughout the simulation period. Variable pressure coefficient values are either read from a file or they are calculated. In both cases, some extra information is required regarding the shape of the building and its surroundings. First, the number of storeys must be specified. If the building has less than three storeys, you must specify the shape of the façade where the opening lies, based on its length-to-width ratio. The level of exposure of the opening to the wind must also be specified as one of three types: *exposed* (there are no obstacles to the wind in front of it), *semi-exposed* (there are some obstacles to the wind at the level of the opening) and *sheltered* (the opening is completely wind shaded by obstacles such as vegetation, plants, trees or buildings). If the pressure coefficient is set so that it takes values from a file, you must specify a file name with an extension '.pco', from which the corresponding values will be read. Each '.pco' file must contain one value in each row, corresponding to the hourly value of the pressure coefficient. The number of rows must be equal to or greater than the *Simulation Period* (the number of hours for which the simulation will be performed). The same '.pco' file can be used for more than one opening.

EXTERNAL CRACKS
This option permits the input of data concerning all the external cracks. It is activated only if the total number of external cracks, defined in the previous menu, is different from zero. For each external crack in each zone the following information must be input:

- Length (m).
- Width (m), defined as the smaller dimension of the opening ranging from 0.0 to 0.1 m.
- Pressure coefficient, ranging from −1 to 1 according to the position of the opening relative to the wind direction. Negative values indicate a leeward position, while positive values indicate a windward position.
- Height above the zone floor (m).
- Orientation, defined as the angle between the normal vector to the opening and due north, moving clockwise and ranging from 0 to 360°.

The pressure coefficient is treated in the same way as described in the section for external openings.

INTERNAL OPENINGS

Only one internal opening can be specified between two zones. The first zone number must always be smaller than the second. The opposite will not be accepted by the program. Consequently, an internal opening between two zones needs to be defined only once. Once the numbers of the zones linked by the internal opening have been specified, the following information must be input:

- Width (m).
- Height of the top and bottom of the opening, as measured from the zone floor (m).
- Discharge coefficient, for which you can find values in the literature. For internal openings a representative value is 0.9.

INTERNAL CRACKS

Only one internal crack can be specified between two zones. As for internal openings, an internal crack needs only to be defined once. Once the numbers of the zones linked by the internal crack have been specified, the following information must be input:

- Length (m).
- Width (m), the smaller dimension, which ranges from 0.0 to 0.1 m.
- Height above the zone floor (m).

SCHEDULES

This option permits editing or saving of the operational schedules used to define the status of each opening for every hour of the simulation.

The schedules are defined on an hourly basis and for a period of one day. The same schedule is then repeated for the whole simulation period. When an operational schedule is to be edited, the schedule number is input first (it ranges from 1 to 99) and the contents of the respective schedule can then be viewed and edited. For every hour of the day a value (1 or 0) is assigned: status 1 means that the opening will be open at that specific hour on every day of the simulation period, while status 0 means that the opening will be taken as closed at that specific hour on every day of the simulation period. In order to change a status value, you may double click on the value. Then, a new box appears in which the new status value must be entered. New or edited schedules can be saved by clicking on *Save Schedule*.

HORIZONTAL TRANSPARENT COMPONENTS

The present version of the software does not handle the problem of airflow through horizontal openings. In fact, existing knowledge on natural ventilation through horizontal openings is very limited. Any horizontal transparent components that the user defines in this option are assumed to be constantly closed. While their presence does affect the thermal behaviour of the building, this is not taken into account in the natural ventilation calculations. First, the total number of horizontal transparent components (up to 10) must be specified and then the *area* (m²) must be input for each.

8.4.4   The *View* menu

This menu enables the user to browse through the inputs of a project and check for possible mistakes. The following options are available:

> *Data of Zones*
> *External Openings*
> *External Cracks*
> *Internal Openings*
> *Internal Cracks*
> *Horizontal Transparent Components.*

In this menu no editing is possible. The user is only allowed to read the inputs as they have been defined through the *Edit* menu. Changes are possible only through the *Edit* menu. However, while browsing through the *External Openings* options the user can *Review Schedules* in order to view and/or edit the operational schedules.

8.4.5   The *Calculations* menu

The *Calculations* menu is activated only after a project has been defined and climatic data have been loaded. It is the option that initiates a simulation. When you ask the program to *Run Simulation* you will be asked for some details regarding the simulation period, the wind velocity data and the terrain type around the building. The following information must be supplied to the program for the simulation to begin:

- *Day of the year at simulation start.* The day of the year on which the simulation will start. This must be an integer between 1 and 365 and must be in the range between the first and the last day of the climatic data. All simulations start at 00:00 hours of the defined day.
- *Simulation Period.* The time period for which the simulation will run. This is given in hours and must be an integer. The simulation period cannot exceed 720 h.
- *Wind Velocity data.* You must first specify whether the values of wind velocity that will be used in the simulation have been measured at the height of the building. If the values have been measured at a different height (usually meteorological measurements of wind velocity are made at a height of 10 m), a terrain type must be chosen that best describes the location of the building. This information will be used in converting the meteorological measurements of wind velocity to reference velocity values at the height of the building. The calculation is based on the 'power law' model. The options are: *Open flat country*, *Country with scattered wind breaks*, *Urban* and *City*.

Warning message regarding *Tilted External Openings*: Although the tilt of an external opening can vary from 1 to 90°, the natural ventilation algorithms used in the airflow model are not accurate for openings with a tilt less than 30°. For this reason it is recommended these openings are not taken into account in the airflow calculations. This can be done by setting the operational schedule of these openings equal to 100 in the *Edit/External Openings* option. Then the program will automatically assume that these openings remain closed throughout the simulation period. If an operational schedule other than 100 is set for openings of such an inclination, a warning message will appear for each one of them, asking whether or not to take the particular opening into account when calculating the airflow rates. If you choose to include these openings in the airflow calculations, there is a high risk of obtaining inaccurate results. If you do not, the operational schedule of the openings will be set equal to 100, indicating that the status of the opening will constantly be equal to 0. In order to take these openings into account during a simulation run, their operational schedules can be changed through the *Edit/External Openings* option.

Warning message regarding the *Correction Factor* (valid only for single-sided ventilation). Single-sided ventilated zones are those that have external openings on one side only and do not communicate with adjacent zones. If such zones are detected, you are given the option to use the *Correction Factor* (CF) model for more accurate airflow rate results for the specific zones (see Chapter 3). If you wish to use the Correction Factor model, you will be asked by the program to input the zone depth, which is defined as the distance between the external wall where the opening(s) is (are) and the wall opposite it in the zone (see Chapter 3 for more details). This information will be required for each single-sided ventilated zone.

Important note: The CF model is based on experiments characterized by a small temperature difference and medium-to-high wind speed. It has so far been validated for wind speeds ranging from 2 to 10 m s^{-1}, temperature differences from 0.5 to 8°C and room depths varying from 3 to 7 m. If there is no single-sided ventilated zone in the studied configuration, the program proceeds with the calculations.

8.4.6   The *Results* menu

This menu permits you to browse through the following results:

> *Flow of Zones*
> *Flow of External Elements*
> *Flow of Internal Elements*

and, finally, the possibility of treating the results statistically through the option:

> *Statistical Analysis.*

FLOW OF ZONES
This option permits you to browse through the simulation results regarding the bulk airflow rates (m^3 h^{-1}) entering and leaving each of the simulated zones.

FLOW OF EXTERNAL ELEMENTS
This option permits you to browse through the simulation results regarding the airflows entering and/or leaving through the external elements (openings and cracks) of the simulated zones.

FLOW OF INTERNAL ELEMENTS
This option permits you to browse through the simulation results regarding the airflows entering and/or leaving through the internal elements (large openings and cracks) connecting the simulated zones.

In all the above cases, results are given in both tabular and graphical modes. In the tabular mode, results are given in two formats: (a) flow results for all the zones/elements that participate in the simulation for user specified hours and (b) airflow results for user-specified zones/elements for the whole simulation period. These results can be printed and exported.

In the second format of the tabular representation of results the possibility of a graph of airflow rate versus time is given through the **Graph of Flow** button. This graph illustrates the incoming and outgoing airflow rate (either in terms of m^3 h^{-1} or in terms of ach) for the specified zone/element versus time. Typical results are shown in Figures 8.1 and 8.2.

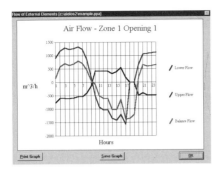

Figure 8.1. Graph of flow in a zone

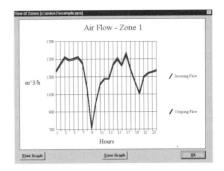

Figure 8.2. Graph of flow through an external element

It is possible to print a high-quality copy of the graph through the **Print Graph** button. The graph can be saved in a file by clicking the **Save Graph** button.

Note: a positive sign indicates an outgoing flow, whereas a negative sign indicates an incoming flow.

STATISTICAL ANALYSIS
This option offers you the possibility of performing a statistical analysis on the results of the simulation.

The frequency distribution (%) and the cumulative frequency distribution (%) of the airflow rate (in ach) for a user-specified number of intervals are calculated for each zone. To start a statistical analysis you must input information on the following: *Day of the Year at Analysis Start*, *Analysis Period* and *Zone Number*.

This analysis can be performed on the results for the whole simulated period or for specific hours of each day during the simulation period, according to a daily schedule. In the second case, a panel appears in which you have to check the hours of the day that you wish to be included in the statistical analysis.

The minimum, maximum and mean values of the analysed results are displayed on a screen. Then you must define the number of intervals into which the sample of data will be divided (the maximum value is 2000).

The results of the statistical analysis are given in tabular or graphical form (Figure 8.3) in terms of *Frequency Distribution* (%) and *Cumulative Frequency Distribution* (%) for the user-specified intervals.

8.4.7   The *Sensitivity Analysis* menu

This menu is used in order to study the impact of a parameter on the air exchange rate in the simulated zones. Note that sensitivity analysis involves changing only one parameter at a time and for the following elements: *External Openings/Cracks*, *Internal Openings/Cracks*. Regarding openings

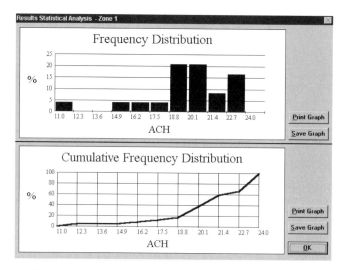

Figure 8.3. Statistical analysis results (graphical form)

(external or internal) the parameter to be investigated is chosen from the following:

- width;
- height of the top of the opening;
- height of the bottom of the opening.

Regarding cracks (external or internal) the parameter to be investigated is chosen from the following:

- width;
- length.

For the chosen parameter **Minimum** and a **Maximum** values for the parameter are defined. The results of the sensitivity analysis are given in a tabular and a graphical form.

During the simulation, all the parameters are kept constant except the one that has been chosen to vary for the purpose of sensitivity analysis. This specific parameter will vary for a range of five fixed values within the limits of variation (minimum and maximum values) that have previously been defined.

The results of the sensitivity analysis are given both in tabular and graphical form. In the tabular mode, results are given in two formats: (a) flow results for all the zones (in ach) that participate in the simulation for user-specified hours and (b) airflow results for user-specified zones (in ach) for the whole simulation period.

These results can be printed and exported. In the second format of the tabular representation of results the possibility for a graph of airflow rate versus time is given through the **Graph of Flow** button. This graph (Figure

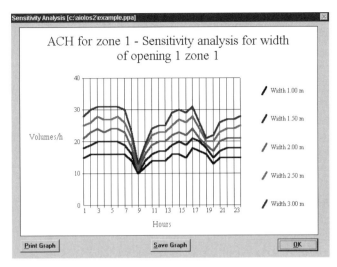

Figure 8.4. Results of **Sensitivity** *Analysis (graphical form)*

8.4) illustrates the airflow rate (in ach) for the specified zone versus time. It is possible to print a high-quality copy of the graph through the **Print Graph** button. The graph can be saved in a file by clicking the **Save Graph** button.

8.4.8   The *Optimization* menu

From this menu you can run an *Optimization Analysis* in order to calculate the optimum dimensions of the external openings for the airflow rate for either the maximum possible value or a value within a specified range.

OPTIMIZATION PARAMETERS
This option permits the user to edit the mathematical parameters needed for the optimization procedure. As these parameters are quite complex, it is recommended that the default values are kept. Using the default values is also recommended in order to obtain accurate results.

On the other hand, keeping the default values usually implies increased computational time. Therefore, you must decide whether or not to compromise the accuracy of results in order to obtain faster calculations.

The general rule is that the *lower* the optimization parameters become, the less accurate the results will be. **Warning**: if the parameters are decreased by too much, there is a risk of obtaining completely inaccurate results.

OPTIMIZATION VARIABLES
The *Optimization Variables* required for an optimization analysis to start are:

Regarding the climatic data: the *Air Temperature* (°C), the **Wind Velocity** (m s⁻¹) and the **Wind Direction** (°). In order to get more realistic results, it is recommended that these values are representative of the location. Therefore, a statistical analysis of the climatic data of the specific location and for specific simulation time periods is necessary.

- Regarding the simulated zones: the **Volume** (m³), the **Temperature** (°C) and the **Reference Height** (m) for each zone.
- Regarding the external openings: for each of the external openings the minimum and the maximum value must be specified for the **Width** (m), the **Height of Opening Top** (m) and the *Height of opening bottom* (m). The optimum value that will be calculated for each of the geometrical characteristics of the opening will be between the defined minimum and maximum values. Also, for each opening the **Discharge Coefficient**, the **Pressure Coefficient**, the **Orientation** (degrees) and the **Tilt** (degrees) must be defined.
- Regarding the type of optimization analysis that will be performed: the user can choose to either **Maximise Airflow** or **Minimise Windows Surfaces**. If the second type of analysis is chosen, a **Maximum** and a **Minimum Airflow Rate** (ach) must be specified. The actual airflow rate that will be achieved after the dimensions of the openings are optimized must be between these two values.

RUN OPTIMIZATION ANALYSIS
You are given the possibility of controlling the execution of the optimization analysis and stopping the process at any time. In case of such an interruption, no access to the **Optimization results** is possible.

8.4.9   The thermal model

The *AIOLOS* software is equipped with a thermal model that can be used in order to calculate the cooling potential of natural ventilation techniques in the simulated building. In order to have access to the thermal model, the airflow model has to be run first.

Important note: The thermal model is a single-zone model. It simulates the building as a single zone, regardless of the number of zones that have been described in the airflow module of the *AIOLOS* program. Data transfer from the airflow to the thermal module is achieved through internal communication between the two modules. Thus, the geometrical characteristics, as well as the global airflow rate of the building regarded as one zone, are transferred. Access to the thermal model is possible either directly, through the **Thermal Model** menu, or soon after the *Sensitivity Analysis* is completed. In either case the user enters a new module, called **AIOLOS – Building**, with a main screen including the following menus:

File
Libraries
Inputs
Calculations
Results
Print
Help

Though this menu you can define a *New Project*, *Open (an existing) Project* and *Save (a) Project*. Existing libraries containing opaque elements may also be loaded through this menu. In order to do this you can select the option *Load Opaque Elements Library* in order to browse through the existing (previously defined) opaque elements that have been derived as combinations of various materials. The option *Save Opaque Elements Library* permits you to save any changes or additions in a new file, which will be available for later use. It is also possible to *Load Existing (previously saved thermal simulation) Results* or *Save (the thermal simulation) Results* if you wish to do so.

Note: As *AIOLOS-Building* is an option in the *AIOLOS* main menu, you are taken back to *AIOLOS* (*Return to AIOLOS*) when you have finished with the thermal model.

THE *LIBRARIES* MENU

Through this menu you can browse through existing (previously defined) libraries. The program uses the following libraries: *Glazing Library*, *Materials Library* and *Opaque Elements Library*. Through this menu you may define your own libraries according to the requirements of the particular project you are working on.

The *Glazing Library* consists of: a user-assigned *Code number*, the *Glazing Type*, which is the name of the glazing (various types are available in text books), the *Transmissivity to Solar Radiation* and the *U-Value* in W m^{-2} K^{-1}. You may edit the existing values, making modifications, or you may *Add (a) glazing* with entirely new characteristics and properties.

The *Materials Library* consists of: The user-assigned *Code number*, the *Material name*, the *Density of the material* (kg m^{-3}), the *Conductivity* of the material (W m^{-1} K^{-1}) and the *Specific Heat* of the material (J kg K^{-1}). You may edit the existing values, making modifications, or you may *Add (a) material* with entirely new characteristics and properties.

The *Opaque Elements Library* contains structures of walls, roofs and floors of buildings. The opaque elements can have up to six layers. Each layer is defined by two inputs: the *Material Code* which refers to the *Code number* in the *Materials Library* and the *Thickness* of the layer (mm). To facilitate the editing of elements, the top of the form displays the **Materials Library**, where you can browse through all the materials with their corresponding **Code Numbers**. You may edit the existing values, making modifications, or you may **Add (an) Element** with entirely new characteristics and properties.

THE *INPUTS* MENU
This menu permits you to define the geometrical and structural characteristics of the building to be simulated. This is achieved through the following options:

- **External Opaque Components**. First, you have to input the total **Number of External Opaque Components** (including: walls, roofs and possibly floors, as long as they are not in direct contact with the ground). For each of the above elements the following data must be entered: **Area of the Element** (m^2) referring to the net area of the opaque elements (the surface area of the windows located on each element must be excluded), the **Absorptivity of the Element**, the **Tilt of the Element** (°), the **Azimuth of the Element** (°), zero in the direction of north and measured positive clockwise (0–360°) and the **Opaque Element Name** defined in the **Opaque Elements Library**.
  To help you, access to the **Opaque Elements Library** is given through the **Elements Library** button at the bottom of the screen. At this point, you may view, change or add new values in this library. On entering the **Opaque Element Name**, the software will calculate the **U-value**, the **Decrement Factor** and the **Time Lag** for the current element. These three values are displayed on the right-hand side of the form.
- **Glazed Surfaces**. If you use this option, you will be asked to define additional characteristics of the **Glazed Surfaces** of the building's envelope. The following parameters, defined in the airflow module of the program, are fixed (displayed, but not changeable): the **Number of Glazed Surfaces**, the **Area of Surface** (m^2), the **Tilt Angle of Surface** (°) and the **Azimuth of Surface** (°). Additionally, for each glazed surface of the building, you must define the following values: **Solar Transmissivity**, **U-value** (W m^{-2} K^{-1}), the **Curtain Factor**, which is defined as the ratio of the average solar energy entering the building with curtains to the energy that could enter the building without curtains. To help you, access to the **Glazing Library** is given through the **Glazing Library** button at the bottom of the screen. At this point, you may view, change and/or add new values in this library. Next, the type of solar control must be defined. The **Type of Shading Device** of the glazed surface is chosen from the following: **None** (no necessary inputs), **Side Fins** (necessary inputs are: **Window Width** (m), **Side Fin Length** (m) and **Window–Side Fin Distance** (m)), **Recessed Windows** (necessary inputs are: **Depth** (m), **Height** (m) and **Width** (m)) and **Overhang** (necessary inputs are: **Window Height** (m), **Overhang Length** (m) and **Overhang–Window Distance** (m)).

- *Internal partitions.* After you have entered the **Number of Internal Partitions**, the following values for each partition must be entered: the **Area of the Partition** (m²), and the **Opaque Element Name** defined in the **Opaque Elements Library**. To help you, access to the **Opaque Elements Library** is given through the **Elements Library** button at the bottom of the screen. At this point, you may view, change and/or add new values in this library.

- *Floor and Operational Data.* In this option the following inputs are required: the **Volume of the Building** (m³) value, which has already been defined in the airflow module and is therefore not changeable, the **Floor Area of the Building** (m²) referring only to the floor in contact with the ground, the **Absorptivity of the Floor**, the **Infiltration Rate** (ach), the **Design Indoor Temperature** (°C) and the **Opaque Element Name of the Floor** defined in the **Opaque Elements Library**. To help you, access to the **Opaque Elements Library** is again given through the **Elements Library** button at the bottom of the screen. At this point, you may view, change and/or add new values in this library. Furthermore, you may define **Occupancy Patterns** in this option. It is possible to define different **Occupancy Patterns** for weekdays, Saturdays and Sundays.

- *Internal Gains.* The following data must be input: **Total Horizontal Area of the Building** (m²). Note: sometimes this value may be different from the **Floor Area of the Building** defined under **Floor and Operational Data**. You should be enter here the reference area used to calculate the **Internal Gains Load** per square metre of floor area. For weekdays, Saturdays and Sundays the following input must be supplied: **Number of Persons in the Building**, **Load Due to Lighting** (W m⁻²), **Load Due to Electrical Equipment** (W m⁻²), **Any Other Load** (W m⁻²).

THE *CALCULATIONS* MENU

This menu starts the calculations for the **Balance Point Temperature** and **Cooling Load**. During the calculation all the results obtained in the *AIOLOS* airflow module are used. If the user has chosen to enter the *AIOLOS-Building* module after a sensitivity analysis, then a sensitivity analysis for the same parameter will also be carried out when the thermal model is run .

THE *RESULTS* MENU

The results include the **Cooling Load** as well as the **Overheating Hours** for the simulation period defined in the *AIOLOS* airflow module. Results from a sensitivity analysis are given in both graphical and tabular form.

THE *PRINT* MENU

Through this menu you may print the input values as well as the results of a simulation.

CᴘCᴀʟᴄ

This is a stand alone facility that offers the user the possibility to calculate the wind pressure coefficient for a specific point on a façade of a building. The user may then use the calculated value as input data for the Cp coefficient required in the **External Openings** and the **External Cracks** menus. The calculation of the pressure coefficient is based on a parametrical model.

8.5   USING *AIOLOS*

In this section examples are given to illustrate the extensive possibilities of the *AIOLOS* software.

8.5.1   Example 1

Consider a two-zone building (Figure 8.5) with one opening (window) in the first zone and two openings (a door and a window) in the second zone. The dimensions of the first zone (length × width × height) are equal to 4 m × 4 m × 3.5 m, while the dimensions of the second zone are equal to 5 m × 4 m × 3.5 m. The window in the first zone is south-oriented. Its dimensions (height × width) are equal to 1 m × 1 m, while the sill height is at 0.9 m from the floor of the zone.

The door and the window in the second zone are north- and east-oriented respectively. Their dimensions are 2 m × 1 m and 1 m × 1 m respectively. The windows sill is at a height of 0.9 m above the floor of the zone. The two zones communicate through a door opening with dimensions 2 m × 1 m. The discharge coefficient of all the external openings is equal to 0.92, while for the internal opening the discharge coefficient is equal to 0.65. The building is located in an urban environment. The first zone is kept at 27°C during the whole day, while the second is kept at 29°C. Perform calculations for Athens and for the period from the 181st to the 182nd day of the year and for 48 h. Consider that the exterior door is closed between 0:00 and 7:00 and between 20:00 and 24:00.

All the walls of the building are composed of 1 cm plaster, 10 cm of brick, 10 cm of insulation, 10 cm of brick and 1 cm of plaster. Both the ceiling and

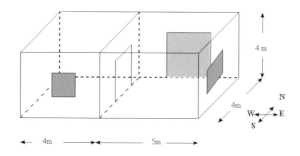

Figure 8.5. Geometry of Example 1

the floor are concrete of 15 cm thickness. All the openings are single glazed. On weekdays, Saturdays and Sundays there is a total of two persons in the building. The load due to lighting is 10 W m^{-2}, the load due to electrical equipment is 10 W m^{-2}. Other internal loads give a total of 25 W m^{-2}.

8.5.1.1 Calculate the hourly airflow rates through each opening and the average hourly air exchange rates in each zone

To start, tell the program that you will be creating a **New Project**. Next, load the extended climatic data for Athens (Athens.met). Edit the data and ask to be shown only the period starting on the 181st and ending on the 183rd day of the year. Save the derived climatic data referring to this 'short' climatic period. Perform a statistical analysis of the data to derive the prevailing outdoor conditions during the simulation period. Get the frequency distribution of the temperature, wind speed and direction in a graphical form, as shown in Figure 8.6.

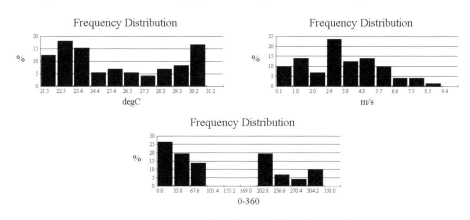

Figure 8.6. Statistical analysis of the climatic data

Next, define the problem geometry through the **Edit** menu. While defining the **External Openings**, ask the program to calculate the pressure coefficient for each opening. Choose the appropriate façade shape: the opening on the east façade belongs to a 'square wall', while other openings belong to 'wide walls'. Check your data through the options in the **View** menu. Then, proceed with **Calculations**. Browse the results through the **Results** menu, first in tabular and then in graphical mode (Figure 8.7).

Ask for a statistical analysis of the results regarding the airflow rates in the two zones (Figure 8.8).

8.5.1.2 Examine the impact of the width of the window of the first zone on the global air exchange rates in the simulated zones

Use the sensitivity menu to perform a sensitivity analysis on the width of the window of the first zone. Let the width vary from 1 m to 3 m. The rest of the

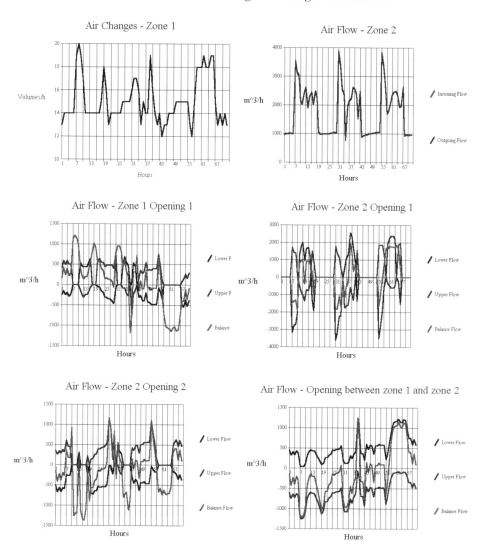

Figure 8.7. Airflow rates through the openings and in the zones

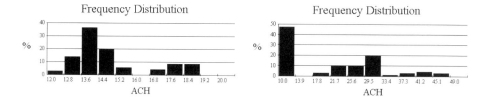

Figure 8.8. Statistical analysis of the derived global airflow rates in the two simulated zones

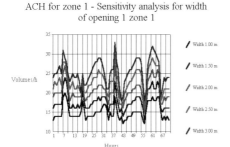 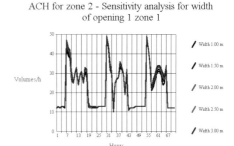

Figure 8.9. Sensitivity analysis on the width of the south window (zone 1)

data will remain unchanged. As shown in Figure 8.9, the resulting global air exchange rates increase with increasing width of the southern window. This effect is more obvious in zone 1.

8.5.1.3 Examine the impact of the top height of the window of the second zone on the global air exchange rates in the simulated zones

Perform the same operation as in Section 8.5.1.2, but change the height of the eastern window from 2 m to 3 m. As shown in Figure 8.10, the resulting global air exchange rates increase with increasing height of the southern window. This effect is more obvious in zone 2.

8.5.1.4 Find the daily cooling load and the number of overheating hours for a design indoor temperature equal to 26°C

Use the thermal model to calculate the cooling load and the number of overheating hours for the simulation period. Create a new *Opaque Element Library*, adding the appropriate type of construction for this application.

Use the *Inputs* menu to define the *External Opaque Components*, the *Glazed Surfaces*, the *Internal Partitions*, the *Floor and Operational Data* and the *Internal Gains*. Refer to the *Glazing Library* in order to chose the values

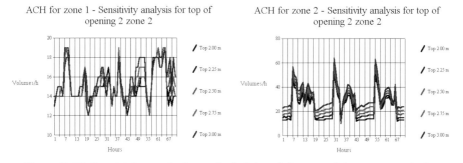

Figure 8.10. Sensitivity analysis on the height of the top of the eastern window (zone 2)

of solar transmissivity and *U*-value for the glazed surfaces (say, solar transmissivity 0.8, *U*-value 6.2 for glazing type clear 5 mm). For the door opening, if it is not glazed, you may use the values 0 and 2 respectively. The curtain factor could be 0.9 for the glazed openings (windows) and 0 for the door, if this opening is not glazed. The absorptivity of opaque elements could be set equal to 0.6. The infiltration rate indicates a minimum air exchange rate in the building taken as whole. If you input a 0 infiltration rate the program will only use the average airflow rate as this is derived after running the airflow module. However, if a value for the infiltration rate is available, it will be added to the average airflow rate derived by the airflow module. The design indoor temperature is input in the ***Floor and Operational Data*** option.

When you have finished with all the options of the ***Inputs*** menu, proceed with ***Calculations*** and then check the ***Results***: total cooling load for the simulation period: 205.5 kWh and total overheating hours for the simulation period: 72 h. At this point it is advisable to save the building description through the option ***Save Project*** in the ***File*** menu of the ***AIOLOS-Building*** module.

8.5.1.5 *Examine the impact of the width of the window of the second zone on the cooling load of the building*

While in the airflow module, perform a sensitivity analysis using the option ***External Openings*** and specify the range of variation of the width of the eastern window (say, from 1 m to 3 m). Run the sensitivity analysis and then chose to proceed to enter the thermal model directly. Load the building description through the option ***Open Project*** of the ***File*** menu. Proceed with ***Calculations***. In this case, the thermal model will perform a sensitivity analysis using the sensitivity analysis results derived from the airflow module that was run previously. In the ***Results*** you will get the impact of the variation of the width of the window of the second zone on the total cooling load and overheating hours (Figure 8.11). As shown, the increase of the width of the eastern window results in an increase of the total cooling load, while it has no impact on the total number of overheating hours for the simulation period.

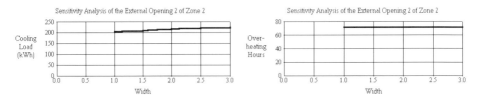

Figure 8.11. The impact of the variation of the width of the window of the second zone on the total cooling load and overheating hours

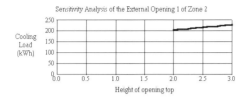 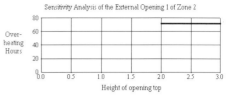

Figure 8.12. The impact of the variation of the door top height level on the total cooling load and overheating hours.

8.5.1.6 Examine the impact of the height of the door of the second zone on the cooling load of the building

Following the procedure described in the previous section, you may derive the impact of the height of the door of the second zone on the cooling load of the building. As shown in Figure 8.12, the increase of the top height of the door results in an increase of the total cooling load, while it has no impact on the total number of overheating hours for the simulated period.

8.5.1.7 What is the minimum surface area of the windows required in order to achieve 5–6 ach?

This calls for an optimization process. It is advisable that you run the optimization process keeping the optimization parameters unchanged. Define the optimization variables. The climatic conditions must be the average values given by the sensitivity analysis of the climatic data (see Figure 8.7): temperature 6°C; wind speed 3.9 m s^{-1}; wind direction: 60°.

Then set the variation ranges for the width, top height and bottom height of each of the openings. For example, use the data given in Table 8.1. This process takes time. In order to be able to interrupt the process, choose the option that allows you to control the execution of the process. If you proceed to the end you will get the results shown in Table 8.2.

Table 8.1. Sample data for the openings

	Width (m)	Top height (m)	Bottom height (m)
Minimum	1	2	0
Maximum	3	4	2

Table 8.2. Optimized window parameters

	Width (m)	Top height (m)	Bottom height (m)
Window 1 (zone 1)	1	2	0.95
Door (zone 2)	1	2	0.99
Window 2 (zone 2)	1	2	1

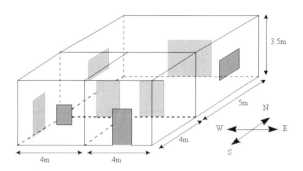

Figure 8.13. Geometry of Example 2

8.5.2   Example 2

Consider a three-zone building (Figure 8.13). The dimensions of the first and second zones are (width × length × height): 4 m × 4 m × 3.5 m, while for the third zone the respective dimensions are: 4 m × 8 m × 3.5 m. The building is fully detached and is situated in an urban environment.

There are two openings in the first zone; a west-facing door and a south-facing window. Their dimensions (height × width) are 2 m × 1 m and 1.2 m × 1m respectively. The window sill is at a height of 0.8 m from the floor. The temperature in this zone is 28°C.

There is one opening in the second zone; a south-facing door with dimensions (height × width) 2.2 m × 0.9 m. The temperature in this zone is 27°C. There are three openings in the third zone; a west-facing window, a north-facing door and an east-facing window. Their dimensions (height × width) are 1 m × 1 m, 2 m × 2 m and 1 m × 1 m respectively. The window sills are at a height of 0.8 m from the floor. The temperature in this zone is 26°C.

Both the first and the second zones communicate with the third zone through a door opening with dimensions (height × width) 2 m × 1 m. All discharge coefficients are taken equal to 1.

All the walls of the building are composed of 1 cm dense plaster, 10 cm of brick, 10 cm of expanded polystyrene (EPS) insulation, 10 cm of brick and 1 cm of dense plaster. Both the ceiling and the floor are concrete of 15 cm thickness.

Interior walls are composed of 2 cm dense plaster, 16 cm of brick and 2 cm dense plaster. The windows are single-glazed (glazing type clear 5 mm), while the door openings are glazed (glazing type grey 5 mm).

On weekdays there is a total of eight persons in the building. The load due to lighting is 10 W m⁻² and the load due to electrical equipment is 15 W m⁻². Other internal loads give a total of 30 W m⁻².

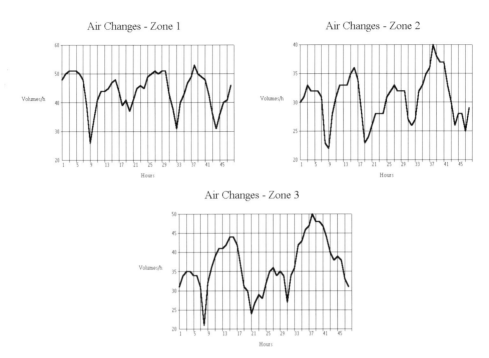

Figure 8.14. Airflow results for each simulated zone

On Saturdays there is a total of two persons in the building. The load due to lighting is 6 W m^{-2} and the load due to electrical equipment is 5 W m^{-2}. Other internal loads give a total of 4 W m^{-2}.

On Sundays the building is closed, so that no internal gains need to be considered.

Perform calculations for a 48 h period starting on day 200. Use the climatic data for Athens.

8.5.2.1 *Calculate the global airflow rate in each zone*
Following the process described in the previous example, input the problem geometry and run the simulation for the appropriate climatic period. Browse the results in tabular and graphical mode. In Figure 8.14 the graphs of the flows in each zone are given.

8.5.2.2 *Calculate the cooling load and the number of overheating hours for the conditions given*

ALL EXTERIOR OPENINGS REMAIN OPEN THROUGHOUT THE SIMULATION PERIOD

Proceed with the thermal model. Input the structural characteristics of the whole building regarded as a single zone. When finished with the *Inputs* menu, proceed with **Calculations**. The derived cooling load and overheating hours for the whole simulation period are 251.7 kWh and 25 h respectively.

EXTERIOR OPENINGS REMAIN CLOSED DURING THE DAY (7:00–21:00)
Re-run the airflow module keeping the initial data and changing only the **Schedules** of the external openings. Use the **Edit** menu to define the appropriate schedule. When the airflow calculations are finished, proceed with calculations in the thermal model. The derived cooling load and overheating hours for the whole simulation period are reduced to 57 kWh and 22 h respectively. This night-ventilation technique reduces the cooling load by 77%. The effect on the number of overheating hours is not so obvious.

EXTERIOR OPENINGS REMAIN CLOSED DURING THE DAY (7:00–21:00)
AND OVERHANGS ARE PLACED OVER THE SOUTH OPENINGS
Perform calculations in the thermal module adding two overhangs through the option **Glazings** in the **Inputs** menu. One overhang should be added to the second opening of the first zone and another to the first opening of the second zone. The **Overhang Length** refers to the length of the overhang protrusion. The derived cooling load and overheating hours for the whole simulation period are reduced to 55 kWh and 22 h respectively.

Index